Creating Enemies of the State
Religious Persecution in Uzbekistan

Human Rights Watch

Printed in the United States of America

ISBN: 1564322998
Cover photos: © 2003 Jason Eskenazi
Cover design by Rafael Jimenez

Human Rights Watch

350 Fifth Avenue, 34th floor
New York, NY 10118-3299 USA
Tel: 1-(212) 290-4700, Fax: 1-(212) 736-1300
hrwnyc@hrw.org

1630 Connecticut Avenue, N.W., Suite 500
Washington, DC 20009 USA
Tel:1-(202) 612-4321, Fax:1-(202) 612-4333
hrwdc@hrw.org

2nd Floor, 2-12 Pentonville Road
London N1 9HF, UK
Tel: 44 20 7713 1995, Fax: 44 20 7713 1800
hrwuk@hrw.org

Rue Van Campenhout 15,
1000 Brussels, Belgium
Tel: 32 (2) 732-2009, Fax: 32 (2) 732-0471
hrwatcheu@skynet.be

9 rue de Cornavin
1201 Geneva
Tel: +41 22 738 04 81, Fax: +41 22 738 1791
hrwgva@hrw.org

Web Site Address: http://www.hrw.org

Listserv address: To receive Human Rights Watch news releases by email, subscribe to the HRW news listserv of your choice by visiting http://hrw.org/act/subscribe-mlists/subscribe.htm

Human Rights Watch is dedicated to protecting the human rights of people around the world.

We stand with victims and activists to prevent discrimination, to uphold political freedom, to protect people from inhumane conduct in wartime, and to bring offenders to justice.

We investigate and expose human rights violations and hold abusers accountable.

We challenge governments and those who hold power to end abusive practices and respect international human rights law.

We enlist the public and the international community to support the cause of human rights for all.

HUMAN RIGHTS WATCH

Human Rights Watch conducts regular, systematic investigations of human rights abuses in some seventy countries around the world. Our reputation for timely, reliable disclosures has made us an essential source of information for those concerned with human rights. We address the human rights practices of governments of all political stripes, of all geopolitical alignments, and of all ethnic and religious persuasions. Human Rights Watch defends freedom of thought and expression, due process and equal protection of the law, and a vigorous civil society; we document and denounce murders, disappearances, torture, arbitrary imprisonment, discrimination, and other abuses of internationally recognized human rights. Our goal is to hold governments accountable if they transgress the rights of their people.

Human Rights Watch began in 1978 with the founding of its Europe and Central Asia division (then known as Helsinki Watch). Today, it also includes divisions covering Africa, the Americas, Asia, and the Middle East. In addition, it includes three thematic divisions on arms, children's rights, and women's rights. It maintains offices in Brussels, Geneva, London, Los Angeles, Moscow, New York, San Francisco, Tashkent and Washington. Human Rights Watch is an independent, nongovernmental organization, supported by contributions from private individuals and foundations worldwide. It accepts no government funds, directly or indirectly.

The staff includes Kenneth Roth, executive director; Allison Adoradio, operations director, Michele Alexander, development director; Carroll Bogert, associate director; Steve Crawshaw, London office director, Barbara Guglielmo, finance director; Lotte Leicht, Brussels office director; Iain Levine, program director; Rory Mungoven, advocacy director; Maria Pignataro Nielsen, human resources director; Dinah PoKempner, General Counsel, Wilder Tayler, legal and policy director; and Joanna Weschler, United Nations representative.

The regional division directors of Human Rights Watch are Peter Takirambudde, Africa; José Miguel Vivanco, Americas; Brad Adams, Asia; Rachel Denber (acting), Europe and Central Asia; Joe Stork (acting), Middle East and North Africa. The thematic division directors are Steve Goose, Arms; Lois Whitman, Children's Rights; and LaShawn R. Jefferson, Women's Rights. The program directors are Arvind Ganesan, Business and Human Rights; Joanne Csete, HIV/AIDS and Human Rights; Richard Dicker, International Justice; and Jamie Fellner, U.S. Program.

Creating Enemies of the State
Religious Persecution in Uzbekistan

ACKNOWLEDGMENTS

This report was researched and written by Acacia Shields, senior researcher on Central Asia. Additional research was conducted by Matilda Bogner, Tashkent-based researcher. It was edited by Cynthia Brown, a consultant to Human Rights Watch, Rachel Denber, acting executive director of the Europe and Central Asia division, and Widney Brown, deputy program director of Human Rights Watch. Veronika Szente Goldston, advocacy director for the Europe and Central Asia division, also reviewed sections of the report. Valuable technical support and assistance was given by past and current associates from the Europe and Central Asia division in New York and Tashkent, including Christina ter Braak, Rebecca Stich, Elizabeth Eagen, Ole Solvang, Kristina Alessi, and Emily Letts.

We extend our thanks to a number of rights defenders in Uzbekistan who were intimately involved in this project. We at Human Rights Watch recognize their incredible courage and commitment to the pursuit of human rights in Uzbekistan. Above all, our unending gratitude goes to the victims and their families, who trusted us with their stories. It was impossible to include in this report the details of all of the instances of abuse and hundreds of testimonies collected, but it is our hope that the cases featured in the report help to speak for the thousands of people who have suffered under this campaign.

I. INTRODUCTION

Summary

For the past decade, with increasing intensity, the government of Uzbekistan has persecuted independent Muslims. This campaign of religious persecution has resulted in the arrest, torture, public degradation, and incarceration in grossly inhumane conditions of an estimated 7,000 people.

The campaign targets nonviolent believers who preach or study Islam outside the official institutions and guidelines. They include independent imams and their followers, so-called Wahhabis—a term used incorrectly by the government to defame people as "fundamentalists." The most numerous targets were adherents of the nonviolent group Hizb ut-Tahrir (Party of Liberation), whose teachings in favor of an Islamic state the government finds seditious. In the early and mid-1990s, the government justified the repression of independent Islam as an effort to preserve secularism. Beginning in 1998 it referred to the need to prevent terrorism, and today the Uzbek government places the arrests firmly in the context of the global campaign against terrorism begun in response to the events of September 11, 2001.

Uzbekistan's campaign against independent Islam is codified in legislation on religion and religious organizations and the country's criminal code. State officials make public statements promoting the campaign and it is implemented by law enforcement agents, the judiciary, and local government officials.

International human rights law guarantees individuals the right to have and to express religion or beliefs. The Uzbek government's policy and practices directly contravene these standards, as they punish certain religious believers for the content of their belief, for expressing their beliefs, exchanging information with others, or engaging in nonviolent association. In their treatment of independent Muslims, the Uzbek authorities' systematic torture, ill-treatment, public degradation, and denial of due process also violate the country's obligations under international law.

This report documents these violations. It explains how the state criminalized legitimate religious practice and belief and how it casts individuals' exercise of their rights to freedom of conscience, expression, and association as attempts to overthrow the government. It details the ordeal independent Muslims have endured from their arrest through to their incarceration, in some cases serving up to twenty years. Most of the people whose stories are documented in this report remain incarcerated. They were tortured and suffered other forms of mistreatment by police trying to obtain confessions. They endured incommunicado detention, denial of defense counsel, denial of a fair trial, and convictions based on fabricated evidence. They continue to suffer torture and ill-treatment as they serve their sentences in Uzbek prisons. We also document the arrest, harassment, and intimidation of their families, including Soviet-style public denunciations that local officials stage against perceived Islamic "fundamentalists."

The majority of independent Muslims arrested in the campaign and whose cases are treated in this report are men. In some cases women were direct targets of the government arrest campaign. In other cases women were subjected to extrajudicial punishment in the context of the campaign. Law enforcement agents have also harassed and pressured women family members of primary suspects in order to force them to reveal information about suspects or to compel detainees to incriminate themselves.

Finally, the report describes the obstacles independent Muslims face in seeking redress through state agencies, including the courts, the ombudsperson's office, and the procuracy. It also recounts the harassment they sometimes face in retribution for appealing to international organizations.

Government officials have referred to the February 1999 bombings in Tashkent and the 1999 and 2000 armed incursions by the Islamic Movement of Uzbekistan (IMU) to justify their intolerance of "Islamic extremism" generally and to cast the net of arrests ever wider in their attempts to eliminate any perceived threat to their power by observant Muslims. Governments have a responsibility to protect citizens from politically motivated violence and to cooperate internationally to bring to justice the perpetrators of such abuse. But despite the government's assertion that these prosecutions are a response to terrorism, in the vast majority of cases we researched, those imprisoned were not charged with terrorism or even with committing any act of violence. The need to prevent terrorism cannot justify persecution of religious dissent, nor can it justify policies of collective punishment that lead to the arrest of suspects' parents, siblings, and spouses. The torture and public shaming rituals that accompany arrests, the planting of drugs and bullets in people's homes, and trials in which evidence that a person prayed five times a day is accepted as proof of intent to overthrow the state are equally indefensible and violate fundamental principles of due process.

Such practices are extremely effective methods of religious repression. They have had a devastating effect on independent Muslim communities. Despite requests from the diplomatic community, the government of Uzbekistan has not made public information regarding the number of people it has arrested and convicted on charges related to religious belief and practice.[1] Only full disclosure by the government of

[1] A Ministry of Internal Affairs statement in 2000 claimed that, "there is no one convicted for political reasons in the republic's correctional facilities" and gave a breakdown of the prison population by the criminal charges under which people were convicted. The statement said that of 63,900 persons serving prison sentences, 36.1 percent of the inmates were serving sentences for theft; 23.7 percent for "especially severe crimes" such as murder, rape, and assault; 11.7 percent for drug-related crimes; 6.2 percent for economic crimes, and 3.8 percent for "hooliganism and various other forms of illegal activity." Another 10.4 percent of the prison population was convicted for disparate crimes, such as dissemination of pornography, criminal negligence, and illegal possession of weapons. Nowhere in the chart are figures given for the number of people convicted for "anti-constitutional activities," distribution of religious literature, or other religion-related crimes. However, another 8.1 percent of prisoners (about 5,176 inmates) are categorized as "other," which no doubt includes those imprisoned on religion-related charges. In addition, given government practices, some percentage of the almost 8,000 people imprisoned on drug-related charges or for illegal weapons possession were convicted on the basis of fabricated evidence and were in fact arrested and jailed for their independent religious activity. "On the Basis of Humanism: The Activities of the Penal System of the Republic of Uzbekistan," *Narodnoe Slovo* (The People's Word), 2000.

Uzbekistan will reveal the actual number of independent Muslims arrested and imprisoned during the course of the campaign.

In August 1999 then-Ambassador of Uzbekistan to the United States of America, Sodyk Safaev (named the country's Minister of Foreign Affairs in 2003), told Human Rights Watch that, "...Hundreds or maybe thousands of others have been arrested for [membership in] Hizb ut-Tahrir and underground activity."[2] Estimates in 2000 from local human rights activists who had followed the pattern of arrests since the beginning of the campaign put the number at between 6,500 and 7,000.[3] These statistics fit with those released by the Uzbekistan branch of Hizb ut-Tahrir, which estimated in 2000 that some 4,000 of its members had been arrested. Since 2000, arrests and convictions of independent Muslims—members of Hizb ut-Tahrir mostly, but also people accused of "Wahhabism"—have continued apace and have outstripped the number of people returned to liberty following implementation of presidential amnesty decrees in 2001 and 2002.[4] As of September 25, 2003, Human Rights Watch had analyzed and entered the cases of 1,229 independent Muslims into its database of religious prisoners in Uzbekistan. The cases of about 150 additional individuals convicted on charges related to religious activity, belief, or affiliation remained to be examined and entered into the database. Researchers from the Russian rights group Memorial have documented the cases of 1,967 independent Muslims.[5]

---

[2] Human Rights Watch interview with Sodyk Safaev, New York, August 18, 1999.

[3] By October 2001 the Russian rights group Memorial Human Rights Center and the Information Center for Human Rights in Central Asia estimated by extrapolating from the data they had gathered and taking into account patterns of release, amnesty, and execution, that there were 8,000 political and religious prisoners in Uzbekistan. Memorial Human Rights Center and the Information Center for Human Rights in Central Asia, List of People Arrested and Tried in Uzbekistan for Political and Religious Reasons (December 1997-August 2001), Moscow, October 2001.

[4] For more information regarding the conditions and results of the amnesty decrees, see Chapter V.

[5] Memorial Human Rights Center and the Information Center for Human Rights in Central Asia, List of People Arrested and Tried in Uzbekistan for Political and Religious Reasons (December 1997-August 2001), Moscow, October 2001. This number is arrived at by taking the total number of cases involving independent Muslims documented by the group—2,297—and subtracting from that the number of such cases where the charge of terrorism

While the campaign was carried out by law enforcement agents nationwide, it appeared that the arrests of independent Muslims occurred on a most massive scale in the capital city Tashkent and certain cities in the Fergana Valley. The overwhelming majority of cases documented by Human Rights Watch and Memorial involved the arrest of people from these regions.[6]

As detailed in this report, the government's actions were intended to eliminate a perceived threat of Islamic "fundamentalism" and "extremism" by silencing and punishing Muslims who rejected government control of religion. The policy was designed and carried out to remove charismatic Islam from the political equation, to prevent any potential contest between the Karimov government and independent-minded Muslim leaders for authority and the loyalty of the people. Fear of religion as a competitor for the hearts and minds of the people is part of the Soviet legacy, but the Karimov government made this project its own, incorporating inherited methods of control and instituting new tactics to prevent religious faith from ever challenging the government's power.

Among the first targets of the government's campaign were Muslim spiritual leaders who declined to limit their sermons and teachings to that which was dictated by state authorities. Other acts of "insubordination" varied from their opposition to the government's ban on loudspeakers to call people to prayer, failure to praise President Karimov during religious services, and open discussion of the benefits of an Islamic state or the application of Islamic law, to their refusal to

---

was levied—330—to reach the number of cases involving independent Muslims not charged with violence that the group documented, i.e. 1,967. Spot-checks have revealed that some, but not all, of the cases documented by Human Rights Watch are also included in the pool of cases collected by Memorial.

[6] These numbers reflect the government's pattern of targeting people in specific regions. The Minister of Internal Affairs, Zokirjon Almatov, head of the agency responsible for carrying out many of the arrests, acknowledged this regional targeting. Speaking of "criminals" acting under the influence of "extremist religious groups" the minister said, "Investigations have shown that those who have committed crimes are mainly citizens who live in Tashkent, Andijan, and Namangan regions." Uzbek Radio first programme, January 27, 2000, English translation in BBC Monitoring, January 27, 2000.

inform on congregation members and fellow religious leaders for security services. Government authorities inappropriately labeled these spiritual leaders "Wahabbis" and harassed or arrested people with close or only casual connection to them: members of their congregations, including those who had occasionally attended their services before their leaders fell out of favor, the imams' students, mosque employees, and even their relatives.

In 1999 the Uzbek authorities began systematically arresting people for membership in Hizb ut-Tahrir, the possession or distribution of the organization's literature, or as with the imams, even casual affiliation with the group. Founded in the Middle East in the 1950s, Hizb ut-Tahrir appeared in Uzbekistan around 1995. At first the group maintained a low profile; it did not declare itself publicly, apply for government registration, or issue public statements. However, by 1998 its members had drawn the attention of the Uzbek government. The group was then increasing its numbers and openly distributing literature that it had not cleared through the state's censorship agencies, such as the publishing house of the Muslim Spiritual Board (MSB), the government institution that regulates all Islamic affairs in Uzbekistan, and the Committee on Religious Affairs, a department of the Cabinet of Ministers.

Hizb ut-Tahrir has semi-autonomous branches in a number of countries, including in the Middle East, Europe, and Central Asia. The program and activities of these branches vary from country to country, as do government policies toward the organization. This report discusses state treatment of Hizb ut-Tahrir in Uzbekistan only. Because Hizb ut-Tahrir's goals and ideas combine religion and politics, the group defies classification as an exclusively political or religious entity. In Uzbekistan, state authorities punish Hizb ut-Tahrir members specifically for their religious beliefs, expression, and activities.

For the purpose of this report, the term "independent Muslims" refers to Muslims who do not defer to government policy in their religious practices, expression, or beliefs. Those in danger of being cast as "fundamentalists" do not share an identical set of beliefs and practices. The Uzbek government judges all Muslims who express their religious beliefs in any way that is outside the parameters it has set as suspect.

Independence in this context does not necessarily mean breaking with traditional religious practice nor does it presume that independent Muslims make an active decision to challenge the will of the state. Uzbekistan's campaign against independent Islam has targeted Muslims who exhibited no objective independence from the state, but who were simply deemed "too pious" by state agents.

Members of Hizb ut-Tahrir, like Muslims labeled "Wahhabi" by the state, are overwhelmingly self-defined Hanafi Sunnis, as are most Muslims in Uzbekistan, and not adherents of Wahabbism as it is understood in the Saudi Arabian context.[7] Some so-called Wahhabis were thus labeled because they prayed five times a day—deemed by some local authorities in Uzbekistan's provinces as evidence of excessive or suspicious piety—or overtly manifested their religious belief by growing a beard or wearing a headscarf that covered the face.

Methodology

Human Rights Watch has maintained an office in Tashkent since 1996. Beginning in 1998, and then regularly from 1999 through 2001 as abuses mounted, Human Rights Watch interviewed some 200 independent Muslims who have been victims of arbitrary arrest and detention or are relatives of victims, as well as numerous other eyewitnesses, human rights defenders, defense attorneys, and government officials. Additional monitoring, including interviews of several former religious prisoners, was conducted in 2002 and 2003. Research for this book was conducted in all eleven districts of Tashkent city and other locations in Tashkent province, and during field missions to other provinces throughout Uzbekistan, including Jizzakh, Khorezm, Samarkand, Bukhara, Andijan, Fergana, Namangan, and Syrdaria as well as to the Autonomous Republic of Karakalpakstan.

[7] According to members of Hizb ut-Tahrir, most members of the group in Uzbekistan are Hanafi Sunnis. In other regions also, they point out, members' identification with a given school of Sunnism reflects the general trend in the area. For instance, in Pakistan and the Middle East many of the members are Shafis. Human Rights Watch interview with Jalaluddin Patel, head of the leadership committee of Hizb ut-Tahrir Britain, London, June 29, 2002.

To provide material for this report, Human Rights Watch researchers attended dozens of trials of independent Muslims and wrote verbatim transcripts of the proceedings, which are otherwise unavailable. We collected police, prosecutorial, and court documents pertaining to the cases of more than 800 independent Muslims. We also reviewed hundreds of supporting documents, including medical records, death certificates, letters of complaint written by victims and their relatives, appeals to government agencies and international organizations, written responses from government agencies, reports and analyses by foreign governments, international organizations, and human rights groups, local and international press reports, official government statements and speeches, and domestic laws and decrees.

Recommendations

To the Government of the Republic of Uzbekistan:

With a view to improving cooperation with the international community,

- Invite the United Nations Special Rapporteur on the Freedom of Religion or Belief to Uzbekistan.
- Invite the United Nations Working Group on Arbitrary Detention to Uzbekistan.
- Invite the United Nations Special Rapporteur on the Independence of Judges and Lawyers to Uzbekistan.

With a view to improving prison conditions,

- In accordance with the recommendation of the U.N. Special Rapporteur on Torture, give urgent consideration to closing Jaslyk prison.
- Ensure and sustain conditions necessary for the International Committee of the Red Cross (ICRC) to conduct visits to post-

conviction and pre-trial detention facilities, in accordance with the agreement to this effect by both parties.

- Make public any Ministry of Internal Affairs or other internal prison regulations regarding the right to observe religious rites and worship in custody.

In order to remedy discriminatory laws,

- Implement recommendations made by the OSCE in June 2003 for reform of certain provisions of the 1998 Law on Freedom of Conscience and Religious Organizations that violate the International Covenant on Civil and Political Rights (ICCPR).

In particular,

- Decriminalize proselytism. Revise article 5 of the 1998 religion law (which criminalizes "Actions aimed at converting believers of one religion into another (proselytism) as well as other missionary activity"). Rescind criminal code article 216-2, part 2 ("Conversion of believers of a faith (proselyte activities) and other missionary activities").

- Decriminalize private religious instruction. Revise article 9 of the 1998 law (which prohibits private teaching of religious principles). Rescind criminal code article 229-2 ("teaching religious dogmas without special religious education and without permission of the Central Administrative Body of [a given] Religious Organization, as well as teaching religious dogmas in private").

- Decriminalize unregistered religious association. Revise articles 8 and 11 of the 1998 law (which specify that only registered religious organizations have the right to function as legal entities and thus engage in rites and worship). Rescind criminal code article 216-2, part 1 (failure to register a religious organization) and criminal code articles 216 (organization of, or participation in, the activities of a "prohibited religious organization"), and 216-1 (persuading others to join a prohibited religious group).

- Decriminalize the exchange of religious extremist, separatist and fundamentalist ideas. Revise article 19 of the 1998 law (which criminalizes the production, storage, and distribution of materials—including printed documents, video and audio cassettes, films, and photographs—that "contain ideas of religious extremism, separatism and fundamentalism"). Rescind criminal code article 244-1 (possession and distribution of literature containing ideas of "religious extremism, separatism, and fundamentalism").

- Decriminalize religious extremist, separatist and fundamentalist association. Rescind criminal code article 244-2 (setting up, leading and participating in a "religious extremist, separatist, fundamentalist" or other banned organization).

- Rescind articles of the administrative code that correspond to the above criminal code limitations on religious practice.

- Reverse the prohibition on religious dress. Revise article 14 of the 1998 law (which outlaws the wearing of religious clothing by non-clerics and which bestows the right to perform religious rites and worship to religious organizations and not to individuals). Rescind administrative code article 184-1 (which penalizes violation of article 14).

In order to remedy unjust convictions,

- Release all people convicted exclusively on religion-related charges—criminal code articles 216, 216-1, 216-2, 244-1 and 244-2.

- Release, pending independent investigation of their cases, all people convicted under criminal code articles 242, 156, and 159, either exclusively or in combination with the above articles.

- Provide for the speedy and thorough independent judicial review of the cases of all people convicted under criminal code article 155 (terrorism).

- Provide for the speedy and thorough independent judicial review of the cases of all people convicted for illegal narcotics possession (criminal code articles 273 and 276) or illegal possession of weapons or ammunition (criminal code article 248), either exclusively or in combination with the above religion-related articles.

- In keeping with the recommendation made by the United Nations Committee against Torture (UNCAT) in May 2002, review all convictions handed down since 1995 that were based solely on confessions, recognizing that many of these may have been obtained through torture or ill-treatment, and, as appropriate, provide prompt and impartial investigation and take appropriate remedial measures. Uzbekistan became a party to the United Nations Convention against Torture in 1995.

To provide for greater transparency,

- Make public a complete list of all people convicted in Uzbekistan under criminal code articles 156 (incitement of national (ethnic), racial, or religious enmity), 159, 216, 216-1, 216-2, 242, 244-1, and 244-2. Include identifying information, including the convicted person's full name, city of origin, date of birth, date of arrest, date of conviction, term of sentence, all charges on which he or she was convicted, location in custody or date of release.

- Make public a complete list of those people who were convicted under the above articles and were subsequently released pursuant to the presidential amnesty decree of 2002.

To protect citizens from retaliation,

- Expunge the criminal records of those people convicted exclusively under criminal code articles 216, 216-1, 216-2, 244-1 and 244-2, and provide for compensation for these people.

- Rescind and publicly announce the reversal of the government policy of collective punishment, namely to hold responsible people who have committed no crime and subject them to punishment for the alleged crimes of their relatives.

To protect citizens from illegal arrest and torture and to ensure that torturers are held accountable,

- Implement the recommendation made by the UNCAT in May 2002 and by the United Nations Special Rapporteur on Torture in 2003 to establish a fully independent complaints mechanism, outside the procuracy, for persons who are held in state custody.

- Introduce judicial review (habeas corpus) in the criminal procedure code of Uzbekistan, as a safeguard against torture and illegal detention and arrest.

- Investigate and prosecute all allegations of torture.

- Provide all detainees with prompt and confidential access to their attorney of choice.

- Provide for timely and thorough independent investigation, including forensic examination and participation by international experts, of all cases of deaths in custody.

To ensure that local government is not an instrument of religious persecution,

- Ensure that mahalla committees stop discrimination against independent Muslims. Specifically, ensure that mahalla committees do not discriminate against independent Muslim families when assessing the latter's need for social services and benefits, and ensure that such services and benefits are delivered without discrimination and through a transparent process.

- Ensure that mahalla committees stop surveillance of independent Muslims that breaches the right to freedom of conscience. Surveillance required for legitimate law enforcement purposes should be carried out by law enforcement officials with appropriate authorization.

- Cease requiring religious prisoners to obtain guarantee letters from mahalla committees in order to be eligible for release under an amnesty. An appropriate government parole body should be charged with supervising released prisoners.

- Stop the practice of extrajudicial punishment through intimidation and humiliation at public meetings organized by government authorities and mahalla committees.

<u>To the Government of the United States:</u>

- Name Uzbekistan a Country of Particular Concern for religious freedom, pursuant to the 1998 International Religious Freedom Act.

- Under U.S. law Uzbekistan may receive assistance under the Cooperative Threat Reduction (CTR) program only after it has been certified by the U.S. government as a country "with a demonstrated commitment to human rights." Similarly, U.S. assistance under the Foreign Appropriations Act requires certification that Uzbekistan has made "substantial and continuing progress" in meeting its human rights and democracy commitments under the "Declaration on the Strategic Partnership and Cooperation Framework" (signed in March 2002).

- The U.S. should withhold certification under both programs until such time as Uzbekistan has, at minimum, reformed provisions of the 1998 Law on Freedom of Conscience and

Religious Organizations that violate the ICCPR, rescinded criminal code articles that violate the ICCPR, released all people convicted exclusively on religion-related charges (criminal code articles 216, 216-1, 216-2, 244-1 and 244-2), and U.S. or independent monitors have verified that the government of Uzbekistan has ceased the arrest of independent Muslims for their religious beliefs and practices.

- In all communications from all agencies of the U.S. government to the government of Uzbekistan, send a clear and consistent message that respect for human rights is an integral part and essential to the success of any security policy, including anti-terrorism operations.

- Review the U.S. counter-terrorism relationship with the government of Uzbekistan to ensure that it does not involve the sharing of intelligence obtained by Uzbek security services through torture.

- Condition all assistance to mahalla committees, including funding for civil society, democracy building, or other similar projects, on reform of those committees.

To the OSCE:

- Charge the OSCE Center in Uzbekistan with the continued monitoring of trials of persons charged under Criminal Code articles 156, 159, 216, 216-1, 216-2, 242, 244-1, and 244-2 and independent Muslims brought up on common criminal charges, including but not limited to, criminal code articles 248, 273, 276 as well as criminal code article 155. Maintain records of the proceedings, including observers' notes and official court documents. Regular reports should be submitted to OSCE participating states.

- Task the OSCE Center in Uzbekistan also with attending, when possible, public demonstrations of persons protesting the illegal arrest or mistreatment of independent Muslims and with reporting to member states on any government abuses that take place during such gatherings.

- Continue the practice of raising concerns with Uzbek government officials regarding religious discrimination, torture, and death in custody.

- Following the practice currently in place in Croatia, make public regular reports by the OSCE Center in Uzbekistan regarding human rights developments in the country and actions taken by the OSCE.

- The Personal Envoy of the OSCE's Chairman-in-Office for Central Asia should make religious freedom a key component of his work in Uzbekistan.

- Tie assistance, including the transfer of supplies and equipment, to the Office of the Ombudsperson on reform of that institution.

<u>To the European Union:</u>

- Publicly recognize that the government of Uzbekistan is in violation of the human rights criteria set out in the Partnership and Cooperation Agreement (PCA) with the E.U. (signed in 1999) and make clear that the PCA will have to be suspended unless significant improvements in the country's human rights record can be noted. Set a clear timeframe for the reforms needed to bring Uzbekistan into compliance with its commitments under the PCA. These reforms include, but are not limited to, reform of the provisions of the 1998 Law on Freedom of Conscience and Religious Organizations that violate the ICCPR, the abolition of criminal code articles that violate the ICCPR, release of all people convicted exclusively under criminal code articles 216, 216-1, 216-2, 244-1 and 244-2, and the cessation of arrests of independent Muslims for their religious beliefs and practices.

- Make use of the Special Envoy of the OSCE Chairman-in-Office to Central Asia to track specific steps taken by the government of Uzbekistan to bring itself into compliance with the human rights requirements of the PCA.

- Continue the practice of issuing formal demarches to the government of Uzbekistan and public statements in the framework of the OSCE Permanent Council in reaction to incidents of particularly egregious government abuse, including religion-related arrests and convictions, and torture and deaths in custody.

<u>To the United Nations Commission on Human Rights:</u>

- Introduce a country-specific resolution on the human rights situation in Uzbekistan, calling on the government to comply with international human rights standards and to cooperate with the international community, including by implementing the recommendations of the Special Rapporteur on Torture and by issuing standing invitations to U.N. special mechanisms. Emphasize in part the urgent need for access to be granted to the Special Rapporteur on the Freedom of Religion or Belief and the Special Representative of the Secretary-General on Human Rights Defenders.

- Give serious consideration to appointing a Special Rapporteur on Uzbekistan.

<u>To the United Nations High Commissioner on Human Rights (UNHCHR):</u>

- Request an invitation to visit Uzbekistan to meet with representatives of the Government of Uzbekistan, local human rights activists, and relatives of those convicted under criminal code articles 156, 159, 216, 216-1, 216-2, 242, 244-1, and 244-2, to investigate the discriminatory arrest and conviction of independent Muslims.

- Appoint a permanent representative of the UNHCHR to the U.N. Mission in Uzbekistan to monitor on-going abuses and report to the HCHR. Charge the representative with ensuring that all confidential communications from victims of abuse submitted to U.N. treaty bodies and special mechanisms are kept confidential and are received by the bodies concerned in a timely manner.

- Encourage the Special Rapporteur on the Freedom of Religion or Belief to request an invitation to visit Uzbekistan.

State-run mosque in Tashkent. © 2003 Jason Eskenazi

II. BACKGROUND

Brief Chronological Overview

At least 80 percent of the population of Uzbekistan identifies as Muslim. The overwhelming majority of Uzbek Muslims are Sunnis and adhere to the Hanafi branch of Sunnism. The balance of the population are Sufis, non-Hanafi Sunnis, Shi'ite Muslims, Russian Orthodox Christians, Jews, Hare Krishnas, Bahais, Catholics, Jehovah's Witnesses, Protestants—including Baptists, Evangelicals, and Seventh Day Adventists—and members of other smaller Christian confessions. Most independent Muslims are Hanafi Sunnis and a small percentage belong to the minority of Muslims who adhere to other branches of Sunnism.

Brief Islamic Revival and Government Backlash

During the Soviet period, the state kept a tight rein on religious practice, including in Uzbekistan. The Soviet government closed places of worship, restricted Islamic study to a few designated institutes, and required the official clergy to serve as informants. The Spiritual Directorate of Central Asia and Kazakhstan, established in 1943 under Stalin, monitored believers and defined the sphere of acceptable religious practice in the region. Meanwhile, those who flouted the restrictions of state-defined Islam practiced and studied in secret.

During the brief period of glasnost, restrictions on religious practice in Uzbekistan, as throughout the region, were loosened. People expressed their belief more openly, and the government and private organizations established new mosques and medressehs (religious schools). The rift between private Islamic practice and state-sponsored Islam narrowed. This process continued through Uzbekistan's coming of age as an independent state. Government and foreign funds contributed to the building of new Muslim houses of prayer. Uzbekistan became the site of some 4,000 mosques, a dramatic increase from the estimated 80 mosques open during the Soviet period.[8] President Karimov, former head of the Communist party in Uzbekistan, took pains to portray himself as an advocate of preserving Uzbekistan's Islamic traditions, even holding the Koran in hand as he took the presidential oath of office in 1991.

As early as 1992, this openness began to shrink. The civil war in Tajikistan broke out in May 1992, pitting the Soviet-era, Russia-aligned elites against a coalition of pro-democracy activists and advocates of an Islamic state. It has been widely conjectured that the war led President Karimov and his advisors to fear the domestic opposition in general and Islamic opposition in particular. Long after the Tajik civil war ended, President Karimov continued to refer to Tajikistan as a cautionary example for Uzbekistan. In 1998 he specifically referred to Tajikistan to justify the passage of Uzbekistan's restrictive law on religion, saying that if harsh anti-fundamentalist measures were not taken, "Tajikistan will come to Uzbekistan tomorrow."[9] In response to questions posed by Human Rights Watch regarding the arrest of independent Muslims, President Karimov's then-Minister of Foreign Affairs, Abdulaziz Komilov, said, "The events that happened in Tajikistan must not happen in Uzbekistan. Tajikistan was planned as the first stage, and the second stage is Fergana, and the third stage is destabilization of all of Central Asia…."[10] Minister Komilov made a similar argument in 1999, when he told Human Rights Watch, "Religious extremism is coming from the south. They want to devastate the country and establish a non-secular system like in Tajikistan…. Uzbekistan is next."[11] A general

---

[8] *Annual Report on International Religious Freedom 2002*, released by the Bureau of Democracy, Human Rights, and Labor, U.S. Department of State, released on October 7, 2002. In this report, the U.S. Department of State noted that the number of mosques had decreased since the early independence period as a result of the Uzbek government's registration policies. While closures were known to have taken place on a wide scale, exact figures were not available to Human Rights Watch as of September 2003.

[9] As quoted in Uzbek radio second program, Tashkent, May 1, 1998, English translation in BBC Monitoring, May 5, 1998.

[10] Human Rights Watch interview with Foreign Minister Abdulaziz Komilov, Tashkent, May 26, 1998.

[11] Human Rights Watch interview with Foreign Minister Abdulaziz Komilov, Tashkent, August 2, 1999.

crackdown ensued against the political opposition, which, like religious groups, had benefited from the brief period of openness. The Karimov government outlawed the existing opposition parties, banned their newsletters, and arrested, beat, and forced into exile the parties' leaders. Also in 1992, the government outlawed membership in the Islamic Renaissance Party (IRP), a political party with an Islamic platform.[12] The leader of the Uzbekistan chapter of the IRP, Imam Abdulla Utaev, disappeared later that year, prompting observers to suspect foul play by state law enforcement agents.[13]

Restored State Control of Religion, 1992-1995

Having banned religious political parties, the government sought to prevent the emergence of other expressions of politicized Islam. It reinvigorated control over Islam and vilified people who defied such controls.

In 1993 the Uzbek government adopted a law on religion that retained many of the restrictive provisions found in the 1991 Soviet law on religion. Two institutions, the Muslim Spiritual Board and the Cabinet of Ministers' Committee on Religious Affairs, were charged with defining acceptable Islamic practices and weeding out Islamic leaders who refused to conform to them. The Muslim Spiritual Board retained much of its predecessor's authority: to register mosques and medressehs, appoint and dismiss individual imams, dictate the content of sermons,

---

[12] The ban was codified in article 57 of the Constitution of the Republic of Uzbekistan, December 1992.

[13] Human Rights Watch, "Crackdown in The Farghona Valley: Arbitrary Arrests and Religious Discrimination," *A Human Rights Watch Report*, Vol. 10, No. 4 (D) May 1998. As of September 2003, Imam Utaev's whereabouts remained unknown. "Disappearance" is defined as any situation where: "...persons are arrested, detained or abducted against their will or otherwise deprived of their liberty by officials of different branches or levels of Government, or by organized groups or private individuals acting on behalf of, or with the support, direct or indirect, consent or acquiescence of the Government, followed by a refusal to disclose the fate or whereabouts of the persons concerned or a refusal to acknowledge the deprivation of their liberty, which places such persons outside the protection of the law." United Nations Declaration on the Protection of All Persons from Enforced Disappearances (A/RES/47/133), December 18, 1992.

and issue religious edicts. Acceptable Muslim practice became limited to that which took place within the framework of these official religious institutions, under the tutelage of religious teachers and imams appointed by the Muslim Spiritual Board.

People who defied these limits were stigmatized as "Wahhabis," regardless of whether they adhered to Wahhabism and even regardless of whether they believed in or advocated an Islamic state or shari'a (Islamic law). Among those labeled Wahhabis were observant Muslims who engaged in private prayer or privately studied religion, or who favored the establishment of an Islamic state in Uzbekistan or incorporation of shari'a as the law of the land. Law enforcement agencies also began to identify as "Wahhabis" those who proselytized, that is, called on fellow Muslims to become observant Muslims by declaring their submission to God and belief in the Prophet Muhammad, shunning alcohol, praying five times per day, observing religious holidays, and learning Arabic in order to study the Koran in its original language. Officials have cast well-known, independent-minded Muslim clerics, imams, as "Wahhabi" for their refusal to pay homage to President Karimov during religious services, to serve as informants for law enforcement agencies, or to comply otherwise with state controls on religion. Authorities now stigmatize virtually any person who has been associated with one of these independent Islamic leaders, who obtained religious instruction from one of them, or who attended religious services at one of their mosques, as a follower of a "Wahhabi" imam and, therefore, a "Wahhabi" himself. In addition, secular and religious authorities came to regard as "Wahhabis" those who manifest their religious beliefs in an overt way, such as by growing a beard or wearing a headscarf. As noted above, observance of the five daily Muslim prayers has also been interpreted as excessive expression of faith. Authorities also regard extensive study of Islamic scholarship as suspect, particularly that written and published outside of Uzbekistan.

Targeting Imams, 1995-1997

The disappearance of Sheikh Abduvali Kori Mirzoev was the first major indication that the government's increasing hostility toward independent Islam would move beyond mere statements. Sheikh Mirzoev was the revered spiritual leader of the Jo'mi (Friday) mosque in Andijan. He was popular throughout Andijan province and was an independent-minded and outspoken member of the Muslim community in Uzbekistan. He allegedly advocated the future establishment of an Islamic state, based on shari'a, and resisted government efforts to control his religious services and beliefs.[14]

On August 29, 1995, Mirzoev and his assistant, Ramazanbek Matkarimov, were scheduled to fly from Tashkent to Moscow to attend an international conference. There were reports that one eyewitness at the airport saw security agents detain Mirzoev as he boarded the plane.[15] There were no confirmed reports of sightings of either Mirzoev or his assistant afterward. An anonymous letter sent by a man claiming to be a former cellmate of Mirzoev contended, however, that the imam had been kept in the basement of the Ministry of Internal Affairs in August 1995 and in Tashkent prison from September 1995 to April 1996.[16] The Uzbek government, for its part, alleged that Imam Mirzoev had

---

[14] According to Munira Nasriddinova, the wife of one of Mirzoev's peers, Imam Obidkhon Nazarov, the authorities targeted Mirzoev because of his popularity and because his allegiance was first to religion and not the state. She told Human Rights Watch, "Mirzoev was disappeared because he read the Koran in his sermons and led a lot of classes and had a lot of influence. So, they [state authorities] had no other way to 'get' him, but to disappear him. The government didn't like that he…put religious law above that of the government." Human Rights Watch interview with Munira Nasriddinova, wife of Imam Nazarov, Tashkent, May 23, 2001.

[15] Author Monica Whitlock recounts the claim made by Mirzoev's followers that they found an ethnic Russian woman who worked at the airport who said she had seen Mirzoev flanked by two plain-clothes men at the boarding gate. When the followers went back to the airport, they were unable to find the woman or anyone who would say they knew her. Monica Whitlock, *Beyond the Oxus: The Central Asians*, London: John Murray (Publishers) Ltd, 2002, p. 208.

[16] Anonymous letter provided to Human Rights Watch in electronic form, December 21, 2000. According to the letter, around March or April 1996 the Supreme Court tried Mirzoev in a closed hearing and sentenced him to an unknown term in prison.

fabricated his own disappearance in order to justify the claim that the government was violating independent Muslims' freedom of religion.[17] The Jo'mi mosque, which the government labeled a "Wahhabi" mosque and a source of "reactionary" religious ideas, was closed after Mirzoev's disappearance in 1995.[18] As of this writing, the whereabouts of Imam Mirzoev and Matkarimov remain unknown. Mirzoev's former assistant, Nematjon Parpiev, followed in the Sheikh's footsteps to become an imam in Andijan. Parpiev disappeared in September 1997.[19]

Among those the government branded as "Wahhabis" by the mid-90s were clerics who had been appointed by the Muslim Spiritual Board. Perhaps the best known was Imam Obidkhon Kori Nazarov, imam of the Tokhtaboi mosque in Tashkent. Nazarov was rumored to be in line for the position of mufti, the highest post in the official Islamic clergy. In 1996, after Nazarov fell out of favor for diverging from the Muslim Spiritual Board's religious guidelines and for refusing to serve as an informant for the National Security Service (SNB, formerly the KGB), the MSB dismissed him from his post at the Tokhtaboi mosque for "disobedience to the Board."[20] The authorities' persecution of Nazarov's family throughout subsequent years is documented in this report.

The Arrests Widen, 1997-2001

The government widened its crackdown on "Wahhabis" in the winter of 1997-98, in response to the December 1997 murder of several police officers and the beheading of a local government official and another prominent community member in Namangan province. At least several hundred, and possibly more than a thousand, independent Muslims in

[17] Indictment against Iuldash Tursunbaev, issued by senior police investigator of special criminal affairs R.A. Gafurov, December 28, 1999.

[18] Ibid.

[19] Human Rights Watch, *World Report 1999: The Events of 1998*, (New York: Human Rights Watch, 1999).

[20] Human Rights Watch interview with Munira Nasriddinova, Tashkent, May 23, 2001; and Human Rights Watch interview, name withheld, Tashkent, May 28, 2001.

Namangan and Andijan provinces in the Fergana Valley were arrested during the first four months following the murders.[21] The police now targeted people even loosely affiliated with imams Nazarov or Mirzoev, or other religious leaders who had fallen out of favor with authorities, as well as those who had sided with Nazarov at the time of his removal from the Tokhtaboi mosque. They placed those who had attended Nazarov's mosque, years before, on special police registers, and subsequently arrested them. Hundreds of young men, labeled "Wahhabis" by the police, were arrested and convicted on falsified charges of possessing narcotics or bullets. Hundreds of others were detained and forced to shave their beards or were placed in administrative custody for ten to fifteen days on false charges and threatened with future arrest.

A marked rise in surveillance of independent Muslims that began in 1998 would contribute to the arrest patterns for several years. Beginning in 1998, official intelligence agencies, local administrators, and mahalla committees came under increased pressure to monitor and inform on citizens' behavior, particularly "suspicious" religious activity. By 1999, for instance, President Karimov tasked mahalla committees to keep their "eyes open" to what was being said in local mosques.[22]

This widespread and highly intrusive surveillance network eventually produced a list of thousands of people, whom officials later identified as "enemies" or opponents of the government. Many of them were arrested after bombings in Tashkent in 1999.

A significant watershed in the effort to eliminate independent Islam was the adoption in May 1998 of the Law on Freedom of Conscience and Religious Organizations. In conjunction with amendments to the

---

[21] Human Rights Watch, "Crackdown InThe Farghona Valley: Arbitrary Arrests and Religious Discrimination," *A Human Rights Watch Report*, Vol. 10, No. 4 (D), May 1998, footnote 11. These estimates reflect the findings of a Human Rights Watch research mission conducted in March 1998 to investigate allegations of mass arrests. One rights defender based in the Fergana Valley estimated that police arrested over one thousand independent Muslims in Namangan and Andijan alone.

[22] Uzbek television first channel, February 16, 1999, English translation in BBC Monitoring, February 16, 1999.

criminal and administrative codes, the law made possession of "extremist" religious literature, membership in "extremist" religious organizations, and proselytizing punishable by long prison sentences. Adoption of the law left no doubt that the arrests underway were an instrument of central state policy, and not rogue activity by certain police forces or local officials.[23] Uzbekistan's foreign policy also spoke to the intentions of the government vis-à-vis independent Islam. In June 1998 Uzbekistan formed a troika with Russia and Tajikistan to counter "Islamic extremism" in Central Asia. The main targets of this anti-fundamentalist front were declared to be the "Wahhabists."[24]

Bombings, Mass Arrests, and Trials

On February 16, 1999, five bombs exploded near government buildings in Tashkent, claiming more than a dozen lives and wounding many others.[25] The bombings marked another turning point in the campaign against independent Islam. President Karimov immediately accused Islamic "extremists," and pointed to the bombings to justify the arrests of independent Muslims that had already taken place.[26] This triggered the arrest of thousands of independent Muslims. President Karimov characterized the bombings as an attempt on his own life and vowed to hold accountable, "The fathers who have brought [enemies of the state] up… together with their children."[27] This signaled a policy of collective punishment that in practice would involve the arrest of suspects' fathers, brothers, and other male relatives absent any evidence other than

[23] See "The Legal Setting" in Chapter II for a detailed explanation of the legislation and restrictions on religion that it imposed.

[24] Shamil Baigin, "Uzbeks, Russia to fight 'militant Islam' together," *Reuters*, June 4, 1998.

[25] Fatality figures range between thirteen (*Agence France-Presse*, February 18, 1999) and sixteen (*Reuters*, February 18, 1999.)

[26] President Karimov suggested that the bombings showed that the concerns of the media and human rights groups regarding arrests prior to the bombings had been nothing more than "gossip" and that the government had acted rightly. "We have not imprisoned a single person unjustly," he said on Uzbek television first channel, February 16, 1999, Worldwide Monitoring, February 16, 1999.

[27] Uzbek television first channel, April 1, 1999, English translation in BBC Monitoring, April 3, 1999.

kinship. Women relatives of suspects were also harassed and briefly detained during this period and, during later phases of the campaign, arrested and convicted.

A series of terrorism trials related to the bombings began in June 1999.[28] Prosecutors repeatedly referred to the defendants as "Wahhabis," and argued that the bombings were the product of a vast conspiracy of Islamic extremists and part of a plan to overthrow the government and create an Islamic state. The state presented no material or forensic evidence linking those on trial with the explosions and committed numerous procedural violations during the course of the trials. The state also tortured the defendants, held them in incommunicado detention, deprived them of legal counsel, and intimidated and coerced witnesses and relatives of defendants. As a result, some observers were left in serious doubt as to the defendants' involvement in the bombings.[29]

Many of the defendants in the bombings trials had been already in prison in February 1999 on charges apparently related to their religious affiliation. The incrimination of "Wahhabis" and other people already in prison at the time of the bombings was in fact directed by President Karimov personally. On the day of the bombings, February 16, 1999, President Karimov announced on national television, "I have instructed my staff. I told them: give me the list of people who have been imprisoned in connection with Namangan, Andijan and in general in connection with the Fergana Valley events. Regarding this list, give me additional information and tell me who among them are true criminals."[30] Those not incarcerated at the time of the bombings and who were charged with participation in the plot were also predominantly observant Muslims with past connections to imams Mirzoev or Nazarov. The prosecution made defendants' religiosity, including the

---

[28] By this time the prosecutor had indicted 128 people. The first trial involved twenty-two defendants.

[29] Human Rights Watch monitored the proceedings in the first of these trials in their entirety. A description of the trial and some of the defendants can be found in Monica Whitlock, *Beyond the Oxus: The Central Asians*, London: John Murray (Publishers) Ltd, 2002.

[30] Uzbek television first channel, February 16, 1999, English translation in BBC Monitoring, February 16, 1999.

number of times a day they prayed, the year they began praying, and the mosques they had attended, the centerpiece of its case, and the courts accepted these factors as evidence of their guilt in the bombings.[31] Court verdicts used the language of a politico-military campaign against Islamic fundamentalism—identifying various dates, for example, as being "after the beginning of the decisive struggle against Wahhabism."[32]

After the bombings, independent Muslims who had been on government surveillance lists, many of whom had been detained or harassed in earlier phases of the campaign, were now re-arrested. Arrests of Hizb ut-Tahrir members, previously scattered and selective, now occurred en masse, even though its members had no known connection to the bombings or any other violent incident. Police raided members' homes as well as public places where the group's members were gathered or proselytizing. While the bombing clearly served as the catalyst for this new pattern of arrests, at least one observer also cites as an explanation Hizb ut-Tahrir's increased visibility and popularity in Uzbekistan. Ahmed Rashid argued that because the group initially made its literature available only in Arabic, the Uzbek government did not view it with much apprehension. But by 1999 Hizb ut-Tahrir produced and distributed its literature in Uzbek and other Central Asian languages. Membership in the group, Rashid relates, also appears to have risen dramatically by 1999.[33]

In the wake of the February bombings, government leaders appeared to have given the police permission to use even the most brazen tactics against "extremists." Masked officers with automatic weapons raided homes at night to seize suspects. They frequently planted drugs or bullets to prove guilt. They sometimes confiscated the Koran or other state-sanctioned religious texts as contraband or evidence of "extremism." Relatives of wanted men were taken hostage pending the

---

[31] Human Rights Watch unofficial transcript, Supreme Court trial of twenty-two men charged with having committed the February 16, 1999 bombings, sessions held from June through July 1999.

[32] Namangan Province Court verdict issued by Judge K. Abduvaliev, October 30, 1999.

[33] Ahmed Rashid, *Jihad: The Rise of Militant Islam in Central Asia*. New Haven: Yale University Press, 2002, p. 120

suspects' appearance. Police also took relatives into custody to increase their leverage with religious detainees who refused to confess to crimes they did not commit. Police used increasingly sophisticated and brutal forms of torture, including electric shock, punctures with metal spikes, rape, and targeted beatings that would not leave marks visible when the defendants appeared in court.

Another government tactic used in the wake of the bombings to root out "extremists" was to offer pardon to those who turned themselves in, and then arrest those who complied. In April 1999 President Karimov and the minister of internal affairs promised to pardon those who asked the state's forgiveness for engaging in unsanctioned religious expression or practice, and encouraged parents to turn in their sons for merciful treatment.[34] The tactic proved effective, although the exact number who sought pardons is unknown. Human Rights Watch estimates that hundreds of independent Muslims turned themselves in to police in the capital alone in the immediate aftermath of the president's promise. A Ministry of Internal Affairs official claimed that 700 people who had

---

[34] President Karimov announced this tactic at a press conference on April 1, 1999. Speaking of "fundamentalists" and those who had left Uzbekistan for military training abroad, he said, "As president and leader, I promise that we will forgive those who give themselves up." Uzbek television first channel, April 1, 1999, English translation in BBC Monitoring April 3, 1999. Minister of Internal Affairs Zokirjon Almatov announced on April 4, 1999, that in accordance with President Karimov's policy, members of "dogmatic and extremist groups" would be spared punishment if they turned themselves over to police. "We will certainly forgive them if they willingly give up and apply to the internal affairs agencies or the prosecutors' offices for forgiveness," Almatov promised on national television. Uzbek television first channel, April 4, 1999, English translation in BBC Monitoring, April 5, 1999. Although the president's promise had been made only in a speech and did not have the quality of legislation, Almatov said he would treat the wishes of Karimov as law and vowed that the actions of the police would be faithful to the president's instructions: "As Internal Affairs Minister, I would like to say that all internal affairs agencies accept our president's views and words as law. Every one of his instructions will be carried out without fail." Then-Procurator General Usmon Khudoikulov, the state official responsible for supervision of the investigation and prosecution of criminal cases, added his voice: "If they surrender and admit their guilt, I repeat, we will forgive them," he promised. In a more menacing tone, he added, "Otherwise, we will without fail find them and make them answer along with their fathers." Ibid. The reference to punishment of fathers for the alleged crimes of their sons would surface frequently during the campaign, and indeed fathers and other relatives would be punished or held hostage by the government to secure arrests and "confessions" from independent Muslims.

sought forgiveness in the first days of the policy had all been pardoned and returned to their families.[35]

Hundreds of men who voluntarily came forward, renounced their religious feelings or affiliations, begged for forgiveness for following the "wrong" religious path, and pledged their loyalty to the state were tried and imprisoned. Once the "confessed extremists" were in custody, the government paraded groups of them at public events designed to unite public opinion against their families and their supporters.

Emergence of the Islamic Movement of Uzbekistan, 1999-2001

By fall 2000 government officials routinely justified the campaign to arrest independent Muslims as necessary to protect the country from violent attack by the Islamic Movement of Uzbekistan (IMU). An armed, militant organization, the IMU seeks the overthrow of the Karimov government through violent means. It was founded in 1997, and is led by political and religious activists who fled Uzbekistan in 1992 under threat of arrest following the crackdown in the Fergana Valley. The IMU's military leader was Juma Namangani (also known as Jumaboi Khojiev), who fought alongside the Islamic opposition against the government of Tajikistan during that country's civil war. Its political leader, Tokhir Iuldash (also known as Tokhir Iuldashev) had led the youth wing of Adolat (Justice), an Islamic patrol group founded in Namangan in 1989.[36] Based in Tajikistan and Afghanistan, the IMU launched armed incursions into Kyrgyzstan in 1999, and into both Uzbekistan and Kyrgyzstan during the summer of 2000.

---

[35] Maj. Fahriddin Islomov, Uzbek TV first channel, April 19, 1999, English translation in BBC Monitoring, April 19, 1999.

[36] Adolat was a registered organization based on the Soviet model of people's patrols (*narodnaia druzhina*). It fought prostitution and street crime, as well as the smuggling of local produce out of the region. While it fiercely opposed "Wahhabism," it sought to impose on the local population observance of such Islamic rules as the banning of alcohol and wearing of headscarves. The government banned Adolat in 1992, arrested some of its members, and fired from local government those civil servants who had been its patrons. Other members, such as Iuldash, fled the country to avoid arrest.

The Uzbek government claimed that Iuldash and Namangani led militants based abroad in a "vast conspiracy" to commit the 1999 bombings, in collusion with the secular opposition, namely exiled politician Muhammad Solikh (also known as Salai Madaminov), and the independent Muslim religious leadership, including missing imams Mirzoev and Nazarov.[37] Similarly, the state claimed that the March 30, 1999 hijacking of a bus carrying local residents in the Bukhara province was the result of collusion among Iuldash, Namangani, Solikh, and their followers inside the country. President Karimov, reacting soon after the hijacking, stated there was no political motivation behind the culprits' actions. He announced on April 1, 1999, that, "These people are not putting forth any political demands, neither [sic] they are adopting any political disguise. They are thieves and robbers through and through."[38] Government authorities later called it a "terrorist" action. In addition, initial reports claimed that police and National Security Service forces had killed three of the five hijackers, but later five residents of the area were sentenced to death for allegedly having a role in the crime. They were scheduled to be executed by firing squad.[39]

In August 1999 armed militants crossed from Tajikistan into Kyrgyzstan and took several hostages. They quickly released the first hostages, but kept another group, including four Japanese geologists, for two months.[40] The Islamic Movement of Uzbekistan, using that name publicly and taking responsibility for the hostage-taking, issued a statement, signed by Tokhir Iuldash, that included its demands: that President Karimov resign; that all religious prisoners in Uzbekistan be released; that those who fled religious persecution and other exiles be

---

[37] The government had not begun yet to use the term IMU to refer to the allegiance of Namangani and Iuldash.

[38] Quoted in "Uzbek head gives details of bus hijack shootout," BBC Monitoring, April 1, 1999.

[39] As of September 2003, there was no further information available regarding whether or not the men had indeed been executed. Death penalty statistics are not commonly made public in Uzbekistan.

[40] Captured on August 23, their release on October 24, 1999 was credited to the alleged payment of a sizeable ransom by the government of Japan.

allowed to return to Uzbekistan; and that the government introduce shari'a.[41]

In August 2000 the IMU launched incursions into Kyrgyzstan and Uzbekistan. The group retreated two months later after pitched battles with government forces in both countries. The only casualty figures came from Kyrgyz and Uzbek government sources. Uzbek spokespeople presented the military's losses to be low, reporting fewer than two dozen soldiers killed in the fighting.[42] Kyrgyz sources reported that they had lost around thirty fighters.[43] Reports ranged from fifteen to one hundred regarding deaths of IMU fighters.[44]

In September 2000 the U.S. government named the IMU a terrorist organization. A little more than a year later, following the attacks on the U.S. on September 11, 2001, President George W. Bush and other world leaders revealed the IMU's close cooperation with the Taliban and Osama Bin Laden's al-Qaeda organization. The IMU bases in

---

[41] "Kyrgyz hostage-takers demand official talks," ITAR-TASS News Agency, Moscow, in English, September 15, 1999, reprinted in BBC Monitoring, September 15, 1999.

[42] Abdumannob Polat and Nickolai Butkevich, "Unraveling the Mystery of the Tashkent Bombings: Theories and Implications," International Eurasian Institute for Economic and Political Research, December 4, 2000 [online], http://iicas.org/english/Krsten_4_12_00.htm, (retrieved September 30, 2003); and "Uzbek President Says Military Underestimated Invaders' Strength," Interfax, August 22, 2000 [online], http://uzland.narod.ru/2000/08_26.htm#militant, (retrieved September 30, 2003).

[43] Official statistics regarding the number of Kyrgyz soldiers killed in the fighting varied from 27 to 32. "Kyrgyz Troops Kill Nine Rebels in Mopping-up Operation," AgenceFrance-Presse, September 25, 2000; and Armen Khanbabyan, "Will the 'Hot Winter' Turn into a 'Hot Spring?'" *Nezavisimaya Gazeta* reprinted by WPS Agency, October 29, 2000; and "Kyrgyz Military still Gives Commands in Russian," *Russian Centre TV*, in Russian, English translation in BBC Monitoring, October 30, 2000.

[44] "Chronology of Uzbekistan, 1924-April 2001," *International Relations and Security Network*, http://www.isn.ethz.ch/onlinepubli/publihouse/fast/suppdata/uzbekistan/uzb_01_chron.pdf; and AFP, "Clashes erupt for third night running on Kyrgyz border," AFP, September 15, 2000. During a series of sweeps before and after the IMU campaign, Uzbek military and police forces permanently displaced an estimated 4,000 residents of Surkhandaria—the location of some of the fighting in 2000 near the Tajikistan border—using force and coercive tactics. They now live in resettlement villages provided by the government in other districts of Surkhandaria province.

Afghanistan were reportedly targets of the U.S. military campaign in Afghanistan. Juma Namangani is believed to have been killed in northern Afghanistan in November 2001.

The Uzbek government has frequently claimed that the IMU, "Wahhabis," and Hizb ut-Tahrir form a united movement, though it has never presented any material evidence to prove this is the case. This has caused many in the international community to conflate the aims and methods of Hizb ut-Tahrir and the IMU. Both the IMU and Hizb ut-Tahrir have an Islamic agenda and have criticized the Karimov administration's crackdown on independent Islam. The two organizations are separate and unique, however, with markedly different aims and methods. In contrast to Hizb ut-Tahrir, the IMU has espoused and used violence to advance its goal of overthrowing the Karimov government. IMU violence has included kidnappings and military tactics, while Hizb ut-Tahrir has an avowed commitment to peaceful action only and has repeatedly decried the use of violence to attain its goals. Hizb ut-Tahrir seeks the re-establishment of the historical Caliphate that existed during the 7th and 8th centuries (and some say even lasted until the end of the Ottoman Empire in 1923). The IMU has expressed only a vague vision of an Islamic state based on shari'a, without elaborating on particular institutional arrangements. Moreover, the primary goal of the IMU is unquestionably the ouster of President Karimov and his administration.

Institutions of Control

Law enforcement and judicial agencies played a highly visible role in the campaign against independent Islam by arresting and imprisoning Muslims. Other institutions also played important roles in maintaining state control over the practice of Islam and expression of religious beliefs. The government's virtually exclusive access to the means of mass communication made it possible for state actors to launch an intense propaganda campaign in coordination with the arrests. Mahalla, or neighborhood, committees provided a vast network of surveillance and social pressure at the local level. The official clergy has actively assisted government officials in formulating, publicly justifying, and implementing the campaign.

The Propaganda Campaign

In Uzbekistan, domestic radio, television and print media are subject to close government scrutiny and censorship.[45] There is no national independent news coverage. The import of most foreign newspapers, magazines, and broadcasts is blocked. Locally broadcast, foreign-run radio programs are available only to a limited degree, as the government assigns them frequencies that are difficult to find on most modern radios. Government control of local newspapers, radio, and television assures the Karimov government a twenty-four-hour vehicle for the propagation of its views. The government re-monopolized access to the internet after a brief period of decentralization, giving it the capacity to more closely monitor communications and to restrict access to web sites. The vast majority of Uzbeks have no access to cable television, which broadcasts foreign news programs.

Control of the mass media has enabled the state to argue, unchallenged, that "religious extremists" pose a serious political and military threat to the country. Television stories about the aftermath of the February 1999 bombings or current events were juxtaposed on a split screen with images of armed Islamic militants fighting in Tajikistan and Afghanistan to illustrate the government's message that Uzbekistan could be next in the region to face a militant Islamic opposition. Television news programs on the arrests or trials of independent Muslims consistently took the side of the state and often declared the accused guilty before a verdict had been reached. People were shown in handcuffs or behind bars while subtitles or voice-over narrative branded them "religious extremists" or "supporters of terrorists" and thereby shamed and judged them before the entire viewing audience.

Government-run media also played a pivotal role in implementing the government's policy of encouraging contrition for religious "misdeeds."

---

[45] In May 2002 Uzbek authorities announced the end of pre-publication censorship. The government, however, continues to use other means of control to restrict the media, which engage in heavy self-censorship to avoid criticism of government policies. For more information, see: Human Rights Watch, "Uzbekistan: Silencing Critical Voices. Dissident Beaten and Ill in Police Custody." *Human Rights Watch Press release*, February 26, 2003, http://www.hrw.org/press/2003/02/uzbekistan022603.htm (Accessed March 17, 2003).

Special broadcasts and nightly news programs aired pre-taped "confessions." In them, young men, sometimes escorted by their parents, confessed to the cameras that they had taken the wrong religious path, begged for the forgiveness of the president and people of Uzbekistan, and then thanked or lauded the Karimov government for its benevolence in pardoning them.[46] This served to bolster the government's contention that these people had done something for which to be sorry, that their religious expression had been wrong and the government had been right. It also led viewers to believe, erroneously, that they could secure pardons from the government. This belief proved disastrous for many who subsequently turned themselves over to police custody to be forgiven and instead found themselves behind bars. Parents, for their part, were shown chastising or denouncing their children, as government and official Islamic policy directed them to do. Parents reiterated the government's message that certain forms of Islamic practice or affiliation were "mistaken" and could bring punishment.

A particularly egregious example of the television propaganda campaign was a two-hour film the government produced and aired on national television that claimed to document the February 16, 1999 bombings and expose those responsible. Men incriminated themselves on screen, and the narrator strung the confessions together into the story of a vast conspiracy against the state of Uzbekistan involving the exiled secular opposition, Uzbek militants abroad, and independent Muslims within and outside the country. Poet Mamadali Makhmudov was one of the men featured in the broadcast incriminating himself and others. His appearance was shocking as, prior to the airing of the film, his whereabouts had not been confirmed and it was feared he had been disappeared. In a letter he wrote following the broadcast, Makhmudov alleged that police had kept him in a basement cell and had threatened to kill him and rape his wife if he did not incriminate himself and others for the television program.[47] Some of the men who appeared in the broadcast were later tried and convicted.

---

[46] For more detail on such "confessions," see "Family Members: Arrests, House Arrest, Harrassment" and "'Hate Rallies' and Public Denunciations" in Chapter III.

[47] Human Rights Watch press release, "Uzbek Torture Victims Sentenced to Prison Terms," August 18, 1999.

Local Government Enforcers (Mahalla Committees)

Agents and officials at all levels of government have assisted and enforced the arrest campaign against independent Muslims since well before the February 1999 bombings. Crucial among these are mahalla, or neighborhood, committees.[48] Together with local mayors, mahalla committees have undertaken surveillance and provided information about community residents' religious beliefs and practices to police.[49] They identify potential "religious extremists" and issue them stern warnings. They have also presided over various methods of social stigmatization, including "hate rallies."

In 2000 Uzbekistan's top leadership singled out the mahalla committees as particularly crucial to the campaign against "extremism." In his January 22, 2000 address to Parliament, President Karimov named the strengthening of mahalla committees and local government authorities a priority of his administration.[50] Following this lead, at a January 28 meeting of Tashkent government officials, state religious leaders, and senior law enforcement officers, Minister of Internal Affairs Zokirjon Almatov promised that police and mahalla committee leaders would support the government's efforts to curb religious "extremism."[51] Following skirmishes between Uzbek military and security forces and the IMU in August 2000, Almatov reiterated the government's call for

---

[48] Traditionally the mahalla is a centuries-old autonomous institution organized around Islamic rituals and social events. After the Soviet period, mahalla committees began to be regulated by law and given the authority to administer a range of activities within the mahalla territory. Although legally the mahalla committees' activities are controlled through general neighborhood meetings, in practice administrative government authorities control their activities. Mahalla committees are effectively state actors. They carry out the policy objectives of senior officials and central government bodies at a local level.

[49] The 1998 religion law tasked mahalla committees, along with other government agencies, with ensuring "observation of the legislation of freedom of worship and religious organizations." Article 6, Law on Freedom of Conscience and Religious Organizations, May 1, 1998.

[50] Uzbek television first channel, January 22, 2000, English translation in BBC Monitoring, January 22, 2000.

[51] Uzbek television first channel, January 27, 2000, English translation in BBC Monitoring, January 28, 2000.

local authorities to play an active role in the campaign against "extremists." He said, "You brothers, parents, imams and leaders, wake up! Where are our young people heading? Why do you not take care of them? Why do you not stop them from becoming bad? You have the right to do many things. You are empowered to decide in your neighborhoods the life and fate of each citizen, each individual who is failing to give their child a proper upbringing, or those who are letting them get involved in these things."[52]

Members of the mahalla committees conducted surveys in villages throughout Uzbekistan, either by visiting homes or by summoning residents to the committee office, to determine each resident's degree of religiosity and possible religious affiliation. The "surveys" included questions such as whether or not one prayed or grew a beard and who had taught the family's children about Islam. Those questioned were encouraged to comment on their neighbors' religious education, practices, and beliefs as well as their own. The committees turned their files on individual citizens, the survey results, and other general surveillance over to local police chiefs.[53]

Memorial Human Rights Center, a Russian nongovernmental organization, obtained a document showing that the Ministry of Internal Affairs directed the surveys and ordered mahalla committees throughout the country to conduct them. The document, issued to the mahalla committee in a Fergana Valley city, describes the kind of information to be gathered by the local officials, and the people to be targeted as "suspicious." The committee members were ordered to make a list of people who encourage women and minors to pray regularly, to list

---

[52] Uzbek television first channel, September 9, 2000, English translation in BBC Monitoring, September 10, 2000.

[53] Human Rights Watch interviews, names withheld, Kokand, May 1998; and *Central Asia Monitor*, "News and Comments" section, Vol. 5, 1998, p. 31. That publication cited a *Vremya MN* article, a credible source, which reported that local leaders were monitoring the movements and behavior of religious and non-religious residents in Uzbekistan and maintaining lists of "potential trouble-makers."

individuals who prayed at unregistered mosques, and to monitor or control men who at the time had or at one time wore a beard.[54]

The surveillance conducted by local officials along with that carried out by law enforcement agents bore substantial fruit. Following the February 1999 bombings, Minister of Internal Affairs Zokirjon Almatov claimed his ministry already had the names of 6,000 people alleged to be members of extremist groups.[55] Memorial reported that during 1999, some 10,700 people were registered or "put on the list" by authorities in mahallas, or neighborhoods, for alleged adherence to "religious fundamentalism."[56] President Karimov himself, referring to Uzbek militants abroad and those he perceived as opponents of his government said, "We have their names on our list."[57]

Court proceedings against independent Muslims frequently revealed the role mahalla committee leaders had played as police informants. Committee members have routinely served as witnesses for the prosecution, testifying to a person's religious activity. They have served also as witnesses for the defense, in particular to testify to a defendant's remorse for having followed the "wrong religious path." They also routinely attest to the mahalla committee's own efforts to steer the accused in the "right" direction. Judges in particular have questioned mahalla committee members about the steps they had taken prior to a defendant's arrest to curb his unregistered religious activity or manifestation of religious belief. In one case involving thirteen men accused of membership in Hizb ut-Tahrir, the mahalla committee chairman was summoned to testify as to why such people had been

[54] "Survey, Distributed in 1998 by the Ministry of Internal Affairs of Uzbekistan among Chairmen of Mahalla Committees," name of Fergana Valley city in which this document was obtained is withheld, provided to Human Rights Watch electronically by Memorial, June 2002. See Appendix for full text.

[55] "President Calls for Extremists to Surrender, Some Heed His Call," *Associated Press Newswires*, April 5, 1999.

[56] Memorial Human Rights Center and the Information Center for Human Rights in Central Asia, *List of People Arrested and Tried in Uzbekistan for Political and Religious Reasons (January 1999 to April 2000)*, Moscow, May 2000.

[57] Uzbek television first channel, April 1, 1999, English translation in BBC Monitoring, April 3, 1999.

participating in unregistered religious activity in his area. One of the lay assessors asked him to confirm whether or not he had received instruction from the hokimiat (mayor's office) to "take care of illegal things."[58] The mahalla committee chairman acknowledged that he had been instructed to inform higher authorities if he discovered any illegal activities in his area. The judge then asked him what he would do if he discovered a member of Hizb ut-Tahrir in his neighborhood. The chairman responded that he would inform fellow members of the mahalla committee and report the person to the police.[59]

President Karimov charged mahalla committees with monitoring local mosques, including the conduct of imams and content of sermons. Speaking just after the February 16, 1999 bombings in Tashkent, he announced on national television:

> ...every neighbourhood committee should supervise the work of its local mosque. What are those mosques there for?... Mosques are designed to improve the life of the neighborhood, to improve people's lives and to inculcate the belief in life after death in the minds of people. They should also explain to people what it's like to have a guilty conscience, and to arouse their conscience. I repeat that if there is a mosque in the neighborhood then the local council should keep their eyes open.[60]

The president tasked the mahalla committees with ensuring that imams used their platform to warn congregations away from "dogmatism." He queried,

---

[58] Lay assessors are non-professional citizens who preside over hearings along with the professional judge, or chairman, of the court. Typically two lay assessors, also called "people's assessors," are appointed to a case. They have full rights to question any member of the defense or prosecution teams. Inherited from the Soviet judicial system, this institution exists in many other post-Soviet states.

[59] Human Rights Watch unofficial transcript, Tashkent City Court hearing held in the Chilanzar District Court building, Tashkent, July 5, 1999.

[60] Uzbek television first channel, February 16, 1999, English translation in BBC Monitoring, February 16, 1999.

> What kind of talk is going on at mosques? Are those chief prayer leaders [imams] performing their duties of defending people?... They should be opening people's eyes and helping them to tell truth from dogmatism... Are they opening people's eyes? Are they warning people? These are legitimate questions. If I am performing my duties well and you are doing yours then those who call themselves chief prayer leaders and religious figures should also perform their duties. Right? Do they have a guilty conscience or not?[61]

Neighborhood Guardians

Several months after the bombings institutional arrangements to implement President Karimov's vision of local control were strengthened. On April 14, 1999, parliament adopted a law regulating the work of mahallas.[62] The Cabinet of Ministers issued a statute creating the position of "neighborhood guardian" (posbon),[63] mahalla committee employees tasked specifically with monitoring residents' behavior and serving as police informants.[64]

The posbon regulation merits more detailed treatment, as these "guardians" essentially serve as morality police, ensuring "adherence to social rules and the norms of manners and morals [in the neighborhood]…" and engaging "deviant" residents in order to alter their behavior.[65]

---

[61] Ibid.

[62] Law on Institutions of Self-Government of Citizens, adopted April 14, 1999.

[63] Second Addition to the Cabinet of Ministers' decision number 180 of April 19, 1999, "About the 'Neighborhood Guardians' Public Organizations Statute" (hereinafter, posbon regulation).

[64]Article 1, posbon regulation.

[65] Articles 17 and 20, posbon regulation. Each "neighborhood guardian," or posbon, is a government employee whose salary is paid from the local budget. (Article 4, posbon regulation.) The mahalla committee selects posbons, who are investigated by both the committee and the local police to determine their acceptability. (Articles 6 and 7, ibid.) Qualification is determined by a person's clean police record, so-called moral health, and

Posbons are subordinate to both the mahalla and to local police, and are described in the law as "the closest helpers of law enforcement organs."[66] As police collaborators, posbons gather information about fellow residents and record the findings from conversations with community residents. They turn these records over to the office of the local police inspector, much the way the mahalla committees hand surveys over to the police.[67] Posbons are explicitly instructed to "identify guilty parties and to carry out searches;"[68] they may also report people to law enforcement officials and summon them to the police station.[69]

The key role played by local informants in the government's campaign against independent Muslims is also alluded to in the posbon regulation. Article 17 states that posbons' duties include "identifying and undertaking preventative and educational measures of [sic] individuals…who invite [youth] to become members of organizations that have the intent to bring them under the influence of various religious extremist ideologies, individuals who undertake various forms of illegal propaganda and propagation activities, those who give religious education to adolescents in a manner contrary to the law and those individuals who spread slander about the constitutional system."[70]

In addition to informing police about residents' religious practices and beliefs, the mahalla committees also carried out their own forms of extrajudicial punishment. They summoned residents to warn them to stop growing beards and fined women who wore headscarves. They demanded that residents forswear Hizb ut-Tahrir membership or sign more general oaths promising not to become involved with "religious

---

lifestyle. (Article 6, ibid.) Significantly, listed among the necessary qualifications of neighborhood guardians is that they be, "volunteers whose spiritual thought is pure and healthy." (Article 3, ibid.)

[66] Articles 11 and 16, posbon regulation.

[67] Articles 11 and 16, ibid.

[68] Articles 19, ibid.

[69] Articles 17, 20 and 22, ibid.

[70] Articles 17, ibid. Other responsibilities of posbons in the social sphere include educating residents regarding public safety and providing social support to alcoholics, drug addicts, and victims of parental neglect.

sects." Harkening back to the Stalinist era, the mahalla committees, along with local police and other government officials, organized community "hate rallies" to publicly shame and denounce independent Muslims and their relatives.

The Role of Official Islam

During the early stages of the campaign, the Muslim Spiritual Board, also called the Muslim Board or Muftiate, took a lead role in cracking down on expressions of faith that did not comply with its dictates.[71] Responsible for the appointment of imams and registration of mosques, the Muslim Spiritual Board was responsible for dismissing leading independent religious leaders and de-registering and closing the majority of mosques that had sprung up after independence. It kept a tight rein on the content of sermons, ensuring that they expressed support for the government, praised the president, and did not expound any views straying from the government line.

In June 1999, the mufti—chairman of the Muslim Spiritual Board and the highest officially sanctioned religious authority in the nation, Abdurashid Kori Bakhromov—went so far as to issue a fatwa, an Islamic decree, against Hizb ut-Tahrir. In it, he called for collective punishment against Hizb ut-Tahrir members, echoing the policy articulated by President Karimov just two months earlier, and called for members of the group to be socially stigmatized and isolated. Mufti Bakhromov declared on national television and radio that members of Hizb ut-Tahrir had criticized "modern Muslims" for failing to pursue jihad, failing to endorse the use of violence, and failing to elect Caliphs.[72] He said, "That is why, as the chairman of the Spiritual Directorate of Muslims in Uzbekistan and mufti, I have issued a fatwa ordering all Muslims to break off all family relations with mercenary-minded people belonging to the Hezb-e Tahrir [sic] sect, with those who have not

---

[71] The Muslim Board of Uzbekistan is the successor institution to the Soviet era Muslim Spiritual Directorate of Central Asia and Kazakhstan, established under Stalin's leadership in 1943.

[72] Uzbek radio first channel, June 11, 1999, English translation in BBC Monitoring, June 11, 1999.

shunned the sect's goals, words, and oaths and have not repented. All neighbourly relations should be eliminated with them. They should not be spoken to. But extremely strict measures should be undertaken against them in order to open their eyes."[73]

Just days after issuing this fatwa, the mufti signed an additional decree, announcing that those who did not recant oaths taken to unregistered Islamic groups would not be given a Muslim burial.[74]

The mufti proved he was willing to act on his own call for the denunciation of Hizb ut-Tahrir members when he had one young man arrested, after the man appealed to him to help stop the persecution of Muslims in Uzbekistan.[75]

The Committee on Religious Affairs

The Committee on Religious Affairs of the Cabinet of Ministers, operating under the authority of parliament and the president, has also played a central role in the criminal prosecution of independent Muslims. The 1998 religion law charged the committee with serving as a liaison between religions organizations and state agencies, and monitoring compliance with the law.[76] Among the committee's main

---

[73] Ibid. The program also reported that the head of the Cabinet of Ministers Committee on Religious Affairs expressed his support for the fatwa.

[74] *Interfax News Agency*, June 15, 1999. Observant Muslim women in Uzbekistan have also claimed to Human Rights Watch that the mufti issued a decree regarding the acceptable and unacceptable ways in which women could wear headscarves. Human Rights Watch interview with two independent Muslim women, names withheld at their request, Tashkent, 1999. Human Rights Watch was unable to obtain the text of such a declaration from the Muftiate.

[75] See below, the case of Usmon Inagamov.

[76] The Committee on Religious Affairs operates under the Cabinet of Ministers, which in turn answers to the president and parliament. The committee is tasked with acting as liaison between religious organizations and state agencies. Specifically, Article 6 of the 1998 Law on Freedom of Conscience and Religious Organizations states, "The coordination of relations between state organizations and religious organizations and control over the observation of the legislation on freedom of worship and religious organizations shall be carried out by the Committee on Religious Affairs under the Cabinet of Ministers of the Republic of Uzbekistan." The committee in fact appears to be engaged

activities is articulating views on the content of religious literature and the significance of certain beliefs, which prosecutors submit to courts as expert testimony.[77] Because possession and distribution of literature are among the most common charges (and in some cases are the only charges) against independent Muslims, the committee's role is significant.

As the government's campaign progressed, such "expert testimony" routinely served as a crucial basis for convictions, along with coerced confessions by defendants. The committee's expert opinions almost always found that statements made in independent Islamic groups' literature were against the constitution. Prosecutors successfully used this opinion to substantiate the frequent charge that possession or distribution of such literature or sympathy with the views expressed therein amounted to anti-constitutional activity punishable by law. Members of the Committee on Religious Affairs did not, with few exceptions, testify in person. Rather, the committee's reports were designed for the prosecution and were not made available to the defense. In a typical court proceeding, no private or impartial examination of the religious literature is provided as an alternative to the committee's views, leaving the Cabinet of Ministers with a monopoly on the interpretation of religious literature. The literature itself is not presented in court. In fact, the content or text of the materials is often not discussed in court beyond an occasional reference to the title of the leaflet or book and a review of the committee's decision.[78]

A few examples:

---

primarily in determining, condemning and censoring the religious activity or ideas that fall outside of the state prescription for acceptable Muslim practice and belief, the religious literature that is "fundamentalist," "extremist" or otherwise "illegal," and those religious groups that, on the basis of their literature or beliefs, are banned.

[77] The Committee also facilitates registration of religious groups of all faiths, and has taken up the issue of registration of smaller Christian groups and problems relating to Christian Sunday schools and day camps. Its staff, comprised of non-clerics with expertise on religious issues, also provides opinions on religious matters to a variety of government agencies, not only the procuracy and judiciary.

[78] For this reason, Human Rights Watch was unable to review much of the literature used as evidence in court, except where our organization obtained it independently.

▪ In his May 1999 verdict concerning Khojiakbar Ergashev (the son of Imam Tulkin Ergashev), Judge V. N. Sharipov relied on the conclusions reached by a group of experts from the Committee on Religious Affairs regarding books that police claimed they found in the Ergashev home. The committee found that Hizb ut-Tahrir used the publications Izzat va sharaf sari and Al-Vai (Consciousness) to spread the group's ideas among the population. According to the committee, these ideas were presented as Islamic but actually "hid under the mask of Islam" so that Hizb ut-Tahrir could first gain public authority and then take power and establish an Islamic state.[79] Judge Sharipov sentenced Ergashev to twelve years in prison for anti-constitutional activities and on other charges, none of which involved acts of violence or the defendant's personally inciting anyone to violence.[80]

▪ Committee experts examined Hizb ut-Tahrir literature that police claimed to have found in the home of Shukhrat Abdurakhimov. They stated that the materials called for the creation of a Caliphate and "contain[ed] illegal ideas regarding changing the existing order, in opposition to the Constitution of the Republic of Uzbekistan."[81] The same committee report contended that Abdurakhimov's co-defendant, Rakhim Umarov, had possessed Hizb ut-Tahrir leaflets that included calls for "the construction of an Islamic state, and seek to take power under the mask of the Muslim religion...."[82] Solely on the basis of this second-hand information about leaflets—and the alleged possession of such literature—the court found Abdurakhimov guilty and sentenced him to seventeen years in prison and Umarov to a fifteen-year term on charges that included article 159, part 3, of the criminal code, an aggravated charge that is meant to apply to those who have repeatedly

---

[79] Tashkent City Court verdict, issued by Judge V.N. Sharipov, Tashkent, May 31, 1999.

[80] Ibid. The Supreme Court reduced Ergashev's sentence to a six-year term on appeal. Supreme Court appeals verdict, issued by R. A. Akbarov, August 9, 1999.

[81] Verdict of the Tashkent Province Court, issued by Judge B. U. Ergashev, August 13, 1999.

[82] Ibid.

or as part of an organized group attempted the overthrow of the constitutional order.[83]

Judge Rakhmonov, who presided over the Tashkent City Court trial of thirteen accused Hizb ut-Tahrir members in July 1999, relied heavily on the interpretation of Hizb ut-Tahrir put forth by the Committee on Religious Affairs. The judge stated in court that he had received a forty-page report from the committee that outlined the origins of Hizb ut-Tahrir and its advocacy of a world Islamic government. The report also stated that the group was intent on converting all Muslims to its way of thinking "by any means" and found the group's literature was being distributed throughout Uzbekistan without government permission.[84] The procurator in this case asserted that the report by the Committee on Religious Affairs proved that the defendants' involvement in spreading the ideas of Hizb ut-Tahrir, including advocacy of a Caliphate and implementation of shari'a, taking an oath of loyalty to the party, and distribution of leaflets were all part of "a plan to overthrow the government."[85] The procurator noted in particular that the committee had examined Hizb ut-Tahrir leaflets and that the draft constitution for an Islamic state contained calls for the overthrow of the government of Uzbekistan.[86] The committee, he said, had designated these books as illegal and against the constitution of Uzbekistan.[87] In a notable

[83] Ibid. Additional information regarding criminal code article 159 is provided in "The Legal Setting" in Chapter II.

[84] Human Rights Watch unofficial transcript, Tashkent City Court trial held in the Chilanzar District Court building, Tashkent, July 8, 1999.

[85] Ibid. The procurator is the investigator and prosecutor of a case.

[86] Human Rights Watch unofficial transcript, Tashkent City Court trial held in the Chilanzar District Court building, Tashkent, July 8, 1999. The procurator referred to a document called "The Islamic Charter," however one Hizb ut-Tahrir representative in the United Kingdom, Imran Waheed, informed Human Rights Watch that there is no Hizb ut-Tahrir document by that name and that it is a mistranslation of the title of the draft constitution issued by Hizb ut-Tahrir. For the draft constitution, see, Hizb ut-Tahrir, "A Draft Constitution," in *The System of Islam* (London: Al-Khilafah Publications, 2002), [also available online], http://www.hizb-ut-tahrir.org/english/ (retrieved February 20, 2004). *The System of Islam* is a basic Hizb ut-Tahrir text. Electronic communication from Imran Waheed to Human Rights Watch, May 30, 2002.

[87] Ibid.

expansion of the application of the committee's mandate, the same procurator revealed that the committee's report had decided also on the validity of the religious beliefs held by Hizb ut-Tahrir and had contained a prescription for proper belief. The committee report, he told the court, "says all the literature found was of a religious extremist group and [that] although you should be religious and recognize Allah, you should never give an oath... even Muhammad said jihad is not good for Muslims... Their activities are in contradiction to the Prophet's words."[88]

Notes on Wahhabism, "Wahhabis," and Hizb ut-Tahrir

Wahhabism and "Wahhabis"

In Central Asia, government leaders and government-aligned clergy use the term "Wahhabism" to denote "Islamic fundamentalism" and "extremism." It is often used as a slur, with strong political implications.[89] There is a common misconception, encouraged by the government of Uzbekistan, that within Islam there are three schools: Sunni, Shi'a, and Wahhabi. In fact, Wahhabism, a revivalist movement that grew out of the Hanbali school, is a branch of Sunni Islam practiced in Saudi Arabia and elsewhere. The name derives from its eighteenth century founder, the Hanbali teacher and reformer Muhammad ibn 'Abd al-Wahhab (1703-1792).

Wahhabism advocates a purification of Islam, rejects Islamic theology and philosophy developed after the death of the Prophet Muhammad, and calls for strict adherence to the letter of the Koran and hadith [the recorded sayings and practices of the Prophet]. In promoting what its adherents view as the precepts of early Islam, Wahhabism maintains a

---

[88] Human Rights Watch unofficial transcript, Tashkent City Court trial held in the Chilanzar District Court building, Tashkent, July 8, 1999.

[89] The "Wahhabi" label has also been used in other parts of the former Soviet Union as short-hand for militant. According to Central Asia scholar Mehrdad Haghayeghi, the term was first used by the Soviets to refer to "fundamentalist" Muslims in general during the 1980s. Mehrdad Haghayeghi, *Islam and Politics in Central Asia*, St. Martin's Press, New York, 1995, p. 227, note 55. In the Tajik civil war, fighters seeking to overthrow the government were nicknamed "vofchiki," a diminutive form of "Vahabit," or "Wahhabi."

strict and puritanical view of religious rites. It eschews "innovations," including practices viewed as polytheistic, such as the worship of saints, mysticism, and decoration of graves. It prohibits dancing and music.

Ibn Wahhab came under the protection of Muhammad ibn Saud and the alliance of the Wahhabi movement and the Saud family, now the rulers of Saudi Arabia, remains formidable to this day. A small number of Sunni Muslims in Uzbekistan are in fact followers of Saudi-style Islam and therefore could be called Wahhabi. They adhere more strictly than adherents of other schools of Sunni Islam to the letter of the Koran and hadith, to the exclusion of other sources.[90]

Views differ as to when Wahhabism first found adherents in Central Asia. Pakistani journalist and author Ahmed Rashid estimates that this occurred in 1912, but that Wahhabism failed to gain much popularity.[91] Haghayeghi argues that Wahhabi principles may have spread from India to Central Asia in the early part of the 1800s.[92]

Haghayeghi draws clear distinction between the Hanafi school and the Wahhabi movement. The Hanafi school of Sunni Islam is another one of the four main schools of law and distinct from the Hanbali school. Haghayeghi writes that adherents emphasize analogy, critical scrutiny, public consensus, and private opinion when implementing and interpreting Islamic principles.[93] The Hanafis' tolerance and even reverence for difference of opinion, according to Haghayeghi "…places the Hanafi school farthest away from the conservative or dogmatic understandings of Islam."[94]

---

[90] Mehrdad Haghayeghi, *Islam and Politics in Central Asia*, New York: St. Martin's Press, 1995, p 95. While the Wahhabi doctrine rejects reinterpretation of the Koran and hadith, it does allow for *ijtihad,* or independent reasoning, in other areas.

[91] *Jihad: The Rise of Militant Islam in Central Asia*, New Haven and London: Yale University Press, 2002, p. 45.

[92] *Islam and Politics in Central Asia*, p. 92.

[93] Ibid. p. 81.

[94] Ibid, p. 81.

Haghayeghi notes that Wahhabism had little resonance with the population of Central Asia because of that branch's "puritanical views" and rejection of private opinion and public consensus.[95] Rashid points to the dramatic difference between actual Wahhabis and the so-called Wahhabis targeted by the Uzbek government:

> In 1992[…] the Uzbek government began to label anyone who was perceived to be an adherent of radical Islam or held anti-government sentiments as part of his Islamic beliefs, a Wahhabi. By 1997 the government was labeling as Wahhabis even ordinary Muslims who practiced Islam in unofficial mosques or engaged in private prayer or study. Any Muslim who associated with unregistered prayer leaders or taught children how to read the Koran was also termed a Wahhabi. Today the government uses Wahhabi to undermine all Muslim believers by associating them with the Wahhabis' record of extremism. Such mislabeling, whilst demonstrating the lack of real knowledge about Islam amongst the ruling elites, enables them to suppress all Islamic activity merely by naming it Wahhabi.[96]

Indeed the vast majority of those branded by the Uzbek government as "Wahhabis" had little in common with the relatively small group that actually follow Wahhabi doctrine. Notably, they were almost without exception adherents of the Hanafi school. Independent Muslims who were followers of the Hanafi school were not necessarily in favor of the establishment of an Islamic state, or application of shari'a in Uzbekistan. Consistent with Hanafi principles, many were believers, but were not all strictly observant practitioners. They often continued to observe pre-Islamic, namely Zoroastrian, rituals.[97] Qualification as a "genuine" Muslim, then, has been for them more dependent on submission to God and his Prophet Muhammad than participation in rituals and strict

[95] Ibid. p. 95

[96] *Jihad*, p. 46

[97] For example, Navruz (celebration of the new year).

adherence to duties.[98] Religious rules regulating marriage, divorce, funerals, and other ceremonies differed dramatically from those followed by Wahhabis.

Many independent Muslims in Uzbekistan objected to the politicization of religion both by Wahhabis and by the government. Many so-called moderate Muslims were branded "extremists" and, ironically, "Wahhabis" for repudiating the government's injection of politics into sermons and rituals. Under President Karimov, a person who moved beyond the official, limited definition of religious observance—by studying Arabic in order to read the Koran in its original language, sticking strictly to the observance of the five daily prayers, or appearing in public dressed in a way that suggested piety—was considered deviant or "Wahhabi." People have also been called "Wahhabi" for showing respect for or declaring allegiance to any authority not sponsored by or directly associated with the state structure—this was viewed by the Karimov government as an affront to its power, a danger to be curbed. Thus, visits to the homes of local religious teachers, attendance at mosques not registered with the state, and most importantly the placement of loyalty to Islam before loyalty to political leaders, were regarded by the state apparatus as displays of excessive independence. Refusals by imams and others to serve as informants for the state security agents regarding the activities and beliefs of their coreligionists was similarly seen as unacceptable insolence.

Hizb ut-Tahrir

Hizb ut-Tahrir members form a distinct segment of the independent Muslim population by virtue of their affiliation with a separate and defined Islamic group with its own principles, structure, activities, and religious texts.

Hizb ut-Tahrir is an international Islamic organization with branches in many parts of the world, including the Middle East and Europe. Hizb ut-Tahrir propagates a particular vision of an Islamic state. Its aims are restoration of the Caliphate, or Islamic rule, in Central Asia and other

[98] *Islam and Politics in Central Asia*, pp. 80-81

traditionally Muslim lands, and the practice of Islamic piety, as the group interprets it, (e.g., praying five times daily, shunning alcohol and tobacco, and, for women, wearing clothing that covers the body and sometimes the face). Hizb ut-Tahrir renounces violence as a means to achieve reestablishment of the Caliphate. However, it does not reject the use of violence during armed conflicts already under way and in which the group regards Muslims as struggling against oppressors, such as Palestinian violence against Israeli occupation. Its literature denounces secularism and Western-style democracy. Its anti-Semitic and anti-Israel[99] statements have led the government of Germany to ban it.[100] The government of Russia has also banned the group, classifying it as a terrorist organization.[101]

---

[99] Hizb ut-Tahrir materials often denounce Israeli occupation of Palestine and Israeli conduct in the conflict there.

[100] The German Ministry of the Interior issued a statement on January 15, 2003 announcing that Hizb ut-Tahrir was banned in the country. http://www.bmi.bund.de/dokumente/Pressemitteiling/ix_91334.htm. The ministry statement cited as grounds for the decision, paragraphs 3, 14, 15, and 18 of the German Vereinsgesetz (congregation laws). German Minister of the Interior Otto Schilly said that, "Hizb ut-Tahrir abuses the democratic system to propagate violence and disseminate anti-Semitic hate-speeches. The organization wants to sow hatred and violence." He also stated that, "The organization supports violence as a means to realize political goals. Hizb ut-Tahrir denies Israel's right to exist and calls for its destruction. The organization further spreads massively anti-Semitic propaganda and calls for killing Jews." See also, Peter Finn, "Germany Bans Islamic Group; Recruitment of Youths Worried Officials," The *Washington Post*, January 16, 2003. That article states that German officials accused Hizb ut-Tahrir of spreading "violent anti-Semitism" and establishing contacts with neo-Nazis. In April, German police searched the homes of more than eighty people suspected of supporting Hizb ut-Tahrir. No arrests were made. See, Associated Press, "Germany stages new raids against banned Islamic organization," April 11, 2003.

[101] On February 14, 2003, Russia's Supreme Court, acting on a recommendation from the Office of the Prosecutor General, designated Hizb ut-Tahrir a terrorist organization. According to a press statement released by Russia's Ministry of Foreign Affairs on June 9, 2003, "The main criteria for the inclusion of organizations in the list of terrorist outfits were: the carrying out of activities aimed at a forcible change of the constitutional system of the Russian Federation; ties with illegal armed bands, as well as with radical Islamic structures operating on the territory of the North Caucasus region, and ties with or membership of organizations deemed by the international community terrorist organizations." "On the Detention of Members of the Terrorist Organization 'Islamic Liberation Party' ('Hizb ut-Tahrir al Islami')," Publication of the Ministry of Foreign Affairs of the Russian Federation, Information and Press Department, June 9, 2003, from the *Daily News Bulletin*, posted June 11, 2003.

Some in the diplomatic community, in particular the U.S. government, consider Hizb ut-Tahrir to be a political organization and therefore argue that imprisoned Hizb ut-Tahrir members are not victims of religious persecution.[102] But religion and politics are inseparable in Hizb ut-Tahrir's ideology and activities, and one of the chief reasons Uzbek authorities arrest members is the religious ideas Hizb ut-Tahrir promotes: the reestablishment of the Caliphate and strict observance of the Koran. Even if one accepts that there is a political component to Hizb ut-Tahrir's ideology, methods, and goals, this does not vitiate the right of that group's members to be protected from religion-based persecution.

Hizb ut-Tahrir in Uzbekistan

Hizb ut-Tahrir is not registered in Uzbekistan and is therefore illegal. It is referred to as a "banned" organization, though in contrast to the means used by German authorities to ban Hizb ut-Tahrir, no single

---

http://www.ln.mid.ru/bl.nsf/0/43bb94f12ad12c7543256d42005a9b49?OpenDocument On June 6, 2003, fifty-five people alleged to be members of Hizb ut-Tahrir were detained in Russia. Two of the men arrested—one a citizen of Kyrgyzstan, the other a citizen of Tajikistan—were accused of illegal possession of grenades and explosive material. Ibid. As of this writing, Human Rights Watch had no further information about the fate of these two men or whether they were convicted on these charges. The Russian rights group Memorial contested the significance of the law enforcement action, however. The group noted that the majority of the men detained were immigrant workers at a bakery and were released soon after the sweep. "Russian rights group: Detention of 55 'Islamic extremists' was sham," *Associated Press*, June 25, 2003.

[102] In a recent expression of this view, Larry Memmot, then-first secretary of the U.S. Embassy in Tashkent, told Human Rights Watch that this is "not an issue of religious repression, but political." Human Rights Watch interview, Tashkent, May 4, 2003. Whether the U.S. government views those arrested on charges related to Hizb ut-Tahrir membership victims of religious persecution has important legal and foreign policy consequences. Under the U.S. International Religious Freedom Act, the U.S. government annually must determine whether governments engage in religious persecution. If the executive finds that governments "have engaged in or tolerated particularly severe violations of religious freedom," it must choose from a menu of actions, ranging from private demarches through sanctions, with regard to that country.

Uzbek administrative or judicial decision has ever prohibited the organization.[103]

Members meet in small groups of about five people, referred to as "study groups" by members and as "secret cells" by Uzbek government officials. Both sides acknowledge that the primary activity of these small groups is the teaching and study of Hizb ut-Tahrir literature, as well as traditional Islamic texts such as the Koran and hadith. Membership in the group is solidified by taking an oath, the content of which has been given variously as: being faithful to Islam; being faithful to Hizb ut-Tahrir and its rules; and spreading the words of the Prophet and sharing one's knowledge of Islam with others.[104] Law enforcement and judicial authorities generally considered both those who had and had not taken the oath as full-fledged members.

In Human Rights Watch interviews and in court testimony, Hizb ut-Tahrir members have overwhelmingly cited an interest in acquiring deeper knowledge of the tenets of Islam as their motivation for joining the group. Hizb ut-Tahrir members in Uzbekistan, and likely elsewhere, regard the reemergence of the Caliphate as a practical goal, to be achieved through proselytism.

Members in Uzbekistan distribute literature or leaflets produced by the organization which include quotations from the Koran, calls for observance of the basic tenets of Islam, and analysis of world events affecting Muslims, including denunciation of the mass arrest of independent Muslims in Uzbekistan.

Peaceful or Violent?

Hizb ut-Tahrir's designation as a nonviolent organization has been contested. Hizb ut-Tahrir literature does not renounce violence in armed struggles already under way—in Israel and the Occupied Territories,

---

[103] See "The Legal Setting" in Chapter II.

[104] Human Rights Watch unofficial transcript, Tashkent City Court trial held in the Chilanzar District Court building, Tashkent, June 30, 1999. For examples of the specific wording of Hizb ut-Tahrir oaths, See "Hizb ut-Tahrir" in Chapter II.

Chechnya, and Kashmir—in which it views Muslims as the victims of persecution. But Hizb ut-Tahrir members have consistently rejected the use of violence to achieve the aim of reestablishing the Caliphate, which they believe will only be legitimate if created the same way they believe the Prophet Muhammad created the original Caliphate, and which can occur only as a result of gradual "awakening" among Muslims.

Human Rights Watch is not aware of Hizb ut-Tahrir members in Uzbekistan charged with undertaking an act of violence.[105] An anonymous leader of Hizb ut-Tahrir reportedly told Ahmed Rashid that "Hizb ut-Tahrir wants a peaceful jihad [struggle] that will be spread by explanation and conversion, not by war."[106] Members of the group in Uzbekistan have uniformly renounced violence and asserted their commitment to peaceful advocacy of Muslim practice and adherence to the goal of a Caliphate. Hizb ut-Tahrir literature states that only God is empowered to determine when the Caliphate will actually come to be. Members also vigorously profess their abhorrence of violence and their belief that the use of violence, particularly murder, is a sin according to Islam.

---

[105] Although not charged with involvement in or responsibility for a specific violent act, some Hizb ut-Tahrir members, particularly in Andijan, have been convicted for terrorism under article 155 of the criminal code. Human Rights Watch's review of these cases found no reference to a violent act having taken place. In one case following the September 11, 2001 attacks in the United States, nine Hizb ut-Tahrir members tried in Tashkent were alleged by the procurator to have links to Osama Bin Laden and al-Qaeda. However, according to trial observers, no evidence was provided to back this claim. One journalist who covered the process described the nature of the alleged connection a "mystery" and quoted defendant Nurullo Majidov's rejection of the state's charges, "We do not have connections to Osama Bin Laden or any other terrorist organizations, as we pursue different methods of struggle. We are fighting for our ideas through peaceful means." Said Khojaev (a pen name), "Tashkent Cracks Down on Islamists," *Institute for War and Peace Reporting*, October 12, 2001. The nine men were convicted in October 2001 to prison terms ranging from nine to twelve years. Hizb ut-Tahrir members in the U.K. also denied that the organization had any ties with Bin Laden or al-Qaeda. Human Rights Watch interview with members of the leadership committee of Hizb ut-Tahrir Britain, London, June 29, 2002.

[106] Ahmed Rashid, "Interview with Leader of Hizb-e Tahrir," *The Analyst*, available on Eurasianet.org [online] http://www.eurasianet.org/resource/cenasia/hypermail/200011/0066.html (retrieved May 9, 2003).

One young member of Hizb ut-Tahrir told Human Rights Watch, "There will not be a jihad, we will not turn to violence. We will spread the ideas of Hizb ut-Tahrir, but we will not fight."[107] When asked by a judge to name the actions Hizb ut-Tahrir planned to take to realize its goal of an Islamic state, accused member Shahmaksud Shobobaev said that the group's principles were consistent with the teachings of the Koran and that, "Hizb ut-Tahrir condemns terrorism, any use of weapons, to establish an Islamic state. When peoples' consciousness changes, when they are pious and want to do good things, the Hizb ut-Tahrir idea is to establish a real, good state."[108] When Judge Rakhmonov later asked Shobobaev whether or not he would kill for Allah at the direction of Hizb ut-Tahrir, the defendant responded, "No. No one would ask such a direct, stupid question… We are not going to kill anybody. We are not reactionaries, we are just expressing our views." He added, "Our idea was to teach, not to use force."[109] When a lay assessor asked Shobobaev's co-defendant, Tolkhon Riksiev, "How can you change the country without [using] weapons?" the accused man answered, "We don't discuss establishing the Caliphate now. We just call people [proselytize] and believe they will decide for themselves how to live."[110] When the lay assessor challenged him, saying that this could take centuries, Riksiev stated, "Allah calls us to be patient."[111]

Judge Rakhmonov noted that Riksiev's co-defendant Aflotun Normukhamedov had expressed dissatisfaction with the current government system in Uzbekistan and embraced a Caliphate as a better system, but acknowledged also, "He does not recognize the use of force or weapons. He only wanted to peacefully establish a Caliphate."[112]

---

[107] Human Rights Watch interview with a member of Hizb ut-Tahrir, name withheld, Tashkent, February 2001.

[108] Human Rights Watch unofficial transcript, Tashkent City Court trial held in the Chilanzar District Court building, Tashkent, June 30, 1999.

[109] Ibid.

[110] Ibid.

[111] Ibid.

[112] Human Rights Watch unofficial transcript, Tashkent City Court trial held in the Chilanzar District Court building, Tashkent, July 20, 1999.

Hizb ut-Tahrir's Religion and Politics

Hizb ut-Tahrir's goals are a mix of religion and politics. According to a statement by the leadership of the international group, "Hizb ut-Tahrir is a political party whose ideology is Islam, so politics is its work and Islam is its ideology."[113] The statement explained, "...politics in Islam is looking after the affairs of the people, either in opinion or in execution or both, according to the laws and solutions of Islam."[114] That is, Islamic politics is the explanation and implementation of Islamic law, shari'a. Hizb ut-Tahrir also claims that the idea of the Caliphate is consistent with Hanafism, and indeed is the truest expression of the teachings of Hanafism's founder.[115]

Many people have been imprisoned for possessing or distributing Hizb ut-Tahrir literature. The political content and consequences of this literature has led some observers, particularly members of the diplomatic community, to regard the literature and the activity of disseminating the literature as primarily political and not religious in nature. The U.S. in particular views the group as political and overlooks the religious ideas and goals its literature contains. To be sure, Hizb ut-Tahrir literature opines on such political phenomena as the repressive policies of the Uzbek government, the arrest and torture of Hizb ut-Tahrir members, corruption in Uzbekistan, and the armed conflicts in Israel and the Occupied Territories, Kashmir, and Chechnya. But it also expounds the duty, which members believe was prescribed by the Prophet Muhammad, for Muslims to reestablish the Caliphate, and reiterates the

---

[113] Hizb ut-Tahrir web site [online], http://www.hizb-ut-tahrir.org/ (retrieved May 9, 2003).

[114] Ibid.

[115] One example of this claim can be found in "The Ideology the President of Uzbekistan, Karimov, Wants to Impose upon Muslims," Hizb ut-Tahrir leaflet, Uzbekistan, July 24, 2000 [online], http://www.khilafah.com/home/lographics/category.php?DocumentID=189&TagID=3 (retrieved May 9, 2003). The leaflet states: "To fight the idea of Khilafah, [the Karimov government] first announced that the Khilafah concept contradicts Islam, they claimed it contradicts the method of the Great Imam Abu Hanifah, but when Muslims realized that the Khilafah is the only way to apply Islam and its shariah in full accordance with Islam and with the method of Abu Hanifah, their plot became obvious and failed."

need to convince others to become observant Muslims. Dissemination of these ideas is considered part of a program of religious proselytism.[116]

Islam as a Complete and Comprehensive System

Members of Hizb ut-Tahrir, like many other Muslims, believe that Islam is a complete system, incorporating rules for all kinds of human conduct, including the direction of politics, economics, family relations, etc. Members' political activities, which consist of propagation of the ideas of Hizb ut-Tahrir, are subservient to the organizing ideology in which they take place, and which they promote—Islam. Politics is viewed as part of a religious doctrine, the implementation or realization of religious belief.[117]

This idea was expressed by Hizb ut-Tahrir member Shahmaksud Shobobaev, who testified that as part of the group he had engaged in Islamic education and the spread of religious ideas. When the Tashkent City Court judge asked Shobobaev whether or not he had been "involved in politics," he responded, "Religion has politics and finance in it, everything. I just wanted people to be religious."[118] He added, "I have nothing against the existing state."[119]

---

[116] The group's writings also hold that criticism of an unjust ruler is the duty of all Muslims. Hizb ut-Tahrir's draft constitution, which envisions the order that would be in place in a future Caliphate, says, "Calling upon the rulers to account for their actions is both a right for the Muslims and a *fard kifayah* (collective duty) upon them." [Article 20 of the draft constitution of Hizb ut-Tahrir ; see, Hizb ut-Tahrir, "A Draft Constitution," in *The System of Islam* (London: Al-Khilafah Publications, 2002), [available online], http://www.hizb-ut-tahrir.org/english/ (retrieved February 22, 2004). Criticizing unjust rulers, then, is a distinctly religious action, as it is viewed as a prerequisite to creation of a worldwide Muslim community, to be awarded by God with an Islamic form of government, or Caliphate.

[117] Hizb ut-Tahrir also says that it does not accept a religious system bereft of politics any more than it would accept a political order that was not based on Islam. This is articulated in the book, *The System of Islam*, a principle Hizb ut-Tahrir text, which reads, "...anything that confines religion to the spiritual dimension, separating it from politics and ruling should be abolished." Hizb ut-Tahrir, *The System of Islam*, p. 40.

[118] Human Rights Watch unofficial transcript, Tashkent City Court trial held in the Chilanzar District Court, Tashkent, June 30, 1999.

[119] Ibid.

Hizb ut-Tahrir also claims that Islam is a superior religion because it contains a comprehensive system of beliefs and governance[120] and because it is a religion revealed by God.[121]

Opposition to Secularism and Democracy

As explained above, Hizb ut-Tahrir rejects the separation of religion and politics,[122] and so also rejects "Western" secularism. An April 2000 leaflet states:

> It is well known that Western laws derived from the doctrine of separation of religion from life and state are applied all over the world, including the Islamic world, with Uzbekistan being part of it. It was well known ahead of time that this doctrine, being false, could not stand [up against] the truth, i.e. Islam, and guarantee

[120] One leaflet states, "Being perfect and complete, Islam has the right to rule the world." See, "Government of Uzbekistan Displays the Decline of Systems of Belief," Hizb ut-Tahrir leaflet, April 9, 2000 [online], http://www.khilafah.com/home/lographics/category.php?DocumentID=84&TagID=3 (retrieved May 9, 2003.)

[121] "The Ideology the President of Uzbekistan, Karimov, Wants to Impose upon Muslims," Hizb ut-Tahrir leaflet, Uzbekistan, July 24, 2000 [online], http://www.khilafah.com/home/lographics/category.php?DocumentID=189&TagID=3 (retrieved May 9, 2003). The leaflet states: "Because Islam is the ideology and system capable of completely solving all problems and leading to an unconditional correct development....Islam is a religion, revealed by Allah to its Messenger Muhammad (the peace and blessings of Allah be upon him). Therefore, we submit ourselves to Islam not because our ancestors did, but because it is a true religion revealed by Allah, and we obey its rules and call to it as Allah orders us."

[122] This idea is expressed in an April 24, 2000 leaflet entitled "The President of Uzbekistan Admits to Being Intellectually Bankrupt." It states: "The creed of the people in the Islamic world is the Islamic creed and the creed of Islam is one from which a system emanates organizing all affairs of the people. And this system is the only correct system for the world because it comes from Allah (swt). And every attempt to separate the creed from the system or to mix and patch together different creeds and systems is a consequence of shallow thinking and its outcome is failure." The leaflet is available at: http://www.khilafah.com/home/lographics/category.php?DocumentID=1&TagID=3 (retrieved May 9, 2003).

> justice in the world by separating religion from the life. That is why today, when Islam together with the Islamic community regains its lost stature, this infamous faith [separation of religion and state] cannot withstand this process and retreats from its own laws, thus showing the rotten decline of its era… Undoubtably [sic], this fallacious doctrine of separation of religion from the life, state, and politics and, derived from it, the western ideology and legislation has corrupted the whole world. Therefore, the western ideology and laws, its states coupled with its menial servants in the Islamic countries, absolutely do not have any right to govern mankind. In the meantime, Islam by means of [rational thought] and clear documentation has proved the ineligibility of all other religions, doctrines, ideologies and systems."[123]

This rejection of secularism and Hizb ut-Tahrir's view of Islam as a superior social, political, and economic system are at the heart of its stance against democracy.

Anti-Americanism

Hizb ut-Tahrir leaflets often portray President Karimov as a proxy of undefined global forces, led by the U.S. government, that seek to impose "alien" western ideas on the people of Uzbekistan.[124]

The U.S. government is seen as the driving force behind Uzbekistan's drive to preserve secularism: "…The USA, watching the unprecedented spread of Islam in Central Asia, specifically the movements to renew the

[123] "Government of Uzbekistan Displays the Decline of Systems of Belief," Hizb ut-Tahrir leaflet, April 9, 2000 [online], http://www.khilafah.com/home/lographics/category.php?DocumentID=84&TagID=3 (retrieved May 9, 2003).

[124] "The Ideology the President of Uzbekistan, Karimov, Wants to Impose upon Muslims," Hizb ut-Tahrir leaflet, Uzbekistan, July 24, 2000 [online], available at: http://www.khilafah.com/home/lographics/category.php?DocumentID=189&TagID=3 (retrieved May 9, 2003).

Islamic life and reestablish the Khilafah State, and wishing to prevent them from spreading, ordered their servant Karimov to create a basis and ideology for the state of Uzbekistan other than Islam."[125]

Hizb ut-Tahrir portrays U.S.-led counter-terrorism actions as an assault on Islam and a transparent attempt to assert cultural hegemony. An April 2000 leaflet, for example, reads:

> America had noticed that Islam was spreading in Central Asia. Thus she feared for her influence and ambitions there. She feared for her culture and herself due to the rise of Islam, which she saw not as a mercy to her but as an affliction on her. That is why she and all the Kufr [unbeliever] states call it terrorism and are holding conferences and draw up plans to fight it.[126]

Anti-Semitism

Hostility to Jews is a recurring theme in Hizb ut-Tahrir literature. This is frequently expressed in denunciations of President Karimov as a Jew or kafir (unbeliever).

Hizb ut-Tahrir blames Karimov's campaign against the group on his alleged Jewish identity. Commenting on an unfair trial that resulted in twenty-year prison sentences for ten members of Hizb ut-Tahrir, an April 9, 2000 leaflet stated:

> …though the prosecutors, having 'proved' trumped-up charges against Members of Hizb ut-Tahrir, which carries an ideological and political call to Islam, asked the judges for [varied] terms, they (the judges) disregarded the request and sentenced all of [the

---

[125] Ibid.

[126] Hizb ut-Tahrir, "The President of Uzbekistan Admits to Being Intellectually Bankrupt," Hizb ut-Tahrir leaflet, April 24, 2000 [online], http://www.khilafah.com/home/lographics/category.php?DocumentID=1&TagID=3 (retrieved May 9, 2003).

> defendants] to 20 years of imprisonment. This is due to the fact that today the Uzbekistan regime led by the Jewish unbeliever Islam Karimov holds trials of Members of Hizb ut-Tahrir, basing its decisions not on the laws in force, but on fear and hatred of Islam... Playing about with ideas like 'legal state' and 'justice,' the Uzbekistan regime shows the people of this country, via such unjust rulings in its court cases, how [tyrannical] and deceitful it is. Moreover, the 'state,' claiming to be legitimate[ly]...led by the Jewish disbeliever Karimov, by all means shows its full ignorance of its own laws in force.[127]

After describing authorities' systematic arrest and torture of Hizb ut-Tahrir members and other Muslims, another leaflet states, "This harshness of Karimov comes from his origins as a disbelieving Jew. The Jews are the most severest [sic] of people in enmity to Islam and the Muslims."[128]

The man interviewed by Ahmed Rashid who claimed to be a leader of Hizb ut-Tahrir, and who was presumably located outside of Uzbekistan, stated point-blank, "We are very much opposed to the Jews and Israel. We don't want to kill Jews, but they must leave Central Asia."[129]

---

[127] "Government of Uzbekistan Displays the Decline of Systems of Belief," Hizb ut-Tahrir leaflet, April 9, 2000 [online], http://www.khilafah.com/home/lographics/category.php?DocumentID=84&TagID=3 (retrieved May 9, 2003.)

[128] Hizb ut-Tahrir, "The President of Uzbekistan Admits to Being Intellectually Bankrupt," Hizb ut-Tahrir leaflet, April 24, 2000 [online], http://www.khilafah.com/home/lographics/category.php?DocumentID=1&TagID=3 (retrieved May 9, 2003). This statement is apparently inspired by sura "The Table" [5:82 of the Koran]: "You will find that the most implacable of men in their enmity to the faithful are the Jews and the pagans..." *The Koran*, Penguin Books, London, England, 1990, p.88. Translated into English.

[129] Ahmed Rashid, "Interview with Leader of Hizb-e Tahrir," *The Analyst*, November 22, 2000.

The Legal Setting

The Uzbek government's campaign against independent Muslims violates the basic rights to freedom of conscience and religion and freedom of expression, which are guaranteed under the International Covenant on Civil and Political Rights (ICCPR). This section first elaborates on key aspects of these rights, drawing on authoritative commentary by the U.N. Human Rights Committee, the body that monitors compliance with the ICCPR, as they relate to the situation in Uzbekistan. The second part of this section describes the abusive restrictions Uzbek law places on freedom of conscience and religion and freedom of expression.

In pressing forth with this campaign, the government violates many other obligations under international law. Not only does the government fail to protect and promote freedom of conscience and religion and freedom of expression, but its attacks on people exercising these rights also involves violations of due process and the right to liberty. Law enforcement and security agents engage in illegal searches and arbitrary arrest and detention. Once in custody, detainees are routinely tortured in violation of the ICCPR and the Convention against Torture and Other Cruel Inhuman or Degrading Treatment or Punishment. The government denies independent Muslim detainees access to counsel and violates their right to a fair trial as guaranteed in the ICCPR. Even after the defendants are convicted and sentenced to prison terms, many continue to be tortured and subjected to other forms of inhuman and degrading treatment. Many aspects of prison conditions in which independent Muslim prisoners serve out their sentences violate U.N. Standard Minimum Rules for the Treatment of Prisoners. More detailed reference is made to these instruments in the relevant chapters of this book.

Freedom of Religion in International Law

In 1995 the Republic of Uzbekistan, under the leadership of President Karimov, voluntarily acceded to the International Covenant on Civil and Political Rights. Uzbekistan ratified the ICCPR the next year, in 1996.

Article 18 of the ICCPR upholds individuals' rights to hold and to manifest their religious beliefs. It states:

> Everyone shall have the right to freedom of thought, conscience and religion. This right shall include freedom to have or to adopt a religion or belief of his choice, and freedom, either individually or in community with others and in public or private, to manifest his religion or belief in worship, observance, practice and teaching. No one shall be subject to coercion which would impair his freedom to have or to adopt a religion or belief of his choice.

Also relevant in the context of this report is the ICCPR's article 19, which protects freedom of expression. Article 19 states:

> Everyone shall have the right to hold opinions without interference. Everyone shall have the right to freedom of expression; this right shall include freedom to seek, receive and impart information and ideas of all kinds, regardless of frontiers, either orally, in writing or in print, in the form of art, or through any other media of his choice.

Articles 18 and 19 allow states to place certain restrictions on the manifestation of religion and on the exchange of information, respectively. With regard to freedom of conscience, article 18 allows only those limitations on the manifestation of beliefs that are "prescribed by law and are necessary to protect public safety, order, health or morals or the fundamental rights and freedoms of others."[130] Similarly, with regard to the right to exchange information and ideas, article 19 permits only those restrictions that are provided by law and are necessary: for respect of the rights or reputations of others; for the protection of national security, or of public order or of public health or morals.

[130] Under article 4, the ICCPR allows state parties to derogate from certain articles of the covenant in times emergency that threaten the life of the nation. Article 4 does not permit states to derogate from a number of articles, among them article 18.

In its General Comments on articles 18 and 19 of the ICCPR, the United Nations Human Rights Committee clarified the scope of religious belief, practice, and expression covered by this instrument. The General Comment to article 18 specifies that freedom of thought, including freedom of conscience and religious conviction, is a right that cannot be limited. In its General Comment 10 on article 19, the committee stated that there could be "no exception or restriction" on the right to "hold opinions without interference." In recognizing the right of state parties to limit the right to free expression, the General Comment reiterates the need for such restrictions to fulfill all of the criteria set forth in the article. Moreover, it emphasizes that such restrictions "may not put in jeopardy the right itself."[131]

In its explanation of the right to hold beliefs without interference, the committee notes that the ICCPR's article 18.2, along with article 17 (stipulating the right to privacy), create a freedom from compulsion to reveal one's thoughts or adherence to a religion or belief.[132] The committee has also detailed particular manifestations of religious beliefs that should be considered protected under article 18. Section four of the General Comment states:

> The freedom to manifest religion or belief in worship, observance, practice and teaching encompasses a broad range of acts. The concept of worship extends to ritual and ceremonial acts giving direct expression to belief, as well as various practices integral to such acts, including the building of places of worship, the use of ritual formulae and objects, the display of symbols, and the observance of holidays and days of rest. The observance and practice of religion or belief may include not only ceremonial acts but also such customs as the observance

[131] Human Rights Committee, General Comment 10, Article 19 (Nineteenth session, 1983). Compilation of General Comments and General Recommendations Adopted by Human Rights Treaty Bodies, U.N. Doc. HRI\GEN\1\Rev.1 at 11 (1994).

[132] Human Rights Committee, General Comment 22, Article 18 (Forty-eighth session, 1993). Compilation of General Comments and General Recommendations Adopted by Human Rights Treaty Bodies, U.N. Doc. HRI\GEN\1\Rev.1at 35 (1994).

> of dietary regulations, the wearing of distinctive clothing or head coverings, participation in rituals associated with certain stages of life, and the use of a particular language customarily spoken by a group. In addition, the practice and teaching of religion or belief includes acts integral to the conduct by religious groups of their basic affairs, such as the freedom to choose their religious leaders, priests and teachers, the freedom to establish seminaries or religious schools and the freedom to prepare and distribute religious texts or publications.[133]

The ICCPR bans coercing an individual to recant his or her religion or belief.[134] The committee commented specifically on the rights of prisoners—who are particularly susceptible to such coercion—not only to hold, but to manifest their religious belief. It stated that, "Persons already subject to certain legitimate restraints, such as prisoners, continue to enjoy their rights to manifest their religion or belief to the fullest extent compatible with the specific nature of the constraint."[135]

Finally, the committee acknowledges that states parties may adopt a state religion or ideology, and clarifies the right not to adhere to it:

> If a set of beliefs is treated as official ideology in constitutions, statutes…or in actual practice, this shall not result in any impairment of the freedoms under article 18 or any other rights recognized under the Covenant nor in any discrimination against persons who do not accept the official ideology or who oppose it.[136]

---

[133] Ibid.

[134] Article 18 (2) states, "No one shall be subject to coercion which would impair his freedom to have or to adopt a religion or belief of his choice."

[135] Human Rights Committee, General Comment 22, Article 18 (Forty-eighth session, 1993). Compilation of General Comments and General Recommendations Adopted by Human Rights Treaty Bodies, U.N. Doc. HRI\GEN\1\Rev.1at 35 (1994).

[136] Ibid.

Uzbek law violates many of the standards protecting freedom of conscience and freedom of expression. It limits or outright bans several of these manifestations of religious belief, including worship, building houses of worship, religious dress, religious teaching, the freedom to choose religious teachers and schools, and the freedom to publish and distribute religious texts. These limitations are described in more detail below. Even where domestic law conforms to international standards, Uzbek government practice violates them in ways documented throughout the report.

The Domestic Legal Context

Beginning in late 1997 the government began arresting suspected members of Islamic religious groups, closing mosques, and carrying out other restrictions in the absence of a legal framework authorizing such measures. In May 1998 Uzbek lawmakers adopted such a law, the Law on Freedom of Conscience and Religious Organizations (hereinafter, the 1998 law).[137]

Also in May 1998 the Oliy Majlis (parliament) adopted a series of amendments to the country's criminal and administrative codes, providing for harsh punishments for violating the 1998 law and for other religion-based infractions.[138] In May 1999 both codes were again amended to impose even stricter penalties on crimes related to religious belief and association.

Key provisions of the 1998 law that were applied against independent Muslims set out restrictions on internationally protected rights to hold and manifest religious beliefs, to freedom of association and assembly, and to freedom of expression, including the right to receive and impart information. Under international law governments may impose

---

[137] The 1998 law replaced the law on religion enacted at the end of the Soviet era on June 14, 1991, three months prior to independence. All citations from the 1998 religion law are from the English translation of the law in BBC Monitoring, May 20, 1998, translated from the original publication of the law in Russian in *Narodnoe Slovo*, May 15, 1998.

[138] Law of the Republic of Uzbekistan on Amendments and Additions to some Legal Acts of the Republic of Uzbekistan, May 1, 1998.

reasonable restrictions on rights for the purpose of regulating a legitimate state interest, but not for the purpose of prohibiting protected rights. The restrictions imposed by Uzbek law, however, are an impermissible violation of religious expression and association. Statements by Uzbek officials make it clear that the law is intended to stifle freedom of religion. President Karimov, for example, said that the new law was necessary because, "Today's main task is to fight against all appearances of Islamic fundamentalism and religious extremism."[139] Another government official said the law was meant to counter the alleged threat of "aggressive Wahhabism."[140] The criminal, in addition to administrative, penalties for violations of the 1998 law also indicate the law's prohibitive intent.[141]

Criminalization of Independent Belief and Practice

The 1998 law proscribes numerous aspects of religious activity. Punishments enforcing these proscriptions were set out in amendments made in 1998 and 1999 to the administrative and criminal codes. Infractions of most articles of the 1998 religion law were to be punished under the administrative code if the infraction was a first offense. Repeat offenses were to be punished by harsh prison sentences, established in two sets of amendments to the criminal code. In practice, courts have handed independent Muslims prison sentences for first-time offenses relating to religious activity.

Most relevant in the campaign against independent Islam are articles of the criminal code relating to illegal distribution of religious literature, membership in a banned religious organization, and unsanctioned

---

[139] Uzbek Radio first program, May 11, 1998, English translation in BBC Monitoring, May 11, 1998.

[140] BBC Worldwide Monitoring, quoting Interfax, May 1, 1998.

[141] Uzbek law enforcement and judicial authorities have also ignored the provision of the religion law recognizing the supremacy of international over domestic law regarding freedom of conscience and religious organizations. Article 2 of the 1998 law states, "If an international agreement of the Republic of Uzbekistan sets rules different from those stipulated in the legislation of the Republic of Uzbekistan, regarding freedom of conscience and religious organizations, the provisions of the international agreement shall apply."

teaching of religion. These legal cornerstones of the campaign are outlined below.

Exchange of Information

Uzbek law criminalizes expression of "religious extremism," "separatism," and "fundamentalism." Article 5 of the 1998 law proscribes such expression, stating: "The state shall not…allow religious or other fanaticism and extremism."[142] Article 19 of the 1998 law states that persons who produce, store, and distribute materials—including printed documents, video and audio cassettes, films, and photographs—that "contain ideas of religious extremism, separatism and fundamentalism" will be held accountable under the law.[143] Neither the law nor any internal regulations provide standards for evaluating at what point religious literature becomes "extremist," or "fundamentalist," and in practice the government has used these vague ideological labels to imprison and silence people whose views it did not want openly expressed.

The 1998 criminal code was amended to include a provision—article 244-1—corresponding to the restrictions under article 19 of the 1998 law, making possession and distribution of literature containing ideas of "religious extremism, separatism, and fundamentalism" a serious offense. These terms and phrases are nowhere defined. Under the new article 244-1 of the criminal code, producing and storing, with the goal of distributing, materials that contain "ideas of religious extremism, separatism and fundamentalism" became punishable by up to three years in prison. Distribution of literature deemed to fall into one of these categories carries with it a maximum sentence of five years in prison. Under such aggravated circumstances as dissemination after agreeing with a group of people to do so, by using one's official position, or using financial assistance from a religious organization, foreign state, group, or person, the offense is punishable by up to eight years in prison.

---

[142] Article 5, Law on Freedom of Conscience and Religious Organizations, May 1, 1998.

[143] Article 19, Law on Freedom of Conscience and Religious Organizations, May 1, 1998.

Article 244-1 emerged as one of the cornerstones of the government's campaign against independent Muslims. Members of Hizb ut-Tahrir, in particular, were tried and convicted under it.

Article 244-1 conflates the above-mentioned ideas with a prohibition on "calls for massacres or the forced eviction of citizens," and materials aimed at "sowing panic."[144] No distinction is made between peaceful expression of "fundamentalist" ideas and outright calls for violence, including massacres. This misleading association of two different types of expression appears to be an attempt by the legislation's authors to associate "fundamentalism" with calls for violence, and to smear certain religious ideas and identities.[145]

The 1998 amendments to the criminal code also included new language outlawing the import of literature "propagating religious extremism, separatism and fundamentalism," labeling it as contraband, and setting a penalty of up to ten years in prison.[146]

The 1999 amendments to the criminal code added article 244-2, which invoked the same undefined "extremist" label to impose stricter criminal penalties for membership in a group that holds certain ideas: "Setting

[144] Law of the Republic of Uzbekistan on Amendments and Additions to some Legal Acts of the Republic of Uzbekistan, May 1, 1998.

[145] Article 244-1 states: "Preparation or possession, with the aim of disseminating, of materials containing ideas of religious extremism, separatism or fundamentalism, calling for pogroms or forcible eviction of citizens, or intended to create panic among the population, committed after administrative punishment has been levied…" carries punishment ranging from a fine equal to fifty times the minimum wage to three years in prison. Meanwhile, "Preparation or possession, with the aim of disseminating, of materials containing ideas of religious extremism, separatism or fundamentalism, calling for pogroms or forcible eviction of citizens, or intended to create panic among the population, as well as use of religion to disturb the harmony of the citizenry, spreading slander, destabilizing the situation through deception, and committing other acts aimed against the established regulations for public conduct and public safety" are punishable with up to five years in prison. Those people found to have committed the above infractions under aggravating circumstances—"by preliminary agreement or as part of a group, by using one's official position, or with the financial or other material help of a religious organization or foreign government, organization or citizen"—can be sentenced to up to eight years in prison.

[146] Article 246 of the criminal code, as amended in 1998.

up, leading and participating in religious extremist, separatist, fundamentalist or other banned organizations are punishable by five to fifteen years of imprisonment with the confiscation of property."[147] The same actions, if they entail "serious consequences," are punishable by fifteen to twenty years of imprisonment with confiscation of property. This charge, particularly when levied in combination with article 216, which bans participation in an illegal religious organization, results in the maximum punishment, twenty years in prison, for holding a set of ideas in conjunction with others.

Proscriptions on Unregistered Religious Rites, Worship, and Association

Article 14 of the 1998 law bestows the right to perform religious rites and worship to religious organizations and not to individuals. It also restricts the types of groups that may exercise this right. Under articles 8 and 11, only registered religious organizations have the right to function as legal entities and thus engage in rites and worship. Article 8 states that, "Religious organizations obtain the status of a legal subject and can carry out their activities after their registration…." Article 11 warns that religious leaders who evade registration will be punished under the law and, further, that "Officials who allow activity of non-registered religious organizations shall bear responsibility in accordance with the law." Since only registered religious organizations have the right to carry out religious ceremonies and worship, the legislation effectively criminalizes unregistered religious rites and observance.

Regarding registration, the prohibitive aspect of the 1998 religion law and related amendments to the criminal code stands in sharp contrast to the 1991 law. Under the latter, a religious organization or group had to have as members ten citizens over the age of eighteen. Such groups had full rights not only to congregate for worship, but also to produce and distribute religious literature and impart religious education. Under the

[147] A number of punishments spelled out in Uzbekistan's criminal code include confiscation of property. Execution of this sentence can result in negative consequences for members of the convicted person's family as well as for the individual.

1998 law, religious organizations—defined by membership of at least 100 citizens over the age of eighteen—have the right to gather for worship. In order to enjoy the right to produce or distribute literature or impart religious education and other essential activities, religious organizations must first establish a "central administrative body." In order to establish a central administrative body, adherents of a given confession must organize a constituent conference of their registered religious organizations from no less than eight separate provinces of the country (thus, 800 members from eight provinces are now required where only ten were previously).[148]

The central administrative body must be headed by an Uzbek citizen deemed by the government to be qualified and registered with the Ministry of Justice, or headed by a foreigner approved by the Committee on Religious Affairs.[149] Only after registering this central body do adherents possess the right to produce and impart information.[150]

The government abuses the legitimate process of registration to ensure the prohibition of religious associations it views as hostile. The registration issue, while at first glance benign, is one of the government's chief weapons against independent Islam.

This restriction of the right to association was one of the main aims of the 1998 religion law. On September 30, 1998, then-Minister of Justice Sirojiddin Mirsafaev wrote, "Registering and re-registering all religious

[148] According to the Ministry of Justice, Presidential Decree 882, signed on August 14, 1998, allows for registration of religious groups with smaller congregations if and when a special commission of the Ministry of Justice deems it appropriate. *Khalq Sozi (*The People's Word) (Tashkent, Uzbekistan), September 30, 1998, English translation in BBC Monitoring, November 11, 1998.

[149] Article 8, Law on Freedom of Conscience and Religious Organizations, May 1, 1998.

[150] Article 19 of the religion law states that "'Religious organizations' central administrative bodies have a right to produce, export, import and distribute the religious items, religious literature and other materials with a religious content in the order established by the law…Delivery and distribution of religious literature published abroad is allowed after its content is examined…Religious organizations' central administration bodies have an exclusive right to publish and distribute religious items provided they have a corresponding license…." Law on Freedom of Conscience and Religious Organizations, 1998.

organizations with the Ministry of Justice and its bureaux [sic] were the most important requirements for ensuring the implementation of this law, because arbitrariness and unruliness in this sphere had gone beyond all measure…."[151] Minister Mirsafaev went on to link unregulated religious leaders with criminality and to equate the disparate phenomena of violent crime and expression of ideas that the minister did not share. He stated: "Self-styled clerics made certain of such establishments as their 'bases,' dens of crime, and committed theft, robbery with violence, and spread false ideas in order to get rich and get publicity."[152]

Under the law, failure to register a religious organization not only means that it will not enjoy certain rights, it means that the group is illegal, and that its membership is criminalized. Article 216 of the criminal code sets out penalties for involvement in an unregistered religious organization. Under article 216, as amended on May 1, 1998, organization of, or participation in, the activities of a "prohibited religious organization" is punishable by up to five years in prison.[153] The way in which a group might earn the status of a "prohibited organization" is not defined. However, the meaning of this language is informed by requirements and limitations elsewhere in the law; broadly but most importantly legal status is realized through registration with and prior sanction by the state.

The 1998 amendments also created article 216-1, imposing sentences of up to three years in prison for the crime of persuading others to join a prohibited religious group, and article 216-2, setting out a three-year

[151] *Khalq Sozi*, September 30, 1998, English translation in BBC Monitoring, November 11, 1998.

[152] Ibid.

[153] In 1999, article 216 was again amended to change the reference to "prohibited" or "banned" groups to "illegal public associations or religious organizations;" the penalty remained unchanged. Law of the Republic of Uzbekistan on Amendments and Additions to Certain Legislative Acts of the Republic of Uzbekistan, dated April 15, 1999, printed in *Narodnoe Slovo*, Tashkent, May 12, 1999, English translation in BBC Monitoring, May 13, 1999. Hizb ut-Tahrir is frequently referred to as a "banned" organization, leading some to believe that the government singled it out for prohibition. However, its "banned" or "prohibited" status derives from its lack of registration and from the "religious extremism" the government ascribes to it.

prison sentence for religious leaders who fail or refuse to register their group.[154]

Under article 201-2 of the administrative code, any person found violating the state rules on religious meetings, street processions, or "cult ceremonies" would be fined or placed under arrest for up to fifteen days. This, like other administrative code articles, appears to have been rarely if ever invoked in the campaign against independent Muslims.

Proselytism Outlawed

Article 5 of the 1998 religion law forbids proselytism, stating, "Actions aimed at converting believers of one religion into another (proselytism) as well as other missionary activity are prohibited." The Soviet version of the law similarly prohibited missionary activity.[155]

The penalties for proselytism and missionary activity are set out in the 1998 amendments to article 240 of the administrative code, and to article 216-2 of the criminal code. As with other offenses under Uzbek law, the first violation carries a fine or period of detention under the administrative code.[156] Persons found guilty of subsequent infractions are punished under article 216-2 of the criminal code and may be fined fifty to one hundred times the monthly minimum wage, sentenced to up

---

[154] Article 216-2 has rarely been invoked. Instead, prosecutors routinely levy and judges employ the principle provision, article 216, which carries a stiffer penalty, up to five years in prison. Also under article 216-2, members of unregistered religious organizations who "organiz[e] and [hold] special meetings for children and youth as well as labor, literature and other circles and groups that are not connected with performance of religious rites by the servants and members of religious organizations" face a sentence of up to three years imprisonment.

[155] Article 7, Law on Freedom of Conscience and Religious Organizations, June 14, 1991.

[156] Article 240, "Violation of the Laws on Religious Organizations," allows authorities to punish proselytism with a fine equal to five to ten times the monthly minimum wage—3,535 som, approximately U.S. $4, in 2003—or administrative arrest for up to fifteen days. In April 2003 the Labor and Social Security Ministry announced this figure for the minimum wage. Uzland.uz web site, in Russian, April 1, 2003, English translation in BBC Monitoring, April 1, 2003.

to six months of administrative arrest, or sentenced to up to three years in prison. In practice, those charged with violation of this and all other provisions of the religion law rarely have been punished under the administrative code, even for a first offense, and, instead, have been tried under the criminal code and given the maximum punishment.

The ban on proselytism has far-reaching implications for individuals and religious groups that see it as their religious duty to call on or encourage others to join in their beliefs or practice. The prohibition on such "missionary" activity violates not only the right to freely express one's belief, and the right to exchange views, it also effectively removes the individual's right to observe his or her own religious faith, a crucial component of which is attempting to convert others. This provision thereby casts legitimate religious practice as a crime.

Limiting Expression and Education: The Ban on Private Religious Teaching

Article 9 of the 1998 religion law prohibits the "private teaching of religious principles." Similar to the right to publish and disseminate religious material, the right to instruct others in religion is conditioned on membership in a registered religious organization that has met all of the requirements set forth in article 8, including establishment of a central administrative body. Once this is done, the central administrative body of a given religious organization must obtain a license and register with the Ministry of Justice before it can legally train clergy and others.[157] Failure to fulfill these requirements brings with it punishment under the law.

With article 9 of the 1998 law, the government of Uzbekistan sought to put a stop to any religious education or activity that was beyond its control. It is illegal to impart religious education outside the framework of a government sanctioned central administrative body of a religious organization. Private citizens may not teach religious subjects. This is a particularly significant prohibition for Uzbek society, given that,

---

[157] Article 9, Law on Freedom of Conscience and Religious Organizations, May 1, 1998.

historically, religious traditions and precepts were passed on to younger generations and largely kept alive during the Soviet period through private religious education. During the Soviet era, this private Islam thrived separately from officially sanctioned Muslim activity that was controlled by the state and therefore has been termed "parallel Islam." This phenomenon of coexistence of official and private Islam characterized the later Soviet period, despite restrictions on paper.

The 1998 amendments to the criminal and administrative codes added penalties for engaging in private religious instruction, showing the seriousness with which the government of Uzbekistan approached this prohibition. Article 241 of the administrative code, as amended in 1998, prescribes a fine of five to ten times the monthly minimum wage or fifteen days administrative arrest for violators.[158] Second offenses are punished under article 229-2 of the criminal code, entitled, "Violation of the Order Regarding Teaching of Religious Dogmas." It states, "Teaching religious dogmas without special religious education and without permission of the Central Administrative Board of [a given] Religious Organization, as well as teaching religious dogmas in private" can result in punishment of up to three years in prison.[159]

Other Aspects of the Religion Law

Religious Attire

Article 14 of the religion law explicitly bans Uzbekistan's citizens from wearing "religious attire," translated also as "cult dress," in public places, unless they are members of the clergy. This provision had no counterpart in the 1991 Soviet law, and has emerged as one of the most controversial new rules in Uzbekistan. The 1998 amendment to the administrative code, article 184-1, envisions penalties ranging from a fine equal to five to ten times the minimum monthly wage to fifteen days under administrative arrest for violation of this clause. The prohibition

---

[158] Law of the Republic of Uzbekistan on Amendments and Additions to some Legal Acts of the Republic of Uzbekistan, May 1, 1998.

[159] Ibid.

on religious garb clearly violates international instruments establishing the right to manifest one's belief.[160]

The application of this law has been one element of the discriminatory government campaign against independent Muslims. Government officials and academic administrators alike used the prohibition on religious dress to retroactively justify expelling from school and university women students who wore headscarves that covered their faces prior to the law's adoption. It has also established quasi-legal grounds for police surveillance and, ultimately, harassment of women in full hijab (meaning clothing that covers the body and face) and many men with beards.[161]

Religious Parties Banned

Article 5 of the religion law reiterates the constitutional ban on political parties with a religious platform. The prohibition on political parties with a religious character was also outlined in the 1991 precursor to this law.[162]

Application of Existing Statutes in the Arrest Campaign

In addition to articles in the statutes amended in 1998 and 1999 to accompany a stricter religion law, three articles of the criminal code that

[160] As noted above, the U.N. Human Rights Committee has stated that, "The observance and practice of religion or belief may include not only ceremonial acts but also such customs as the observance of dietary regulations, the wearing of distinctive clothing or head coverings, participation in rituals associated with certain stages of life, and the use of a particular language customarily spoken by a group." Human Rights Committee, General Comment 22, Article 18 (Forty-eighth session, 1993). Compilation of General Comments and General Recommendations Adopted by Human Rights Treaty Bodies, U.N. Doc. HRI\GEN\1\Rev.1at 35 (1994).

[161] For more information, see: Human Rights Watch, "Class Dismissed: Discriminatory Expulsions of Muslim Students," *A Human Rights Watch Report*, Vol. 11, No. 12 (D), October 1999.

[162] Article 7, Law on Freedom of Conscience and Religious Organizations, June 14, 1991.

do not derive from the religion law are also among the primary legal tools used to prosecute independent Muslims. These relate to subversion, organization of a criminal group, and inciting ethnic, racial, or religious enmity.

Subversion

Perhaps the most important and common legal statute invoked in the state campaign against independent Muslims has been criminal code article 159, entitled Encroachment on the Constitutional Order of the Republic of Uzbekistan. In the years since 1997, prosecutors and judges have almost uniformly applied this charge, commonly referred to as "anti-state or anti-constitutional activities," to cases involving Muslim religious dissidents.[163]

Article 159 states:

> Public appeals to unconstitutionally change the existing governmental system, to seize power to remove from office legally elected or appointed representatives, or to unconstitutionally disrupt the territorial unity of the Republic of Uzbekistan, as well as distribution of material with such content are punishable with a fine of up to fifty times the minimum wage or imprisonment up to three years.

The law goes on to say that violent actions against the constitutional authorities carries a penalty of up to five years in prison. When

[163] The primary exception to the application of article 159 to those charged with religious infractions is in cases involving membership in Hizb ut-Tahrir under so-called mitigating circumstances. Specifically, if a person charged with membership in the group claims that he or she became a member "accidentally," that he or she is in fact not a member at all, or that he or she stopped attending the group's study sessions and did not participate in distribution of the group's literature, then that person has, in some cases, avoided prosecution under article 159 and is most routinely charged under article 216, punishing membership in an illegal religious organization, which carries a shorter maximum prison term.

undertaken repeatedly or by a group, perpetrators can be imprisoned for up to ten years.

Of particular significance to cases dealt with in this report is the provision in article 159 punishing conspiracy to "overthrow the constitutional order of the Republic of Uzbekistan" with ten to twenty years imprisonment and confiscation of property. Any call for an Islamic state, including the call by Hizb ut-Tahrir members for restoration of a Caliphate, absent any other actions and absent any threats or acts of violence, is considered by Uzbekistan's authorities to be a crime under article 159.

Organizing a Criminal Group

In addition to invoking criminal code article 216, prescribing punishment for membership in an illegal religious group, Uzbek state authorities employed article 242, "organizing a criminal group," to prosecute independent Muslims for their presumed membership in unregistered religious groups. Categorized as a crime against national security and social order, it punishes the establishment or leadership of a criminal society or group with up to twenty years in prison or the death penalty.[164]

Inciting National, Racial, or Religious Enmity

Article 156 refers to incitement of national (ethnic), racial, or religious enmity. In addition to outlawing acts that directly infringe on the rights of others or lead to the physical harm of others, it states that, "Willful action that denigrates national (ethnic) honor or dignity or which offends citizens on the basis of their religious (or atheistic) beliefs, committed with the goal of inciting animosity, intolerance, or discord…is punishable by imprisonment of up to five years." If actions deemed to fall under this statute are undertaken by prior collusion or by a group, or under other aggravated circumstances, they are punishable with up to ten years in prison. Uzbek prosecutors and judges routinely

[164] As of this writing, there were no known cases of an independent Muslim being sentenced to death under this particular article.

interpreted this provision as applicable to the possession or distribution of literature. Neither the criminal code nor any other legislation or government regulation defines denigration of a group's honor and dignity or an offense to an individual, leaving the interpretation to judicial and executive authorities. The opportunities for arbitrary application of this article are apparent and examples are provided in subsequent chapters of this report.

It is worth clarifying that the government of Uzbekistan does not prosecute Hizb ut-Tahrir members for hate speech, if defined as incitement to violence.[165] Rather, Hizb ut-Tahrir members and other independent Muslims have been charged under article 156 of the criminal code, which punishes speech that "insults" ethnic, national or other groups. The International Covenant for Civil and Political Rights, article 19, which provides for freedom of speech and expression, allows for exceptions only when necessary "For respect of the rights or reputations of others" or "For the protection of national security or of public order (ordre public), or of public health or morals." The government of Uzbekistan has failed to recognize the right of Hizb ut-Tahrir members to freedom of speech and has instead jailed, tortured, and tried them, with no due process, for their belief in a Caliphate, for exchange of opinions including those in favor of a Caliphate, and for membership in a pro-Caliphate organization.

Common Crimes: Drugs and Weapons Charges

Independent Muslims were routinely brought up on fabricated charges of illegal possession of narcotics (criminal code articles 273 and 276) or illegal possession of weapons or ammunition (criminal code article 248). These charges do not relate directly or logically to religiosity, but were fabricated by police and applied in an arbitrary way by state prosecutors and judges so universally that they became core elements of the government campaign. These phenomena are explained further in other chapters of this report.

---

[165] In none of the cases cited in this report are independent Muslims prosecuted for speech that was demonstrated to be a direct and imminent incitement to violence.

Usman Iusupov, age 64, with a photograph of one of his sons, an imprisoned independent Muslim. Two of his sons are currently in prison for membership in Hizb ut-Tahrir. Margilan city, Fergana Valley.
© 2003 Jason Eskenazi

Oiparcha Mirzamatova and her daughter-in-law, with photographs of male relatives imprisoned on religion-related charges. Mirzamatova's son, Ibrokhim Khaidarov, is serving a sixteen-year sentence for membership in Hizb ut-Tahrir. Her daughter-in-law's brother, Khurshid Oripov, was arrested on religion-related charges and died apparently from torture in custody. At least two other male relatives are in prison on similar charges. Margilan city, Fergana Valley.
© 2003 Jason Eskenazi

Akhmedjon Madmarov, age 58, with a letter from his son, Hamidulla, imprisoned in Karshi on religion-related charges. Madmarov has two other sons in prison on similar charges. Margilan city, Fergana Valley.
© 2003 Jason Eskenazi

Former religious prisoner Bakhodir Ulmasov, who suffered head trauma and other serious injury from mistreatment in prison. His brother (shown in smaller photograph) was also imprisoned on religion-related charges. Margilan city, Fergana Valley.
© 2003 Jason Eskenazi

Sadik Vahobov, age 75. His son was arrested while praying in public in commemoration of a friend who had died in prison. He is serving an eighteen-year sentence on religion-related charges. Margilan city, Fergana Valley.

III. TARGETS OF THE CAMPAIGN

This chapter describes and documents the harassment, detention, prosecution, and imprisonment of independent Muslims from 1998 through the present.

The campaign's original targets were individual religious leaders, imams, some of whom were imprisoned or disappeared as early as 1992. Since that time, prosecutors have brought charges against people for being "Wahhabi," for membership in "extremist" or illegal organizations, and on trumped-up weapons and narcotics charges. Those convicted have been subject to long prison sentences. Authorities used incommunicado detention, beatings, and torture during pre-trial detention to obtain testimony to support these charges, as is detailed in "Torture and Mistreatment in Pre-trial Detention" below. Those detainees whose charges were dropped or who were paroled or released under amnesty face ongoing harassment.

The government's campaign later expanded to target large numbers of actual associates or disciples of the independent imams, and even some persons merely perceived to be affiliated with them. In cases brought against such people, participation in religious discussion, ownership of a copying machine and cell phones, even playing soccer, have been cited as evidence of criminal activity or intent. As in cases involving the imams themselves, the dangerously elastic charge of "Wahhabism" appears frequently in the case reports, as do lengthy prison sentences.

Beginning in 1998, the Uzbek government began to target members of Hizb ut-Tahrir. Unlike the imams, their followers, and others branded "Wahhabi," they are identifiable members of an organized group that advocates a particular ideology: the establishment of a Caliphate. But like those accused of "Wahhabism," the group's members face charges of conspiring to overthrow the government, as well as criminal charges relating to membership in a banned organization. The government has shown little patience for distinguishing among religious principles, political beliefs, and actual subversion. Case materials show that merely distributing Hizb ut-Tahrir's religious leaflets and engaging in discussion of Hizb ut-Tahrir religious ideas have been criminalized as acts hostile to the state, and prosecuted aggressively.

Chapter III reports these developments in two sections. "Imams, Their Followers, and 'Wahhabis'" documents the government's actions against the imams, their associates, and those alleged to be affiliated with them. Because of important differences in the target group itself and in the issues raised, the campaign against Hizb ut-Tahrir is treated separately in "Hizb ut-Tahrir."

Imams, Their Followers, and "Wahhabis"

Uzbek authorities justify the campaign against independent Islam as necessary to fight terrorism. But years before the Uzbek government faced armed threats from the IMU, suffered bombings in the capital, or became a partner in the U.S.-led campaign against terrorism, it took action to limit the nonviolent challenge to its authority posed by an organized and independent religious movement. It did so not to stave off threats of terrorism, but to prevent the emergence of politicized Islam.

As explained above, a well-known and elemental part of the Soviet project was eradication of religion as an organizing principle for society and social interaction. In Central Asia, this policy was modified and expressed in terms of state efforts to control and co-opt religious belief and expression. The government of independent Uzbekistan inherited the Soviet program of state control of religion, as well as suspicion of segments of society whose first allegiance was not to the state, or more specifically not to the ruling state elites. Coming out of the glasnost era, having witnessed the birth of political opposition parties in the country and seen the challenge they posed to their political monopoly, Uzbekistan's elites reinvigorated Soviet methods to reestablish control over politics and religion. Once the political opposition was effectively neutralized or marginalized in 1992, the elites assessed any further threats to their hold on power. It was in this moment that state focus turned to religious Muslim leaders who displayed any form of independence from state authority. This independence was manifested in a variety of ways: through a refusal to praise the president and his policies during religious services; expression of a desire for a state governed by Islamic law; refusal to work for state law enforcement to spy on fellow religious leaders or members of the congregation, to root out disloyalty to the state or its doctrine; or, simply, exhibition of popularity and influence with a congregation. The state viewed these dynamic, renegade, or dissident imams as a threat, as a potential organizing force for religious-based opposition to the existing power elites. With the program and tools of religious repression already at their disposal, the former-Soviet authorities made use of the state's monopoly on power and initiated their campaign to rid the country of religious expression that was independent of state control.

One of the first steps the government took was to persecute individual dissident spiritual leaders. One of them was Imam Abdulla Utaev, who disappeared in 1992. Then, in 1995, the state-appointed Imam Abduvali Mirzoev and his assistant vanished, many believe, at the hands of state agents. In 1997, Nematjon Parpiev, an assistant to Mirzoev, was disappeared.[166] Other well-known religious leaders, including imams Barnoev, Iuldashev, and Abdurakhmonov, were imprisoned in the late 1990s and in 2000 on charges of anti-state activity. The campaign of religious persecution began with these individuals, then expanded to their followers, and more recently has focused on the organization Hizb ut-Tahrir.

The government's campaign extended to members of the official clergy. Among the first clergymen targeted was Imam Obidkhon Nazarov, one of the most popular—and, at one time, officially most favored—of the state-appointed imams. He was fired in 1996 for speaking out about the disappearance of Imam Mirzoev, refusing to serve as an informant for the national security services, and allegedly for objecting to policies of

---

[166] U.S. Department of State, *1997 Country Report on Human Rights Practices*, released by the Bureau of Democracy, Human Rights, and Labor, January 30, 1998 [online], http://www.state.gov/www/global/human_rights/97hrp_index.html (retrieved January 6, 2004). Nematjon Parpiev was last seen in August 1997.

the Muslim Board.[167] In 1998 after two years of harassment, he either was disappeared or fled the country fearing arrest.[168] Nazarov was placed on a police wanted list for having been a leader of a "criminal extremist organization." Following his vanishing, even a loose association with Imam Nazarov became the basis for arrests, conspiracy charges, and long prison sentences. According to one witness of this early phase of the crackdown, silencing these state religious leaders weakened the moderate, alternative expression of Islam and may have contributed to the growth of Hizb ut-Tahrir, the only formalized expression of religious dissent that currently exists in Uzbekistan.[169]

Imams

Police arrested Imam Akhad Barnoev on March 15, 1999. Barnoev had served as imam-khatib (prayer leader and chief orator) of the well-known Otallohon, or Gumbas, mosque in Namangan from 1991 to 1995. Specifically, the state charged that Imam Barnoev allowed "Wahhabis" to attend his mosque, which was registered with the Muslim Board. Barnoev denied the charge in court, retorting that some of his congregation were given this label only because they raised their hands during prayers and said "amen" out loud following the reading of the

---

[167] According to Nazarov's wife, three SNB officers—including Tohir Ibrahimov and Riksibai Bikhambaev, and the Tashkent city procurator, Ergash Juraev—took Nazarov from his mosque and threatened the imam as early as 1995, when he gave a sermon in which he asked the congregation to pray to God to protect Mirzoev. Nazarov's wife also reported that the imam received anonymous letters containing death threats in 1995 and that SNB officer Tohir Ibrahimov threatened Nazarov's life in 1996. Human Rights Watch interview with Munira Nasriddinova, Tashkent, May 23, 2001. Another person close to the case pointed to the imam's refusal to work as an informant for the SNB as well as his growing popularity as the factors that propelled him into disfavor with state authorities. Human Rights Watch interview, name withheld, Tashkent, May 28, 2001. As with Imam Mirzoev, Nazarov's true "crime" in the eyes of the state may well have been his popularity, his ability to garner the loyalty and enthusiasm of thousands of young people. Nazarov's wife estimated that some 5,000 people had attended her husband's services. Human Rights Watch interview with Munira Nasriddinova, Tashkent, May 23, 2001.

[168] The family of Imam Nazarov maintains that he was disappeared by state security forces.

[169] Open letter by Muharramkhon Nazarova, mother of Imam Nazarov, to Minister of Internal Affairs Zokirjon Almatov, February 1, 2000.

fotikh sura (the fotikh sura is the first sura, or chapter, of the Koran, repeated several times in daily prayers).

Barnoev testified in court that his only fault was having been imam of a mosque that was later labeled "Wahhabi." The state alleged, however, that those associated with the imam's mosque created an organization composed of "reactionary religious extremists."[170] Also cited against the imam were police claims to have found "Wahhabi leaflets" and weapons in his home.[171] The court, finding that during his spiritual leadership of the Otallohon mosque Barnoev had "significantly contributed to the spread of Wahhabism," and "had been an instructor and leader of Wahhabis," sentenced him to eighteen years in prison and confiscation of his property.[172] Imam Barnoev was held in Tashkent prison for at least five months following his conviction.[173] As of December 2002, the imam was incarcerated in Zangiota prison in Tashkent province.[174]

Kyrgyz citizen Imam Iuldash Tursunbaev, born in 1955, served as a state-appointed spiritual leader in Uzbekistan from 1989 to 1996. He also presided over the congregation of Otallohon mosque in Namangan, the mosque later led by Imam Barnoev and branded by the government as "Wahhabi."[175] He then worked at a medresseh in Tashkent and later as imam of a mosque in the Kattakurgan district of Samarkand, before

---

[170] Namangan Province Court verdict issued by Judge K. Abduvaliev, October 30, 1999. Numerous observant Muslims who attended services at the mosque were arrested on religion-related charges beginning in late 1997, according to official court documents and courtroom testimony recorded by Human Rights Watch. The state further claimed that Barnoev was a member of such a criminal group, the goals of which—according to the court's verdict—were to "use the cloak of religion … to create an Islamic state in Uzbekistan, to take advantage of the religiosity of citizens of Namangan province…."

[171] Indictment of Akhad Barnoev, issued by the head of the Criminal Investigations Department of the Namangan Province Procuracy, October 15, 1999.

[172] Namangan Province Court verdict issued by Judge K. Abduvaliev, October 30, 1999. A Supreme Court review of the case resulted in a reduced sentence of sixteen years.

[173] Human Rights Watch telephone interview with rights defender Akhmat Abdullaev, April 18, 2001.

[174] Human Rights Watch interview, name withheld, Tashkent, December 4, 2002.

[175] Indictment issued by senior police investigator of Special Criminal Affairs R.A. Gafurov, December 28, 1999.

returning to his native Kyrgyzstan, where he took over the leadership of a mosque in Bazar Kurgan, in Jalal-Abad province.[176] On August 29, 1999,[177] Uzbek law enforcement agents roughly seized him in Bazar Kurgan on the street outside a mosque and before some sixty to seventy witnesses.[178] They then transported him across the border to Uzbekistan, where they held him incommunicado, first in Namangan and later in Tashkent, until his January 2000 trial.[179]

The indictment charged him with attempting or conspiring to commit terrorism, inciting ethnic, racial, or religious enmity, conspiracy to overthrow the government, attempt or conspiracy to commit subversive activity, organization of, or participation in, a criminal association, and illegal possession of weapons. It also charged Tursunbaev with being a "Wahhabi," associated with disappeared Imam Mirzoev and aligned with militants who later became the leadership of the IMU. It did not accuse him of involvement in any specific violent act or specific plot to overthrow the government.[180] As evidence of the imam's criminality the prosecution charged that he was an active participant in a goup called *Tavba (*Repentance), a charge he did not deny. Tavba—established in Azerbaijan in 1991 with the aim of uniting Muslim factions and

---

[176] Human Rights Watch interview, name withheld, Tashkent, February 23, 2000.

[177] Uzbek state authorities claimed that they only arrested the imam on September 27, 1999, as noted in the verdict of the Tashkent Province Court, issued by Judge Mansura Jalilova, February 29, 2000. But eyewitness statements, including three on file with Human Rights Watch, establish the correct date.

[178] Written report to Human Rights Watch, author's name withheld, undated; and written report to Human Rights Watch from the Organization for Human Rights Protection "Justice," based in Kyrgyzstan, April 18, 2000. The arrest was a breach of a neighboring country's national sovereignty, and it occurred at a particularly tense time in Uzbek-Kyrgyz relations. During August 1999 the Uzbek military were unilaterally bombing territory in Kyrgyzstan with the presumed aim of routing out or killing Uzbek militants who had taken hostage several Japanese citizens and members of the Kyrgyz military and who demanded the release of religious prisoners in Uzbekistan. *Human Rights Watch World Report 2000*, p. 277.

[179] Tursunbaev testified about the incommunicado detention at his trial, according to a written report by the Kyrgyz rights group Justice, present at trial as non-lawyer advocates for him, February 3, 2000.

[180] Indictment against Iuldash Tursunbaev, issued by senior police investigator of Special Criminal Affairs R.A. Gafurov, December 28, 1999.

eliminating dissension among religious leaders—reportedly included future IMU leaders Tokhir Iuldash and Juma Namangani among its members. According to knowledgeable rights defenders in Uzbekistan, the organization's aims did not resonate with many Central Asian Muslims and garnered negligible support in Uzbekistan.[181] Nor was the group forbidden at the time of Tursunbaev's association with it.[182] While the Uzbek government labeled Tavba a "religious extremist group," Tursunbaev in his testimony recalled that his interest in it was sparked in 1991 by its goal to bring harmony to the Muslim community, its apolitical nature, and its status as an officially registered organization in Azerbaijan.[183]

Testimony by prosecution witnesses did not strengthen the state's case: Imam Barnoev, for example, stated that he did not know Tursunbaev and that his pre-trial written testimony incriminating the other imam had been dictated by police investigators.[184] The charge of weapons possession was based on a single unsubstantiated allegation, taking up just one sentence of the ten-page verdict against him. This stated that during the summer of 1991 (before Uzbekistan's independence from the Soviet Union), the imam had received a shipment of an unspecified number of pistols with silencers from an unspecified person and had transported them to Namangan, with the aim of arming his "criminal group," and showed them to people at a meeting.[185] This charge ostensibly rested on testimony provided to the court by men—some of whom were themselves in prison at the time of the trial—who claimed to have known the imam during the early 1990s. However, two witnesses testified that a man other than Imam Tursunbaev had brought guns to a meeting, while a third witness cited a completely different meeting where Tursunbaev supposedly showed off not pistols, but a

[181] Human Rights Watch interview with rights defender Vasila Inoiatova, Tashkent, March 8, 2001; and Human Rights Watch interview with Mikhail Ardzinov, chair, Independent Human Rights Organization of Uzbekistan, Tashkent, March 9, 2001.

[182] Written report by the Kyrgyz rights group Justice, February 3, 2000.

[183] Tashkent Province Court verdict, issued by Judge Mansura Jalilova, February 29, 2000.

[184] Written report to Human Rights Watch by Justice, February 3, 2000.

[185] Tashkent Province Court verdict, issued by Judge Mansura Jalilova, February 29, 2000.

single hunting rifle he had been given as a gift. The remaining witnesses for the prosecution did not address the weapons charge.[186]

The Tashkent Province Court judge denied Human Rights Watch access to Tursunbaev's trial on the day the defendant himself testified, January 13, and to a subsequent hearing on January 27, 2000. In a highly unorthodox move, the afternoon session of the January 27 hearing was, in fact, held behind closed doors in Tashkent prison. On February 29, 2000, repeating the prosecution's indictment almost verbatim, the judge ruled Imam Tursunbaev guilty as charged and sentenced him to twenty years in prison.[187]

Imam Tulkin Kori Ergashev, along with Imam Nazarov, was put on an official "wanted" list in 1998 for alleged anti-state activities.[188] As imam-khattib of the Sahobilar mosque in Tashkent, Ergashev had reportedly continued using a loudspeaker to broadcast the mosque's call to prayer, in contravention of a 1998 government decree prohibiting this.[189] As a result, the Muslim Board dismissed him for disobedience.[190] It has also been reported that the Sahobilar mosque was unregistered—efforts to

---

[186] Ibid; and Human Rights Watch telephone interview with a person close to the case, February 23, 2000. According to Justice, at least two of the witnesses who testified were prisoners and those who were unable to testify in person were in police custody and under investigation in Namangan and Samarkand, respectively. Written report to Human Rights Watch by Justice, February 3, 2000

[187] Verdict of the Tashkent Province Court, issued by Judge Mansura Jalilova, February 29, 2000.

[188] Memorial Human Rights Center and the Information Center for Human Rights in Central Asia, *List of People Arrested and Tried in Uzbekistan for Political and Religious Reasons (January 1999 to April 2000)*, Moscow, May 2000.

[189] *The List of Muslim Victims of Uzbek Government Repression (1990-1999)*, p. 52. On file with Human Rights Watch. The authors of this report, a group of independent activists working to document abuses against independent Muslims, submitted it to Human Rights Watch as an anonymous document to protect their safety. Decree No. 6, Muslim Board of Uzbekistan, January 8, 1998, issued by Mufti Abdurashid Kori Bakhromov, bans the use of the loudspeaker for the call to prayer. This decree is reprinted in "Crackdown in the Farghona Valley: Arbitrary Arrests and Religious Discrimination", *A Human Rights Watch Report*, May 1998, Vol. 10, No. 4 (D), Appendix C.

[190] *The List of Muslim Victims of Uzbek Government Repression (1990-1999)*, p. 52. On file with Human Rights Watch.

register the mosque with authorities reportedly failed—and that it drew a significant number of young people to Friday prayers.[191] The unofficial status of the mosque and its popularity may also have been motivation for state antagonism toward Ergashev.[192] Ergashev's whereabouts are unknown, and he is believed to be in hiding since he left home in early 1998. In his absence, police arrested his son and brother and detained his wife.[193]

Law enforcement agents arrested Imam Ergashev's protégé soon after. Forty-one-year-old Imam Kobil Murodov had also been linked with Nazarov. After Ergashev's dismissal, Murodov had taken over as imam of the Sahobilar mosque.[194] The U.S. Department of State reported that in early October 1998, Murodov was arrested on charges of illegal possession of narcotics and teaching religion without permission.[195] He died on October 30 in pre-trial detention at Tashkent prison.[196] According to the U.S. government report, "Murodov's body showed severe bruising, his teeth were knocked out, and his collarbone and

---

[191] Carlotta Gall, "The Great Game-Glitz Cannot Hide Terror in Uzbekistan," The Moscow Times, November 20, 1998.

[192] The mosque was later branded by the state as a "religious-extremist" one in court documents. For example, the court verdict against Imam Iuldash Tursunbaev lists the Sahobilar mosque along with the Tokhtaboi mosque in Tashkent, the Gumbas or Otallohon mosque in Namangan, and the Jo'mi mosque in Andijan as places where "religious-extremist" schools of thought were developed and spread. Tashkent Province Court verdict, issued by Judge Mansura Jalilova, February 29, 2000.

[193] For accounts of persecution of Ergashev's son, brother, and wife, please see "Family Members: Arrests, House Arrest, Harrassment" in Chapter III.

[194] U.S. Department of State, *1998 Country Reports on Human Rights Practices*, released by the Bureau of Democracy, Human Rights, and Labor, February 26, 1999 [online], http://www.state.gov/www/global/human_rights/98hrp_index.html (retrieved January 6, 2004); and Carlotta Gall, "The Great Game-Glitz Cannot Hide Terror in Uzbekistan," *The Moscow Times*, November 20, 1998.

[195] U.S. Department of State, *1998 Country Reports on Human Rights Practices*, released by the Bureau of Democracy, Human Rights, and Labor, February 26, 1999.

[196] Ibid.

several ribs were broken."[197] The official explanation for his death was either that he fell in his cell or was beaten by fellow inmates.[198]

Nazarov's former deputy, Abduvahid Iuldashev, served as imam of the officially registered Ilonli Ota, or Borijar, mosque in Tashkent for one year.[199] Iuldashev, born in 1968, is reputed to have been a popular and dynamic prayer leader. When Nazarov was removed from his post as imam of Tokhtaboi mosque in 1996 Iuldashev was detained and held for fifteen days on misdemeanor charges of "hooliganism."[200] In February 1999 the police arrested him after services at the Ilonli Ota mosque, and allegedly beat him and planted drugs on him.[201] He was convicted on drug possession charges. An appeals court released him on parole in August 1999, but his release was conditional and authorities kept him under tight surveillance. Notably, the appeals court determined that Iuldashev was not a member of any illegal religious organization, even though he was not charged with this infraction.[202] He was compelled to report every Saturday to the Sobir Rakhimov district police station to be filmed or photographed, to give fingerprints, and to sign a statement avowing that, "I, Abduvahid Iuldashev, am not a member of any religious sect and do not approve of these sects."[203] The content of

[197] Ibid.

[198] Ibid.

[199] Iuldashev was appointed by the Muslim Board as Nazarov's deputy upon his graduation from Islamic institute in the early 1990s. Electronic communication from Omina Iuldasheva to Human Rights Watch, September 14, 2000; and Human Rights Watch interview with "A.A.," a person close to the case, Tashkent, August 1, 2000.

[200] According to a person close to Iuldashev's case, several of Nazarov's other students were also detained on charges of "hooliganism" around the same time. Nazarov's second deputy, a citizen of Tajikistan who did not have a residence permit to live in Tashkent, was reportedly deported by force. Human Rights Watch interview with A.A., Tashkent, August 1, 2000.

[201] Unofficial transcript, Iakasarai District Court, Tashkent, May 11, 1999, written by independent trial monitors, names withheld, June 1999; Human Rights Watch interview with Iuldashev's attorney, Irina Mikulina, Tashkent, June 10, 1999; and Human Rights Watch interview with A.A., Tashkent, August 1, 2000.

[202] The appeals court considered the sentence overly harsh. Tashkent City Court appeals verdict, issued by Judge T. Kh. Nazarov, August 10, 1999.

[203] Human Rights Watch interview, with A.A., Tashkent, August 1, 2000.

these avowals is particularly revealing—police had ostensibly arrested Iuldashev for a narcotics violation, not on religion-related charges.

Police rearrested Iuldashev in July 2000 and held him incommunicado for more than five months at the Tashkent municipal police headquarters (MVD). They denied his lawyer access to him with the implausible explanation that he had elected to reject legal counsel.[204] At trial, where he was charged along with twelve other men who had attended his mosque or were otherwise associated with him, Iuldashev testified that police had tortured him and other defendants to produce statements that he was the leader of an extremist religious group and had purchased weapons to prepare for the violent overthrow of the state.[205] In April 2001 Judge Najimov of the Tashkent City Court found Iuldashev guilty of conspiracy to overthrow the state, leadership of a criminal group, leadership of a religious extremist, separatist, fundamentalist or other banned organization, possession and distribution of literature containing ideas of religious extremism, separatism, and fundamentalism, and illegal acquisition of foreign currency and sentenced him to nineteen years in prison.

The state's case against Iuldashev was largely based on the allegation that lessons he gave on the Koran and other Islamic texts while serving as a state-appointed imam were actually lessons in "Wahhabism" and calls for holy war. Judge Najimov questioned co-defendant Ulugbek Vakhidov on this point. Vakhidov, who testified that he had asked Iuldashev to teach him more about Islam and was invited in 1998 to join a small class of three to four people, had the following exchange with the judge:

> Judge: Abduvahid Iuldashev was your teacher. What did he teach you?
> Vakhidov: To read the Koran and hadith and doa [supplication or prayer].

[204] Human Rights Watch telephone interview with Irina Mikulina, August 9, 2000.

[205] Human Rights Watch unofficial transcript, Tashkent City Court trial held in the Akmal Ikramov District Court building, Tashkent, February 7, 2001.

> Judge: And the Arabic alphabet?
> Vakhidov: I already knew that.
> Judge: Did he ever say anything about jihad or infringing on the constitutional order?
> Vakhidov: No.
> Judge: He didn't tell you about these things?
> Vakhidov: No, he didn't…
> Judge: What is your attitude regarding an Islamic state in our country?... We just want to know your thoughts.
> Vakhidov: I was not involved in politics before. I never paid attention, even to television. If [it is done] peacefully, if everyone supports it, if no one is hurt, I could support an Islamic state. But, if [it were established] by other means, I would be against it.
> Judge: Is there anything else you would like to add?
> Vakhidov: Our classes were like in school: we waited for the teacher and he came and taught us about the Koran and gave us sura [chapters of the Koran] to learn by heart, and we just prayed and went home. There is nothing else I can add.[206]

Another defendant, Jamshid Azimov, stated simply, "I didn't think it was a crime to go to a house for classes."[207] He and Vakhidov were each sentenced to eight years in prison and confiscation of their property.

Abdurakhim Abdurakhmonov worked as a religious teacher in the government-run Kokoldosh medresseh in Tashkent from 1991 to 1995. His case includes a number of features typical of the arrest campaign—multiple arrests, torture, incommunicado detention, and conviction on highly suspect charges—and merits detailed description. Abdurakhmonov served as imam of the religious school from 1995 to

[206] Human Rights Watch unofficial transcript, Tashkent City Court trial held in the Akmal Ikramov District Court building, Tashkent, February 7, 2001.

[207] Human Rights Watch unofficial transcript, Tashkent City Court hearing held in the Akmal Ikramov District Court building, Tashkent, February 8, 2001.

1996, when the Muslim Board dismissed him for stating his agreement with Imam Nazarov in the debate over the elder imam's alleged disobedience.[208] Abdurakhmonov reportedly had attended Nazarov's sermons at Tokhtaboi mosque before the imam was removed and had gone occasionally to the well-known religious leader for advice.[209]

He was first detained on January 17, 1998, along with four other men, following a visit to Imam Nazarov's home in Tashkent.[210] All five men were released, but police burst into Abdurakhmonov's house the next night, January 18, dragged him from bed, beat him, stuck a gun in his elderly father's mouth, and arrested them both. Police held him in detention overnight and beat him severely in custody.[211] According to his wife, when she saw him next day—police brought him along as they searched his home—he was pale and could barely speak or stand. He later told her that police had beaten him on the head until he lost consciousness, and that they resumed the beatings each time he woke.[212] He was released with the payment of a fine (it is unclear whether or not he was formally charged under the administrative or criminal code). A person close to the case reported to Human Rights Watch that the imam

---

[208] Human Rights Watch interview with the imam's wife, Muborak Abdurakhmonova, Tashkent, May 26, 2000.

[209] Human Rights Watch interview with independent rights defender, Mukhtabar Akhmedova, Tashkent, June 23, 1998. Court documents state that Abdurakhmonov was, at various times, a student of Nazarov and of "Kobil Kori," presumably a reference to Kobil Murodov, the one-time imam of Kokoldosh medresseh. Akmal Ikramov District Court verdict, issued by Judge F. B. Shukurov, July 7, 2000. For information regarding Murodov, who died in prison in 1998, see above, in this chapter.

[210] Human Rights Watch interview with independent rights defender Mukhtabar Akhmedova, Tashkent, June 23, 1998.

[211] Ibid; Human Rights Watch interview with the imam's wife, Muborak Abdurakhmonova, Tashkent, May 26, 2000; and open letter from Muborak Abdurakhmonova, 1998. Abdurakhmonov's father was also a well-known religious leader, the former imam-khattib of a mosque in Zarafshan, in Novoi province (1991-1992) and later the head of a mosque in Tashkent province (1994-1995).

[212] Human Rights Watch interview with Muborak Abdurakhmonova, Tashkent, May 26, 2000.

was diagnosed with brain damage and had required an operation and long-term hospitalization for his head injuries following his release.[213]

Abdurakhmonov was again arrested in June 1998 on charges of falsifying his passport and narcotics possession.[214] The judge stated in his verdict that Abdurakhmonov and a co-defendant had "partially confessed" that they had arranged to have their passports altered to facilitate doing business in Kyrgyzstan. The judge dismissed the charge of illegal possession of narcotics.[215] Convicted of having a falsified passport, he was sentenced to two years in prison, but as this statute fell under the presidential amnesty of 1998, Abdurakhmonov was released from the courtroom on December 5, 1998.[216] The doctor who examined Abdurakhmonov upon his release found that he had a concussion, a broken rib, and bruised kidneys, as well as nerve damage to his spine so severe that the then-thirty-year-old man could no longer sit or stand upright.[217]

---

[213] Human Rights Watch interview with a close relative of Imam Abdurakhmonov, name withheld, Tashkent, July 23, 1998.

[214] Iunusabad District Court verdict, issued by Judge R. Abdulkhasanov, December 5, 1998. According to Abdurakhmonov's wife, his passport indicated that he was a citizen of Kazakhstan, whereas he is in fact an Uzbek citizen. It was rumored that he had planned to leave the country with the false documents. Human Rights Watch interview with the imam's wife Muborak Abdurakhmonova, Tashkent, May 26, 2000. Human Rights Watch was unable to verify grounds for this charge. It is plausible that Abdurakhmonov would desire to leave the country as had other imams who are believed to have fled to neighboring states when they came under pressure from authorities for displaying independence from state doctrine on religion.

[215] Iunusabad District Court verdict, issued by Judge R. Abdulkhasanov, December 5, 1998. In his verdict, Judge Abdulkhasanov noted Abdurakhmonov's testimony and that of his wife that police planted the narcotics, that he (Abdurakhmonov) was subjected to physical and psychological coercion to force him to confess to the drugs charge, and that the procurator had failed to prove this charge. The judge similarly dismissed a charge against Abdurakhmonov's co-defendant that the man had a grenade in his car.

[216] The 1998 presidential amnesty, like other amnesties announced by the Uzbek government, was a presidential decree ordering the release of certain categories of prisoners, including those charged under article 228 (preparation or use of false identification documents). The judge recognized that this statute was named in the decree and so released Abdurakhmonov and his co-defendant directly from the courtroom.

[217] Human Rights Watch interview with Muborak Abdurakhmonova, Tashkent, May 26, 2000.

Abdurakhmonov was later obliged to report for police questioning about the activities and possible whereabouts of Obidkhon Nazarov, but he refused to become an informant.[218] At one point, police accused him of having taught members of Hizb ut-Tahrir.[219] Police re-arrested him shortly thereafter, on or about April 27, 2000, and held him incommunicado for two months, the duration of the pre-trial investigation.[220]

During this period, investigator Khalkhon Juraev of the Procuracy General denied Abdurakhmonov's wife any contact with him and refused to inform her of the reason for his arrest.[221] She did not know his whereabouts but was too frightened of the authorities to pursue the question aggressively, which reflects the experience of other detainees' relatives. She explained that she was "afraid to go to the MVD because they will lock me up in a room and threaten to do things to me if my husband doesn't confess, then they will threaten my husband that they will rape me and then he'll confess to everything. This is what I've been told."[222]

The family reported that during the investigation—from April to July 2000—at least three attorneys refused to defend Abdurakhmonov. They explained to the family that security agents had followed them and had put them under intimidating surveillance when they had represented him in the past.[223] But the defendant did not have state representation either.

---

[218] Human Rights Watch interview with a person close to the case, name withheld, Tashkent, August 1, 2000.

[219] According to Abdurakhmonov's wife, some of the young men whom Abdurakhmonov taught while he was working as imam at Kokoldosh medresseh later became members of Hizb ut-Tahrir and named him as their teacher. The imam's wife claimed that Abdurakhmonov has no connection to Hizb ut-Tahrir. Human Rights Watch interview with Muborak Abdurakhmonova, Tashkent, May 26, 2000.

[220] Human Rights Watch interview, name withheld, Tashkent, August 1, 2000; and Human Rights Watch interview with Muborak Abdurakhmonova, Tashkent, May 26, 2000.

[221] Human Rights Watch interview with Muborak Abdurakhmonova, Tashkent, May 26, 2000.

[222] Ibid.

[223] Ibid.

The state failed to appoint any lawyer to represent Abdurakhmonov during the investigation of his case and to attend police interrogations. A state-appointed lawyer for the defense appeared for the first time at trial, and then only for the first two hearings.[224]

In its indictment of Abdurakhmonov, the state charged him with "Wahhabism" and with being part of a criminal group along with Imam Nazarov. He was accused of having recruited young men for terrorist training camps abroad and plotting to explode the Charvok dam, north of Tashkent. The court sentenced him to seventeen years of imprisonment on charges of attempt or conspiracy to commit terrorism, conspiracy to overthrow the state, attempt or conspiracy to commit subversion, incitement of national (ethnic), racial, or religious enmity, organization of a criminal group, polygamy, and illegal possession of arms or ammunition.[225]

The most damning evidence against Abdurakhmonov at his second trial was a written statement confessing to all of the state's charges. When given the opportunity to testify in court, however, Abdurakhmonov recanted this confession, stating it was coerced under torture, and conceded only that he had previously met with several so-called Wahhabis. He insisted that he had not been involved in any criminal act. According to an observer at the trial, "He said, 'If you think it is a crime to talk with religious people, then I confess to that.'"[226] But the verdict states that Abdurakhmonov—along with the disappeared imam Abduvali Mirzoev, the IMU leaders Tokhir Iuldash and Juma Namangani, and Bakhrom Abdullaev and others—had led a criminal group aiming to destabilize the government of Uzbekistan and establish an Islamic state by force.[227] The judgment loosely links Abdurakhmonov

---

[224] Human Rights Watch interview, name withheld, August 1, 2000.

[225] Akmal Ikramov District Court verdict, issued by Judge F. B. Shukurov, July 7, 2000.

[226] Human Rights Watch interview, name withheld, Tashkent, August 1, 2000.

[227] Akmal Ikramov District Court verdict, issued by Judge F. B. Shukurov, July 7, 2000. Bahrom Abdullaev was sentenced to death in the first of several trials related to the February 16, 1999 bombings. For more information on this bombing trial and the Abdullaev case, see Monica Whitlock, *Beyond the Oxus: The Central Asians*, London: John Murray (Publishers) Ltd, 2002.

to well-known militants and people labeled "religious extremists," but relies on sweeping allegations. Furthermore it does not detail specific actions of his that violated the law, nor, therefore, any evidence connecting Adburakhmonov to a crime.

With regard to the recruitment charge, Judge Shukurov's verdict makes allegations as to Abdurakhmonov's allegiance and intentions, without providing evidence. For example, the verdict states that Abdurakhmonov "supported" a call to establish an organization called "Tizhoratchi" (tradesmen) and that this group's members sent five hundred men to military training camps abroad. Abdurakhmonov himself is not named as a member of Tizhoratchi, is not alleged to have sent anyone to a military camp, and his "support" of the group is not elaborated upon in the verdict. It is unclear whether the court reviewed other evidence that was not presented at trial. The verdict also asserts that Abdurakhmonov conspired with others to explode a water reservoir in Charvok, but again points to no specific act to uphold this statement.[228]

The verdict states that police arrested Abdurakhmonov while he was in the process of "preparing together with members of a religious extremist movement to carry out pogroms and terrorism in Uzbekistan," but devotes only one sentence of the verdict to this assertion and gives no indication that any evidence was available to prove it.[229] The judge further claimed that witness testimony offered proof of Abdurakhmonov's guilt, but examination of the testimony as recounted in the verdict reveals that seven of the eight witnesses stated only that Abdurakhmonov prayed and that he had been arrested previously in 1998. None of the seven witnesses' testimony, which was summarized in the verdict, referred to Abdurakhmonov having committed a crime.[230] The eighth witness claimed to know that Abdurakhmonov was part of a "Wahhabi movement" but did not define the term. He also testified that the imam and another man had asked him to make copies of a tape about jihad and that he had once overheard a conversation in

---

[228]Akmal Ikramov District Court verdict, issued by Judge F. B. Shukurov, July 7, 2000.

[229] Ibid.

[230] Ibid.

Abdurakhmonov's house about authorities' arrest of Muslims and the need to change the system and to establish an Islamic state through jihad.[231]

The verdict focused heavily on Abdurakhmonov's Islamic studies and influences, including studies with Imam Nazarov and attendance at that imam's Friday prayer services.[232] The ruling acknowledges that Imam Abdurakhmonov stated that he had no relationship to Hizb ut-Tahrir or any other "religious extremist organizations." It further notes that Abdurakhmonov testified that he had not committed any crime against the government nor any crime related to extremism, fundamentalism, or separatism. He said he had had no thoughts of undertaking terrorism or aggression. And he admitted only to having studied Islam during the period in question.[233] The verdict does not elaborate in any way on the origins of the charge of possession of illegal weapons or ammunition. It does not discuss the charge or provide support for it. The judge nonetheless ruled that Abdurakhmonov was guilty on this charge. Human Rights Watch attended the twenty-minute Tashkent City Court appeals hearing of Abdurakhmonov's case.[234] His state appointed lawyer failed to note the procedural violations in the first trial and presented a defense of her client seen often in earlier political cases, a defense that conceded the state's charges and asked simply for leniency on the basis of his youth and for the sake of his children.[235] After a two-minute break to deliberate, the three-judge panel ruled to uphold the lower court's decision. At this writing, Imam Abdurakhmonov is in Zangiota prison.

Followers

Over the years, local rights defenders agree, not only well-known imams but also many of their followers or perceived followers have been

[231] Ibid.

[232] Ibid.

[233] Ibid.

[234] As is common in Uzbekistan, the defendant was not present at the appeal.

[235] Human Rights Watch unofficial transcript, Tashkent City Court, Tashkent, August 8, 2000.

detained or arrested during the government campaign against independent Islam. The government has particularly targeted people it perceived as followers of Imam Nazarov. Their estimates of numbers vary from several hundred to several thousand,[236] but this discrepancy is not surprising, as some detainees are released uncharged and others held incommunicado, or on misdemeanor charges for varying periods. In addition, many detainees are picked up more than once, as part of a pattern of ongoing harassment and surveillance of independent Muslims. Those who are released are often reluctant to discuss their detention with human rights organizations; sometimes because they were forced to name friends or acquaintances as criminals, pay a bribe to police, or agree to inform on others after being released, and sometimes simply out of fear of re-arrest. Others were detained multiple times before being formally arrested, convicted, and sentenced to prison terms.

Police action against people associated with Imam Nazarov began as early as 1996, just after the Muslim Board dismissed Nazarov from his position as imam.[237] Later, police arrested not only those with a direct relationship with Nazarov, but also those with only a loose affiliation to the imam, including people who at one time attended his mosque, listened to his sermons, or possessed tapes of those sermons. Local human rights activist Vasila Inoiatova, who has attended dozens of trials of men brought up on religion-related charges, spoke of the on-going persecution of those "connected" with Nazarov, "...[A]ll these people who listened to his sermons or kept tapes [of Nazarov] are being arrested because of it."[238] As noted above, Imam Nazarov's wife testified to the same phenomenon. "About 5,000 people went to his mosque," she said of her husband, "but there are also many [who've been] arrested as his followers, but who never really went to his mosque, … who didn't know him at all. Just because they had his tapes, they were arrested."[239] Another person close to the Nazarov case told

---

[236] Human Rights Watch interview with Vasila Inoiatova, Tashkent, March 8, 2001; and Human Rights Watch interview with Mikhail Ardzinov, Tashkent, March 9, 2001.

[237] See above, case of Imam Iuldashev.

[238] Human Rights Watch interview with Vasila Inoiatova, Tashkent, March 8, 2001.

[239] Human Rights Watch interview with Munira Nasriddinova, Tashkent, May 23, 2001.

Human Rights Watch that police targeted not only his students and congregants, but also those who "invited him to their homes at one time or were in the same room [as he] one day or drove him home—just people who showed him respect. Law enforcement agents followed [him] and video taped him and found those people—even people who only met him once."[240] "People who listened to his tapes were also arrested," the source reported, recalling that one man had been arrested for listening to a tape of the imam reading from the Koran.[241]

The cases of two men, arrested together in 1998, typify what Human Rights Watch has learned about prosecutions of those accused of following independent imams in their alleged anti-state activity.

Abdurashid Isakhojaev was a worker in an industrial plant who frequented many mosques, including that of Imam Obidkhon Nazarov, with whom he formed a loose friendship and from whom he obtained basic religious instruction. Isakhojaev attended the Friday services at Nazarov's Tokhtaboi mosque. He also met the imam at celebrations at the Nazarov home; he attended a wedding there and also the birthday of a child. When he suffered a work-related spinal injury in 1991—an injury that made him an invalid—Imam Nazarov visited him in the hospital. Isakhojaev and some of his schoolmates invited Imam Nazarov to participate in a "gap," a men's discussion group. At the "gap" Nazarov taught the young men basic Islamic rituals, such as how to pray and how to prepare bodies for a Muslim funeral. He also called on them to live clean lives, to be honest, and not to drink alcohol.[242] According to Isakhojaev's family, these interactions formed the extent of the young man's relationship with the famous imam.

After Nazarov vanished in March 1998, local police briefly detained and interrogated Isakhojaev, along with estimated hundreds of other "followers" of Nazarov. At the precinct house, officers beat the young man while barraging him with questions about his religion and Imam

[240] Human Rights Watch interview, name withheld, Tashkent, May 28, 2001.

[241] Ibid.

[242] Human Rights Watch interview with Sharifa Isakhojaeva, the young man's mother, Tashkent, June 1, 2000.

Nazarov. He pleaded with the officers not to beat him on his injured back, but while questioning him about Nazarov, they focused their physical abuse on the area of his injury. The police asked him, "Where is Obid Kori?"[243] and "Why do you wear a beard?"[244] They released him after instructing him to find a cassette of Nazarov's sermons that they were seeking, bring it to them, and shave his beard.[245] Isakhojaev's mother (born 1937) told Human Rights Watch, "I told him he was ill and would not survive torture, and I pleaded with my son to shave."[246] But Isakhojaev did not shave his beard.

On June 21, 1998, after his place of work closed unexpectedly, Isakhojaev's friend Odil Isaev drove him to the Chilanzar mayor's office, where he intended to make inquiries about it. As he approached the office, two men roughly detained both Isakhojaev and his friend. They pulled Isaev out of the car, beat him, and planted narcotics in his car before moving both detainees to MVD police headquarters in Tashkent.[247] That evening eight or nine officers, saying they were MVD and entering without a warrant, searched Isakhojaev's family's house. They focused on one room they evidently believed to be his.[248] Police concluded their search with the triumphant assertion: "We've got all we needed"—holding up a grenade.[249] When Isakhojaev's father-in-law accused them of planting the weapon, the officers forcibly removed him from the premises. Then the police took religious literature from the house, including copies of hadith. Later they compelled Isakhojaev's wife to sign their report verifying the search, reportedly telling her: "Your husband is in our hands. If you want to give him food and a

[243] A reference to Obid Kori or Obidkhon Kori is a reference to Obidkhon Kori Nazarov. The term Kori is an honorific indicating that the person has memorized the Koran.

[244] Human Rights Watch interview with Sharifa Isakhojaeva, Tashkent, June 1, 2000.

[245] Ibid.

[246] Ibid.

[247] Ibid.

[248] According to Isakhojaev's lawyer, it was in fact the bedroom of the detainee's mother and father. Written complaint addressed to the chairman of the Tashkent City Court, from Hamid Zainutdinov, December 24, 1998.

[249] Human Rights Watch interview with Sharifa Isakhojaeva, Tashkent, June 1, 2000.

jacket, you'd better sign."[250] The religious materials were later deemed permissible and returned to the family.[251]

Police informed Isakhojaev's family that the young man had refused legal representation, but then assigned a state lawyer to him. That lawyer told the family that Isakhojaev had confessed to all of the charges against him but did not specify those charges.[252] On February 14, 1999, seeing his mother for the first time since his arrest, Isakhojaev told her that police had held him in the basement of the MVD for twenty-four days and that officers had tortured him there.[253] He reportedly said that during interrogation, police beat him badly and tried to force him to give testimony against Imam Nazarov. Police questioning had focused exclusively on Nazarov, with no questions at all about the narcotics they claimed to have found in Isakhojaev's possession.[254] In response, Isakhojaev wrote a statement about Nazarov's kindness to him after his accident and participation in the men's discussion group. The investigator allegedly tore up Isakhojaev's statement, saying, "We don't need your fairy tales."[255] Eventually, police succeeded in extracting a

[250] Ibid. The procedure of signing a search report is meant to protect citizens from illegal searches and to give them recourse to complain about any wrongdoing by police during the course of the search. If a person has objections to any part of the report, he or she has the right to write his/her version of events and describe police behavior. When a person signs the document without writing in objections, he or she is confirming the veracity of the police officers' account of the search. The report then serves as an important piece of evidence verifying the legality of the search as it states, for instance, that the search was undertaken in the presence of witnesses, that everything the officers claim to have found was indeed found in the home or on the property, and it accounts for all property taken into possession by police. In Uzbekistan, however, the procedure has been turned around from what was originally intended. Rather than being a tool for recourse, it serves as an obstacle to obtaining justice later in court, and is, in effect, the first in a series of coercive measures to force a detainee or suspect to incriminate him or herself or to force family members to bear witness against the detainee or suspect.

[251] Human Rights Watch interview with Sharifa Isakhojaeva, Tashkent, June 1, 2000.

[252] This state-appointed and state-paid lawyer demanded 40,000 som (at least ten times the average monthly wage) from the family as a fee. Ibid.

[253] Ibid.

[254] Isakhojaev's torture was so severe that he was partially paralyzed. Human Rights Watch interview with Sharifa Isakhojaeva, Tashkent, June 1, 2000.

[255] Ibid.

statement from Isakhojaev that incriminated him for helping Imam Nazarov spread ideas of "Wahhabism."[256]

Isakhojaev's trial at the Chilanzar District Court began on October 30, 1998. The judge, K.H. Toshmatov, allegedly recommended that the family hire his court secretary as the lawyer for the defense and said that this would help the young man's chances. The family hired the judge's secretary and paid her for this service, but said they felt afterwards that she had not helped at all.[257]

At trial, according to the defendant's mother, Isakhojaev was bent over and barely able to sit up. The only witnesses called were two men who had been stopped on the street by police after Isakhojaev was detained and who signed a document saying that police had shown them the drugs they claimed to have found on the young man.[258] There were discrepancies in the state's assertions about the "discovery" of the drugs on Isakhojaev, but this did not affect the trial.[259] What the trial, like the investigation, focused on was Imam Nazarov and the defendant's relationship to him. When the judge questioned Isakhojaev about Imam Nazarov, the young defendant recalled the imam's visit with him in the hospital and the development of his own spiritual faith, which sprang from having survived his infirmity and being able to have children.[260]

---

[256] Written statement to then-U.S. Ambassador-at-Large for International Religious Freedom Robert Seiple, from Sharifa Isakhojaeva, May 20, 2000.

[257] Human Rights Watch interview with Sharifa Isakhojaeva, Tashkent, June 1, 2000.

[258] Ibid.

[259] The court verdict alleges on the first page that narcotics were found in Isakhojaev's right pants pocket, but later the document states that witnesses saw police take something wrapped in white paper out of his left pants pocket. Chilanzar District Court verdict, Tashkent, issued by Judge K. Kh. Toshmatov, November 3, 1998, translated from Uzbek. During the trial, the judge reportedly asked no questions about the narcotics charges, nor about the grenade allegedly found in Isakhojaev's home. Human Rights Watch interview with Sharifa Isakhojaeva, Tashkent, June 1, 2000.

[260] Human Rights Watch interview with Sharifa Isakhojaeva, Tashkent, June 1, 2000.

The judge ruled that Isakhojaev was an active participant in a forbidden religious movement.[261] Judge Toshmatov further found that from February 1992 to July 1998, Isakhojaev "...actively participated in the activities of the religious trend 'Wahhabism,' led by Obid Kori Nazarov, [who] illegally operated in the territory of the Republic under the mask of religious belief, for the purposes of spreading the ideas of this religious trend among the population, gathered people in his neighborhood and mosques and called them to join the 'Wahhabi' movement..."[262] The judge's verdict goes on to point to Nazarov's participation in the men's discussion group or "gap" as further evidence of Isakhojaev's active involvement in calling people to "Wahhabism." In the court's opinion, the imam's participation in the group was directed to discussing establishment of an Islamic state based on Islamic law.[263]

Judge Toshmatov sentenced Isakhojaev to eight years in a general-regime prison for illegal possession of narcotics, possession of weapons or ammunition, and organization of, or participation in, a banned social association or religious organization.[264]

Initially unable to learn where he was incarcerated, Isakhojaev's family finally succeeded in locating him, in Jaslyk prison, the country's harshest facility, where his poor condition and bruised body indicated that he had been beaten by guards.[265] All of the family's attempts to have him transferred to the central prison infirmary in Tashkent failed, as authorities either handed off the requests to other bureaucrats or responded with hostility.[266] Meanwhile, after the trial authorities

---

[261] Chilanzar District Court verdict, Tashkent, issued by Judge K. Kh. Toshmatov, November 3, 1998.

[262] Ibid.

[263] Ibid.

[264] Ibid; and Tashkent City Court appeals verdict, issued by Judge I. E. Kabilova, Tashkent, December 18, 1998. The Tashkent City Court upheld the lower court's ruling on appeal.

[265] Human Rights Watch interview with Sharifa Isakhojaeva, Tashkent, June 1, 2000.

[266] Written statement to the Organization of the Islamic Conference, U.N. Commission on Human Rights and various human rights organizations, from Sharifa Isakhojaeva, January 30, 2000; and Human Rights Watch interview with Sharifa Isakhojaeva, Tashkent, June 1, 2000.

intimidated and harassed Isakhojaev's family—detaining a younger brother, Muzafar, and harshly interrogating him because of his older brother's perceived religious affiliation and his own religious practices.[267]

Odil Isaev, born in 1968, was arrested along with his friend, Abdurashid Isakhojaev, and accused of having been part of a "Wahhabi trend" led by Imam Nazarov.[268] Isaev wore a beard and participated in the same men's discussion group as Isakhojaev and Imam Nazarov.

On June 21, 1998, after driving his friend and co-worker, Isakhojaev, to the Chilanzar mayor's office, he was detained by plainclothes agents who attempted to plant drugs on him. When he managed to get the narcotics, wrapped in a twenty-five-som note, out of his pocket, police reportedly laughed at his attempt to avoid having the contraband planted on him. "What, are you so rich that you can throw away money?" they taunted. Then they reportedly planted an even larger amount of marijuana in Isaev's car and placed him under arrest.[269]

Odil Isaev was tried before Judge Toshmatov in the Chilanzar District Court just one day before Isakhojaev's trial. He was sentenced to nine years in a strict-regime prison on charges of illegal possession of narcotics.[270] In the decision against Isakhojaev, Judge Toshmatov noted that Odil Isaev was a member of the men's discussion group that had included Imam Nazarov and that he and Isakhojaev were responsible for first inviting the imam to participate.[271] Isaev was sent to Jaslyk prison.

---

[267] Human Rights Watch interview with Sharifa Isakhojaeva, Tashkent, June 1, 2000.

[268] Chilanzar District Court verdict convicting Abdurashid Isakhojaev, Tashkent, issued by Judge K. Kh. Toshmatov, November 3, 1998; and Tashkent City Court appeals verdict against Abdurashid Isakhojaev, issued by Judge I. E. Kabilova, Tashkent, December 18, 1998. Odil Isaev's own court documents were not available to Human Rights Watch at the time of this writing.

[269] Human Rights Watch interview with Sharifa Isakhojaeva, Tashkent, June 1, 2000.

[270] Ibid. On appeal, the Supreme Court reduced the term to eight years in a general-regime prison and confiscation of Isaev's car.

[271] The appeals verdict for Isakhojaev further portrays Isaev as an Islamic activist, stating that, ".. he, together with his friends Rashid [Abdurashid Isakhojaev] and Mirbosit [full name not available], went to Toi-tepe [on the outskirts of Tashkent] and called people to become

Fourteen Accused "Wahhabis:" Fergana, June 2002

In June 2002 the Fergana Province Court convicted fourteen men for having been "active members of an organized criminal religious extremist group that follows Wahhabism."[272] The verdict was based on confessions that, according to the defendants' testimony, had been coerced under torture.[273] The defendants recanted their confessions in court, but the judge ignored the torture claims and sentenced the men to terms ranging from nine to seventeen years of imprisonment.

The prosecution charged that the defendants were "religious exremists" who recruited militants for the IMU and made plans to commit acts of terrorism on various factories in the Fergana Valley. The evidence brought forth to support these charges included a grenade, several bullets, and small quantities of narcotics. The defendants acknowledged only that they helped others to leave Uzbekistan to escape religious repression.[274]

Eight Accused "Wahhabis:" Tashkent, September 2001

On September 21, 2001, the Tashkent City Court handed down a verdict convicting and sentencing eight people for being members of a "Wahhabi organization" led by Imam Nazarov and another imam, Rukhiddin Fakhruddinov.[275] One of the defendants was Fakhruddinov's wife, Rakhima Akhmedalieva, whom the judge sentenced to seven years in prison.[276] The verdict presented as compelling evidence against

---

believers…." Tashkent City Court appeals verdict, issued by Judge I. E. Kabilova, Tashkent, December 18, 1998.

[272] Fergana Province Court verdict issued by Judge N. Iakubjanov, June 3, 2002.

[273] Ibid.

[274] Ibid.

[275] Verdict issued by Judge F.K. Shodmonov, Tashkent City Court, hearing held in the courthouse of the Iunusabad District Court, Tashkent, September 21, 2001.

[276] For an account of the harassment her daughter faced, see "Family Members: Arrests, House Arrest, Harrassment" in Chapter III.

defendant Bakhtior Karimov police data from Andijan indicating the young man had attended Imam Mirzoev's sermons prior to 1995.[277] Another defendant testified that he had been a student of Imam Mirzoev in Andijan in the early 1990s, but denied the government's charge that the imam had taught him and other students from "Wahhabi" books, saying Mirzoev only instructed them in prayer and the Koran.[278]

Thirteen Accused "Wahhabis:" Tashkent, December 2000-April 2001

Twelve men were arrested in 2000 and tried along with Imam Iuldashev. The state charged that during religion classes with Imam Iuldashev, the men had received not Koranic instruction, but lessons on "Wahhabism" and jihad. They were indicted on charges that included participation in a criminal group, distribution of extremist religious literature, and membership in a religious extremist organization. As to specific acts cited as evidence of their guilt, these related almost exclusively to expression and ideas. First, Iuldashev and his co-defendants were charged with distributing "Wahhabi" literature under orders from Imam Nazarov. No such literature is known to exist, and none was presented in court. The state also alleged that the men recorded and distributed broadcasts of Radio Free Europe/Radio Liberty and BBC, which included criticism of government policies.[279] Some of the defendants allegedly possessed audio and video cassettes of speeches made years earlier by imams Nazarov and Mirzoev. As the indictment noted, Islamic scholars from the official Kokoldosh mosque had reviewed the tapes for the Cabinet of Ministers and found that they contained "ideas of

---

[277] Verdict issued by Judge F.K. Shodmonov, Tashkent City Court, Tashkent, September 21, 2001.

[278] Ibid. The judge's verdict acknowledges that this co-defendant, a young father (born in 1968, father of two), testified in court that police had forced him to say he had been against the government and had been "emir" of a Wahhabi organization and that he recanted that false confession.

[279] Indictment of Tashkent city procurator M. I. Naimov, signed by police investigator A. Karshiev, December 18, 2000.

extremism, separatism, and fundamentalism."[280] One co-defendant, Dilmurod Sagdullaev, was supposedly caught in possession of "leaflets" titled, "Hurry to her, Muslims, the month of charity has arrived" and "Textbook for charitable people."[281] The Cabinet of Ministers ruled that these materials advocated the establishment of an Islamic state through jihad.[282]

The men also allegedly owned a xerox machine, cell phones, a tape recorder, pagers, and a computer. These were not produced in court, but were mentioned in the indictment as evidence of criminal intent.[283] The state further alleged that the men met twice in 1997 at public sports centers in Tashkent for exercise classes in preparation for "combat training for jihad."[284] The prosecution charged that the men collected money for a so-called baitulmol al-mal fund and were in possession of U.S. dollars.[285]

Dilmurod Sagdullaev denied all of the charges against him, including possession of "leaflets," and acknowledged only that he took lessons in Islam.[286] He was sentenced to ten years in prison.[287] Defendant Khusan Maksudov "confessed" to having worked at Tokhtaboi mosque and having cooked for others during a trip to the mountains for "physical preparations" and lessons on religion led by Imam Nazarov. He also testified that he possessed tapes of Nazarov's speeches and religious

---

[280] Ibid.

[281] Ibid.

[282] Ibid.

[283] Ibid.

[284] Ibid.

[285] In Uzbek the term is given as *baitulmol*. It is frequently identified as an organization in indictments and court verdicts in Uzbekistan. However, the Arabic term *bayt al-mal* refers to a treasury. In an Islamic state, it refers to the state treasury.

[286] Indictment of Tashkent city procurator M. I. Naimov, signed by police investigator A. Karshiev, December 18, 2000.

[287] Human Rights Watch unofficial transcript, Tashkent City Court hearing held in the Akmal Ikramov Disctrict Court building, Tashkent, April 9, 2001.

literature. He denied that he was a "Wahhabi."[288] Forty-nine-year-old Maksudov recounted that police tortured him in pre-trial detention and threatened to rape his wife.[289] The court convicted Maksudov and fellow defendants Ulugbek Vakhidov, Abdukarim Mirzakhmedov, Jamshidbek Azimov, and Shukrullo Turaev and sentenced each to eight years in prison for organization of, or participation in, a religious extremist, separatist, fundamentalist or other banned organization and attempt to overthrow the constitutional order.[290] Imam Iuldashev's assistant in 1998 and 1999, Shukhrat Tajibaev, denied the state's allegations that he established a religious extremist organization and plotted the overthrow of the state. He was treated the most harshly and was sentenced to eighteen years in prison.[291] Five of the thirteen defendants—Botir Amanov, Nizomiddin Alavutdinov, Rashid Makhmudov, Zhavlon Tokhtakhanov, and Ravshan Irmatov—were found guilty of failing to report a crime and given two-year suspended sentences, and fined 20 percent of their salary for two years.

Seventeen Accused "Wahhabis:" Tashkent, June-August 2000

The trial of seventeen men from Tashkent who studied Islam at home starkly typifies the government's campaign against religious activity outside state controls. The state charged that their activities were part of a "Wahhabi trend" and that their "Wahhabi" group operated under the

---

[288] Ibid; Maksudov is identified in court documents as a former security guard for the mosque from 1993 to 1998. Indictment of Tashkent city procurator M. I. Naimov, signed by police investigator A. Karshiev, December 18, 2000.

[289] Human Rights Watch unofficial transcript, Tashkent City Court trial held in the Akmal Ikramov District Court building, Tashkent, February 7, 2001.

[290] Human Rights Watch unofficial transcript, Tashkent City Court hearing held at the Akmal Ikramov District Court building, Tashkent, April 9, 2001; and Tashkent City Court verdict, issued by Judge G. Z. Najimov, April 9, 2001. Maksudov was additionally convicted on charges of distribution of literature containing ideas of religious extremism, separatism and fundamentalism.

[291] Indictment issued by Tashkent city procurator M. I. Naimov, signed by police investigator A. Karshiev, December 18, 2000; and Human Rights Watch unofficial transcript, Tashkent City Court trial held at the Akmal Ikramov District Court building, Tashkent, April 9, 2001.

leadership of Imam Nazarov. In fact, at least two of the defendants had never met Nazarov. The group's activities, according to the indictment, included study of the Koran and discussions on the need to establish an Islamic state and live by the rules of Islamic law.[292] According to the state prosecutor, "They pursued ideas of extremism, Wahhabism, and terrorism, and invited others to join..." He charged that the men obtained, copied, and distributed "religious extremist books" and propagated "Wahhabism."[293] The state alleged that money the men claimed to have collected for shared meals and to help poor neighbors was meant to buy weapons—though none was charged with weapons possession. Further, the state characterized the men's participation in a semi-regular soccer game at a stadium in the city center as part of their "preparation to build an Islamic state."[294]

The state indicted the men for conspiracy to seize power or overthrow the constitutional order of the Republic of Uzbekistan; organization of, or participation in, an illegal religious organization; establishment or leadership of, or participation in, a religious extremist, separatist, fundamentalist, or other banned organization; and distribution of "materials containing ideas of religious extremism, separatism, and fundamentalism" by a group and through abuse of office. Five of the seventeen defendants were charged with organizing a criminal association. The main defendant, Gafurjon Toirov, was also charged with illegal sale or acquisition of currency.

Some of the most appalling incidents in the case against the seventeen men took place long before they were brought to court. Police compelled at least six of the seventeen men to make public statements of contrition before congregations at state mosques, where government-sponsored Islamic leaders denounced them and warned others not to follow their example. The men were promised freedom in exchange for

[292] Indictment of seventeen men issued by the Tashkent City Procuracy, signed by senior police investigator K. Khujanov and department chief S.V. Shiniaev, June 20, 2000.

[293] Human Rights Watch unofficial transcript, Tashkent City Court, Judge Sharipov presiding, August 4, 2000. The trial was held in the building of the Sobir Rahimov District Court, Tashkent.

[294] Ibid.

this public humiliation and vow of penitence, but police arrested them again soon after. Conditions of pre-trial detention were brutal for the seventeen men. Police allegedly kept them incommunicado for months, denied them access to legal counsel, and tortured them to force them to sign confessions. At trial, the men and their lawyers recounted the torture in detail, but Judge Sharipov ruled their testimony not credible and concluded, "No one tortured them."[295]

The defendants[296] denied that they were "Wahhabis" or involved in any kind of anti-state activity and claimed that their only "crime" had been to study Islam in private. They further claimed that the state failed to show that they had committed any act beyond this. The lawyer for Gairat Sabirov noted in his closing arguments, "During the trial...just one thing was proven, that he was studying religion."[297]

Defendant Anvar Mirakhmedov said, "I lived in this country, was educated here. I never had anything against my country. I just wanted to learn the Koran, hadith, and be a real, pious Muslim. I just wanted to increase my knowledge." Explaining his choice to participate in private religious instruction, defendant Otabek Makhmudov said, "Everybody asks us 'Why do you learn religion at home, not at a mosque or university?' If I go to the university, who will feed my family?" In an apparent attempt to bridge the gap between his legitimate practice of religion and the state's demand that he ask for forgiveness, he added, "If reading the Koran is against the law, we admit that we made a

[295] Human Rights Watch unofficial transcript, Tashkent City Court, Judge Sharipov presiding, August 21, 2000. Their torture is described in some detail below, in "Torture and Mistreatment in Pre-trial Detention" in Chapter IV.

[296] The seventeen defendants were: Gafurjon Toirov, Mansur Juraev, Otabek Maskudbekov, Agzam Astankulov, Ibrahim Obidov, Gairat Sabirov, Faizullo Saipov, Murod Kasymov, Hamidullo Rakhmatullaev, Avazkhon Boimetov, Shukhrat Islamov, Anvar Mirakhmedov, Dilshod Iunusov, Shavkhat Bobokhonov, Shukhrat Umarov, Tahir Obidov, and Bahodir Rakhimov.

[297] Human Rights Watch unofficial transcript, Tashkent City Court, Judge Sharipov presiding, August 4, 2000. Unless otherwise noted, remaining information on this case derives from this transcript.

mistake."[298] "I just want you to distinguish between real Muslims and militants," defendant Faizullo Saipov told the judge.

Defendants Mansur Juraev, a twenty-two-year-old student at the Islamic university, and Gafurjon Toirov, had taught the others about Islam using the Koran. The state alleged that they had also taught the others that it was necessary to create an Islamic state by violent means and that they were leaders of a secret, illegal "Wahhabi" group intent on the violent overthrow of the government. In his testimony, Juraev said, "I proudly admit to the charges, I really taught these young men the Koran." Regarding the men's supposed participation in secret gatherings, Juraev noted, "The procurator asked us why we met secretly. I can't distinguish between open and secret [here]. If we get together, should we hang a poster outside? We had dinner, we talked about prayer, but we didn't hide from anybody." Toirov echoed his co-defendants, explaining how he came to instruct the others in Islam, "I heard that there was an Islamic institute called Al Bukhari. I was preparing to join the Islamic university, and I don't think I did anything wrong. Then I started teaching other people. I didn't call anyone to go against our country."

The defendants further rejected the state's claim that the religious books found in their possession were "forbidden" or anti-constitutional. "Calling people to overthrow the country wasn't our business. We did have religious books, though. If you go to any market, you can buy these books...they were not books against the constitution," defendant Juraev told the court. As to charges that the group's computer was purchased to produce anti-constitutional literature, Otabek Makhmudov's lawyer noted, "Out of forty-eight diskettes, eleven had religious ideas, but nothing against the government or constitution... They're being accused of having anti-government diskettes."

Defendants acknowledged that they collected money for the needy, including at least one family of an accused "Wahhabi," but denied that this amounted to wrongdoing. Outside the courthouse, a witness for the prosecution told Human Rights Watch that her brother had been

---

[298] Ibid.

convicted to five years in prison on fabricated charges of illegal possession of narcotics and a grenade. She said that a friend—one of the defendants—had given her family money, to help out, and that she had been summoned by police to serve as a witness in this case, to say that the defendants gave her family money.[299] The state saw a conspiracy in the way the men had played soccer. They had taken part in "physical exercises in a Tashkent stadium," according to the prosecutor, "in preparation for building an Islamic state..."[300] The lawyer for Dilshod Unusov argued, "If they played soccer or exercised, does it mean they wanted to use it against someone? The President encourages sports, and now we're accusing them of playing soccer!"[301]

On August 21, 2000, Judge Sharipov ruled that the men had been members of a "Wahhabi" group involved in spreading "Wahhabi literature" and engaged in "physical exercises and military training in Pakhtakor stadium" with the aim of establishing an Islamic state.[302]

Some of the sentences passed down by the court shocked even the most experienced observers. Long-time rights defender Mikhail Ardzinov commented, "I thought they would get five or six years; this was frightening."[303] Judge Sharipov sentenced Gafurjon Toirov and Shukhrat Umarov to nineteen years in prison and Mansur Juraev to an eighteen-year term. Maksudbekov and Sobirov were sentenced to fifteen and fourteen years, respectively, while Mirakhmedov, Boimetov, Astankulov, Rakhmatullaev, Ibrahim Obidov, Iunusov, and Rakhimov received sentences ranging from ten to thirteen years. The court imposed slightly lighter sentences, nine years in prison or less, on defendants Bobokhonov, Islamov, Saipov, Kosymov, and Tokhir

[299] Human Rights Watch interview, name withheld, Tashkent, August 4, 2000.

[300] Human Rights Watch unofficial transcript, Tashkent City Court, Judge Sharipov presiding, August 4, 2000.

[301] Ibid.

[302] Human Rights Watch unofficial transcript, Tashkent City Court, Judge Sharipov presiding, August 21, 2000. Also in his decision, Judge Sharipov accused the men of harboring the goal of creating a Caliphate, a system of government desired by members of Hizb ut-Tahrir and not usually ascribed to so-called Wahhabis.

[303] Human Rights Watch interview with Mikhail Ardzinov, Tashkent, August 21, 2000.

Obidov. The latter, Obidov, was found guilty only of participation in a banned religious organization and was sentenced to three years and six months incarceration, reduced pursuant to a December 1998 presidential amnesty to one year and three months.[304]

Fifteen Accused "Wahhabis:" Tashkent, June-November 2000

In a related case, Tashkent City Court Judge Yusupov convicted fifteen men in November 2000 for taking classes on Islam.[305] The fifteen men[306] were accused of having studied the Koran and hadith in private classes or gatherings with a man named Rakhmatullo. As in the case against the seventeen accused Wahhabis, the state charged that these fifteen men took classes about the Koran and learned basic Arabic and that, as classes progressed, Rakhmatullo and other private instructors discussed holy war with them.[307] Also reminiscent of the earlier case, the

[304] Tashkent City Court verdict issued by Judge Sharipov, August 21, 2000.

[305] Witness and written testimony of defendants in the group of fifteen men was used to incriminate those in the two group cases described above. One of the defendants in the case of fifteen, Shukhrat Balikov, used the opportunity of his "last word" in court to say that police had coerced him to make false statements incriminating others, including the group of seventeen alleged Wahhabis: "I am not an actor. These are real tears…[S]eventeen young men were convicted because of me… Why should they be blamed because of me? Please let them be released." Human Rights Watch unofficial transcript, Tashkent City Court hearing held in the Akmal Ikramov District Court building, Tashkent, November 1, 2000; Memorial Human Rights Center and the Information Center for Human Rights in Central Asia, *List of People Arrested and Tried in Uzbekistan for Political and Religious Reasons (January 1999 to April 2000)*, Moscow, May 2000; Indictment of fifteen men, criminal case number 20/1517, issued by senior investigator, police Capt. I. S. Umirzakov, signed also by the head of the investigative department of the Ministry of Internal Affairs, Col. S. V. Shimiaev, June 16, 2000; and unofficial U.S. Embassy transcript of the Tashkent City Court hearing held at Akmal Ikramov District Court building, April 9, 2001. Meanwhile, the court decision condemning Imam Abduvahid Iuldashev and his twelve co-defendants in April 2001 named Kakhramon Saidkhojaev, one of the fifteen accused Wahhabis, as the source that incriminated the imam and others.

[306] The fifteen men were: Shukhrat Balikov, Kakhramon Saidkhojaev, Mamurjon Musaev, Makhmud Abdullaev, Tokhir Azimov, Munirjon Aliev, Kudratullo Valiev, Dilshod Alimov, Bakhtior Mirdjalilov, Mirzokhid Mirdjalilov, Ravshan Iunusov, Kamol Shokasimov, Bakhromjon Taimuradov, Anvar Khalilov, and Murodjon Rikhziev.

[307] Indictment of fifteen men, criminal case number 20/1517.

state charged that the men played sports in a local stadium as part of their preparation for establishing an Islamic state and were engaged in military training during a two-day trip to a children's recreation camp.[308] The defense argued that all the men did at the children's camp was play soccer and go swimming.[309]

The state indictment of the fifteen men labeled them "Wahhabis" and "members of a Wahhabi trend."[310] It alleged that they were operating under the leadership of Imam Nazarov, but failed to flesh out the supposed connection with Nazarov.[311] For their part, the defendants denied that they had even met the famous imam.[312]

Defendant Kakhramon Saidkhodjaev acknowledged that he had participated in religious study with one Rakhmatullo since 1996, but said that the supposed anti-state content of the classes was fabricated by police, who had forced him to sign a statement saying that Rakhmatullo had taught him about jihad.[313] Defendant Mamurjon Musaev testified, "We were never involved in terrorism. We were just following God's Koran and hadith and following Muhammad's sunna [example]."[314] Other defendants claimed that police had arrested them for praying and for their strong belief in God. Defendant Makhmud Abdullaev said, "When I was taken to the basement of the MVD, they asked me if I prayed. When I said yes, they asked why. They asked why I didn't drink and go out with girls. It was then that I found out that I could be

---

[308] Human Rights Watch unofficial transcript, Tashkent City Court hearing held in the Akmal Ikramov District Court building, Tashkent, November 1, 2000; and Indictment of fifteen men, criminal case number 20/1517.

[309] Human Rights Watch unofficial transcript, Tashkent City Court hearing held in the Akmal Ikramov District Court building, Tashkent, November 1, 2000.

[310] Indictment of fifteen men, criminal case number 20/1517.

[311] Ibid.

[312] Human Rights Watch unofficial transcript, Tashkent City Court hearing held in the Akmal Ikramov District Court building, Tashkent, November 1, 2000.

[313] Ibid.

[314] Human Rights Watch unofficial transcript, Tashkent City Court hearing held in the Akmal Ikramov District Court building, Tashkent, November 3, 2000.

arrested for praying."[315] Meanwhile, defendant Kamol Shokasimov declared simply, "We're here for praying, for believing in God. All the rest is false."[316]

The court sentenced the fifteen men to prison terms ranging from six to nineteen years. They were all found guilty of attempted overthrow of the state; organization of, or participation in, a banned religious group; and organization of, or participation in, a religious extremist, separatist, fundamentalist or other banned organization. Defendant Shukhrat Balikov, who was sentenced to nineteen years, was also convicted of illegal possession of weapons or ammunition (on the basis of a signed confession to the state's claim that he had detonators in a tape recorder) as well as the import of contraband, organization of, or participation in, a criminal association, and distribution of literature that contains fundamentalist, separatist, or extremist ideas.

Hizb ut-Tahrir

Hizb ut-Tahrir is an unregistered—effectively, banned—organization.[317] At trial, members recounted their main activities as the study of Arabic (in order to read the Koran in its original language), study of the sura, or chapters, of the Koran, and study of Islamic literature produced by Hizb ut-Tahrir, including "The Islamic Charter."[318] They observed the five daily prayers, and many said that upon involvement in the group they abandoned smoking and drinking alcohol, generally believed to be prohibited under Islamic guidelines. They also condemned the use of narcotics and "immodest" forms of dress for women. They proselytized, calling on others to observe these practices as well. When asked to explain the reasons behind their advocacy for a Caliphate and

[315] Ibid.

[316] Ibid.

[317] For an analysis of Hizb ut-Tahrir's legal status in Uzbekistan, see above "Notes on Wahhabism, 'Wahhabis,' and Hizb ut-Tahrir" in Chapter II.

[318] This is a reference to Hizb ut-Tahrir's draft constitution, published in *The System of Islam*. Electronic communication from Imran Waheed, member of the leadership committeee of Hizb ut-Tahrir Britain, to Human Rights Watch, May 30, 2002; and Human Rights Watch interview with Imran Waheed, London, June 29, 2002.

implementation of shari'a, the members interviewed by Human Rights Watch, almost to a person, cited a desire to rid the country of corruption and prostitution.

As with followers of independent imams, there are divergent estimates of how many members of Hizb ut-Tahrir have been arrested. Human Rights Watch has documented 812 cases of arrest and conviction of the group's members in Uzbekistan.[319] The group itself estimated in June 2000 that police had arrested some 4,000 of its members in Uzbekistan during the government's campaign against independent Islam since 1998.[320] By November 2002 the German section of Hizb ut-Tahrir estimated that the government of Uzbekistan had imprisoned as many as 10,000 of the group's followers.[321] The Russian rights group Memorial reported 2,297 religiously and politically motivated arrests it had documented as of August 2001; the group estimated that more than half of the Muslims arrested for nonviolent crimes were those accused of Hizb ut-Tahrir membership.[322] In addition to being arrested for

[319] As of September 25, 2003, there were 812 people convicted for membership in, affiliation with, or possession of literature by Hizb ut-Tahrir whose cases had been reviewed by Human Rights Watch and entered into the Human Rights Watch database of religious prisoners. The remaining 417 cases in the database were those of people accused of Wahhabism or affiliation with an independent imam. As noted above, the cases of approximately 150 individuals remained to be examined and entered into the database.

[320] Hizb ut-Tahrir statement addressed to human rights organizations, June 15, 2000. On file with Human Rights Watch.

[321] "Statement Regarding the False Accusations Levelled against Hizb ut-Tahrir by the German Press and German Politicians to the Members of Parliament, the Political Wings, and to All the Citizens of this Country," issued by Shakir 'Aasim, Hizb ut-Tahrir representative, Germany, November 4, 2002.

[322] Of the 2,297 cases documented by the group, 1,967 of them were cases of people not charged with violence. At least 33 of these people were not independent Muslims, but other categories of prisoners, such as Christians or journalists. The group estimated that fifty-five percent of the 1,967 people were targeted for membership in Hizb ut-Tahrir. The group noted that the states' case against those 330 people charged with political violence should be looked at with skepticism given the pattern of state fabrication of evidence and use of criminal pretexts to justify politically and religiously motivated arrests. Memorial Human Rights Center and the Information Center for Human Rights in Central Asia, *List of People Arrested and Tried in Uzbekistan for Political and Religious Reasons (December 1997 to August 2001),* Moscow, August 2001. This report was updated in August 2002; the later report cited new data about another 269 political and religious prisoners.

membership and gathering to study, adherents of Hizb ut-Tahrir have been arrested, sometimes en masse, for possession or distribution of the group's literature or, in some cases, because of simple, accidental proximity to those proselytizing for Hizb ut-Tahrir. For example, during a three-day Hizb ut-Tahrir effort to spread its literature in June 1999, police swept through public markets in Tashkent, arresting hundreds of men. A few were released after brief questioning, but the majority were held and charged.[323]

This section is divided into three parts. The first part describes three typical group arrests and prosecutions that took place in 1999, when the number of Hizb ut-Tahrir arrests rose dramatically in the wake of the Tashkent bombings. The second part describes two more recent cases of arrest and trial that took place in 2002 and 2003. The third part describes the prosecution's special focus on the religious ideology of Hizb ut-Tahrir and the content of its publications.

Twelve Members: Tashkent, May 1999

Local human rights activists point to an August 1998 case as the first Hizb ut-Tahrir trial. Unfortunately, no documentation of this trial, nor any testimony, was available at the time of this writing. One of the better-documented early cases of criminal prosecution of members of Hizb ut-Tahrir in Uzbekistan was heard in the Tashkent City Court in May 1999 and involved twelve men.[324] Human Rights Watch attended

[323] Human Rights Watch interview with Mikhail Ardzinov, Tashkent, June 19, 1999. Some of these cases are described below in this chapter.

[324] Human Rights Watch is aware of two earlier relevant trials. Two men—Rustam Mirzaev and Abdulla Shodmonov—were tried by the Chinoz District Court in Tashkent province for Hizb ut-Tahrir membership in April 1999. The men were arrested as early as November 1998. Both were found guilty of attempted overthrow of the state and possession or distribution of "extremist, fundamentalist, or separatist" literature. Mirzaev was sentenced to thirteen years in prison while his codefendant, Shodmonov, who was also accused of illegal narcotics possession, received a fourteen-year term. While relatively little information was available regarding their case, the official court documents do reveal the religious nature of the allegations. More is known regarding the case of Abdurashid Isakhojaev, who frequented Imam Nazarov's mosque and was charged primarily with "Wahhabism," but who was also accused of affiliation with Hizb ut-Tahrir in November 1998. His case is described above in "Imams, Their Followers, and 'Wahhabis'" in Chapter III.

the reading of the verdict in that trial. Judge Mansur Akhmadjonov's decision stated that the defendants[325] had been intent on establishing Islamic rules and an Islamic state, or Caliphate, in Uzbekistan.

In addition to bringing forth legal arguments, the judge expressed his objection to the group's religious beliefs. "Real Muslims cannot join this party, and people cannot believe this is the real way of Islam. The Prophet said that the Caliphate will continue for thirty years after his death and [therefore] this is not a contemporary idea. The idea of a Caliphate and converting all people to Islam is not the true way of Islam."[326] The judge made contradictory remarks about Hizb ut-Tahrir's propensity toward violence. At one point he said that, "They [members of Hizb ut-Tahrir on trial] said they were willing to die on the way [to] Islam and [that] they were ready to use weapons to establish Islamic rules."[327] A moment later the judge declared that, "They [the defendants] say it is necessary to change the government by constitutional will…"[328]

The judge noted the status of Hizb ut-Tahrir as an illegal party in other countries, including Jordan and Egypt. His verdict was based, however, not on his own analysis of the facts at hand but on a determination passed down from another government agency, the Committee on Religious Affairs (of the Cabinet of Ministers). The committee claimed that Hizb ut-Tahrir literature was against the government and territorial integrity of Uzbekistan and was, therefore, anti-constitutional. Judge Akhmadjonov interpreted this to mean that membership in Hizb ut-Tahrir, and possession and distribution of literature or exchange of ideas of Hizb ut-Tahrir, constituted anti-constitutional activity punishable by law. The court held that the defendants' ideas constituted a threat to territorial integrity and were a form of anti-state activity.

---

[325] The twelve defendants were: Abdurauf Zuparov, Shoaziz Iliasov, Khairullo Islamov, Akhror Abdurakhmonov, Faisullo Sadykov, Abdusalom Sattarov, Beksot Juraev, Abduvali Guliamsov, Abduaziz Inoiatov, Sirojiddin Tojikhojaev, Nozim Maksudov, and Asadullo Mirsamadov.

[326] Human Rights Watch unofficial transcript, Tashkent City Court, Tashkent, May 14, 1999.

[327] Ibid.

[328] Ibid.

Regarding defendant Khairullo Islamov, Judge Akhmadjonov emphasized the young man's commitment to the ideas of Hizb ut-Tahrir as evidence of his guilt and discounted Islamov's charges of police wrongdoing:

> He says that the party ideas are correct and he won't abandon this path and he said he will continue the propaganda. During the search, in the police station, drugs were found on him and he said they were not his... He confessed that he participated in an unofficial party and spread propaganda and carried out tasks for the party and was appointed nakib [a position of responsibility within Hizb ut-Tahrir]...He said he did not do anything against the government.

In conclusion, the judge noted, "In Islamov's car a grenade was found and he said this was planted."[329] Islamov was sentenced to nineteen years in prison, a term later reduced to sixteen years.[330]

In summarizing the charges against Akhror Abdurakhmonov, Judge Akhmadjonov remarked simply, "...he carried out tasks for the party and took lessons in the ideas of the party," he noted that Abdurakhmonov, "...only confessed to membership in an unofficial party."[331] The judge sentenced Akhror Abdurakhmonov to nine years in prison, reduced to eight years on appeal.[332] The judge's enumeration of Faisullo Sadykov's supposed misdeeds similarly rested on criminalization of Hizb ut-Tahrir's ideas and exchange of party literature. The judge noted that Sadykov did not confess in court, but charged, "He was aware of the party's activities and spread literature of the party in Uzbekistan." The judge remarked that, like Abdurakhmonov, Sadykov confessed only to

[329] Ibid.

[330] Ibid.

[331] Ibid.

[332] Supreme Court appeals verdict, issued by Judge Akbarov, August 13, 1999.

party membership.[333] He sentenced Sadykov to nine years in prison, which the Supreme Court reduced to eight years.[334]

Enumerating the crimes of Sirojiddin Tojikhojaev, the judge stated, "In 1993, he met Sharof...and agreed to take lessons...He knew the party was unofficial, but he continued to take lessons. He read "The Islamic Charter"[335]...he joined the party...he distributed religious literature to party members...and collected money for the party."[336] Tojikhojaev too accused police of wrongdoing: "… [W]hen he was arrested, [he alleged,] the officers planted drugs. He said that the narcotics were not his and that he never takes drugs," the judge read out from Tojikhojaev's earlier testimony.[337] Judge Akhmadjonov sentenced Tojikhojaev to ten years in prison, but the Supreme Court elected to release him from the courtroom, on three years of parole.[338]

Defendant Abdurauf Zuparov was found guilty of possessing Hizb ut-Tahrir leaflets, a grenade, and heroin. His sixteen-year sentence was reduced by the Supreme Court to fourteen years in prison.[339] On charges of illegal possession of heroin and a grenade, and membership in Hizb ut-Tahrir, co-defendant Shoaziz Iliasov—who testified in court that police had planted the grenade—was sentenced to nineteen years in prison, which the Supreme Court reduced on appeal to sixteen.[340]

On the experience of Beksot Juraev, born 1975, Human Rights Watch has more detailed information. Arrested on a Tashkent street the night of August 5, 1998, he was taken to the Akmal Ikramov district police

---

[333] Human Rights Watch unofficial transcript, Tashkent City Court, Tashkent, May 14, 1999.

[334] Supreme Court appeals verdict, issued by Judge Akbarov, August 13, 1999.

[335] As noted above, this is a reference to the draft constitution of Hizb ut-Tahrir. It is found in *The System of Islam*, the first text covered in Hizb ut-Tahrir study circles.

[336] Human Rights Watch unofficial transcript, Tashkent City Court, Tashkent, May 14, 1999.

[337] Ibid.

[338] Supreme Court appeals verdict, issued by Judge Akbarov, August 13, 1999.

[339] Ibid.

[340] Ibid.

station; en route police allegedly put marijuana in his pocket.[341] The same night some twenty armed men—nineteen of them in civilian clothes and presumed by eyewitnesses to be agents of the SNB—searched the family home without showing a warrant.[342] The sole uniformed officer present was from the Akmal Ikramov district police station.[343] When the detainee's father asked to invite neighbors to witness the search, officers refused. They said, "We brought our own [witnesses]."[344] Relatives present said that, after ransacking the apartment, police claimed to have found a hand grenade among the mattresses in Beksot Juraev's room.[345] They also took literature and cassette tapes in Arabic and English, which Juraev studied at home.[346] Officers threatened Juraev's father, saying that if he refused to sign the police report verifying the search, they would arrest him too.[347]

Juraev's family was informed neither of his official arrest nor his place of detention. Family members could not locate him for almost four months. Later, relatives learned that the young man had spent those months incommunicado, in the basement of the MVD in Tashkent.[348]

[341] Letter from Rakhim Juraev and Umida Juraeva, parents of Beksot Juraev, to Ombudswoman Sayora Rashidova, October 18, 1999; and Human Rights Watch interview, names withheld, Tashkent, February 10, 2000.

[342] Human Rights Watch interview, names withheld, Tashkent, February 10, 2000; and written statement from Umida Juraeva to the United Nations Human Rights Committee, March 2, 2000.

[343] Ibid. The name of the uniformed officer is on file with Human Rights Watch.

[344] Written statement from Umida Juraeva to the United Nations Human Rights Committee, March 2, 2000.

[345] Human Rights Watch interview, names withheld, Tashkent, February 10, 2000; and written statement from Umida Juraeva to the United Nations Human Rights Committee, March 2, 2000.

[346] Written statement from Umida Juraeva to the United Nations Human Rights Committee, March 2, 2000.

[347] Human Rights Watch interview, names withheld, Tashkent, February 10, 2000; and letter from Rakhim Juraev and Umida Juraeva, parents of Beksot Juraev, to Ombudswoman Sayora Rashidova, October 18, 1999. For information on the importance of search reports to a case, see above, "Imams, Their Followers, and 'Wahhabis'" in Chapter III.

[348] Human Rights Watch interview, names withheld, Tashkent, February 10, 2000.

According to Juraev's mother, it was six months before authorities allowed a lawyer to see her son.[349] According to his parents, Juraev was physically and psychologically mistreated in detention. Officers beat him with nightsticks, kicked him when he asked to see a doctor, and threatened to kill him if he told anyone they had tortured him.[350] The abuse was especially damaging, as Juraev had a frail constitution and a history of illness.[351] Police also allegedly told Juraev, "If you do not confess that the grenade we found in your home is yours, we will arrest your brother or father."[352]

The judge convicted Juraev on charges of calling for the overthrow of the constitutional order and illegal possession of narcotics and weapons, based on drugs and grenades that witnesses said were planted. He was sentenced to eighteen years in prison.[353] The Supreme Court slightly reduced his sentence on appeal to a fifteen-year term.[354] Summarizing Juraev's testimony on the final day of the trial, Judge Akhmadjonov noted that the young man had objected to the charges against him. The judge stated, "He said he only prayed and that he met Jahongir and that of his own [free] will he took lessons and read Islamic literature and of

---

349 Written statement from Umida Juraeva to the United Nations Human Rights Committee, March 2, 2000.

350 Letter from Rahim Juraev and Umida Juraeva, to Ombudswoman Sayora Rashidova, October 18, 1999.

351 Juraev has reportedly been ill since childhood, but does not possess any official documents certifying his disability. In a letter to President Karimov, Juraev's mother noted that his illnesses were considered grave enough to excuse him from military service. Letter from Umida Juraeva to President Karimov, March 2, 2000. In an earlier letter, his parents also describe their son's chronic ailments in detail: born with a dislocated hip, he had complications following surgery as a child, and thus contracted hepatitis, heart disease, and a form of meningitis. His parents state that his illnesses were registered with a doctor and that he is still in need of treatment today. Letter from Rakhim Juraev and Umida Juraeva, to President Karimov, December 7, 1999.

352 Letter from Rahim Juraev and Umida Juraeva, to Ombudswoman Sayora Rashidova, October 18, 1999; and written statement from Umida Juraeva to the United Nations Human Rights Committee, March 2, 2000.

353 Tashkent City Court verdict, issued by Judge Mansur Akhmadjonov, May 14, 1999.

354 Supreme Court appeals verdict, issued by Judge Akbarov, August 13, 1999.

his own will participated in the party."[355] The judge noted that Juraev had acknowledged that he studied Hizb ut-Tahrir ideas and learned about Islam from one of his co-defendants and that he later gave lectures on Islam himself. The judge said of Juraev, "He feels that the party ideas are correct and not against the government."[356]

In November 1999 almost six months after Juraev's conviction, authorities finally allowed relatives to visit him in Zangiota prison. His health had worsened, allegedly due to poor sanitary conditions and lack of medical care, and his weight had dropped dramatically.[357] He was later transferred to Jaslyk prison, where conditions were even harsher. Persons close to Juraev point out that he was sentenced to imprisonment in a general-regime facility but that Jaslyk prison is in fact the harshest place of detention in Uzbekistan, where strict-regime convicts are often sent.[358] After a subsequent family visit with Juraev in Jaslyk prison in May 2000, a person close to the case told Human Rights Watch that the young man had looked weak and thin and was barely able to lift the bag of food that relatives had brought him.[359] When they probed about conditions in the prison, Juraev put his fingers to his lips, indicating it was forbidden to speak of such things.[360]

Thirteen Members: Tashkent, July 1999

In July 1999 the Tashkent City Court sentenced thirteen men to prison for membership in Hizb ut-Tahrir.[361] The men were among those arrested during law enforcement agencies' first sweeps of Hizb ut-Tahrir

---

[355] Human Rights Watch unofficial transcript, Tashkent City Court, Tashkent, May 14, 1999.

[356] Ibid.

[357] Letter from Rakhim Juraev and Umida Juraeva, to President Karimov, December 7, 1999; and Human Rights Watch interview, names withheld, Tashkent, February 10, 2000.

[358] Jaslyk is officially designated as a general-regime prison, but convicts sentenced to both general and strict-regime incarceration are sent to that facility. For a description of the "regime" categories of Uzbek prisons, see "Treatment in Prison" in Chapter IV.

[359] Human Rights Watch interview, name withheld, Tashkent, June 5, 2000.

[360] Ibid.

[361] Hearings were held in the Chilanzar District Court building.

members, in late 1998 and early 1999, before the government campaign against the group was intensified in the wake of the February 1999 Tashkent bombings. Ten of the men received sentences of eight to twelve years in prison on charges that included attempted overthrow of the state, while the other three were convicted only on the charge of membership in a banned religious organization and given two years in prison each.[362]

State authorities repeatedly pointed to the fact that the men took an oath as part of their initiation into Hizb ut-Tahrir as evidence of their status as full-fledged members of the unregistered group and, therefore, as criminals. The content of the oath that provided grounds for incriminating the men was recalled by Tolkhon Riksiev, at the request of the judge: "On behalf of Allah, to become faithful to Islam and spread the Prophet's words among Muslims."[363] One co-defendant recalled it as a vow: "To be faithful to Islam, protect Islam, [and] be faithful to the rules of Hizb ut-Tahrir."[364] Yet another man described the words of the oath as "On behalf of Allah, I promise to share my knowledge with others."[365]

When the attorney for defendant Khikmat Rasulov stood to argue on behalf of his client, he said that he had learned about the ideas of Hizb ut-Tahrir through discussions with his client and by listening to the other defendants. He stated that, "They answer within religion, refer to the Koran. I never heard anything [from them] against the system or the president."[366] He cautioned the court to remember that a desire to become a pious Muslim did not make a person a criminal, and warned the judge to be wary of the future review of his actions and the judgments of history. "Years will pass," said the lawyer, "maybe they will

[362] Human Rights Watch unofficial transcript, Tashkent City Court hearing held in the Chilanzar District Court building, Tashkent, July 20, 1999.

[363] Human Rights Watch unofficial transcript,Tashkent City Court hearing held in the Chilanzar District Court building, Tashkent, June 30, 1999.

[364] Ibid.

[365] Ibid.

[366] Human Rights Watch unofficial transcript, Tashkent City Court hearing held at the Chilanzar District Court building, Tashkent, July 9, 1999.

go to jail now, but maybe in ten years your policy will change...in ten years, these men will not be considered guilty, so be careful."[367]

Speaking on his own behalf, defendant Bahodir Ikramov told the judge, "You should not count me as an enemy of my own people...I am guilty of only one thing and that is my membership in Hizb ut-Tahrir and activities in Hizb ut-Tahrir."[368]

Twenty-Six Members: Andijan, April-August 1999

On August 23, 1999, the Andijan Province Court convicted twenty-six men on charges related to their alleged membership in Hizb ut-Tahrir and sent them to prison for terms ranging from three to eighteen years.[369] In this case, according to a news story carried on BBC monitoring, which reported on a local paper's coverage of the trial, the court ruled that Hizb ut-Tahrir was a terrorist organization.[370] However, none of the defendants was charged with involvement in a terrorist act.[371]

---

[367] Ibid.

[368] Ibid.

[369] The defendants were: Ismatullo Urmanov, Pulatjon Jabbarov, Mohammad-ali Iunusov, Tavakkaljon Akhmedov, Abdummanob Iakubov, Muhammad-sharif Urmanov, Zokirjon Mamadjonov, Ulugbek Abdullaev, Shukhratbek Kuchkarov, Boburjon Akiulov, Abduvahob Akhmedov, Ravshan Mekhmonov, Abdumajid Iuldashev, Ibrohimjon Juraev, Doniorbek Abdurakhmonov, Abduvohid Urmanov, Kudratullo Mamatov, Nematullo Babokhonov, Tursunboi Mamatov, Shodmonbek Oripov, Muminjon Ibragimov, Abdujalil Akhmedov, Zievuddin Akhmedov, Zoidjon Islamov, Yadgarbek Boltabaev, and Fakhriddin Urmanov. Memorial Human Rights Center and the Information Center for Human Rights in Central Asia, *List of People Arrested and Tried in Uzbekistan for Political and Religious Reasons (January 1999 to April 2000)*, Moscow, May 2000.

[370] *Kriminalnye Vesti Fergany* newspaper, In Russian, February 8, 2000, English translation in BBC Monitoring, February 14, 2000.

[371] Indictment, issued by the Andijan province procurator, June 14, 1999.

The defendants were all from Asaka, a city in Andijan province, in the Fergana Valley, and fourteen of the twenty-six were neighbors in Okchopon, a neighborhood of Asaka.[372]

Among the fourteen neighbors were Tavakkaljon Akhmedov and Kudratullo Mamatov, along with the latter's father, Tursunboi Mamatov. Kudratullo Mamatov was the first of the three to be arrested. Officers came to his home late at night on April 19, 1999, and took him to the Asaka police station. They accused him of illegally teaching children about Islam and calling young people to Islam.[373] Acquaintances recalled that in a meeting with his wife, the twenty-three-year-old Mamatov said that authorities mistreated him during his detention in the Asaka police station.[374] A search of the Mamatov household conducted by MVD and SNB officers one week after his detention failed to turn up any incriminating evidence. Mamatov was transferred to Andijan prison and taken daily to the SNB for questioning. There, SNB investigator Dilshod Akhmedov allegedly demanded that Mamatov reveal the names of the Hizb ut-Tahrir members in his area. Persons close to Mamatov charge that authorities forced the young man to sign a confession.[375]

Less than a month after police arrested Kudratullo Mamatov, authorities returned to the Mamatov home to arrest the young man's father. Police conducted a search of the premises at 6:00 a.m. on May 15, 1999.[376] Police then claimed to have found one Hizb ut-Tahrir leaflet, which witnesses said was planted on a bookshelf in the house. On the basis of a single leaflet they took Tursunboi Mamatov into custody. He was held in Andijan prison and taken to the Asaka department of the SNB for

[372] Human Rights Watch interview with relatives of Tavakkaljon Akhmedov, Asaka, Andijan, May 2000; and Memorial Human Rights Center and the Information Center for Human Rights in Central Asia, *List of People Arrested and Tried in Uzbekistan for Political and Religious Reasons (January 1999 to April 2000)*, Moscow, May 2000.

[373] Human Rights Watch interview with persons close to Mamatov, names withheld, Asaka, Andijan, May 18, 2000.

[374] Ibid.

[375] Ibid.

[376] Human Rights Watch interview with persons close to Tursunboi Mamatov, names withheld, Asaka, Andijan, May 18, 2000.

interrogation each day for a week. Authorities denied relatives permission to visit him for the first eighteen days.[377]

Tursunboi Mamatov, father of four, stood trial alongside his son, Kudratullo. Father and son faced identical charges of inciting national (ethnic), racial, or religious enmity; conspiracy to overthrow the constitutional order of the republic; organization of, or participation in, a banned religious group; organization of, or participation in, a criminal group; and preparation of, or possession with intent to distribute, materials containing ideas of religious extremism, separatism, and fundamentalism.[378] At trial, Judge Abdumajid Iormatov suggested that the elder Mamatov should ask for forgiveness.[379] Tursunboi Mamatov refused to express contrition, and the judge sentenced him and his son to sixteen years each in a strict-regime prison and ordered confiscation of their property.[380]

On the same morning that police arrested Tursunboi Mamatov, they also detained his neighbor, thirty-nine-year-old Tavakkaljon Akhmedov, a father of four. Seven officers—three of them SNB agents in civilian clothes and the others police officers in uniform—searched the family home.[381] According to a female relative, the officers found nothing in their search and promised the man's family that they were only taking Tavakkaljon in for questioning and would bring him home right away.[382] But they remained in the detainee's home for three hours. One SNB

---

[377] Ibid.

[378] Memorial Human Rights Center and the Information Center for Human Rights in Central Asia, *List of People Arrested and Tried in Uzbekistan for Political and Religious Reasons (January 1999 to April 2000),* Moscow, May 2000.

[379] Human Rights Watch interview with persons close to Tursunboi Mamatov, names withheld, Asaka, Andijan, May 18, 2000.

[380] Memorial Human Rights Center and the Information Center for Human Rights in Central Asia, *List of People Arrested and Tried in Uzbekistan for Political and Religious Reasons (January 1999 to April 2000),* Moscow, May 2000.

[381] The name of one of the SNB officers who conducted the search is on file with Human Rights Watch.

[382] Human Rights Watch interview with relatives of Tavakkaljon Akhmedov, names withheld, Asaka, Andijan, May 2000.

agent questioned Akhmedov's wife in a separate room of the house, without showing any document authorizing him to interrogate her and without offering her the option of legal representation. She said that the agent asked her about her husband's acquaintances and activities during the previous ten years.[383] She further reported to Human Rights Watch that, before her husband's arrest, the neighborhood police officer had been coming to the house as often as three times a week, pushing open the door and entering without permission or a warrant of any kind. After her husband's arrest, the officer continued to come to the house and had threatened family members with physical abuse for speaking to Human Rights Watch. "The children are now afraid of the police," she reported.[384]

After police arrested Akhmedov, they took him to the Andijan SNB, charged him with Hizb ut-Tahrir membership, and allegedly tortured him for seventeen days to force him to confess.[385] The family was not informed about the place or date of Akhmedov's trial, just as they had never been officially notified of his arrest.[386] They reported having to pay bribes to guards to attend the court proceedings. When called upon to testify in court, Akhmedov said, "If there were enemies of Uzbekistan, I would give my life to save the motherland. But we are not trying to take power. We are praying and calling people to become good Muslims."[387] According to relatives present, Akhmedov refused to ask for forgiveness.[388] The court sentenced him to seventeen years in prison, under a strict regime, and ordered confiscation of his property.[389]

---

[383] Human Rights Watch interview with the wife of Tavakkaljon Akhmedov, Asaka, Andijan, May 2000. Human Rights Watch has withheld her name at her request.

[384] Ibid. For details regarding the threats made to the Akhmedov family, see Chapter IV.

[385] Ibid.

[386] Human Rights Watch interview with relatives of Tavakkaljon Akhmedov, names withheld, Asaka, Andijan, May 2000.

[387] Ibid.

[388] Ibid.

[389] Memorial Human Rights Center and the Information Center for Human Rights in Central Asia, *List of People Arrested and Tried in Uzbekistan for Political and Religious Reasons (January 1999 to April 2000),* Moscow, May 2000.

Musharraf Usmanova

Police officers and approximately forty unidentified men in civilian clothes raided the house of Musharraf Usmanova on the night of April 14, 2002.[390] Although a search of the premises failed to produce any illegal materials, the officers placed Usmanova (born 1963) under arrest and took her to an undisclosed location.[391] She was missing in custody for seven days, during which time police refused to inform her relatives of her whereabouts or even confirm that she had been detained. Official confirmation of her arrest was given only on April 22, when the judge in a relative's case announced that Usmanova would soon be tried.[392] During pre-trial detention, authorities repeatedly denied Usmanova access to the lawyer of her choice.[393]

Prosecuting officials said she was the leader of a Hizb ut-Tahrir women's study circle and charged her with attempted overthrow of the constitution and distribution of extremist literature. On July 16 a Tashkent judge, citing mitigating circumstances in her case, gave Usmanova a two-year suspended sentence and released her from the courtroom. Usmanova had remarried during the years since her husband's death and was six-months pregnant at the time of her trial.[394]

---

[390] Human Rights Watch press release, "Uzbekistan: Round-up of Women Linked to Islamic Groups," May 1, 2002. Usmanova is the widow of Farhod Usmanov, who was accused of possession of a Hizb ut-Tahrir leaflet and who died in police custody in June 1999. For details regarding his case, see below, "Torture and Mistreatment in Pre-trial Detention" in Chapter IV.

[391] Ibid.

[392] Ibid. The relative was Nasiba Uzakova, a woman from Tashkent who was charged along with three other women with Hizb ut-Tahrir membership. Uzakova was sentenced to three and a half years in prison on April 24, 2002. Human Rights Watch attended the trial where the defendants testified that their religious activities consisted of meeting privately for prayer and Islamic study. One of the women testified in court that police beat them or threatened physical violence to coerce confessions and to punish them for their activities. Uzakova's husband had been convicted on similar charges and sentenced to a fifteen-year term in 2000. Ibid.

[393] Ibid.

[394] Her second husband, Istam Khudoiberdiev, and a son-in-law, Ismail Ortikov, were reportedly also arrested and convicted for membership in Hizb ut-Tahrir and are currently in prison serving lengthy terms. Associated Press, July 18, 2002.

According to a local rights defender, Usmanova was compelled upon release to sign a statement vowing that she would not participate in "meetings" or give information to journalists or others regarding her case.[395]

The Keston News Service quoted the reaction of Usmanova's sixteen-year-old daughter, Mahbuba Usmanova, to the authorities' persecution of her family: "Our mother's only crime was to be a very pious woman. Since the authorities murdered our father, all our male relatives have spent time in prison. At present, five of our relatives are in prison…"[396]

Fifteen Members: Tashkent, May-July 2003

On July 4, 2003, the Akmal Ikramov District Court convicted fifteen people on charges of involvement with Hizb ut-Tahrir.[397] Charges included anti-constitutional activity, membership in an illegal religious organization, preparing and distributing literature threatening the security of society, and involving minors in anti-social behavior. With the exception of two defendants who were given suspended sentences, the defendants were sentenced to prison terms ranging from seven to fifteen years.[398]

[395] Human Rights Watch telephone interview with Vasila Inoiatova, February 18, 2003. The statement is presumed to be similar to those signed by other persons released from prison or police custody or otherwise on a list of suspect people and the scope of topics on which Usmanova promised not to speak presumably includes the cases of other family members.

[396] "Uzbekistan: Murdered Muslim Preacher's Widow Arrested," Igor Rotar, *Keston News Service*, April 19, 2002. The cases of Usmanova's relatives are dealt with below, "Family Members: Arrests, House Arrest, Harrassment" in Chapter III.

[397] The defendants were: Ravshan Shonasyrov, Ravshan Iusupkhojaev, Olimkhon Maksumkhanov, Shavkat Khojev, Komiljon Gafurov, Khairullo Arziev, Kobiljon Abdurasulov, Ibrokhimjon Okulkhujaev, Ikrom Narkhojaev, Khikmat Buriev, Khasan Bomuratov, Abdukhalil Omonov, Zakhid Kasymov, Khasanbek Saidbekov, and Khojiakbar Nuriddinov. Human Rights Watch unofficial transcript, Akmal Ikramov District Court, Tashkent, May 29, 2003.

[398] Human Rights Watch unofficial transcript, Akmal Ikramov District Court, Tashkent, July 4, 2003.

As evidence of the defendants' guilt, the judge emphasized that the police had confiscated a number of Hizb ut-Tahrir leaflets about harassment of Muslims, economic and other problems in Uzbekistan, and U.S. involvement in Uzbekistan, as well as literature from international human rights organizations.[399] As with many similar cases, the state's evidence also included a statement by a Committee on Religious Affairs expert averring that the confiscated literature was anti-constitutional. The defendants repeatedly asked the judge to summon the expert. When the judge denied their request, the defendants announced a hunger strike and refused to appear in court after a break. The expert never appeared before the court.

Other important pieces of evidence, according to the judge, included testimony given by defendants to police during the pre-trial investigation, although several defendants stated in court that they gave such testimony under duress of torture.[400]

Punishing the Exchange of Ideas

Police and judicial authorities have regarded any person who distributed Hizb ut-Tahrir literature as a criminal, as when Hizb ut-Tahrir activists carried out a three-day campaign to distribute the group's leaflets in Tashkent bazaars from June 14 to 16, 1999. According to Mikhail Ardzinov, chairman of the Independent Human Rights Organization of Uzbekistan, police arrested some 200 leafletters on just June 15 and 16, in public markets including Chorsu bazaar in the old city, Kulyuk bazaar, and the Hippodrome, the capital's largest market.[401] The majority of those picked up during the sweeps were placed under arrest and, as of late June that year, were being held in police stations in the Sobir Rakhimov, Akmal Ikramov, Shaikhantaur, and Biktimir districts of Tashkent.[402]

---

[399] Ibid.

[400] Ibid.

[401] Human Rights Watch interview with Mikhail Ardzinov, Tashkent, June 19, 1999.

[402] Ibid.

▪ Ziadullo Abdullaev was among those arrested from the Hippodrome bazaar on June 14. Police claimed to have found leaflets in his car. Abdullaev confessed to being a member of Hizb ut-Tahrir and distributing the group's literature, but said that he did not believe this to be against the law.[403] He allegedly told authorities that, if released, he would do it all again.[404] Police transferred him to Tashkent prison, where authorities claimed he had rejected legal counsel. A Tashkent city police investigator in charge of the case refused to give family members access to Abdullaev in custody.[405]

▪ Police arrested Irkin Omon, then twenty-six years old, on June 15 for distributing leaflets in the Hippodrome bazaar and sent him to Tashkent prison. As of July 21, 1999, authorities had failed to appoint him an attorney and had refused him any visits with relatives.[406]

▪ Human Rights Watch spoke to a person close to another young man, Musratullo Komilov, who was arrested from a bazaar in Tashkent on June 15. Hizb ut-Tahrir members reportedly told Komilov that distributing the group's literature would constitute a good deed and he agreed to do it.[407] Komilov was tried alone in the Bekobad District Court less than a month after his arrest. Facing charges related to affiliation with Hizb ut-Tahrir and distribution of the group's materials, Komilov received an eleven-year sentence. He was sent to Zarafshan prison, where he reportedly contracted tuberculosis. A person close to him expressed fear for his health and chances of survival in prison.[408]

---

[403] Human Rights Watch interview with rights defender Vasila Inoiatova, Tashkent, July 21, 1999.

[404] Ibid.

[405] Ibid. At the time of this writing, Human Rights Watch had no further information on Abdullaev's fate. His name did not appear on a September 1999 list of released prisoners.

[406] Human Rights Watch interview with Vasila Inoiatova, Tashkent, July 21, 1999. No further information regarding his fate was available as of November 2002.

[407] Human Rights Watch interview by telephone, name withheld, February 13, 2001.

[408] Ibid.

Authorities also arrested individuals who were in possession of Hizb ut-Tahrir literature and leaflets but who did not distribute them to others.

- Police arrested Feruza Kurbanova, at 10:00 a.m. on December 23, 2000, during Ramadan. They found her at home, with three friends. About a dozen officers from the Shaikhantaur district police station, some in uniform and some in civilian clothes, arrived to search the house without presenting identification or authorization.[409] During the six-hour search, police found or claimed to find copies of "The Islamic Charter" and several Hizb ut-Tahrir leaflets. Kurbanova's possession of these texts was cited as the basis for her arrest and the three-day detention of her guests. The Shaikhantaur District Court sentenced Kurbanova to a one year suspended sentence for membership in Hizb ut-Tahrir.

- During the trial of thirteen men charged with Hizb ut-Tahrir membership in the Tashkent City Court in June and July 1999 (see above), the prosecution made no secret of the fact that the men were being charged because they had engaged in the exchange of ideas about religion and had proposed the establishment of a religion-based government. The procurator accused the men of "poisoning young people" with the ideas of Hizb ut-Tahrir, specifically with spreading the idea of a Caliphate.[410] Arguing for conviction of the defendant Khasan Akhmedov, the procurator stated, "He was active with teenagers and filled their minds with his ideas, called them to join the group, explained shari'a and why a Caliphate is the best system. He gave them books and leaflets."[411] On the basis of this argument Akhmedov was found guilty of conspiracy to overthrow the state and sentenced to eight years in prison.

---

[409] Human Rights Watch interview with an eyewitness, name withheld, Tashkent, February 14, 2001; and Human Rights Watch interview with a second eyewitness, name withheld, Tashkent, February 26, 2001.

[410] Human Rights Watch unofficial transcript, Tashkent City Court hearing held in the Chilanzar District Court building, Tashkent, July 8, 1999.

[411] Ibid.

The presiding judge in this case portrayed Hizb ut-Tahrir literature as contraband, declaring, "Books were used as weapons."[412] When questioned by the judge about the content of the Hizb ut-Tahrir literature he had studied, defendant Shahmaksud Shobobaev said that the books called on people "...to restore Islamic life, to make Muslims' lives accord with Islamic rules."[413] Shobobaev's co-defendant, Tolkhon Riksiev, was also called upon to describe the content of "The Islamic Charter," the study and possession of which was used as grounds for the conviction of at least dozens of men. "It calls for praying and other issues, such as how to behave if someone dies. It does not include advocacy for overthrowing the government or contradicting the government," he asserted.[414]

Co-defendant Danior Khojimetov went further, contending that the men's religious activities and even what he characterized as their opposition to the constitution of Uzbekistan fell within the parameters of the right to free expression: "Uzbekistan is a democratic state, and in a democratic state there is freedom of conscience and freedom of ideas, and this is the basis of democracy. Each citizen has the right to express his views. We expressed ideas against the constitution, but I think this is freedom of expression."[415] Danior Khojimetov was sentenced to twelve years in prison on charges of illegal possession of narcotics and attempted overthrow of the constitutional order.

- Presiding over a May 1999 trial of twelve men before the Tashkent City Court (see above), Judge Akhmadjonov condemned Hizb ut-Tahrir literature, stating, "All literature of Hizb ut-Tahrir was propaganda about the real meaning of Islamic ideas." He further noted that such literature

---

412 Human Rights Watch unofficial transcript, Tashkent City Court hearing held in the Chilanzar District Court building, Tashkent, July 9, 1999.

413 Human Rights Watch unofficial transcript, Tashkent City Court trial held in the Chilanzar District Court building, Tashkent, June 30, 1999.

414 Ibid.

415 Human Rights Watch unofficial transcript, Tashkent City Court trial held in the Chilanzar District Court building, Tashkent, July 9, 1999.

was forbidden in Uzbekistan.[416] Explicating the alleged crimes of the defendants, he declared, "They wanted to establish an unofficial religious organization to spread ideas and spread this religious literature."[417]

With specific reference to defendants Juraev, Iliasov, and others, the judge added, "...[T]hey said they did not carry out actions against the government, but only wanted to discuss the Islamic way of life. But, it is evident that this propaganda itself is against the constitution of Uzbekistan...."[418] He further cited the conclusions of the Committee on Religious Affairs of the Cabinet of Ministers, which ruled that Hizb ut-Tahrir literature, "is against the territorial integrity of Uzbekistan and its government."[419] Judge Akhmadjonov condemned not only the use of the written word but also spreading religious ideas verbally. He warned, "They propagandized youth, and young people are the future of our country..."[420] "Propagandizing" or discussing ideas of Hizb ut-Tahrir was found by Judge Akhmadjonov to be particularly incriminating evidence against the defendants, whom he accused of having held "underground lessons" in Hizb ut-Tahrir ideas.[421]

Based on the report of the Committee on Religious Affairs, the judge told the courtroom:

> ...[T]he examination of the literature by experts was correct...Hizb ut-Tahrir means Party of Liberation, and its aim was to establish an Islamic state and reorganize

---

[416] Human Rights Watch unofficial transcript, Tashkent City Court, Tashkent, May 14, 1999. There is in fact no law or decree in Uzbekistan forbidding Hizb ut-Tahrir literature and no law against creation of "propaganda" about Islam. But, as described above in "The Legal Setting" in Chapter II, laws in the criminal code criminalize "extremist" "fundamentalist" or "separatist" speech, without providing criteria for these categories. While the judge was not strictly accurate in his interpretation of the law, he was able to exploit the law's vagueness.

[417] Human Rights Watch unofficial transcript, Tashkent City Court, Tashkent, May 14, 1999.

[418] Ibid.

[419] Ibid.

[420] Ibid.

[421] Ibid.

> all life in the Islamic way. That means they wanted to take power and administer the government under Islamic rules...They say it is necessary to change the government by constitutional will and to establish an Islamic state; this was the real aim of the party.[422]

At the heart of the government's persecution of Hizb ut-Tahrir's ideas is the contention that the group's support for an Islamic government or Caliphate, ruled by Islamic law, is a call to subvert the existing government of Uzbekistan. The government portrays discussion of alternative forms of government based on religion as active attempts to overthrow the state. This was in evidence when Judge Rakhmonov of the Tashkent City Court declared the thirteen men on trial guilty of anti-state activity because, "They said the democratic system is not good and shari'a should be established instead through a Caliphate."[423]

In this case as in many others, the court conflated belief in Hizb ut-Tahrir doctrine with action against the state. In other words, it found the very belief that a Caliphate would be a good form of government, preferable to the current government, and expression of this belief are tantamount to trying to seize power, or take violent action to overthrow the existing state. A belief in the desirability of applying a different set of laws over a territory, however, even an outright endorsement of a new form of government, is not the same as taking action or inciting action against the state. A religious belief is not an action against the state. Even if the Uzbek government were to claim that Hizb ut-Tahrir's expression is political and not religious, because it is nonviolent expression, the government does not have the right to repress it.

Hizb ut-Tahrir literature advocates the Caliphate. It states that only Muslims can be legitimate leaders of Muslims and asserts that only Islam can be the legitimate basis for political, social, and economic order.

---

[422] Ibid.

[423] Human Rights Watch unofficial transcript, Tashkent City Court trial held in the Chilanzar District Court building, Tashkent, July 20, 1999. As noted above, the thirteen men were convicted to prison terms ranging from two to twelve years.

Significantly it does not provide a roadmap or guidance of law to effect the political change necessary to implement such a vision.

Hizb ut-Tahrir leadership based outside the country does not contest that it seeks to change Uzbekistan's form of government, but maintains that it seeks change through persuasion and not force. In an interview with Human Rights Watch, British members of Hizb ut-Tahrir, part of the leadership committee of the group in the U.K., told Human Rights Watch that the group indeed objects to the governing system in Uzbekistan and elsewhere. These representatives told Human Rights Watch that the group seeks the establishment of a new system. Specifically, when asked by a Human Rights Watch representative, "Would you agree with the Uzbek government that members of Hizb ut-Tahrir are attempting to encroach the constitutional order of Uzbekistan?" The leading member of the group's U.K. chapter, Jalaluddin Patel, replied, "We've made it clear that we want to replace the system in Uzbekistan with the Islamic system. I think our members haven't kept that quiet there, as you know."[424] Another member of the leadership committee, when asked about any plans on the part of Hizb ut-Tahrir to attempt to register with the government of Uzbekistan, said that the issue of registration was moot, "…unless they allow for a registration process which allows entities to call for the removal of the Uzbek constitution…."[425]

Hizb ut-Tahrir's vision for change, often described as Utopian by outside observers, appears to rely on the spread of the group's ideas and the belief that these ideas will become irresistible and then will become the dominant ideas of a given society. This was articulated also by the group's leading U.K. representative when he was asked how Hizb ut-Tahrir would replace the existing system in Uzbekistan without using violence, as it claims is it's goal. Jalaluddin Patel told Human Rights Watch:

---

[424] Human Rights Watch interview with Jalaluddin Patel, head of the leadership committee of Hizb ut-Tahrir Britain, London, June 29, 2002.

[425] Human Rights Watch interview with Sajjad Khan, member of the leadership committee of Hizb ut-Tahrir Britain, London, June 29, 2002.

> We say that you need to target…all of the people that exist in society, in particular those who have influence. And this is a method the Prophet of Islam used, that he targeted both the general people and the others, those who hold influence, the policymakers, those who can change the situation in their country. We believe that in the Muslim world, where Islam still exists in the deepest sentiments of the majority of the people, this is not hard to do. And [there are] many people there, whether amongst policymakers or otherwise, who belong to the political medium or the intellectual medium that we can access, who can open doors for us. And it happens that in the Muslim world on many occasions we've successfully won such people over, and that we continue to do that.[426]

Emphasizing the group's view of the power of ideas, another member of the U.K. chapter's committee remarked, "With this confidence in thought, we believe that there is no regime that cannot be toppled, and that can't be toppled by thought. And this is the strongest weapon that exists."[427]

Punishing the Study of Religious Texts

Law enforcement authorities and courts have treated involvement in Hizb ut-Tahrir study groups, where participants read traditional Islamic texts as well as literature published by Hizb ut-Tahrir, as evidence of anti-state sentiment and intent to commit subversion.

Local human rights defenders claim that around one hundred residents of General Uzakov Street, a long boulevard in Tashkent, were arrested in a matter of weeks and charged with membership in Hizb ut-Tahrir.[428]

---

[426] Human Rights Watch interview with Jalaluddin Patel, head of the leadership committee of Hizb ut-Tahrir Britain, London, June 29, 2002.

[427] Human Rights Watch interview with Dr. Abdulla Robin, member of the leadership committee of Hizb ut-Tahrir Britain, London, June 29, 2002.

[428] Human Rights Watch interview with Vasila Inoiatova, Tashkent, August 11, 2000.

Human Rights Watch independently confirmed the arrest or detention of five of these neighbors—Mirabid Iakiaev, Komil Masudov, Sarvar Masudov, Sanjar Masudov, and also the Masudovs' sister, Shoknoza Musaeva—on religion-related charges.

Shoknoza Musaeva was arrested in June 1999, and sent to prison by a Tashkent court. She was charged with membership in Hizb ut-Tahrir and teaching other young women about Islam using books that favored establishing an Islamic state.[429]

Police arrested the twenty-nine-year-old Musaeva, mother of two, at her home on June 1, 1999, for membership in Hizb ut-Tahrir and, according to one relative, "Koran distribution."[430] The state accused her of teaching several religious women using "The Islamic Social Charter" (presumably a reference to the Hizb ut-Tahrir publication "The Social System of Islam") and the published work "Hizb ut-Tahrir," both introductory texts that set out the aims and principles of the group. The state also accused Musaeva of having sold copies of this literature to her students for 150 som, the equivalent of about U.S. $0.25.[431] The court justified her arrest and conviction by reference to an expert evaluation of the religious literature that she had allegedly taught. The evaluation found that, "...in these books, the idea of struggling to establish an Islamic state controlled by a Caliph is propagated."[432] These allegations that Musaeva was a member of Hizb ut-Tahrir, taught others about Islam using Hizb ut-Tahrir and other Islamic literature, possessed and sold such literature, and that this literature was deemed by government experts to contain ideas about establishing an Islamic state, formed the entirety of the prosecution's case against the young woman.

---

[429] Musaeva was sentenced to seven years in prison on charges of attempting to overthrow the state and organizing an illegal religious group. These serious charges were based on no allegation or evidence other than her membership in the group, possession and sale of Hizb ut-Tahrir literature, and the accusation that she taught others about Islam.

[430] Human Rights Watch interview, name withheld, Tashkent, November 3, 1999; and Human Rights Watch interview with rights defender Mahbuba Kosymova, Tashkent, June 22, 1999.

[431] Urta-Chirchik District Court verdict, issued by Judge T. Sh. Zainutdinov, August 12, 1999.

[432] Ibid.

In court, Musaeva acknowledged that she was a member of Hizb ut-Tahrir, but stated that the ideas of the group were not against the government.[433] Speaking of Shoknoza and their other arrested children—Sarvar, Komil, and Sanjar Masudov—Musaeva's parents told Human Rights Watch, "They taught their friends Islam; how to live well….The government couldn't tolerate this."[434]

- "Mukhtabar M." (not her real name), born 1943, was arrested by police on September 23, 1999. Mukhtabar M. told Human Rights Watch that police detained her and five other women from a private home where they had been conducting a religious meeting.[435] At the local police station, officers accused them of membership in Hizb ut-Tahrir and showered them with insults.[436] According to Mukhtabar M., who acknowledges her own membership in the group since 1998, some of the women were members of Hizb ut-Tahrir, but others were not.[437]

After holding the women in detention for four days, police took them to a "courtroom" in the district police station. Mukhtabar M. described the police trial, "The police called a lawyer and the judge tried us and yelled at us. He said, "Why don't you like Karimov?" I said, "I don't know about politics, I used to live well...but now I am on pension and don't have enough to live. I can't even get half a bag of flour. I can't feed my children...Maybe where you work, you make enough money, but we don't. We choose the Will of Allah."[438] The judge ordered Mukhtabar M.'s arrest, saying to her, "You will find the 'Will of Allah' in a prison cell."[439]

---

[433] Human Rights Watch interview with the mother and father of Shoknoza Musaeva, Tashkent, April 13, 2000; and Urta-Chirchik District Court verdict, issued by Judge T. Sh. Zainutdinov, August 12, 1999.

[434] Human Rights Watch interview with Shoknoza Musaeva's mother and father, Tashkent, April 13, 2000.

[435] Human Rights Watch interview with "Mukhtabar M." (not her real name), Tashkent, February 2001.

[436] Ibid.

[437] Ibid.

[438] Ibid.

[439] Ibid.

The other women were fined and released. Mukhtabar M. was taken to the women's prison on the outskirts of Tashkent where she served a ten-day sentence and was released. Authorities failed to provide her with any document certifying her arrest or release.[440] Authorities continued to monitor Mukhtabar M.'s activities after release, compelling her to report regularly to her local mahalla committee, which also organized a public denunciation of her and other independent Muslims.

- Accused Hizb ut-Tahrir member Muzafar Avazov was charged with having given classes based on the group's principal document, "The Islamic Charter."[441] Avazov was convicted on this and related charges to twenty years in prison, reduced to nineteen years on appeal.[442] Avazov died, apparently from torture, in Jaslyk prison in August 2002.[443]

Judicial authorities joined government leaders and official Muslim clerics in calling on observant Muslims to restrict their study of Islam within the confines of state structures. Judge Rakhmonov of the Tashkent City Court told one Hizb ut-Tahrir member who said he joined the group in order to study Islam, "...there is no objection if you want to study Islam...we have an Islamic Institute and a religious board [the Muslim Board]. Why don't you go to that institute? You can go abroad [to study], if you join the government channels."[444] When the judge later suggested again that those interested in learning about Islam could "go to the Mufti," defendant Shahmaksud Shobobaev pointed out, "We have our own way of teaching Islam."[445]

---

[440] Ibid.

[441] Indictment of nine accused members of Hizb ut-Tahrir, including Muzafar Avazov, issued by Tashkent City Procurator M. I. Naimov, June 23, 2000.

[442] Human Rights Watch interview, name withheld, Tashkent, February 26, 2001.

[443] For more information see "Uzbekistan: Two Brutal Deaths in Custody," Human Rights Watch press release, August 10, 2002.

[444] Human Rights Watch unofficial transcript, Tashkent City Court trial held in the Chilanzar District Court building, Tashkent, June 30, 1999.

[445] Ibid.

In fact, according to the testimony of men convicted for Hizb ut-Tahrir membership by various courts, an overwhelming majority of them joined the group in order to obtain instruction in Islamic rules and principles. Hizb ut-Tahrir member Tolkhon Riksiev told the court of a conversation with an acquaintance who attended his mosque. Riksiev expressed to the man a desire to learn more about Islam. "We used to pray and we studied Islamic rules. We used to talk about religion, and he asked if I wanted to learn it better and said if I joined the party, they would teach me, so I decided to join," he said.[446] His co-defendant, Abdukhalil Gafurov, echoed Riksiev, "I joined it to learn [about] religion," he said.[447]

- Another of the thirteen men convicted along with Riksiev was English professor Zafar Avasov, who was accused of teaching young people about Islam after class using "The Islamic Charter" and other Hizb ut-Tahrir literature. His lawyer told the court that, "He admitted he wanted to be a pious Muslim. He just read the Koran and wanted to be a real, good Muslim."[448] He was sentenced to eight years in prison.[449]

- The catalogue of Nozim Maksudov's alleged crimes included having taken lessons in the ideas of Hizb ut-Tahrir and having read "The Islamic Charter." Judge Akhmadjonov acknowledged that "[Maksudov] said that there were no anti-government ideas in these books," but nevertheless sentenced him to four and a half years in prison.[450] Maksudov was later released on appeal and given three years parole.[451]

---

[446] Ibid.

[447] Ibid.

[448] Human Rights Watch unofficial transcript, Tashkent City Court held in the Chilanzar District Court building, Tashkent, July 9, 1999.

[449] Human Rights Watch unofficial transcript, Tashkent City Court held in the Chilanzar District Court building, Tashkent, July 20, 1999.

[450] Human Rights Watch unofficial transcript, Tashkent City Court, Tashkent, May 14, 1999.

[451] Supreme Court appeals verdict, issued by Judge Akbarov, August 13, 1999.

Family Members: Arrests, House Arrest, Harrassment

Uzbekistan's law enforcement extended the scope of punishment and persecution of independent Muslims to include their relatives. This followed directly from President Karimov's declaration of a collective punishment policy against independent Muslims.[452] The police arrest the fathers, mothers, spouses, children, and siblings of wanted persons, and in some cases harass and arrest members of the extended families of suspects. These tactics enable the authorities to coerce suspects into surrendering to the police and confessing to crimes they did not commit. The authorities also stage "hate rallies" to exhibit prisoners and their relatives as examples of turpitude. The mahalla committees reinforce these persons' social isolation and bring the weight of the state down upon the targeted community as a whole. The policy is, in effect, extrajudicial punishment of anyone associated with independent Muslims.

Arrests

Tracking subversion through family networks is a legitimate law enforcement strategy. But in Uzbekistan, police do not merely "track" families of suspected independent Muslims. They use relatives—sometimes including young children—as leverage to compel a wanted person to turn himself in, or to compel testimony from a detainee. They also at times hold under house arrest the family members of detained individuals. In many cases, particularly those involving female relatives, family members are themselves accused of no crime. The way in which police detain and question relatives, or force them to sign self-incriminating statements, makes clear that beyond seeking to "track" subversion or conspiracy, the authorities seek to spread fear throughout the independent Muslim community, to compel its members to desist from independent prayer or study, and to convince others to do the same.

Below are details about the cases of arrest, detention, and physical mistreatment of the relatives of independent Muslims. A description and

[452] See above, "Brief Chronological Overview" in Chapter II.

examples of the infamous "hate rallies" organized against family members of "enemies of the state," can be found below in this chapter.

The Nazarov Family

Official pressure on Imam Obidkhon Nazarov's family began in December 1997, the earliest days of the government campaign against independent Muslims. The pretexts for the arrests and harassment that followed the imam's disappearance in 1998 failed to hide the real motive behind the police actions, according to the family's lawyer, Irina Mikulina, who said, "None of them [Imam Nazarov's relatives] was questioned about drugs or leaflets, they were only asked, 'Where is Obidkhon?'"[453] Relatives living in the Fergana Valley, especially Namangan, appeared to be particular targets of law enforcement. One family member explained that these relatives were "more vulnerable in Namangan, where police treat people like animals."[454]

Abdumalik Nazarov

On December 26, 1997, at 8:30 a.m., Fergana province police detained the imam's father, Sobitkhon, and two brothers, Umarkhon and Abdumalik. The men were taken to Fergana police headquarters, where their car was searched. Having found no incriminating materials during the first search, police took the keys to the car, and then searched the car a second time during the evening at which point they "discovered" twelve grams of marijuana in the trunk.[455] Fergana authorities kept Sobitkhon and Umarkhon Nazarov in custody several days and then released them without charge, apparently in reaction to diplomatic outrage about the case.[456]

---

[453] Meeting with then-United States Ambassador-at-Large for Religious Freedom Robert Seiple and Human Rights Watch, Tashkent, May 23, 2000.

[454] Human Rights Watch interview with a Nazarov family member, name withheld, Tashkent, May 28, 2001.

[455] Human Rights Watch, "Crackdown in The Farghona Valley: Arbitrary Arrests and Religious Discrimination," *A Human Rights Watch Report*, Vol. 10, No. 4 (D) May 1998.

[456] Ibid.

Abdumalik Nazarov, the imam's youngest brother, was, however, placed under arrest on December 31, 1997, and charged with narcotics possession. Eyewitnesses present at his interrogation told Human Rights Watch that police threatened even more serious charges if the young man did not confess and said that he had been arrested so that "at least one Nazarov" would be in state custody.[457] On May 4, 1998, Abdumalik, a citizen of Kyrgyzstan, was tried in a Fergana district court and convicted on charges of narcotics possession and possession of falsified documents and sentenced to nine years in prison.[458] The court's verdict noted supposedly incriminating witness testimony that, "although young, he wore a beard."[459]

Authorities transferred Abdumalik Nazarov (born 1973) to the infamous Jaslyk prison on May 29, 1999.[460] His mother, Mukharramkhon Nazarova, told Human Rights Watch that during his meeting with his father, Sobitkhon, Abdumalik said that from May until December 1999 he was forced to sit in his cell and not allowed any exercise or fresh air. She said that he was being kept in a cell with sixteen other men, that four guards beat him seven times a day every day, that prayer is forbidden and that if any man in the cell attempts to pray, all of the men are beaten.[461] This situation is yet another example of collective punishment which violates fundamental human rights principles.

Despite repeated appeals made on his behalf to the Uzbek authorities and requests for assistance from the government of Kyrgyzstan, he was

---

[457] Ibid.

[458] The falsified documents charge was based on the discovery of several pieces of paper in the home of Abdumalik Nazarov's parents and which had the words "Asian Muslim Committee" printed on them in several languages, including Arabic. Verdict issued by Judge A. Khudoinazarov of the Fergana District Court, May 4, 1998.

[459] Ibid.

[460] For a detailed description of the physical mistreatment he encountered upon arrival at that prison, see below, "Treatment in Prison" in Chapter IV.

[461] Human Rights Watch interview with Muharramkhon Nazarova, Tashkent, February 19, 2000.

denied access to his lawyer, Irina Mikulina. She was not allowed to meet him after May 1999.[462]

Abdumalik Nazarov was released on January 18, 2003, pursuant to a presidential amnesty decree of 2002.[463] However, less than three months later police again took him into custody. According to his mother, who wrote to Human Rights Watch about the incident, Abdumalik went to the home of his brother, Imam Nazarov, to visit with his nephews on April 4, 2003. It was his first such visit since his release. As soon as he got to the door, armed police grabbed him and, after conducting a search of the Nazarov home, took him to the Sobir Rakhimov district police station. From there, police transferred him to the Tashkent city police department, where they kept him in a basement cell.[464] Nazarov's mother expressed her grief at the cruel turn of events, "Now, after all those years of waiting and hoping…they've taken him again…"[465]

Munira Nasriddinova

Police detained Munira Nasriddinova, Imam Nazarov's wife, and Mukharramkhon Nazarova, his mother, on February 21, 1999, during the initial round of sweeps following the Tashkent bombings. Officers reportedly physically mistreated the two women. Nazarova was released eight hours after her detention. Nasriddinova, however, was charged

---

[462] Human Rights Watch interview with Irina Mikulina, Tashkent, February 19, 2000. People can visit Jaslyk prison only by official "invitation" from authorities. As of January 2003, Ministry of Internal Affairs officials, who run the prison system in Uzbekistan, had denied Mikulina permission to see her client. During a visit to the town of Jaslyk in July 1999, a Human Rights Watch representative was told by a local police chief that the permission of President Karimov was required even to enter the city limits. People arriving by train to the area who are not in possession of an official letter granting them access are not allowed to disembark at Jaslyk. Human Rights Watch interview with Irina Mikulina, Tashkent, October 30, 1999. Relatives of prisoners were first granted access to the prison visiting area by invitation in December 1999.

[463] Human Rights Watch interview with Nazarov's lawyer, Irina Mikulina, Tashkent, March 25, 2003.

[464] Written appeal to Human Rights Watch and other organizations, from Muharramkhon Nazarova, Abdumalik's mother, April 8, 2003, transmitted electronically.

[465] Ibid.

with "hooliganism" and held under administrative arrest for ten days.[466] Nasriddinova's lawyer was unable to locate her in custody for at least four days following her arrest.[467] It was later revealed that she was held in a basement cell.[468] According to an Amnesty International report, police interrogated Nasriddinova regarding her husband and Imam Tulkin Ergashev.[469]

Abdurashid Nasriddinov

Abdurashid Nasriddinov (Imam Nazarov's brother-in-law) was arrested on or around March 1, 1999, and taken into police custody in Namangan. According to Mukharramkhon Nazarova, Nasriddinov, born in 1970, was held in a basement cell and deprived of food for seven days during pre-trial detention.[470] Namangan Province Court Judge T.Z. Ibragimov sentenced him to eleven years in prison on charges of encroachment on the constitutional order and distribution of religious "extremist" literature.[471] Much of the verdict dwells not on Nasriddinov but on Nazarov.[472] In so far as the verdict discusses the

---

[466] Amnesty International Urgent Action (UA 34/99), Fear for Safety/alleged ill-treatment in detention/incommunicado detention, EUR 62/02/99, February 25, 1999; and Human Rights Watch interview with rights defender Mukhtabar Akhmedova, Tashkent, June 1999.

[467] Amnesty International Urgent Action (UA 34/99), Fear for Safety/alleged ill-treatment in detention/incommunicado detention, EUR 62/02/99, February 25, 1999.

[468] Interview with Irina Mikulina at a meeting with Robert Seiple, then-United States Ambassador-at-Large for Religious Freedom, and Human Rights Watch, Tashkent, May 23, 2000.

[469] *Amnesty International Annual Report 2000*, Uzbekistan chapter [online], http://www.web.amnesty.org/web/ar2000web.nsf/58f967f150817f77802568f500617d07/c08e32af31b6d49e802568f200552981!OpenDocument (retrieved May 1, 2003).

[470] Human Rights Watch interview with Muharramkhon Nazarova, Tashkent, February 19, 2000.

[471] Verdict issued by Judge T.Z. Ibragimov of the Namangan Province Court, May 20, 1999.

[472] The first half of the verdict is dedicated to a history and denunciation of the so-called Wahhabi movement in Uzbekistan. It names Obidkhon Nazarov's mosques as those that housed "followers of an Islamic religious-political movement of an ultra-reactionary character." Verdict issued by Judge T.Z. Ibragimov of the Namangan Province Court, May 20, 1999.

case against Nasriddinov himself, it states that he was part of the "religious extremist movement" purportedly led by Obidkhon Nazarov, Tokhir Iuldash, and Juma Namangani. Supporting evidence included ten audio cassettes that he had given a friend for safe-keeping that were later found by police to contain verses from the Koran, as well as ten copies of a leaflet entitled, "Jihad: a pillar of Islam and its peak," which police found in his home.[473] One of the most striking moments in the verdict is when the judge asserts that although Nasriddinov maintained his innocence, the court found that in fact he did attend Gumbas (also known as Otallohon) mosque—revealing that affiliation with the so-called Wahhabi mosque was among the "crimes" in question.[474] The court similarly ignored Nasriddinov's rejection of the other charges against him. Judge T.Z. Ibragimov found Nasriddinov guilty of encroachment on the constitutional order, and preparation or distribution of materials containing ideas of religious extremism, separatism, and fundamentalism, and sentenced him to eleven years in a strict-regime prison, along with confiscation of his property. The evidence including the leaflets was ordered destroyed.[475] Destruction of evidence is common in cases involving charges of narcotics or weapons possession, but less common when the material evidence is paper documents.

Abdurashid Nasriddinov was imprisoned in Kashkadaria (prison number 64/51). In February 2000 the Nazarov family's lawyer, Mikulina, reported that she had visited Nasriddinov in prison in December 1999 and at a prison infirmary in February 2000, where she saw that he was seriously ill.[476] She said, "They beat him so badly, his nerves are shot.... Now he has a nervous disorder.... He can't stand on his own, he can't even talk.... If he has to go back [to the regular prison facility], he will be in bad shape."[477] She reported that the infirmary's chief physician had told her there was no way to treat Nasriddinov at the

---

473 Ibid. According to the verdict, the Jordan branch of Hizb-ut-Tahrir published the leaflet.

474 Ibid.

475 Ibid.

476 Human Rights Watch interview with Irina Mikulina, Tashkent, February 19, 2000.

477 Ibid.

infirmary because he had been convicted under criminal code article 159 and "we can't treat political prisoners."[478]

Akhmadali Salamov and Umarkhon Nazarov

On March 17, 1999, fifteen armed police officers raided the Namangan home of Akhmadali Salamov, Imam Nazarov's uncle, and arrested him and Nazarov's brother, Umarkhon Nazarov, who was visiting.[479]

Salamov and Nazarov were tried in the Namangan Province Court and sentenced on May 20, 1999, by separate judges. Umarkhon Nazarov, a Kyrgyz citizen, and Salamov were charged with encroachment on the constitutional order and preparation or distribution of materials containing ideas of religious extremism, separatism, and fundamentalism. Nazarov and Salamov denied all of the charges against them.[480]

Salamov told the court that he believed he had been arrested because of his relation to Obidkhon Nazarov.[481] Indeed, the first half of the verdicts against the two men were identical and contained references to Imam Obidkhon Nazarov's mosques as among the "Wahhabi" mosques and to the imam as one of the leaders of a supposed "ultra-reactionary" Islamic movement and criminal group.[482]

---

[478] Ibid.

[479] Amnesty International Urgent Action (UA 55/99), Possible prisoners of conscience/ fear for safety/ incommunicado detention, March 24, 1999, EUR 62/07/99. On March 24, a full week after the arrest, Amnesty International reported that police continued to hold Salamov incommunicado, denying him access to his lawyer and relatives.

[480] Namangan Province Court verdict, issued by Judge K. Safarov, May 20, 1999; and Namangan Province Court verdict, issued by Judge B. Makhmudov, May 20, 1999.

[481] Namangan Province Court verdict, issued by Judge B. Makhmudov, May 20, 1999.

[482] The first part of the verdicts for all three men—Salamov, Nazarov, and Nasriddinov—were in fact the same. Namangan Province Court verdict, issued by Judge K. Safarov, May 20, 1999; and Namangan Province Court verdict, issued by Judge B. Makhmudov, May 20, 1999; and Namangan Province Court verdict, issued by Judge T.Z. Ibragimov, May 20, 1999. See discussion of Nasriddinov case above.

The court, in its decision against Umarkhon Nazarov, cited "incriminating" witness testimony certifying that police had found a "Sharp" brand tape recorder, several audio tapes, and unidentified books in Arabic in a trunk in Salamov's house, where Umarkhon Nazarov was a guest.[483] It was further alleged that in Nazarov's jacket police had discovered four copies of a leaflet entitled, "The Prophet says: Jihad is a pillar of Islam and its peak." The Namangan Province Court sentenced Umarkhon Nazarov to eleven years in a strict-regime prison and confiscation of his property.[484]

The specific evidence presented against Salamov was witness testimony that five of the aforementioned leaflets were supposedly found in a variety of rooms during a police search of his home.[485] Salamov was sentenced to four years in prison.

Like his brother, Abdumalik, Umarkhon Nazarov also had a harrowing tale to tell regarding his transport to prison in the Kashkadaria province (prison number 64/51). His mother, Mukharramkhon Nazarova, said that she and other relatives had visited him in September 1999 and that he had told them that he'd been transported by train in July (a particularly hot month in Uzbekistan) and had been forced to stand in the train car along with about seventy other men during the three-hour trip from Tashkent. He said that by the time the train arrived at Karshi city in Kashkadaria, one of the men in his wagon had died.[486]

Akhmadali Salamov was also sent to the prison in Kashkadaria in August 1999. According to the family's lawyer, Salamov's mother reported that during a visit in September 1999 she saw bruises on his body and could tell that he had been badly beaten.[487] According to his attorney, Salamov was released under a presidential amnesty decree

---

[483] Namangan Province Court verdict, issued by Judge K. Safarov, May 20, 1999.

[484] Namangan Province Court verdict, issued by Judge K. Safarov, May 20, 1999.

[485] Namangan Province Court verdict, issued by Judge B. Makhmudov, May 20, 1999.

[486] Human Rights Watch interview with Muharramkhon Nazarova, Tashkent, February 19, 2000.

[487] Human rights Watch interview with Irina Mikulina, Tashkent, October 30, 1999.

issued in 2002, approximately seventy days before his scheduled release.[488]

Authorities used other methods of intimidation against the Nazarov family in addition to the arrest of the imam's relatives. Pursuant to a court order, Tashkent police attempted to evict Nazarov and his family from their home on April 21, 1998. The effort, illegal since the Nazarov family had not yet exhausted its right to appeal the court ruling, failed when the Organization for Security and Cooperation in Europe (OSCE) and U.S. diplomatic representatives joined journalists and local supporters of the imam to observe the police action and prevent the eviction.[489]

Imam Nazarov's wife and mother were also subjected to humiliating and intimidating public denunciations by police and local authorities.[490]

The Wife and Step-daughter of Imam Fakhruddinov

On March 17, 2001, officers from Tashkent police headquarters arrested Rakhima Akhmedalieva, wife of Imam Rukhiddin Fakhruddinov.[491] Authorities had labeled Fakhruddinov a "Wahhabi" and he was believed to be in hiding since at least 1998, fearing arrest.[492] Police held the

---

[488] Human Rights Watch interview with Salamov's lawyer, Irina Mikulina, Tashkent, March 25, 2003.

[489] Human Rights Watch, "Crackdown in The Farghona Valley: Arbitrary Arrests and Religious Discrimination," *A Human Rights Watch Report*, Vol. 10, No. 4 (D) May 1998.

[490] See "'Hate Rallies' and Public Denunciations" in Chapter III.

[491] Written report to Human Rights Watch, name withheld, March 22, 2001; and letter to U.N. Secretary General Kofi Annan from Odina Maksudova, March 26, 2001, received in English. Rakhima Akhmedalieva married Rukhiddin Fakhruddinov in 1993, while he was an imam in Tashkent. Verdict against Rakhima Akhmedalieva and others, issued by Judge F.K. Shodmonov, Tashkent City Court hearing held in the courthouse of the Iunusabad District Court, Tashkent, September 21, 2001.

[492] Imam Fakhruddinov had led the S. Darbaza mosque in Tashkent from 1992 until sometime in 1996. He also worked at the popular Tokhtaboi mosque, where Imam Obidkhon Nazarov was spiritual leader, and was fired along with Nazarov in 1996. Court documents report that following Fakhruddinov's dismissal, police went to his home to question him. Verdict of Rakhima Akhmedalieva and others, issued by Judge F. K.

imam's wife hostage, conditioning her release on his surrender. Police mistreated her, using psychological and physical pressure. When her nineteen-year-old daughter, Odina Maksudova, sought her mother, she too was detained and was forced to incriminate and verbally abuse her mother, as well as threatened with police reprisals against her very young siblings.[493] Maksudova was detained again later in March as retribution for her complaints to the international community and in an attempt by police to intimidate her into silence. Throughout, as she wrote in a letter to the international community, police pressured both Maksudova and her mother for information on Imam Fakhruddinov's whereabouts.[494]

According to Maksudova, Tashkent police ambushed the family home on March 17, 2001, and began breaking down the door and banging on the barred windows. When the family opened the door, out of fear, officers rushed in and initiated a search of the house without presenting a warrant or order of any kind.[495] Maksudova, who was present during the police search, reported that officers planted leaflets in the house and then claimed to have "found" them.[496] In the course of the search, which was videotaped by police, officers also confiscated the family's Koran. Akhmedalieva was arrested on unspecified charges, and authorities failed to inform her children of her whereabouts in custody.[497] After searching the house, police searched Akhmedalieva's son's car, in which they claimed to find additional leaflets.[498]

Shodmonov, Tashkent City Court, September 21, 2001. It is believed Imam Fakhruddinov left Uzbekistan in 1998.

[493] Maksudova is Akhmedalieva's daughter from a previous marriage and, therefore, the imam's step-daughter.

[494] Letter to the Mission of the U.N. and OSCE in the Republic of Uzbekistan, embassies of foreign countries in Uzbekistan, and human rights organizations, from Odina Maksudova, March 21, 2001, received in English.

[495] Ibid.

[496] Ibid.

[497] Written report to Human Rights Watch, name withheld, March 22, 2001.

[498] Letter to the Mission of the U.N. and OSCE in the Republic of Uzbekistan, embassies of foreign countries in Uzbekistan, and human rights organizations, from Odina Maksudova, March 21, 2001, received in English.

Odina Maksudova went to Tashkent police headquarters on March 20, seeking her mother. Instead of assisting her, police detained the young woman for twenty-four hours.[499] Maksudova reported being taken down to the basement where her mother was held and finding her mother exhausted. She had been deprived of sleep and of medicine she needed for a chronic heart condition.[500] Threatening the young woman with physical abuse, officers forced her to write a statement incriminating her mother and to curse and renounce her verbally.[501] Officers removed the headscarves of both women in the basement, and the officer in charge ordered Maksudova not to wear religious dress or to pray anymore.[502] In the days that followed, the knowledge that police had used her to exert psychological pressure on her mother tormented Maksudova, who wrote, "Now I can't forgive myself for these deeds, because my mother is a good and pure woman."[503]

The officers made clear Akhmedalieva's status as their hostage by demanding as a condition for her mother's release that Maksudova provide them with information on her step-father's whereabouts.[504] In addition to threatening the young woman with violence, the officers beat a prisoner in front of her and threatened to place her six-year-old sister and three-year-old brother in an orphanage, "so they [won't] become 'Wahhabi.'"[505]

---

[499] Written report to Human Rights Watch, name withheld, March 22, 2001; and written report to Human Rights Watch, name withheld, March 24, 2001.

[500] Letter to U.N. Secretary General Kofi Annan from Odina Maksudova, March 26, 2001, received in English.

[501] Ibid.

[502] Ibid. The officer Maksudova identified as Edik is presumed to be Edik Tsoi, an officer who for years has been infamous in Tashkent police headquarters for mistreatment of prisoners and the subject of numerous complaints by victims of torture. According to rights defender Vasila Inoiatova, Tsoi was fired along with a large number of other officers from the MVD department against corruption, racketeering and terrorism in a "purge" of that division in 2002. Human Rights Watch telephone interview with Vasila Inoiatova, March 4, 2003.

[503] Letter to UN Secretary General Kofi Annan from Odina Maksudova, March 26, 2001, received in English.

[504] Ibid.

[505] Ibid.

Maksudova was detained again for four hours on March 26, 2001, when she went to the U.N. Mission in Tashkent to deliver the appeal letter she had written on behalf of her mother. The letter was confiscated by Tashkent police who forced her to disavow the appeal.[506]

Imam Fakhruddinov did not turn himself over to police and Akhmedalieva was formally placed under arrest and charged with conspiracy to overthrow the state, membership in a religious extremist group, and possession of religious extremist literature. The state alleged that she and her seven co-defendants had been members of a "Wahhabi organization" led by her husband, Imam Fakhruddinov, together with Imam Nazarov.[507] In September 2001 the Tashkent City Court sentenced her to seven years in prison.

Following Akhmedalieva's incarceration, police repeatedly compelled Odina Maksudova to report for questioning, searched her home, and threatened criminal charges against her. As of February 2003, concern expressed by rights defenders regarding the case appeared to have forestalled further police action against the imam's children.[508]

The Nephew and Brother of Nakhmiddin Juvashev

When Nakmiddin Juvashev, a member of Hizb ut-Tahrir, asked the authorities for forgiveness, as President Karimov had called on people to do, he was arrested, tortured, tried, sentenced, and released on appeal. He was subsequently re-arrested, physically mistreated, tried, sentenced, and sent back to prison.[509] A nephew, Yadgar Sodykov, arrested with him on August 5, 2000, was held by National Security Service officers in Jizzakh and beaten in order to coerce the young man to incriminate his

---

[506] Letter to U.N. Secretary General Kofi Annan from Odina Maksudova, March 29, 2001, provided to Human Rights Watch in English. Additional information regarding this incident is provided in Chapter V.

[507] Verdict issued by Judge F.K. Shodmonov, Tashkent City Court, September 21, 2001.

[508] Human Rights Watch telephone interview with Vasila Inoiatova, February 18, 2003.

[509] Juvashev's case is described in "Torture and Mistreatment in Pre-trial Detention" in Chapter IV.

uncle. Officers released Sodykov the same day they detained him but in dire physical condition. He was hospitalized with a concussion and ruptured aural membrane.[510] The next day, National Security Service agents came to the hospital and took Sodykov, on a stretcher, back to detention.[511] At the National Security Service department in Jizzakh, they forced him to write that his uncle had resisted arrest and other testimony they wanted regarding Juvashev. Sodykov charged: "...they beat me terribly and then released me, saying, 'If you go back to the hospital, next time we'll bring back your corpse!'"[512] A few days later, after he was interrogated and released again, Sodykov vanished; a relative close to the case told Human Rights Watch he had "probably fled" to seek medical treatment and avoid further abuse.[513] In his own letter to authorities before his departure, Sodykov wrote: "Because of the poor state of my health, I am forced to get treatment in a hospital, even in another country…in Uzbekistan there is no more justice…"[514]

At 5:30 a.m. on September 6, 2000, the day after Sodykov's detention, seven men in civilian clothes came to the home of Idrisbek Umarkulov, Nakhmiddin Juvashev's brother. When the family refused to open the door, the officers entered by charging over the fence. They showed no warrant to enter the premises or conduct a search. When Umarkulov demanded to see a warrant, an officer grabbed him and pulled him away. Police grabbed his nineteen-year-old daughter by her hair and pulled her out of the way as well.[515] "E.E.," a family member present at the time,

---

[510] Letter to the Jizzakh regional procurator, from Yadgar Sodykov, August 14, 2000; written statement to Human Rights Watch from rights defender Vasilia Inoiatova, August 9, 2000; and written report of the Jizzakh regional branch of the Human Rights Society of Uzbekistan, August 29, 2000.

[511] Written statement to Human Rights Watch from Vasilia Inoiatova, August 9, 2000; and Human Rights Watch interview with a relative close to the case, name withheld, Jizzakh, November 1, 2000.

[512] Letter to the Jizzakh regional procurator, from Yadgar Sodykov, August 14, 2000.

[513] Human Rights Watch interview with a relative close to the case, name withheld, Jizzakh, November 1, 2000.

[514] Letter to the Jizzakh regional procurator, from Yadgar Sodykov, August 14, 2000.

[515] Human Rights Watch interview with Umarkulov's wife, Jizzakh, November 1, 2000. Umarkulov's wife requested not to be identified by name.

said the plainclothes officers identified themselves as National Security Service and announced they were there to conduct a search. E.E. recalled, "Idrisbek Umarkulov came out and they twisted his arms behind his back and hit him."[516] According to Umarkulov's wife, who was present, he cried out to neighbors, who came over to the house.[517] "Then police said they were going to put my son and daughter and Idris in handcuffs, and I fainted," Umarkulov's wife recalled.[518]

She regained consciousness half an hour later to find that the house had been ransacked and that police officers were stationed in a car outside her gate.[519] Then the officers, who had discovered nothing incriminating during their first search of the premises, said that the head of the Jizzakh branch of the National Security Service, Abdumannob Makhmudov, had ordered a second search.[520] Officers forced Umarkulov's wife and children, altogether eight family members, into the bathroom, preventing them from witnessing this second search. But neighbors allegedly saw the security forces approach a woodpile near the cow pen, where the agents claimed to find a plastic bag containing a sawed-off shotgun and sixteen bullets for a Makarov pistol.[521] E.E. noted that the officers did not conduct any further search of the premises after they had "found" the items in the woodpile.[522]

Security agents took Idrisbek Umarkulov and his son Sahobiddin Umarkulov, then twenty-three years old, into custody. E.E. reported that officers at the Jizzakh National Security Service beat Sahobiddin to force him to say that the gun belonged to his father, to incriminate himself as a member of Hizb ut-Tahrir, and to say that his uncle, Nakhmiddin

[516] Human Rights Watch interview with family member "E.E." (not the person's true initials), Jizzakh, February 8, 2001.

[517] Human Rights Watch interview with Umarkulov's wife, Jizzakh, November 1, 2000.

[518] Ibid.

[519] Ibid.

[520] Ibid.

[521] Human Rights Watch interview with Umarkulov's wife, Jizzakh, November 1, 2000; and letter to Human Rights Watch from Juvashev's wife, November 1, 2000.

[522] Human Rights Watch interview with E.E., Jizzakh, February 8, 2001.

Juvashev, had been his religious teacher and had been living in his home during the months he was missing.[523] Sahobiddin, who reportedly was not a member of Hizb ut-Tahrir, refused to incriminate himself and his relatives. According to E.E., a security officer handcuffed one of Sahobiddin's wrists to the leg of his chair and hit him in the ribs, stomach, and on the head to force him to sign the "confession."[524] He eventually signed a statement acknowledging that police had found a gun on the family's woodpile but saying that he did not know how it got there.[525] However, the officers in charge were dissatisfied with his testimony and subjected the young man to further coercion and physical abuse to compel him to incriminate his relatives.[526]

The Umarkulov family had hired a private lawyer, Birboi Mamatov, immediately after father and son were detained, and he secured the release of Sahobiddin at 11:00 p.m. According to his mother, one of the young man's hands was swollen, his cheek was red from being hit by the officer, and he complained that his kidneys hurt because officers had hit him repeatedly in the small of his back.[527]

Idrisbek Umarkulov was placed under arrest and went on trial for possession of the shotgun and ammunition and a later-added charge of anti-constitutional activity. On that latter charge, the evidence against him consisted mainly of neighbors' statements—all later recanted. The people in question testified that the statements had been fabricated by the National Security Services and were false, forcing the prosecution to drop this charge.[528] One of the neighbors who witnessed the search testified in court that she had seen the officers plant the plastic bag

---

[523] Ibid.

[524] Ibid.

[525] Ibid; and Human Rights Watch interview with Sahobiddin Umarkulov's mother, Jizzakh, November 1, 2000.

[526] Human Rights Watch interview with E.E., Jizzakh, February 8, 2001.

[527] Human Rights Watch interview with Sahobiddin Umarkulov's mother, Jizzakh, November 1, 2000.

[528] Human Rights Watch telephone interview with rights defender Bakhtior Hamroev, January 16, 2001.

(containing the gun) in the woodpile.[529] The Jizzakh Province Court ignored these exculpatory statements and sentenced Umarkulov to six years in prison for illegal weapons possession.[530]

The Brother of Muzafar Avazov

Twenty-nine-year-old Mirzakarim Avazov was arrested on July 24, 2000, while his older brother, Muzafar Avazov, was in National Security Service custody on charges of membership in Hizb ut-Tahrir. Human Rights Watch interviewed a person close to the case, who witnessed the arrest and followed closely the details of the brothers' detention, trials, and subsequent incarceration. According to this source, police arrested Mirzakarim Avazov to coerce his brother to sign self-incriminating statements that, even under torture, he had refused to sign.[531] The same person pointed out that Mirzakarim Avazov "had no leaflets on him or anything."[532] This source told Human Rights Watch that officers at the Tashkent police headquarters beat him in front of his older brother.[533] The U.S. State Department reported in 2001 that, "Members of the National Security Service reportedly tortured Mirzakarim with electric shocks in front of his brother until Mirzafar [sic] agreed to sign a statement incriminating himself and others."[534]

Mirzakarim Avazov remained incommunicado for seven months, and was not provided with a lawyer.[535] Authorities charged him with

---

[529] Human Rights Watch interview with E.E., Jizzakh, February 8, 2001.

[530] On appeal, the Supreme Court upheld this ruling in April 2001.

[531] Human Rights Watch interview, name withheld, Tashkent, February 26, 2001.

[532] Ibid.

[533] Ibid. The elder Avazov was originally held in SNB custody, but some of these beatings and interrogations of his younger brother in his presence allegedly took place at the Tashkent police headquarters. Transfer of prisoners back and forth for interrogations is routine in Uzbekistan. Interrogations typically take place at the MVD even when a person is being held in an SNB cell or housed in Tashkent prison during the pre-trial period.

[534] U.S. Department of State, *Annual Report on International Religious Freedom 2001*, released by the Bureau of Democracy, Human Rights, and Labor, October 26, 2001.

[535] Human Rights Watch interview, name withheld, Tashkent, February 26, 2001.

distribution of materials containing ideas of religious extremism, separatism or fundamentalism; organization of or participation in an illegal religious group; participation in a religious extremist, separatist, fundamentalist or other banned organization; and "activity as part of a group to encroach upon the constitutional order of the Republic." He was tried together with twenty-three other accused members of Hizb ut-Tahrir in a Tashkent City Court trial held at the Akmal Ikramov District Court in Tashkent. According to the verdict, Mirzakarim Avazov denied having distributed Hizb ut-Tahrir leaflets and testified that statements given to police during the investigative period of the case had been coerced and extracted "under pressure."[536]

Avazov was sentenced to sixteen years in prison while twelve of his co-defendants received prison terms ranging from fifteen to eighteen years.[537] Another ten men were sentenced to seven to ten years in prison.[538] Mirzakarim Avazov was imprisoned in a Novoi province facility, where, it was reported, he contracted a serious form of tuberculosis.[539] According to a person close to the case, police threatened to kill him if his family discussed the circumstances of his brother Muzafar's death in custody and the government cover-up that followed.[540]

---

[536] Tashkent City Court verdict, Judge Mirzarakhimov, May 17, 2001. The trial was held in the Akmal Ikramov District Court building in Tashkent.

[537] These co-defendants were Abdulvosit Abdurakhimov, Kudratullo Rakhmatullaev, Rakhmonberdi Khamroev, Abdujabar Abdukadirov, Shukhrat Alimov, Saidgani Islamov, Sherzod Akhmedov, Ziomitdin Shokhobitdinov, Solikhodja Abdullaev, Sadriddin Ashparov, Salokhitdin Ashrapov, and Sherzod Kholmukhamedov.

[538] The other ten men were Akilkhodja Turakhodjaev, Khairullo Ubaidullaev, Abdukakhar Khasanov, Danior Kosimov, Khurshid Usmanov, Khamid Shermukhamedov, Abdukarim Komilov, Akmal Iusupov, Odiljon Umarov, and Jamolitdin Khakimov. Lutfullo Abdullaev was given a three-year sentence, but was released from the courtroom on the judge's determination that a presidential amnesty decree applied to his case.

[539] Human Rights Watch telephone interview with local rights defender Vasila Inoiatova, February 18, 2003.

[540] Human Rights Watch interview with a person close to the case, name withheld, Tashkent, August 9, 2000. For details on Muzafar Avazov's death, see "Treatment in Prison" in Chapter IV.

The Family of Imam Tulkin Ergashev

Uzbek authorities were unable to locate the independent imam Tulkin Ergashev, so they arrested his son and brother instead.[541] State authorities targeted both men, mistreated them, and sentenced them to long prison terms solely because of their relationship with the imam.

Police arrested the imam's younger brother, Abdullo Mirazimov, from his home on the night of February 17, 1999.[542] In court, Mirazimov testified that police had previously summoned him many times for questioning about his brother's whereabouts, and that when he—Mirazimov—was detained in February, questioning again focused exclusively on the imam, not on the charges that Mirazimov himself was facing.[543] According to a person close to the case, officers beat Mirazimov during interrogation to force him to reveal his brother's location.[544]

Although the imams Ergashev and Nazarov were accused of being "Wahhabis," Mirazimov was charged with membership in Hizb ut-Tahrir.[545] According to the judge's verdict, supporting evidence amounted only to a police claim that officers had found Hizb ut-Tahrir leaflets and a copy of Al-Vai, a magazine published by Hizb ut-Tahrir, in Mirazimov's home along with other unspecified religious books.[546]

---

[541] Imam Ergashev, charged with anti-state activity along with Imam Nazarov in 1998, is believed to have fled Uzbekistan.

[542] Human Rights Watch interview with "Z.Z." (not the person's true initials), a person close to the case, Tashkent, March 3, 2000. Court documents give the date of Mirazimov's detention alternately as February 19 and February 20, 1999. Tashkent City Court verdict issued by Judge G. U. Maksumova, Tashkent, July 20, 1999.

[543] Tashkent City Court verdict, issued by Judge G.U. Maksumova, Tashkent, July 20, 1999; and Human Rights Watch interview with Z.Z., Tashkent, March 3, 2000.

[544] Ibid.

[545] Tashkent City Court verdict, issued by Judge G. U. Maksumova, Tashkent, July 20, 1999.

[546] Tashkent City Court verdict, issued by Judge G. U. Maksumova, Tashkent, July 20, 1999.

An additional charge of illegal possession of narcotics was based on the police claim that officers found about four grams of heroin in Mirazimov's shirt pocket. The court ruled that Mirazimov had stored the literature in order to distribute it later and thereby create a "destabilizing atmosphere," and he was convicted of attempted overthrow of the state and illegal possession of narcotics.[547]

The night after Mirazimov's arrest, police came for the imam's son, Khojiakbar Ergashev, born 1975.[548] Ten men carried out the arrest, some in civilian clothes and others in special forces (OMON) uniforms, wearing black masks and carrying Kalashnikov rifles. Storming over the wall and into the courtyard of the Ergashev home, they demanded to know the whereabouts of Imam Ergashev and showed a search warrant. While the masked officers stood on the rooftop, plainclothes officers went to the sitting room, where they allegedly planted narcotics under the carpet.[549] Not finding Khojiakbar Ergashev at home, police threatened that if he did not return soon they would detain his mother instead.[550] They confiscated religious books belonging to the imam's family and said there would be additional charges brought regarding the books.[551] According to those close to the case, however, these were all mainstream religious books and included no prohibited materials or even religious leaflets.[552] At that point, Khojiakbar Ergashev returned home from the hospital where his wife, who had recently given birth, had received treatment. Officers informed him that they had found narcotics in the house, that they would take him in for questioning and

[547] Ibid.

[548] The actual date of arrest was February 18, 1999, but official court documents give the date as February 19; this discrepancy may be due to his not having been registered at the police station until the morning hours.

[549] Human Rights Watch interview with Z.Z., Tashkent, March 3, 2000; and Human Rights Watch interview with "Y.Y." (not the person's true initials), a person close to the case, Tashkent, May 15, 1999.

[550] Human Rights Watch interview with Y.Y., Tashkent, May 15, 1999.

[551] Human Rights Watch interviews with Z.Z. and Y.Y., Tashkent, March 3, 2000 and May 15, 1999.

[552] Ibid.

would then release him.[553] They took Khojiakbar Ergashev directly to the Ministry of Internal Affairs, where they held him incommunicado for one week under the supervision of investigator Yadgar Makhmudov. Police then transferred him to Tashkent prison, where his family was initially unable to see him, but was eventually allowed to meet with him. According to a person close to the case, Ergashev told his lawyer that Ministry of Internal Affairs agents had tortured him.[554] As they had done with the imam's brother, police questioned Ergashev's son exclusively about his father and his father's whereabouts and disregarded the charges that had served as pretext for his arrest.[555]

Khojiakbar's mother, Shahzoda Ergasheva, the imam's wife, was picked up on February 23 and held for fourteen days. According to a source close to the case, the police interrogation of her also revealed that the young man had been taken into custody only because his father was wanted by police; and that authorities were essentially holding the son hostage in order to compel the family to disclose Imam Ergashev's whereabouts.[556] One officer told Ergasheva, "If your husband returns, we will release you on the spot, but if he doesn't come back, your son will go to jail and so will you."[557] Upon her release on March 8, Ergasheva returned home to find that police had occupied her house. For the next week, three to four officers held her under house arrest—resting in her courtyard, sitting in her kitchen, and eating the food she was obliged to prepare for them—until they received a call saying that the detention period was over.[558] Ergasheva became seriously ill and was sent to hospital, where relatives were allegedly afraid to visit her, knowing that anyone seen with the family would be considered suspect by the police.[559]

---

[553] Human Rights Watch interview with Z.Z., Tashkent, March 3, 2000.

[554] Ibid.

[555] Ibid.

[556] Human Rights Watch interview with Y.Y., Tashkent, May 15, 1999.

[557] Ibid.

[558] Ibid.

[559] Ibid.

The Tashkent City Court under Judge V.N. Sharipov tried Khojiakbar Ergashev in May 1999. When called to testify, the young man denied all charges against him and refused to ask for forgiveness.[560] Judge Sharipov ruled that young Ergashev, under the leadership of his father and two other men, used the "mask of Islamic religion" to call for the overthrow of the established state of Uzbekistan in order to form a Caliphate, or Islamic state, "armed with destabilizing books."[561] The verdict, citing a decision of the Committee on Religious Affairs of the Cabinet of Ministers, found that the literature that police claimed they found in the Ergashev home was anti-state. The judge sentenced Khojiakbar Ergashev to twelve years in prison for anti-constitutional activities and illegal possession of narcotics, later reduced to six years by the Supreme Court.[562] The imam's son is incarcerated in Novoi prison.

The Usmanov Family

Farhod Usmanov, an accused Hizb ut-Tahrir member and son of a prominent imam, died in police detention in June 1999 (his case is described in "Torture and Mistreatment in Pre-trial Detention" in Chapter IV). His youngest brother had been arrested in April, his son was arrested in June. After his death, two more of his brothers were arrested in December 1999 and January 2001, as were his uncle and widow, all on charges of Hizb ut-Tahrir membership.[563] While his widow is a member of Hizb ut-Tahrir, it is unclear whether Usmanov's other arrested relatives rejected the charges of membership in the group.

---

[560] Human Rights Watch interview with Z.Z., Tashkent, March 3, 2000.

[561] Tashkent City Court verdict, issued by Judge V.N. Sharipov, Tashkent, May 31, 1999. This quote is given as it appeared in the verdict, which is on file with Human Rights Watch.

[562] Tashkent City Court verdict, issued by Judge V.N. Sharipov, Tashkent, May 31, 1999; Supreme Court appeals verdict, issued by R. A. Akbarov, August 9, 1999.

[563] Details on the arrest of Usmanov's widow are in "Hizb ut-Tahrir" in Chapter II. His youngest brother, Muhammadjon Usmanov, was arrested on April 24, 1999, after police officers searched his home and property and claimed to find a 1988 copy of the Islamic magazine *Al-Vai*, which family members say was planted by police. A Tashkent court tried Muhammadjon Usmanov without a lawyer, charging him with possession of the magazine, and sentenced him to eleven years in prison. Letter from Masuda Kosimova, Muhammadjon's mother, addressed to the Uzbekistan Parliament, August 11, 1999.

The vigor with which government agents pursued the Usmanov family suggests that charges against many of the Usmanovs may have been brought because of their family connection to Farhod Usmanov.

Seventeen-year-old Oyatullo Usmanov, Farhod Usmanov's son, was arrested by officers from the Ministry of Internal Affairs sometime in June 1999 and charged with attempted overthrow of the government. He was sentenced to six years in prison by Judge Bashorad Jalilova of the Tashkent Province Court in March 2000.[564] According to local rights defender Ismail Adylov, the sentence was later reduced and, when he had served his term, Oyatullo Usmanov was released on January 3, 2001.[565] Human Rights Watch was unable to obtain details regarding the conditions of his release.

Police arrested one of Farhod Usmanov's brothers, Ravkhat, on December 31, 1999. Authorities charged him with attempted overthrow of the state, distribution of religious extremist literature, failure to report a crime, and organization of a criminal association.[566] Ravkhat Usmanov's trial was scheduled to begin on April 23, 2000, at the Chilanzar District Court in Tashkent, and Human Rights Watch attempted to monitor the hearing. The judge postponed it, declaring that the defense lawyer had failed to arrive. But Human Rights Watch's representative spoke to a woman exiting the building who had been in the judge's chambers when he made the declaration about postponement and who in fact was the defense lawyer. Human Rights Watch later learned that Judge Meliev sentenced Ravkhat Usmanov to fourteen years in prison.[567] A relative expressed concern for him, as he suffers from epilepsy.[568]

---

[564] Human Rights Watch interview with rights defender Vasila Inoiatova, Tashkent, March 15, 2000, and April 5, 2000.

[565] Human Rights Watch interview with rights defender Ismail Adylov, Tashkent, March 26, 2003.

[566] Human Rights Watch interview with "W.W." (not the person's true initials), Tashkent, April 23, 2000.

[567] Human Rights Watch interview with "V.V." (not the person's true initials), Tashkent, May 22, 2000.

[568] Human Rights Watch interview with W.W., Tashkent, April 23, 2000.

On January 14, 2001, police detained Farhod Usmanov's brother-in-law, Faizullo Agzamov, born 1969. A local rights defender reported Agzamov was held incommunicado in the basement of Tashkent police headquarters during pre-trial detention and that the same police investigator responsible for Farhod Usmanov's case was in charge of his brother-in-law's investigation.[569] The officer denied Agzamov's family any meetings with him.[570]

Agzamov was accused of membership in Hizb ut-Tahrir and was tried along with nine other men on charges of anti-constitutional activity, possession and distribution of "extremist" religious literature, and, in Agzamov's case, illegal sale or acquisition of foreign currency.[571] Agzamov denied the charges, declaring that he was not a member of Hizb ut-Tahrir at all.[572]

The state claimed that the late Farhod Usmanov had "drawn" Agzamov into Hizb ut-Tahrir and that, under Usmanov's leadership, Agzamov had subsequently taken an oath to the group and assumed a central role among its Tashkent leadership. In the verdict's discussion of the charges against Agzamov, the court named Usmanov as one of the supposed founders of Hizb ut-Tahrir in Uzbekistan—he was not listed as a founder of the group in the discussions of the cases of the other nine men on trial.[573] Despite the emphasis on Usmanov in the sections of the verdict dealing with Agzamov, nowhere is it mentioned that the two men were related.[574] Tashkent City Court Judge M.A. Abdujabarov sentenced Agzamov to seventeen years in prison on September 25,

---

[569] Human Rights Watch interview with rights defender Mahbuba Kosymova, Tashkent, April 26, 2001.

[570] Ibid.

[571] Verdict issued by Tashkent City Court Judge M. A. Abdujabarov, September 25, 2001. The trial was held in the Chilanzar District Court building.

[572] Ibid.

[573] Ibid.

[574] Ibid.

2001. His co-defendants were given sentences ranging from three years probation and a fine to seventeen years in prison.[575]

Shukrullo Agzamov, another of Farhod Usmanov's brothers-in-law, was sentenced to a seven-year prison term.[576] He was subsequently released in August 2002. Farhod Usmanov's uncle, the brother of Imam Nosir Kori Usmanov, was also arrested following Farhod's death and sentenced to an unknown number of years in prison.[577]

Father and Mother of Uigun and Oibek Ruzmetov

Local police in Khazorasp in the western province of Khorezm branded the Ruzmetov family "Wahhabi," and arrested and tortured brothers Uigun and Oibek Ruzmetov. They also detained and physically mistreated their mother, Darmon Sultanova, held Sultanova and her daughter and grandchildren under house arrest, and arrested Sultanova's husband Sobir Ruzmetov on trumped-up charges.

Arrested in late December 1998, Uigun and Oibek Ruzmetov were tortured and forced to confess to serious anti-state crimes, including terrorism, sentenced to death, and executed.[578]

---

[575] Verdict issued by Tashkent City Court Judge M. A. Abdujabarov, September 25, 2001. The trial was held in the Chilanzar District Court building. The nine other co-defendants were: Khusnutdin Khikhmatov, Khakhramon Sultanov, Talgar Bulegenov, Khairullo Juraev, Abdukodir Rakhimov, Abdurazzok Erinov, Muradullo Shirmukhamedov, Naim Rashidov, and Kanat Duisenbaev.

[576] "Uzbekistan: Round-up of Women Linked to Islamic Groups," Human Rights Watch press release, May 1, 2002.

[577] Human Rights Watch interview with rights defender Vasila Inoiatova, Tashkent, March 15, 2000.

[578] The trial of Uigun and Oibek Ruzmetov was held in Tashkent in July 1999, without any due notification of the family that the hearings had begun. The trial had to be postponed at least once because the defendants had no lawyer. Human Rights Watch interview with the presiding judge, Tashkent, July 6, 1999. They were tried with a group of six other men, the majority of whom were also from Khorezm province, and charged with being part of a criminal group that sought to undermine the Uzbek constitution and "create an Islamic state founded on the principles of religious extremism and Islamic fundamentalism." Verdict of the Tashkent Province Court, July 29, 1999. The state further accused the men of having

According to Sultanova, police began harassing the family in November and December 1998. She told Human Rights Watch:

> An officer from either the GUVD [city police department] or ROVD [district police department] in Khorezm came to my home when I was there with my daughter, who is mentally ill. The officer's name was Komil. He insulted me and said, "You are a Wahhabi and so is your daughter and we will shoot you all. None of you will be left alive."[579]

On the day police came to arrest her sons, police made clear that they had targeted the family for its members' religious beliefs and activities. Sultanova recalled, "On December 28 seven guys with weapons came to our house at night. I remember two of them: Kadir Saparov and Kodir

---

promoted or advanced the ideas of the "ultra-reactionary, religious-political, extremist movement of Islam: Wahhabism." Ibid. In court, the state alleged that the men had plotted to explode the dam at Charvok, just outside Tashkent, as an act of terrorism. However, the men were not actually charged with terrorism (article 155 of the criminal code) or with plotting terrorism.

One observer who attended the proceedings recounted for Human Rights Watch the young men's testimony. According to this source, Uigun Ruzmetov told the judge that he signed a prepared confession because police had threatened to arrest his wife and parents if he did not. Human Rights Watch interview with a journalist who attended the trial, name withheld, Tashkent, July 22, 1999. The same person told Human Rights Watch that one of the Ruzmetov's co-defendants, Utkur Iusupov, also from Khorezm province, testified that police threatened to rape his wife in front of him if he did not sign the prepared confession and said, "we will do it so that you will have no choice but to sign." The court accepted the allegedly coerced confessions as evidence and sentenced to death the Ruzmetov brothers and three others on charges including murder and weapons possession, charges springing from the men's confessions to having committed a series of hitherto unsolved crimes throughout the country, including the murder of border police. The court also found them guilty of membership in an illegal religious organization (criminal code article 216). The remaining defendants were sentenced to twenty years in prison.

The executions are believed to have been carried out in August or September 1999. In October, Sultanova reported she had received an official letter stating that the verdict against her sons had been carried out. Human Rights Watch interview with Darmon Sultanova, Tashkent, October 21, 1999. In Uzbekistan, the death penalty is carried out by firing squad. Bodies are not returned to the families.

579 Human Rights Watch interview with Darmon Sultanova, Tashkent, October 21, 1999.

Atabaev. They demanded to know who in the house prays, and who reads the Koran."[580] Five officers occupied the house that night and continued to keep family members under armed house arrest for the next forty days.[581]

On December 29 some 200 to 300 armed officers raided the Ruzmetov home and claimed to find bullets in a jar and morphine in the room of Sultanova's mentally disabled daughter. Police also confiscated a copy of the Koran in Arabic, a book of the hadith of Imam al-Bukhari,[582] and six copies of sura (chapters) of the Koran in Uzbek.[583] Uigun, Oibek, and Sobir Ruzmetov were placed under arrest that day.

Darmon Sultanova

Darmon Sultanova and Sobir Ruzmetov were interrogated at the Urgench police station on January 5, 1999. Sultanova was taken into custody during the night and held at the station for twenty-four hours. She recalled the police interrogation, "They insulted me. They asked me, 'Who comes to visit you? Who reads the Koran in your house?'"[584] The officers' primary motive for taking Sultanova into custody appears, however, to have been as a means of psychological torture and coercion of her sons. According to Sultanova, the officers stripped her down to her underwear in a basement cell at the police station and handcuffed her to a radiator.[585] Then, they paraded her bruised and bloody sons past her to force the young men to sign self-incriminating statements.[586] It

[580] Human Rights Watch interview with Darmon Sultanova, Tashkent, June 9, 2000.

[581] Human Rights Watch interview with Darmon Sultanova, Tashkent, November 2, 1999; and Meeting with Darmon Sultanova, then-U.S. Ambassador-at-Large for Religious Freedom Robert Sieple, and Human Rights Watch, Tashkent, May 23, 2000.

[582] Muhammed ibn Ismail abu Abdolah al-Juti al-Bukhari (810-870) is a famed Uzbek theologian and collector of the sayings and deeds of the Prophet Muhammed.

[583] Letter to Human Rights Watch from Darmon Sultanova, November 2, 2000.

[584] Human Rights Watch interview with Darmon Sultanova, Tashkent, October 21, 1999.

[585] Human Rights Watch interview with Darmon Sultanova, Tashkent, November 2, 1999; and Meeting with Darmon Sultanova, then-U.S. Ambassador-at-Large for Religious Freedom Robert Sieple, and Human Rights Watch, Tashkent, May 23, 2000.

[586] Human Rights Watch interview with Darmon Sultanova, Tashkent, November 2, 1999.

was later revealed in court that police had threatened to imprison the young men's parents.[587] Officers also allegedly threatened to arrest or rape Uigun's wife if he did not sign a confession and told him his children had already been placed in an orphanage.[588] The Ruzmetov brothers both signed confessions on serious anti-state charges.

Sultanova was released to police who were occupying her house. Sultanova, herself a nurse by profession, said that her health was so poor during the first four hours after her release that emergency medical assistance had to make several visits to the house.[589] Sultanova, her daughter Zioda, and her grandchildren were held under armed house arrest for the next month, until February 6, 1999. In interviews and written communications with Human Rights Watch, Sultanova detailed valuable possessions—including a gold watch awarded to her as a "Veteran of Labor"—she claims police stole from her during their occupation of her home. She reported that police destroyed household appliances and furniture before they departed in February.[590] Sultanova described the police treatment of her and her daughter during house arrest as unbearable. "They beat me several times, saying I was a Wahhabi and asking me where I got my books," Sultanova recalled, "I said I just pray five times a day and only in Uzbek, I don't even read Arabic."[591] She reported that the five male officers confined her daughter to her room for the forty days and did not allow her to come out even to use the bathroom. She said that the officers occupying her home made repeated threats to kill members of the family.[592] Sultanova also told Human Rights Watch about actions the police took to further isolate the family. She said, "Police officers went around to all our

[587] Human Rights Watch interview with a journalist who attended the trial, name withheld, Tashkent, July 22, 1999.

[588] Human Rights Watch interview with Darmon Sultanova, Tashkent, November 2, 1999; and letter to President Islam Karimov and others, from Darmon Sultanova, November 19, 1999.

[589] Human Rights Watch interview with Darmon Sultanova, Tashkent, November 2, 1999.

[590] Human Rights Watch interview with Darmon Sultanova, Tashkent, June 9, 2000.

[591] Darmon Sultanova at a meeting with Robert Seiple, then-United States Ambassador-at-Large for Religious Freedom, and Human Rights Watch, Tashkent, May 23, 2000.

[592] Human Rights Watch interview with Darmon Sultanova, Tashkent, November 2,1999.

relatives carrying weapons, automatic rifles, and said that our family is Wahhabi and told them not to help us or talk to us. They went to our neighbors and friends and relatives and said this. They threatened our neighbors and others and said not to help that 'Wahhabi family' that has weapons."[593] In this case, the threats appeared to have successfully frightened others from interacting with or supporting the Ruzmetovs. Sultanova said, "Now, when I walk down the street, everyone runs away. They were all threatened and told mine is a bad family."[594]

Sobir Ruzmetov

Sobir Ruzmetov, a retired medical doctor, was interrogated on January 5, 1999. He was arrested on trumped-up charges of illegal narcotics possession, tried, convicted, sentenced, and sent to prison. Three years later he was released pursuant to the 2001 presidential amnesty decree.

Police subjected Ruzmetov to physical abuse during pre-trial detention. According to Sultanova, who met with him afterwards, police beat the sixty-five-year-old Ruzmetov on the genitals and he was unable to walk for some time after.[595] According to Sultanova, Ruzmetov was denied the right to counsel, "They took him to trial…in leg irons… and tried him without a lawyer. He asked for a lawyer, but they said, 'he didn't come.'"[596] The Khazorasp District Court convicted Ruzmetov on charges of illegal possession of narcotics on May 29, 1999, and sentenced him to five years in prison. He was sent to a facility in Novoi province. After meeting with him in June 2000, Sultanova told Human Rights Watch that her husband had cried and asked about their sons. She said he told her, "They'll kill you if you pray here, they don't allow

[593] Human Rights Watch interview with Darmon Sultanova, Tashkent, October 21, 1999.

[594] Ibid.

[595] Human Rights Watch interviews with Darmon Sultanova, Tashkent, October 21, 1999 and November 2, 1999.

[596] Human Rights Watch interview with Darmon Sultanova, Tashkent, October 21, 1999.

it."[597] Sultanova told Human Rights Watch that her husband had stopped praying because he feared the beatings.[598]

The ill-treatment Ruzmetov endured in prison, combined presumably with the execution of his sons, left him in poor physical and psychological condition upon his release.[599]

A Brother of Abdurashid Isakhojaev

Persecution of the Isakhojaev family for Abdurashid Isakhojaev's alleged affiliation with Imam Nazarov did not stop with the young man's conviction or his transfer to the harsh Jaslyk prison. After the February 1999 bombings in Tashkent, local police began to summon Abdurashid's younger brother Muzafar for questioning nearly every week. Police called him on the telephone repeatedly and visited his parents' home looking for him. According to his mother, as of June 2000, Muzafar had been detained once and taken in for questioning some fifty times since the Tashkent bombings.[600] He shaved his beard to avoid problems with the police, but this apparently failed to satisfy them. According to his mother, police continued to harass him because "...his brother is in jail and ... he prays."[601] The combination of being related to a so-called enemy of the state and overtly manifesting his own piety through his appearance and religious practice served to put Muzafar at particular risk. Sharifa Isakhojaeva told Human Rights Watch that her other two sons who did not pray had not reported harassment by police.[602]

---

[597] Human Rights Watch interview with Darmon Sultanova, Tashkent, June 9, 2000.

[598] Human Rights Watch interview with Darmon Sultanova,Tashkent, November 2, 1999.

[599] Human Rights Watch interview with Darmon Sultanova, Tashkent, August 31, 2002.

[600] Human Rights Watch interview with Sharifa Isakhojaeva, Tashkent, June 1, 2000.

[601] Ibid.

[602] Ibid.

Azim Khojaev, Father of Polvonnazar Khojaev

Along with his brothers, Polvonnazar Khojaev was known throughout his community as particularly devout, and was wanted by police on charges of "Wahhabism" and "religious extremism." Unable to locate him, police in Khiva, the main city in Khorezm province in western Uzbekistan, focused their attention on his father, Azim, a local metal worker and father of six. (Polvonnazar, it was later discovered, had been living in Russia). According to a person close to the case, beginning in January 1999, local police would come to the house twice a week to summon Azim Khojaev to the police station where officers interrogated him about the whereabouts of Polvonnazar and his other sons.[603] Nazira Ishchanova, Azim Khojaev's wife, reportedly said that the police were "interested in the religious devotion of [the] sons."[604] But the young men were abroad and Azim Khojaev either could not or would not compel them to turn themselves over to police. According to one report, as police intimidation increased, Nazira Ischanova asked officers on April 2, 1999, what they were planning to do. A policeman answered matter-of-factly, "We will arrest your husband instead of your sons."[605] Police also told a member of the Khojaev family, "If we wanted, we could put a tank in your yard and say it was yours."[606] Police arrested the forty-eight-year-old Azim Khojaev on charges of possession of marijuana on April 4, 1999—the very day that a senior government official publicly announced a policy to make fathers pay for the supposed wrongdoings of their sons. Police held Khojaev in custody until his June 11 trial. The Khiva District Court convicted him in just forty-five minutes and sentenced him to eight years in prison on charges of narcotics possession.[607] A person present at the court hearing gave the following account:

---

[603] Human Rights Watch interview with a person close to the case, name withheld, Tashkent, May 9, 2000.

[604] Oleg Panfilov, electronic bulletin, Center for Journalism in Extreme Situations, May 23, 2000.

[605] Ibid.

[606] Human Rights Watch interview with a person close to the case, name withheld, Tashkent, May 9, 2000.

[607] Verdict issued by Judge R. Duschanov, Khiva District Court, June 11, 1999.

> Before his arrest he'd been healthy, but at trial he looked pale and unwell. The lawyer asked the judge to apply the amnesty law, but the judge refused. Azim said he was not guilty and didn't even know what he was being charged with. In the trial, they didn't ask about drugs, the judge just asked about his sons and the religious practices of the family. The judge asked if his sons read namaz [prayed] and Azim said yes. The procurator asked if they got some kind of financing from someone somewhere. He asked Azim if he was part of a group.... There was no break to consider the verdict, they just gave it immediately.[608]

Azim Khojaev died in Jaslyk prison on July 2, 1999 (just twenty days after his conviction). The official death certificate gave the cause of his death as "acute failure of the left stomach."[609] The family was denied the right to view his body or to be present during the Muslim burial rites when the body was delivered some eleven days after Khojaev's death.[610] A person who saw the body briefly and who spoke with someone who washed Khojaev's body in preparation for burial, told Human Rights

---

[608] Human Rights Watch interview with a person close to the case, name withheld, Tashkent, May 9, 2000. The one-and-a-half page verdict does mention the narcotics charge, stating that half a kilogram (approximately one pound) of marijuana was found on a shelf in the house and that while Khojaev denied it was his, he agreed, as head of household, to answer for the charge. The verdict also noted that in their search police had confiscated two typewritten letters with religious content, religious books, and "documents of a religious nature." Verdict of the Khiva District Court, issued by Judge Ruzimboi Duschanov, June 11, 1999. The verdict also explains the judge's refusal to apply the April 30, 1999 presidential amnesty to Azim Khojaev with a statement claiming that Khojaev had violated several, unspecified, prison regulations while in pre-trial detention during the investigative period.

[609] Death certificate No. 0005094, issued February 1, 2000, on file with Human Rights Watch.

[610] Oleg Panfilov, electronic bulletin, Center for Journalism in Extreme Situations, May 23, 2000.

Watch that the body showed signs of torture.[611] This source told Human Rights Watch that Khojaev's body was bruised on the right-hand side, that there was grazing on his side and buttocks, a cut to the back of the head, and that he had no fingernails.[612]

Father of a "Wahhabi"

In some cases, police harassment of relatives appeared aimed more at exacting revenge than at extracting information. The case of "Abdulaziz Azimov" (not the man's true name) illustrates this pattern. Azimov suffered social pressure immediately after his son was taken into custody for "Wahhabism" in 1998.[613] The private shop where Azimov worked in Andijan fired him explicitly because of the charges against his son. Two months later, local police summoned Azimov for interrogation. He did not comply with the police request for two days, and when he did go to the station, police treated him with extreme brutality. The officers kept Azimov for twelve hours, 9:00 a.m. to 9:00 p.m., during which time they beat him continuously with nightsticks, on the back and kidney area,

---

[611] Human Rights Watch interview with a human rights defender, name withheld, Tashkent, March 2003.

[612] Ibid. Polvonnazar Khojaev was subsequently arrested by Russian law enforcement agents, in April 2000, extradited to Uzbekistan, and sentenced to death on charges that included religious extremism and terrorism. His youngest brother, Muzafar Khojaev, was arrested on September 18, 1999, in Uzbekistan. When a female relative went looking for him in detention, police told her he was not there, that he had gone "to Tajikistan, to Chechnya." The officer said Muzafar had shot people and when the relative rejected this accusation, the officer threatened, "You need to be shot too." Human Rights Watch interview with a person close to the case, name withheld, Tashkent, May 9, 2000. Muzafar Khojaev was sentenced to eleven years in prison and, as of March 2003, was incarcerated in Zangiota prison in Tashkent. Human Rights Watch interview with a human rights defender, name withheld, Tashkent, March 2003. In May 2000 Urgench police were seeking the arrest of Polvonnazar's brother Hamza Khojaev. According to a source close to the case, police said he was wanted for his religious beliefs and anti-state activities. Human Rights Watch interview with a person close to the case, name withheld, Tashkent, May 9, 2000. In March 2003 Human Rights Watch learned that Hamza Khojaev had been sentenced to death and executed in 2000. Human Rights Watch interview with a human rights defender, name withheld, Tashkent, March 2003.

[613] His son was tried and convicted in a high-profile and highly publicized religion-related case.

accusing him of being a "Wahhabi," just as they had his son. The police brutality was visible, according to a person who saw Azimov immediately after his release. "He returned home at 9:00 p.m. only half-alive. His whole body, except for his face, was covered in bruises, four of his ribs were broken, and he had serious problems with his kidneys…He lay at home for twenty days to rest,"[614] the source told Human Rights Watch. He declined to go to the doctor because police had warned him that if he complained about the beatings they would arrest him. Two years after the incident, Azimov still reportedly suffered from trauma. A person close to the case told Human Rights Watch that he shook and trembled all the time and appeared to be psychologically damaged.[615] In June 2000 he was re-arrested on charges of illegal narcotics possession.

Harassment of Relatives

Family members of convicts were forced to report monthly to local police to recount their activities and swear that they had not attended any protests or prohibited gatherings. Some were compelled to sign loyalty oaths to the government and statements avowing that they were not members of any religious sects. Numerous relatives of religious prisoners were "put on the list," that is, registered with police as suspicious individuals. In at least one episode, authorities pressured family members of imprisoned independent Muslims to publicly "confess" to their own involvement in "extremist" activities in exchange for the state's forgiveness.

- Local police compelled the wife of Imam Iuldashev, Omina Iuldasheva, to sign statements swearing that she was not involved in any "religious sects." Officers also summoned her to force her to abandon the hijab.[616] The neighborhood police officer threatened Imam Iuldashev that he would inform the National Security Service if the

---

[614] Human Rights Watch interview, name withheld, Andijan, May 19, 2000.

[615] Ibid; and Human Rights Watch telephone interview with rights defender Muzafarmirzo Isakhov, August 12, 2000.

[616] Human Rights Watch interview, name withheld, Tashkent, August 1, 2000.

imam's wife did not remove her Islamic clothing. He told Iuldashev that information regarding his wife had already been entered into computer files at the Ministry of Internal Affairs.[617] Indeed, when Iuldashev was first arrested, local police officer Jozilboi Suvankulov allegedly threatened the imam's wife directly, saying, "If you don't uncover your face, I'll put you in prison with your husband."[618] As detailed below, she was also made the object of a local "hate rally."

The Wife of Shukhrat Abdurakhimov

Just days before the presidential election, around January 6, 2000, officers from the Biktimir police station on the outskirts of Tashkent detained the wife of Shukhrat Abdurakhimov, who had been arrested in April 1999 and sentenced to seventeen years in prison on "religious extremism" charges.[619] A relative reported that the officers who detained her in January 2000 kept Abdurakhimov's wife for three days.[620] Her arrest was among other administrative measures authorities took against religious dissidents in the run-up to the elections.

When Abdurakhimov was arrested in April 1999, his wife followed police officers as they dragged her husband from the family's apartment in handcuffs. According to an eyewitness, one officer beat her there in the corridor, hitting her on the back of the neck three times with a crowbar that officers initially had used to try to force their way into the house.[621] After the beating, when the family reported to the Biktimir department of criminal investigations that they planned to take her to

---

617 Ibid.

618 Ibid.

619 Human Rights Watch interviews with the mother of Shukhrat Abdurakhimov, Tashkent, April 5, 2000 and July 19, 2000. Abdurakhimov's mother asked to be identified only in this way and not named.

620 Human Rights Watch interview with the mother of Shukhrat Abdurakhimov, Tashkent, July 19, 2000.

621 Human Rights Watch interview, name withheld, Tashkent, November, 1999; and Human Rights Watch interview with the mother of Shukhrat Abdurakhimov, Tashkent, July 19, 2000.

the hospital for a medical exam, the deputy of criminal investigations threatened her saying, "If you do, we will open a case against you too."[622] She did not seek medical treatment for her injuries or a doctor's report regarding their origin.[623]

- One woman whose son was accused of being a "Wahhabi" and imprisoned in 1999 on charges of anti-state activity and possession of two bullets, said that she was forced to report every month to the procuracy. "I was told I was 'registered' and that I had been 'warned.' They think I am agitating people to pray and believe in God, and, because I am a teacher, that I am agitating children to be against the government," she said.[624] The woman, who lives alone and has sole responsibility for her grandchild, told Human Rights Watch, "I am always afraid. They are always coming to me, always questioning me...When I am called in for questioning, they yell at me and address me as if I am guilty. If I refuse [to go], they scare me, and say, 'We'll arrest you too. We'll put leaflets on you or find some excuse to punish you, but you won't be able to prove it.'"[625] In November 2000 local police came to her door late at night to summon her to the station again. She objected, saying she didn't want to go so late at night, but "They took me by the arms and neck to the station, so they could take my photograph."[626]

- Similarly, police reportedly compelled the wife of disappeared Islamic leader Imam Abdulla Utaev to report monthly to the local station for questioning.[627]

[622] Human Rights Watch interview with a relative of Shukhrat Abdurakhimov, name withheld, Tashkent, November 4, 1999.

[623] Human Rights Watch interview with the mother of Shukhrat Abdurakhimov, Tashkent, July 19, 2000.

[624] Human Rights Watch interview, name withheld, Tashkent, February 27, 2001.

[625] Ibid.

[626] Ibid.

[627] Human Rights Watch interview, name withheld, Tashkent, February 2000.

▪ In some cases, rather than summon family members of a religious prisoner to the police station, authorities paid repeated and intimidating visits to their homes. The wife of accused Hizb ut-Tahrir member Tavakkaljon Akhmedov reported to Human Rights Watch that three police officers made repeated visits to her home to force her to sign a document stating that she would not attend any forbidden meetings or demonstrations. "They came every week and ordered me to sign and eventually I did," she said.[628] Akhmedova also reported that the visits intimidated family members, "The children are afraid and have stopped going to school. They don't trust the authorities anymore."[629]

Some prisoners' relatives were required to report their activities not only to the police but also to their local mahalla committee. These committees also conducted their own door-to-door surveillance of relatives of religious suspects and convicts. According to a local rights defender in Fergana city, the mahalla committees there have been tasked with intense surveillance of residents, including physically following their movements.[630]

▪ Mukhtabar M. (not her real name) told Human Rights Watch in February 2001 that every month since her release from prison in September 1999 her local mahalla committee had summoned her to write a statement swearing that she had not proselytized, was not a member of any unofficial organization and stating that she understood she would "answer for it" if she were a member of such a group.[631] The elderly woman explained, "I'm on the list of dangerous people."[632]

One important goal of this campaign is to stigmatize independent Muslims in the eyes of their fellow citizens, to halt proselytizing on the one hand and, on the other, to cut off neighbors' support for the

---

628 Human Rights Watch interview with the wife of Tavakkaljon Akhmedov, Asaka, Andijan, May 2000.

629 Ibid.

630 Human Rights Watch interview, name withheld, Tashkent, February 27, 2001.

631 Human Rights Watch interview, name withheld, Tashkent, February 2001.

632 Ibid.

religious prisoners' families. In addition to the "hate rallies" organized by local officials, even stricter measures are sometimes employed. One acquaintance of the Abdurakhimov family was detained and held for ten days by local police who threatened that if he continued to help families of those arrested the police would "destroy you all." After police detained him, the man stopped helping Abdurakhimov's family.[633]

- According to relatives of convicted Hizb ut-Tahrir member Tavakkaljon Akhmedov, the local mahalla committee, which is charged with distributing assistance to the elderly and families with small children, has failed to give benefits for the Akhmedov children. The village council, a similar government structure functioning under the supervision of the district mayor's office, is also responsible for giving benefits to families with young children. The Akhmedov family alleged in May 2000 that this office also had been refusing them assistance since January.[634]

- The wife of one convicted independent Muslim, arrested because of his participation in private religious classes, reported that when she complained to the state housing office about a leaking roof, the civil servants there refused to help her because of her husband and expelled her from the office.[635]

Fear for the safety of relatives appears to have been one of the motives for some independent Muslims to turn themselves in to police and to ask for forgiveness for their independent religious activity. What appeared to be several such instances were broadcast on national television in 2001. President Karimov had declared on September 6, 2000, that the government would pardon those people who had "mistakenly" joined "terrorist groups." By January 2001 Tashkent prosecutors claimed to have begun implementation of the presidential decree. National television broadcast the news along with statements by

---

[633] Human Rights Watch interview with the mother of Shukhrat Abdurakhimov, Tashkent, May 9, 2000.

[634] Human Rights Watch interview with relatives of Tavakkaljon Akhmedov, Asaka, Andijan, May 2000.

[635] Human Rights Watch interview, name withheld, Tashkent, November 3, 2000.

young men who allegedly had been members of Hizb ut-Tahrir and had been released as a result of this review process. Their statements gave reason to fear that the men had been coerced to appear on television out of concern for the well-being of their fathers. One man said he surrendered to police and asked for forgiveness after his father was imprisoned. Another, Umidjon Inoiatov, introduced as a member of Hizb ut-Tahrir, told the television camera, "They told us that they would teach us Arabic and Koran and then we agreed. They taught us from a book, but then I gradually gave it up. Then in line with the decree, I returned and apologized and was pardoned."[636] The television presenter's next statement spoke volumes, "It turns out a search has been announced for your father in connection with this. What would you like to say, taking this opportunity?" The young man replied, on cue, "We want him to take advantage of the decree and return to his family."[637]

"Hate Rallies" and Public Denunciations

Uzbek authorities have staged public denunciations of independent Muslims and their families, calling primarily on mahalla committees and the official clergy to carry them out. Public denunciations are carefully staged spectacles at which independent Muslims and their families are vilified, humiliated, and called upon to make statements of contrition. They serve to punish and ostracize their victims, alienating them from their local networks of support, and spreading fear among communities about the dangers of involvement in unsanctioned religious activity.

Public denunciations of independent Muslims organized by the Karimov government echoed meetings held during the Soviet era. In particular the gatherings mirrored those in the late 1920s and 1930s that condemned individuals whose behavior was contrary to the goals and dictates of the Communist Party or whose social origins made them

[636] Uzbek television, January 22, 2001.

[637] Ibid.

"enemies of the people."[638] Attended by ranking party officials, the Soviet-era meetings featured denunciations of fellow community members or co-workers and self-recrimination by participants. The "hate rallies" of present-day Uzbekistan are carefully staged spectacles organized by mahalla committees and city mayors. They are held in school auditoria or other large halls and include participation by police and procuracy officials as well as members of the officially sanctioned clergy. They are an important propaganda exercise in the government's campaign against independent Muslims. They have also served to make average citizens complicit in the persecution of their friends and neighbors.

Structure and Content of Public Denunciations

Attendance at a public denunciation is obligatory both for its targets—some of whom are awaiting trial on religion-related charges—and for spectators, whom mahalla and other local officials have summoned to the events. Officials' speeches at the meetings serve as warnings, aimed at frightening people into abandoning religious practices the state finds objectionable or into disavowing relatives who have been branded "enemies." Officials give general warnings against taking the "wrong" religious path and then vilify the meetings' subjects as "terrorists" and "extremists." State officials accuse their targets of being worthless to society, bad parents, and bad neighbors. These public denunciations isolate the subjects from the support networks that their community would otherwise provide. The hundreds of assembled community residents then have a turn at lambasting the targets, sometimes calling for their incarceration or execution. In some cases the targets, often detainees at the time, are forced to endure hours of verbal abuse, but are rarely given a chance to speak in their own defense.

Targets of hate rallies may be those awaiting trial on religion-related charges, or their relatives. Both categories of people are branded "enemies of the state" or "enemies of the people." Relatives of leading

[638] Shiela Fitzpatrick, *Everyday Stalinism: Ordinary Life in extraordinary Times: Soviet Russia in the 1930s* (New York: Oxford University Press, Inc., 1999), pp. 29, 116, 135, 199-200, and passim.

religious dissidents, either missing or in jail, have found themselves the subjects of repeated "hate rallies" that can also involve criticism of their own religious practice, such as the wearing of hijab (Muslim attire ranging from a scarf covering the hair to clothing covering the entire body and face). The subjects of the assembly are called upon to disavow their loved ones, outline their own supposed misdeeds, and to beg for forgiveness not only of their neighbors and the gathered law enforcement agents, but also President Karimov and all of the people of Uzbekistan.

Denunciations Organized by Mahallas and Other Local Officials

An example of the structure and content of a typical "hate rally" was the public denunciation organized by local officials in Namangan against forty-seven-year-old Omina Muidinova, her three sons, and other male relatives on April 5, 2000. These family members were accused of Wahhabism" and charged with attempted overthrow of the state.[639] Held in the Namangan mayor's office, the meeting was presided over by

[639] According to Judge Eronov's verdict for the Namangan Province Court issued on June 29, 2000, the state accused Muidinova of maintaining contact with her relative, Akmal Ergashev, who had been on a police wanted list. She was also accused of recruiting people for terrorist training camps in Tajikistan. The main evidence supporting the charges was a videotape of the training camp, which Akmal Ergashev allegedly gave her.

Police also claimed to have found religious literature in her home, which state officials examined and found to contain "opinions contrary to the constitutional order and relating to political organizations and religious trends," as well as "calls for the overthrow of the existing government order and creation of a Caliphate."

The state's charges against Muidinova's relatives were identical to those brought against her, with the additional accusation that her brother had a copy of the training video in his car and that police found ten copies of a document with the heading "Come holy day, hurry good people" and four additional pieces of paper in his home titled "Beginning the Year." Court records reveal that none of the defendants in the case conceded the charges against them, save that they knew of Akmal Ergashev's whereabouts in hiding and that they had viewed the videotape in question. According to the verdict, Muidinova testified that she had met with Ergashev while he was in hiding and that she and her relatives had watched a video he gave her depicting terrorist training camps in Tajikistan. The judge also reported that Muidinova said she had initially agreed to send one of her sons to Tajikistan, but then changed her mind; none of her sons attended the camp.

Deputy Mayor A. Lukmanov.[640] Other officials who convened the meeting included Deputy Minister of Internal Affairs B. R. Parpiev; chief of the Namangan province police department, B. Subkhanov; the mayor of Namangan province, T.A. Jabbarov; Namangan province procurator Kh. Sabirov; and representatives from the Namangan city mahalla committee.

Following a pattern seen in other "hate rallies," the meeting began with a broad warning to area residents to shun religious trends deemed harmful to the state. Speakers called for the defense of citizens from "religious extremism" and particularly from the influence of the Islamic organization Hizb ut-Tahrir.[641] Officials hailed fidelity to the motherland, condemned her traitors, and warned citizens of the consequences of encroachment on the existing order.[642]

In the second stage of the "hate rally," the officials offered a live illustration of the dangers of following unsanctioned religious trends. Omina Muidinova, three of her sons, her brother, and her son-in-law, all of whom had been arrested by police during the preceding months, were brought into the hall in handcuffs. The family was made to stand before the crowd, surrounded by guards, to hear the officials' accusations against them. One observer commented that the proceeding resembled a court hearing, and indeed it featured charges and judgment but it lacked a defense. The officials charged that Muidinova had conspired, "under the mask of Islam" with "ferocious religious extremists" such as IMU leader Juma Namangani, to establish an Islamic state in Uzbekistan.[643] The officials then called on citizens in attendance to give their opinions of Muidinova and her family. Several men stood up to condemn Muidinova, and some of these called even for punishment of her parents. Others demanded that the accused family be executed.[644] When

---

[640] Written report to Human Rights Watch from Akhmat Abdullaev, Namangan representative of the Human Rights Society of Uzbekistan, undated.

[641] Ibid.

[642] Ibid.

[643] Ibid.

[644] Ibid.

the officials instructed Muidinova to address the crowd, she said only that her relative, Akmal Ergashev, had persuaded her to become an observant Muslim and that she had subsequently urged others to become observant Muslims, to "embark on the true path of Islam."[645] After the rally, Muidinova and her relatives were returned to pre-trial detention. Two months later they were tried and sentenced to prison terms ranging from eleven to thirteen years on charges of Wahhabism and attempt to overthrow the state.

The technique of forced public humiliation has also been used against relatives of detainees. For example, after Imam Iuldashev's release, in late 1999, the authorities compelled his wife to attend a public denunciation of so-called Wahhabis.

Prior to the public denunciation, local authorities summoned Iuldashev's wife to two separate meetings at which they privately warned her and other independent Muslims about their religious practices. At the first meeting, at the mahalla center (a meeting house of the neighborhood council) in the Sobir Rakhimov district of Tashkent, the presiding officials included deputy police chief Jamal Suliev and the Sobir Rakhimov district procurator. In all, they had summoned about ten people "on the list," or registered with police, whom the meeting organizers referred to as "Wahhabis." The authorities explained that they had been brought there to receive a warning and charged that they were members of religious sects and "people who cover their faces."[646] A man introduced as an imam told participants that it was necessary to wear hijab only in Arab countries with desert sand and that Uzbekistan's climate did not require one to cover one's face. Moreover, he said, the directive to cover one's face, to wear hijab, is not written in the Koran.[647] One participant at the meeting recalled, "[Officer] Suliev scared us all. He said, 'We have helped the local police officers and they have guns and nightsticks and handcuffs [to use on you], and they can do anything, if you step out of line…' He said, 'This meeting is a

[645] Ibid.

[646] Human Rights Watch interview, name withheld, Tashkent, August 1, 2000

[647] Ibid.

warning and if you take another step out of line, the next place you'll be going is Jaslyk.'"[648]

The following day, the same individuals were instructed to visit Muhayo Saidova, from the district mayor's office, for one-on-one meetings. At these meetings, Saidova required that each person write a note swearing off any involvement with "religious sects."[649]

Two days later, twenty or so "Wahhabis," including Iuldashev's wife, were ordered by the local police officer to appear at the local schoolhouse, where about one hundred local residents also gathered. Presiding over the meeting were Dilbar Guliamova, chair of the central government Women's Committee; Muhayo Saidova; the district mayor; the district procurator; and representatives from the local mahalla committee.[650] "One by one, we were called up to say that we were against sects," recalled a participant. "They made one man take the Koran and swear he was not part of a sect."[651] Others were directed to ask forgiveness from the assembly, although Imam Iuldashev's wife was reportedly allowed to leave without being forced to do this.[652]

During the two-hour public meeting, the procurator focused his comments on well-known imams Obidkhon Kori Nazarov and Tulkin Kori Ergashev, calling them "murderers and terrorists."[653] He charged, "Your leaders, Tulkin Kori and Obid Kori, took your money and used you for terror, they leave blood on your hands, and we must punish them. These leaders must be punished; [otherwise] those who do not understand and follow them will end up answering for them."[654]

---

[648] Ibid.

[649] Ibid.

[650] Ibid.

[651] Ibid.

[652] Ibid.

[653] Ibid.

[654] Ibid.

Hate rallies organized against Imam Nazarov's wife, Munira Nasriddinova, and mother, Mukharramkhon Nazarova, followed a similar line. Nasriddinova described the first public denunciation that the two women were compelled to attend, on February 10, 2000, at a local school:

> They called me to the neighborhood meeting. The mahalla organized it. More than three hundred people were there. Most were from Beruni [her neighborhood in Tashkent]. Officials from the district police station and mahalla attended, as well as representatives from mosques, including the imam…Gulamkodir [presumably imam Gulamkodir Mirzaiakubov of the Al-Bukhari mosque in Tashkent]. Jamal Suliev, the deputy chief of the district police station was there. At first, the meeting started with officials calling Hizb ut-Tahrir followers terrorists and then they accused Obidkhon of being against democracy, saying that we [the family] were criminals and against independence.[655]

Nasriddinova said that a second meeting was held on February 17 and that Dilbar Guliamova, the head of the government's Women's Committee, and a representative of the Muslim Board of Uzbekistan were among the officials there who spoke against Nazarov and denounced his mother. Nasriddinova told Human Rights Watch:

> The head of the mahalla warned our neighbors not to talk to us, or else they would go to jail. At the meeting on the seventeenth, they said that from each mahalla there are already thirty or forty women on a list of people to arrest. Someone from the women's committee said this and also said that women shouldn't think that they will not be arrested [just because they are women]. 'We will arrest the women and put the children in orphanages,' they threatened.[656]

---

[655] Human Rights Watch interview with Munira Nasriddinova, Tashkent, February 19, 2000.

[656] Ibid.

In addition to issuing their own threats and condemnations, government officials called on others in the crowd to denounce the Nazarovs. Nasriddinova said, "One supposed witness said we hold religious meetings in our home. We now fear they will bring more pressure on us."[657]

The authorities also called on other subjects of the hate rally to address the gathering and express their contrition. Nasriddinova recalled that during the meeting on February 17, the officials called on a woman named Muiasar Azimjonova, who wore a headscarf with her face uncovered, "They called on her to ask for forgiveness. She instead began to criticize [officer] Suliev, so they turned off the microphone."[658] Another young woman from the neighborhood, named Halida, who prayed regularly and wore a headscarf, was also called upon to speak at the meeting.[659] Nasriddinova said, "They asked Halida why she was on the 'black list' and she said, 'because I wear a headscarf.' The officials got furious and said she was messing with politics."[660]

The public denunciations are also attempts to convince individuals, particularly those accused of "extremism," that they should inform on and condemn others like themselves, in order to show support for the state and official Islam. The elderly "Mukhtabar M." (not her real name) was released from prison in September 1999 after serving a ten-day administrative sentence for membership in Hizb ut-Tahrir and meeting with other women to discuss Islam. Local police and the mahalla committee in her area called a public meeting to denounce her and Hizb ut-Tahrir members in general.[661] According to Mukhtabar M., all the women in her neighborhood who wore headscarves were summoned to

[657] Ibid

[658] Ibid.

[659] According to Nasriddinova, a National Security Service agent regularly followed Halida and threatened her with arrest if she refused to give him information about her family members.

[660] Human Rights Watch interview with Munira Nasriddinova, Tashkent, February 19, 2000.

[661] Human Rights Watch interview, name withheld, Tashkent, February 2001.

the meeting. There, Tashkent City Imam Anvar Kori announced that all those in hijab were not required to wear this type of dress, and authorities called on those present to locate and report others who wore it. They warned the women that Hizb ut-Tahrir members were "dangerous" and told participants they should fear them and shun relatives who were members.[662]

While isolating independent Muslims from the rest of the community was evidently a goal of this public denunciation, it was not the result. Mukhtabar M. asserted that her neighbors understood and supported her, "They never scold me and are not afraid to talk to me; they help me."[663]

Authorities have organized repeated public denunciations of some families. Female relatives of independent Muslim prisoners staged a series of protests in Andijan in March and April 2001. Local mahalla committees there allegedly responded by intensifying the frequency of public denunciations, described by one Andijan rights activist as "little inquisitions."[664] The activist reported that in each neighborhood local authorities had targeted half a dozen relatives of religious prisoners whom they routinely harassed and publicly shamed.[665]

Even after authorities convicted Shukhrat Abdurakhimov, they did not cease persecution of his family. Local government authorities made Abdurakhimov's mother the subject of public denunciations at three public meetings, organized by the mahalla committee in her neighborhood. At those meetings, officials charged that the family was engaged in anti-state activities and branded Abdurakhimov an "enemy of the state." "Family members of arrested Muslims live in fear, because they [authorities] follow our every move," wrote one of Abdurakhimov's

---

[662] Ibid.

[663] Ibid.

[664] Human Rights Watch interview with a rights activist from Andijan, name withheld, Tashkent, April 20, 2001.

[665] Ibid.

relatives in an international appeal.[666] Abdurakhimov's mother was also compelled to report to police and representatives of her mahalla committee regarding her own activities, even her preferred candidate in the presidential elections.[667] Moreover, according to a person close to the case, the city procurator visited the school where she taught, to ask her supervisor if she was against the state, and then required her to write a statement to her students attesting that her son had "followed a wrong path."[668]

One woman told Human Rights Watch, "I have three sons in prison—one in Nukus, one in Karshi, and one in Tavaksai. They were accused of being members of Hizb ut-Tahrir...When there was a meeting, they called my sons 'enemies of the state.' There were people from the procuracy and the mayor's office there, and they called me there, and I was the only mother of Hizb ut-Tahrir members present."[669] Referring to herself and other mothers of arrested independent Muslims, she added, "We are all afraid."[670]

The Role of Quasi-official Actors and Groups

Sometimes it is not government officials and clergy who promote public humiliations but representatives of other state-approved entities—

[666] Written statement to then-U.S. Secretary of State Madeleine Albright from a relative of Shukhrat Abdurakhimov, name withheld, May 9, 2000.

[667] A representative of the Biktimir district mahalla committee visited Shukhrat Abdurakhimov's mother in October 1999, prior to parliamentary and presidential elections. The representative allegedly presented her with a document and told her, "If you are for Karimov, sign. If you are against him, don't bother." Human Rights Watch interview, name withheld, Tashkent, November, 1999. Commenting on this incident, Abdurakhimov's mother told Human Rights Watch, "They only came to me, not to other neighbors." She told them she had not made up her mind, and refused to sign. Human Rights Watch interview with the mother of Shukhrat Abdurakhimov, Tashkent, November, 1999. Police later detained Abdurakhimov's wife just prior to the presidential election.

[668] Human Rights Watch interview with a person close to Shukhrat Abdurakhimov, name withheld, Tashkent, November 1999.

[669] Human Rights Watch interview, name withheld, Tashkent, March 1, 2000.

[670] Ibid.

operating with at least the tolerance of the state. A young schoolteacher in Andijan told Human Rights Watch that members of a pro-government political party organized a "hate rally" against her because a relative had been arrested for membership in Hizb ut-Tahrir: "After my brother was arrested, I had problems at work. The leader of Fidokarlar [a registered political party] organized a public meeting and called my brother an 'enemy of the state.' They said I was from a bad family. They organized the meeting at the school where I work."[671] The government's conduct encourages this sort of initiative. A rights activist from the Fergana Valley reported that officers from the Ministry of Internal Affairs and procuracy officials, as well as members of the state-sponsored Komolot youth group (formerly the Young Communist League), regularly attend meetings organized by mahalla committees to denounce independent Muslims.[672] He said that the meetings usually include announcements of arrests of independent Muslims and warnings to other residents not to follow their example.[673]

Denunciations in State-Run Mosques

Public denunciations also take place in official mosques, just prior to or after prayer services. In these cases the state-appointed imam makes a general statement warning of the consequences of following the "wrong" religious path and then calls on "volunteers" to come forward to admit their guilt to the congregation and ask for forgiveness. The pool of "volunteers" is, however, comprised of detainees who have been brought to the mosque by police and who sit, in some cases, handcuffed to plain clothes security agents, while waiting their turn at self-denunciation. Judging from the statements of contrition Human Rights Watch was able to obtain, they are highly scripted. Those who "volunteered" to make such speeches had been promised that they would be released in exchange, but in fact some remained in custody after the event, and others were released but rearrested within months or even days, and were subsequently convicted and sent to prison.

---

[671] Human Rights Watch interview, name withheld, Andijan, May 18, 2000.

[672] Human Rights Watch interview, name withheld, Tashkent, February 27, 2001.

[673] Ibid.

Official clergy have on occasion incorporated denunciations of independent Muslims into their religious services. For example, according to a local resident and human rights defender in Fergana city, Imam Tokhir Kori of the state-sanctioned Juma mosque, the largest in that area, called on worshipers at his services to shun "Wahhabis" and members of Hizb ut-Tahrir and to "drive them from our midst."[674]

A more elaborate example of the role of official clergy appears in the case of six men detained in January 2000 for private study of Islam. They were forced to make public statements of contrition at state-run mosques in exchange for promises that their cooperation would absolve them.[675] A relative of Murat Kosymov recalled the police manipulation to coerce him to beg for forgiveness before the congregation in exchange for promises of freedom:

> He was detained on January 7 for the first time, along with others in this case. They were told, 'If you ask for forgiveness, the state will forgive you.' [Police] took them to a mosque and then released them, but later detained them again. The police shamed them on television, where they [also] asked for forgiveness. They said they would let them go.[676]

At the subsequent trial, others described the public shaming. Tokhir Obidov's attorney pointed out that his client was detained first in May 1998, then again in January 2000, when he was taken to a mosque, interrogated before others, and required to ask for forgiveness, which he

---

674 Human Rights Watch interview with a local rights defender, name withheld, Tashkent, February 27, 2001.

675 These men would later be tried among seventeen so-called Wahhabis in August 2000 in Tashkent City Court. See "Imams, Their Followers, and 'Wahhabis'" in Chapter III.

676 Human Rights Watch interview, name withheld, Tashkent, August 4, 2000. Dilshod Unusov's lawyer also confirmed in court that the men were first detained "and released after asking forgiveness, although they didn't commit any criminal acts." Human Rights Watch unofficial transcript, Tashkent City Court, Judge Sharipov presiding, August 4, 2000.

did. Then he was detained again in February 2000.[677] After police allegedly tortured Anvar Mirakhmedov and forced him to confess to false charges, they took him to a series of mosques where he was compelled to call on young people not to follow the path of "Wahhabism."[678] Faizullo Saipov told the court that police also had compelled him to give a penitent speech before those assembled for prayer at a mosque, to warn those in attendance of the harmfulness of "Wahhabism" and "extremism."[679] Saipov recalled, "The first time we were detained, they said, 'There are thirty of you, the President knows who you are.' They took me to meetings three times, and I asked for forgiveness."[680]

The detainees were brought to a number of mosques for public shaming, among them to the Kokcha mosque in Tashkent. Human Rights Watch obtained a videotape of the imam's sermon given on January 21, 2000 at the Kokcha mosque and the detainees' pleas for forgiveness. Police brought the detainees in handcuffs during prayer time; the video shows Imam Rakhmatullo opening the event by pointing out the detainees and plainclothes police in the front row of the assembly. He then proceeded with a markedly political sermon that illuminated his role as state functionary and blurred the line between the mosque and the Ministry of Internal Affairs.[681] Among his comments:

> What was the greatest quality that our Prophet Muhammad possessed? He always generously forgave guilt if a guilty person came to him with a confession

---

[677] Human Rights Watch unofficial transcript, Tashkent City Court, Judge Sharipov presiding, August 4, 2000.

[678] Ibid.

[679] Ibid.

[680] Ibid.

[681] Imam Rakhmatullo allegedly testified in court against accused Wahhabi Ziakhonov, stating that the defendant traveled with Obidkhon Nazarov to Mecca in 1985. Rakhmatullo allegedly testified that Nazarov met there with "Wahhabis" and that since Nazarov was a "Wahhabi" and Ziakhonov was his student, he claimed, then Ziakhonov was also a "Wahhabi." Ziakhonov was sentenced to eight years in prison. Human Rights Watch interview with rights defender Vasila Inolatova, Tashkent, July 2000.

> and asked forgiveness. Even in cases where someone came to him intending to kill him, he called on that person with kind words to become a Muslim and forgave him...Our respected President also possesses these same qualities. Even though criminals, hating our independence, slander the President and work against his policies, if they come to him and ask for forgiveness, regretting what they have done, even if they came back from abroad, the President will say, "I forgive them!" Despite it all he sticks to his conviction. Those who have gone astray can come to the court, to the procuracy, to law enforcement agencies, to their police departments, mahalla committees, or local mosques and ask forgiveness, and the government will forgive them. No one will cause them harm.[682]

The imam then went on to detail his interview with a recent group of religious detainees on police premises:

> A few days ago we were invited to the Tashkent UVD [city police station], where several people detained for distributing leaflets were being held. We talked with them about how it's considered a crime to call for a coup d'etat, and that it is punished with imprisonment of five to twelve years. Then they told us that, wanting to study religion and the Koran, they had started down the wrong path. "Here in the basement we're suffering, our parents and families are suffering... Now we understand that we went astray. It won't happen again. We ask for forgiveness, we repent."[683]

The next stage of the "sermon" involved a live, public shaming of the detainees in question, introduced by the imam, who presented the men's

---

[682] Unofficial transcript, videotaped speech of Imam Rakhmatullo Kori, in Kokcha mosque, Tashkent, January 21, 2000, translated from Uzbek.

[683] Ibid.

experience as a cautionary tale of the dangers of studying Islam outside of the state mosque:

> You are all witnesses to the fact that they will in fact, taking the Koran in their hands and swearing in the name of Allah, ask for forgiveness and they will here and now be released from custody. And they will return to their families. If anyone among you wants to study religion, to study Koran, come to the mosque. Our respected imams will teach you Islam, religion, the Koran, and won't take a single som from you for it... Now I will give the floor to our misguided sons.[684]

One detainee told the congregation:

> We started some lessons, beginning by learning the Koran and hadith, it then turned into instruction in Wahhabism and we unwittingly fell into this path. Thank you to the authorities who took us and told us that this path which we were on was incorrect... they sat with us for three days without any sort of force and explained to us in a correct way that the path we were on was damaging to our religion and our politics. We came to understand that we had entered onto a mistaken path. After that I would say to my contemporaries that if they were studying these things in secret or were reading unofficial literature that they should repent and turn away from this path. Or they should go to the authorities and repent and appeal to them. Nobody is going to pressure anyone. Here from among us, there are some guys who went and repented; they were then let be, nothing at all happened to them. I stand before you holding the Koran in my hand admitting my fault and I swear before Allah never to return to that path.[685]

---

[684] Ibid.

[685] Ibid.

The remarks of subsequent detainees followed the same pattern. One man identified as Alisher Zakhidov reiterated Imam Rakhmatullo's message that private study of Islam was incorrect and that those interested in obtaining Islamic education should turn to the state-run mosques, "We were secretly acquiring knowledge... we later embarked on the Wahhabi path. I swear to Allah that I'm never going to return to that path and if I decide that I'm going to acquire knowledge, like the respected imam said, everyone should go to his local mosque and if this is asked of them the imams will help to the extent that they are able."[686]

As noted above, the men who expressed their contrition were not all freed exactly as promised. Ibrahim Obidov's lawyer said that, even after his client's participation in the Kokcha gathering, police refused to release Obidov until he also asked forgiveness at a public denunciation organized by his mahalla committee, and paid a fine. Less than a month later, on February 10, police detained Obidov again. Forced, according to his lawyer, to "admit to things he did not do," Obidov was sentenced to ten years in prison on August 21, 2000.[687]

---

[686] Ibid.

[687] Human Rights Watch unofficial transcript, Tashkent City Court, Judge Sharipov presiding, August 4, 2000

Fatima Mukhadirova with photos of her dead son, Muzafar Avazov, in Tashkent. Avazov, convicted for membership in Hizb ut-Tahrir, was apparently tortured to death in 2002 while in custody in Jaslyk prison.

IV. TORTURE AND DUE PROCESS VIOLATIONS

The process by which law enforcement agents carry out the arrest, detention, and interrogation of independent Muslims involves a series of violations of due process and other basic rights. Save for exceptional cases, criminal suspects are kept in custody prior to trial. Uzbekistan's legal system does not allow for habeas corpus, or judicial review of arrest.[688] Police and security agents exploit this legal void by carrying out unsanctioned detentions, illegal searches, and planting or fabricating evidence to justify arrests. They also deny detainees the right to legal counsel, fail to notify their families of their detention, and then isolate them from their families.[689] In addition, the torture of independent Muslim detainees has become an unmistakable element of the campaign against independent Islam. Police and security agents use torture to coerce confessions and testimony from detainees and witnesses, in violation of Uzbekistan's obligations under the International Covenant on Civil and Political Rights and the Convention against Torture and

---

[688] The lack of judicial oversight of detention is a glaring violation of the ICCPR's article 9(3), which states: "Anyone arrested or detained on a criminal charge shall be brought promptly before a judge or other officer authorized by law to exercise judicial power and shall be entitled to trial within a reasonable time or to release." Because the procuracy exercises executive, not judicial, power, procuracy review of arrest cannot be interpreted as the judicial review of detention envisaged in the ICCPR's article 9.

[689] Denial of access to counsel violates principle 8 of the U.N. Basic Principles on the Role of Lawyers, which states that, "All arrested, detained or imprisoned persons shall be provided with adequate opportunities, time and facilities to be visited by and to communicate and consult with a lawyer, without delay, interception or censorship and in full confidentiality. Such consultations may be within sight, but not within the hearing, of law enforcement officials." Abuse of these rights are common in all criminal investigations in Uzbekistan. The Uzbek criminal justice system lacks procedural safeguards for detainees and criminal defendants, which police and security agents exploit in the campaign against independent Islam. It grants the prosecution wide powers concerning pre-trial custody and access to lawyers, and access to forensic evidence. Detainees do not have the right to appeal the lawfulness of their detention or to protest ill-treatment before a judge until their case goes to court, an egregious violation of international law governing detainees' rights. While the code of criminal procedure provides for release of accused persons on bail during the preliminary investigation phase, custody during investigation and prior to trial is the rule, rather than the exception. The domestic legal framework for due process is detailed in "'And It Was Hell All Over Again…': Torture in Uzbekistan," *A Human Rights Watch Report*, Vol. 12, No. 12(D), December 2000.

Other Cruel and Inhuman or Degrading Treatment or Punishment.[690] This chapter documents these abuses during the preliminary investigation phase, before suspects are formally charged, when the most severe abuse takes place. Due process violations that occur during investigation: unsanctioned arrests and searches, the planting of evidence, incommunicado detentions, and the denial of access to counsel are described in "Unsanctioned Arrests, Searches, and Planting of Evidence." "Torture and Mistreatment in Pre-trial Detention" presents evidence of torture of independent Muslim detainees in pre-trial custody.

Agents from the Ministry of Internal Affairs' Department for Combating Corruption, Racketeering, and Terrorism, and the ministry's special forces (OMON), have taken the lead in searches, detentions, interrogations, and torture of independent Muslims.[691] As the testimony of numerous witnesses indicates, the National Security Service is also involved in this campaign and in particular the torture of Muslim detainees.

Unsanctioned Arrests, Searches, and Planting of Evidence

The right to protection from unlawful and arbitrary interference in one's privacy, family, and home is set out in international legal instruments. In particular, articles 9 and 16 of the ICCPR. The General Comment to article 16 states that, "Searches of a person's home should be restricted

---

[690] The ICCPR's article 7 states, "No one shall be subjected to torture or to cruel, inhuman or degrading treatment or punishment." Uzbekistan became a party to the Convention against Torture and Other Cruel and Inhuman or Degrading Treatment or Punishment on August 31, 1995. Its failure to comply with many of the convention's articles regarding the prevention of torture and accountability is detailed in Human Rights Watch, "And It Was Hell All Over Again."

[691] OMON is an acronym for Otriady Militsii Osobogo Naznachenia, Russian for Special Task Militia Unit.

to a search for necessary evidence and should not be allowed to amount to harassment."[692]

Domestic law in Uzbekistan similarly sets out guidelines for law enforcement in conducting detentions and searches.[693] Uzbekistan's Criminal Procedure Code stipulates that, except in cases of particular urgency, searches must be sanctioned by a warrant from an interrogator, investigator, or court prior to being carried out. The warrant must be presented to the subject and should declare specifically what is being sought and who is accused of possession of material relevant to a case. Persons presented with such an order are to be given the opportunity to voluntarily hand over the materials being sought. Uzbekistan's law also provides that subjects of a search have the right to be present during all stages of the police investigation, to have any comments recorded in the search report, and to have witnesses present during the search. It states that law enforcement officials must also have due cause to carry out a detention. Uzbek police must identify themselves upon detaining someone, including by providing identification documents to the detainee upon request.

The reality of the police conduct of searches and detentions or arrests departs radically from the guidelines in the law books. Police have consistently violated due process in conducting arrests and searches of independent Muslims. Officers not only fail or refuse to identify themselves, but often take measures to disguise their identity, such as by wearing black ski masks during raids. Charges brought subsequent to a detention often have only a remote connection to the purpose used initially to justify searching a home or placing someone in custody. The laws on search and seizure are routinely undermined, as when police conduct searches without a warrant, without announcing themselves or giving any declaration regarding the materials being sought. In flagrant violation of due process is the regular police practice of planting

---

[692] Paragraph 8, Human Rights Committee, General Comment 16, (Twenty-third session, 1988), Compilation of General Comments and General Recommendations Adopted by Human Rights Treaty Bodies, U.N. Doc. HRI\GEN\1\Rev.1 at 21 (1994).

[693] Articles 157 to 161, 221 and 224 refer specifically to the rules regulating searches and detentions, Criminal Procedure Code of the Republic of Uzbekistan, 1999.

evidence on a person or in his or her home in order to justify a detention. Measures meant to protect the subjects of a search, such as recourse to comment in the search report and the right to have witnesses present are often not complied with; and in many cases police simply force the subjects of a search to relinquish these rights.

Contrary to the spirit of Uzbekistan's domestic law and the stipulations of international law, police and security forces also harass and intimidate the subjects of searches and detentions. The force deployed to conduct arrests and raids merits mention here. Uniformed officers and armed agents in civilian clothes typically work together; soldiers are used to block off entire neighborhoods during raids on private homes. The raids themselves have often been conducted at night. Masked armed officers in dark clothes scale the walls of domestic courtyards and invade family homes, often in the presence of small children. The operations have been conducted as though the suspects were heavily armed and militarily organized. In many cases, however, even after one or more thorough police searches, the suspects are found to "possess" perhaps a few bullets, a lone hand grenade, a religious magazine, or some leaflets.

- Police used the tactics outlined above when they stormed the home of Imam Abdurakhim Abdurakhmonov well after midnight on June 18, 1998. According to an eyewitness, some ten to fifteen armed officers in civilian clothes climbed over the wall into the family courtyard, broke into the house, and pulled the imam from his bed.[694]

- The mother of one young man tried along with fourteen others in December 1998 on religion-related charges, in a case that came to be known as "the Andijan 15," recalled her terror the day police raided her home to arrest her son. She told Human Rights Watch that before dawn one day in April 1998, an entire busload of armed and uniformed OMON officers stormed the family home and surrounded the area. They arrested the woman's son from his place of work nearby, but continued to occupy the house until evening. Without showing any

---

[694] Human Rights Watch interview with Muborak Abdurakhmonova, Tashkent, May 26, 2000; and open letter from Muborak Abdurakhmonova, 1998. This case is described in detail in "Imams, Their Followers, and 'Wahhabis'" in Chapter III.

warrant for a search, the OMON officers ransacked the premises, tore up floorboards, and confiscated five books of hadith in Arabic.[695]

Arrests without Warrant

Security agents carrying out arrests of independent Muslims have often lied about their purpose. They have stated, for instance, that a person was being taken in for "informal questioning" or was needed as a witness in a case. This obviates the need for an arrest warrant, quiets relatives' protests, and buys time before the family starts making inquiries regarding the detainee's status, whereabouts, and physical condition.

- When Ministry of Internal Affairs officers took Imam Iuldashev into the ministry's custody in February 1999, they told him that he was being taken in for informal questioning and would be released promptly.[696] Upon arrival at the ministry, Iuldashev was beaten and placed under arrest on charges of illegal possession of narcotics.[697]

- One woman whose son was arrested in May 2000 told Human Rights Watch, "The police came and said they just wanted to question him, to show him some photographs because he had witnessed a murder."[698] The woman's son did not serve as a witness in any murder trial and was instead arrested and convicted for violation of laws against unregistered religious activity.[699]

- "He was taken on February 10, 2000, at around 5:00 or 6:00 a.m. They said he would be back at 3:00. It was four days before we even

---

[695] Human Rights Watch interview, name withheld, Andijan, May 19, 2000.

[696] Unofficial transcript, Iakasarai District Court, Tashkent, May 11, 1999, written by independent trial monitors, names withheld, June 1999. The Ministry of Internal Affairs building in Tashkent contains an investigative isolator and is the site of interrogations.

[697] Human Rights Watch interview with Irina Mikulina, Iuldashev's attorney, Tashkent, June 10, 1999; and Human Rights Watch interview, name withheld, Tashkent, August 1, 2000.

[698] Human Rights Watch interview, name withheld, February 27, 2001.

[699] Ibid.

found out where he was," recalled a relative of one of fifteen men arrested in Tashkent for studying Islam in private and convicted on charges of anti-state activity in November 2000.[700]

- The mother of one religious Muslim prisoner described her son's arrest in his home in Tashkent in late 1999, "…They took him and said it would be only for one hour. The next day I went to the station. They opened a door to let me hear that he was alive…."[701]

Unsanctioned Searches

In some cases the arresting officers show a search or arrest warrant, but in many cases they do not. Identifying documents are sometimes shown, sometimes not. The officers often act with violence toward unarmed relatives of the person they have come to detain. Detainees and family members are forced, through threats, to sign search reports confirming what officers have done and what they have supposedly found. Relatives are seldom given a copy to keep for future reference or use in legal proceedings.

During earlier stages of the campaign against independent Muslims, the courts regularly convicted defendants based on the claims made by police that they had found narcotics, weapons, or ammunition in the defendants' homes or on their person. In more recent years, such evidence continues to be produced and used to justify arrest, but has sometimes been discarded and excluded from the criminal case once police have secured a confession.[702] In order to verify that evidence has been "found" at the suspect's home, police sometimes bring their own witnesses for use in court.

---

[700] Human Rights Watch unofficial transcript, Tashkent City Court hearing held in the Akmal Ikramov District Court building, Tashkent, November 3, 2000. The case of the fifteen accused "Wahhabis" is described above, in "Imams, Their Followers, and 'Wahhabis'" in Chapter III.

[701] Human Rights Watch interview with the mother of a man accused of membership in Hizb ut-Tahrir, name withheld at her request, Tashkent, March 1, 2000.

[702] See "Threats of Torture" in Chapter IV.

- Police forced their way into the home of Abdurashid Isakhojaev and failed to present his wife with a warrant certifying their right to search the premises.[703] In the absence of witnesses, the officers then claimed to find a grenade in the home; this was used to justify Isakhojaev's arrest—which had actually taken place hours earlier.[704]

- According to eyewitnesses, thirteen armed SNB officers dressed in camouflage raided the Andijan home of Shukhrat Parpiev on April 19, 1998. The officers failed to produce a warrant to search the home or to summon independent witnesses to observe the operation.[705] Persons close to Parpiev told Human Rights Watch that the SNB officers searched the house for nine hours, until one officer planted four bullets and one wire meant for explosives in the family home.[706] Family members witnessed the officer's actions and called out to alert Parpiev's father.[707] The planted evidence was used to justify Parpiev's arrest, but the charges were later dropped when the case went to court.[708]

Human Rights Watch received reports from rights activists in the Fergana Valley and Tashkent that men feared the planting of false evidence by police to such an extent that some resorted to sewing up the pockets of their pants. During its research into arrests of independent Muslims in the Fergana Valley in 1998, Human Rights Watch also found that, "…men in that area tried to wear clothing without pockets to help

---

[703] Written complaint addressed to the Chairman of the Tashkent City Court, from attorney Hamid Zainutdinov, December 24, 1998; and Human Rights Watch interview with Sharifa Isakhojaeva, Tashkent, June 1, 2000. This case is described above, in "Imams, Their Followers, and 'Wahhabis'" in Chapter III.

[704] Human Rights Watch interview with Sharifa Isakhojaeva, Tashkent, June 1, 2000.

[705] Human Rights Watch interview with persons close to Shukhrat Parpiev, names withheld, Andijan, May 18, 2000.

[706] Ibid. The name of the officer is on file with Human Rights Watch.

[707] Ibid.

[708] Ibid. Parpiev was nonetheless convicted on unrelated charges and sent to Jaslyk prison, where he died from torture. See "Torture and Mistreatment in Pre-trial Detention" in Chapter IV.

deter such commonly used set-ups."[709] One young man detained by police in Tashkent in 1998 kept his hands in his pockets during police interrogation to avoid having contraband planted on him.[710]

- Even crude planting of evidence has proven effective for police. The first time police arrested Shukhrat Abdurakhimov was on September 19, 1998. Officers entered the family home without a warrant and, searching the premises, claimed to find marijuana on his person.[711] Authorities later claimed the search was part of a regular passport check in the area.[712] The next day, Abdurakhimov's relatives were told that he had escaped from police custody, a story they did not believe.[713] Abdurakhimov reportedly came home from time to time and was in the family apartment on the night of April 12, 1999, when police raided the house and arrested him again.[714] Arresting officers allegedly struck Abdurakhimov's wife repeatedly. After taking Abdurakhimov away, police returned to search the family home, without producing a search warrant and refusing to identify themselves.[715] An eyewitness to the search told Human Rights Watch, "I watched them ransack the apartment and they found nothing. Then I saw one man take a paper out of his sleeve, drop it among the children's toys and then 'find' it and unwrap it. It had a bullet in it. He was in civilian clothes and he refused

---

[709] Human Rights Watch, "Crackdown in The Farghona Valley: Arbitrary Arrests and Religious Discrimination," *A Human Rights Watch Report*, Vol. 10, No. 4 (D) May 1998.

[710] Human Rights Watch interview with Sharifa Isakhojaeva regarding the detention of her son, Abdurashid Isakhojaev, Tashkent, June 1, 2000.

[711] Written statement delivered to Human Rights Watch, signed by a relative of Shukhrat Abdurakhimov, name withheld, October 31, 1999.

[712] Tashkent Province Court verdict issued by Judge B.U. Ergashev, August 13, 1999.

[713] Human Rights Watch interview with persons close to Shukhrat Abdurakhimov, names withheld, November 4, 1999.

[714] Human Rights Watch interview with a person close to Shukhrat Abdurakhimov, name withheld, Tashkent, November 4, 1999; and Human Rights Watch interview, name withheld, Tashkent, July 19, 2000.

[715] Human Rights Watch interview with persons close to Shukhrat Abdurakhimov, names withheld, Tashkent, November 4, 1999; and Tashkent Province Court verdict, issued by Judge B.U. Ergashev, August 13, 1999. Court documents place the date of arrest as March 12, 1999, not Aprll 12.

to identify himself."[716] Abdurakhimov's mother, present during the search, accused the officer of wrongdoing and tried to snatch the bullet away from him, whereupon he grabbed the elderly woman, twisted her arm behind her back and threw her to the floor.[717] The officers pulled the family's religious books off the shelves and photographed them. They also asked Abdurakhimov's mother where he had gotten his copy of the Koran and from whom.[718] Officers wrote up a report of the search, claiming they had found marijuana on Abdurakhimov and religious books and one bullet in his home, and had the report signed by the witnesses they had brought along. The police investigator returned later to the Abdurakhimov home and forced the young man's mother to sign the report as well, despite her objections that the evidence supposedly found had in fact been planted.[719] The family was not given a copy of this report.

In August 1999 the Tashkent Province Court tried Shukhrat Abdurakhimov and two others on charges related to alleged membership in Hizb ut-Tahrir. Among the charges against Abdurakhimov were allegations of possessing marijuana and one bullet. The police held Abdurakhimov incommunicado for five months during which time he was interrogated and eventually signed a statement incriminating himself on the charges of illegal possession of narcotics and ammunition. He is currently serving a seventeen-year term in Jaslyk prison. In the court verdict against Abdurakhimov the judge noted that among other evidence of criminality police had found "eight notebooks with religious notes" in the young man's home.[720]

- The wife of one of the defendants in the Tashkent City Court trial of twelve men accused of Hizb ut-Tahrir membership in May 1999

---

[716] Human Rights Watch interview with persons close to Shukhrat Abdurakhimov, names withheld, Tashkent, November 4, 1999.

[717] Ibid.

[718] Ibid.

[719] Human Rights Watch interview, name withheld, Tashkent, July 19, 2000.

[720] Tashkent Province Court verdict issued by Judge B. U. Ergashev, August 13, 1999.

similarly charged that evidence of drug possession had been falsified.[721] She claimed she had never seen narcotics in her home and further noted that the judge in the case failed to ask where or how her husband had supposedly obtained the narcotics.[722]

The defendant's wife described the incident and noted that the planting of evidence on her husband had been denounced by witnesses, in spite of police pressure. During the summer of 1998, she said, police had stopped her husband's car, badly beaten him and some of his co-workers in the street, and then arrested them.[723] Her husband, she said, felt police put something in his pants pocket. At the police station, he reportedly refused to take the planted evidence out of his pocket, stating that it did not belong to him. Eventually he removed the narcotics from his pocket, again insisting that the drugs were not his. Two strangers brought in off the street to serve as witnesses to the body search saw him remove the packet and heard his protests. They refused to sign the police report stating that drugs were found on the man.[724] Police found their position unacceptable. The arrest had taken place at about 11:30 a.m. The witnesses were kept at the police station until 2:00 a.m. the next day, at which point they finally agreed to sign the police statement. In court, however, they testified that they had been threatened by police and frightened into signing the statement.[725]

Planting of Islamic Literature

Particularly after February 1999, police planted banned Islamic literature, often Hizb ut-Tahrir literature and the Al-Vai magazine, to incriminate independent Muslims, including those who were not affiliated with or sympathetic to the Hizb ut-Tahrir organization. This phenomenon

---

[721] This case is described in detail in "Hizb ut-Tahrir" in Chapter II.

[722] Human Rights Watch interview with the wife of one defendant, interviewee asked not to be named, Tashkent, May 14, 1999.

[723] Ibid.

[724] Ibid.

[725] Ibid.

seemed especially prevalent in the Namangan province of the Fergana Valley.

- Following the June 1999 arrest of Hizb ut-Tahrir member Shoknoza Musaeva, Tashkent police conducted a search of her home without family members or witnesses present.[726] During the search, which was videotaped, police allegedly planted Hizb ut-Tahrir books and leaflets, which they then claimed to find among Musaeva's belongings.[727] The possession of this literature along with the allegation that Musaeva used it to teach others the ideas of Hizb ut-Tahrir provided the basis of the state's case against the twenty-nine-year-old woman.[728] Musaeva was sentenced to seven years in prison.[729]

- An eyewitness charged that police also planted Hizb ut-Tahrir literature in the home of Musaeva's neighbor, who was arrested along with one of Musaeva's brothers just two weeks after her own detention. Police claimed to have found the group's literature in Mirabid Iakiaev's home, but an eyewitness present during the police search told Human Rights Watch that officers found nothing incriminating.[730] The eyewitness further stated that she saw the report that officers originally wrote at the scene attesting to having found nothing illegal.[731] The later police claims were included in the indictment against Iakiaev but, interestingly, the Chirchik City Court found that the relevant charge—that Iakiaev possessed "materials containing ideas of religious extremism, separatism, or fundamentalism"—had not been proven

---

[726] Human Rights Watch interview, name withheld, Tashkent, November 3, 1999.

[727] Human Rights Watch interview, name withheld, Tashkent, November, 3, 1999; and Human Rights Watch interview with rights defender Mahbuba Kosymova, Tashkent, June 22, 1999.

[728] Urta-Chirchik District Court verdict, issued by Judge T. Sh. Zainutdinov, August 12, 1999.

[729] Ibid. This case is described above, in "Hizb ut-Tahrir" in Chapter II.

[730] Chirchik City Court verdict, issued by Judge A. A. Kamilov, August 15, 1999; and Human Rights Watch interview with Iakiaev's mother, Bakhrid Iakiaeva, Tashkent, April 13, 2000.

[731] Ibid.

during the trial. The judge, however, found Iakiaev guilty of anti-state activity and sentenced him to five years in prison.[732]

According to a rights activist in Fergana city, the majority of independent Muslims arrested in the Fergana province were charged with "Wahhabism" rather than membership in Hizb ut-Tahrir.[733] He noted, however, that police officers and investigators often failed to distinguish between so-called Wahhabis and members of Hizb ut-Tahrir. For example, police planted Hizb ut-Tahrir leaflets on suspected "Wahhabis" to justify arrest. "Leaflets are more popular now than bullets or drugs," the activist said, describing police tactics.[734] In court, the accused were referred to as "Wahhabis" and not tried for Hizb ut-Tahrir membership.[735]

- In May 1999 police arrested an elderly man from Namangan for "illegally going on Hajj" and accused him of Wahhabism. According to the man, officers planted Hizb ut-Tahrir leaflets in his house to justify the arrest. On the strength of police claims regarding the literature and testimony given by a witness whom the accused man said was a complete stranger, the Namangan Province Court sentenced him to three and a half years in prison on charges of anti-constitutional activity.[736] The man was imprisoned in Almalik prison and later released under the 2001 presidential amnesty.[737] Another Namangan man, who was also sent to prison for three years and subsequently released under presidential amnesty gave a similar account of local police planting leaflets in his home.[738]

---

[732] Chirchik City Court verdict, issued by Judge A. A. Kamilov, August 15, 1999.

[733] Human Rights Watch interview with a local rights defender, name withheld, Tashkent, February 27, 2001.

[734] Ibid.

[735] Ibid.

[736] The man was also indicted and convicted on charges of crossing the Uzbek border without an exit visa.

[737] Human Rights Watch interview with released prisoner, name withheld at his request, Namangan, July 11, 2001.

[738] Human Rights Watch interview with a second released prisoner, name withheld at his request, Namangan, July 11, 2001.

Police have also frequently confiscated sanctioned religious texts—such as the Koran and works of Islamic scholar Al-Bukhari—and called them prohibited or "extremist" literature. Such materials, if used in prosecutions, has not generally been cited as evidence of criminality but rather of a general fanaticism in religious matters. In the cases reviewed by Human Rights Watch, sanctioned literature was usually returned to the family of a detainee after he had signed a self-incriminating statement.

Incommunicado Detention

Many of those arrested on religion-related charges have been kept for days and even months in the basements of police stations, where conditions were particularly harsh. They were held incommunicado, isolated from family visitors, legal counsel, fellow detainees, and any possible impartial police authorities. This in turn facilitated torture. The three cases described below illustrate this pattern of detention in basement cells:

- Abdurashid Isakhojaev told his mother that police kept him in the basement of the Ministry of Internal Affairs for the first twenty-four days of his detention in 1998. Isakhojaev alleged that officers tortured him while he was confined to the basement, causing serious injury.[739]

- Accused of being a Wahhabi, Khusan Maksudov testified in court to his fear of the Ministry of Internal Affairs (MVD) basement, where he was held from July 21 to August 10, 2000. "When I was taken in on July 21, the next day, I heard a story that some people die in the MVD, and I saw a person who had lost consciousness during interrogation. Even before that, I heard a lot of rumors about the basement...so I was very afraid to be there [and] I admitted easily to anything they accused me of…."[740]

---

[739] Human Rights Watch interview with Sharifa Isakhojaeva, Tashkent, June 1, 2000.

[740] Human Rights Watch unofficial transcript, Tashkent City Court hearing held in the Akmal Ikramov District Court bulding, Tashkent, February 7, 2001.

▪ A relative of accused Hizb ut-Tahrir member Ulmasbek Khakimov, arrested on December 15, 1998, alleged that police kept him in the basement of the Ministry of Internal Affairs for a month and a half.[741] Police also kept his co-defendant, Danior Khojimetov, in the basement for the first month of pre-trial detention.[742]

Police routinely fail to notify families of religious detainees as to their relatives' whereabouts. And even when a family is notified of a detainee's whereabouts in custody or is told the identity of the arresting officers and is therefore able to deduce a detainee's whereabouts, police and procuracy authorities routinely deny anyone access to the detainee. In addition to being an abuse in itself, preventing relatives from seeing detainees in custody increases the risk of torture. It also impedes a family's efforts to arrange for legal counsel to protect the detainee's rights during the initial investigation period. In various cases described above in this report, detainees have endured weeks or months incommunicado: Shukhrat Abdurakhimov, five months; Mirzakarim Avazov, seven months; Imam Abdurakhim Abdurakhmonov, two months; Komoliddin Sattarov, three months; and Gairat Sabirov, five months.

▪ A relative of accused Hizb ut-Tahrir member Tolkhon Riksiev told Human Rights Watch that police had held the twenty-nine-year-old incommunicado for six months during pre-trial detention. Officials failed even to officially notify his family of his arrest or his whereabouts in custody.[743]

▪ In November 1999 a relative of Dilmurod Juraev who witnessed his arrest told Human Rights Watch, "He was arrested two months ago and I am still looking for him... They took him from home and planted drugs on him, after they found nothing in a search of our house."[744]

---

[741] Human Rights Watch interview, name withheld, Tashkent, July 12, 1999.

[742] Ibid.

[743] Human Rights Watch interview, name withheld, Tashkent, June 21, 1999.

[744] Human Rights Watch interview with a relative of Dilmurod Juraev, name withheld, Tashkent, November 18, 1999. Court documents indicate that police arrested Juraev on

▪ A relative of accused Hizb ut-Tahrir member Khikmat Rasulov recalled the family's difficulty in locating the young man following his January 12, 1999 arrest by armed soldiers and plainclothes officers from Tashkent police headquarters: "We tried to go to the MVD and called [the police], but they never answered. After two to three weeks, I saw him in Tashkent prison."[745]

The mother of one of Rasulov's co-defendants related police obfuscation at the time of her son's arrest. She said that when officers took him into custody on the night of February 20, 1999, they refused to show identification and said that they were simply taking him in for a few questions and would release him shortly. That night, his relatives went to their local police station and waited until 3:00 a.m., at which time officers said they would receive news at 5:00 a.m. At 5:00 a.m. the family was told that the young man had been taken to the Ministry of Internal Affairs. There, they were told to go to the Tashkent city police station. The officers at the Tashkent city police station told them to go back to Tashkent police headquarters. There, almost twenty-four hours after the young man's arrest, at 11:00 p.m., the authorities told the family to come back the next day. Finally, on February 23, 1999, police investigator Ilias Umarzakov of Tashkent police headquarters acknowledged that he had the young man in custody, and that he was under arrest and would not be released.[746]

▪ In at least one case, the whereabouts of a man taken into custody presumably on charges related to his religious belief or affiliation were never confirmed. Bahodir Hasanov, thirty-eight years old at the time of his arrest, was a French language instructor at the Alliance Francaise in Tashkent. Although not particularly pious himself, he came from a family of observant and strongly independent Muslims.[747] Hasanov was reportedly taken by police from his home in Chirchik, just outside

---

September 5, 1999. Verdict of the Collegium of the Supreme Court of the Republic of Uzbekistan, April 3, 2000.

[745] Human Rights Watch interview, name withheld, Tashkent, July 12, 1999.

[746] Human Rights Watch interview, name withheld, Tashkent, July 12, 1999.

[747] Human Rights Watch interview with a person close to Hasanov, name withheld, place withheld, June 15, 2000.

Tashkent, on July 17, 2000, and never seen or heard from again.[748] When "F.F." (not the person's true initials), a person close to Hasanov, inquired at the National Security Services (SNB) headquarters in Tashkent regarding Hasanov's whereabouts, an agency representative told him, "Find him yourself."[749]

- The mother of one young man branded a "Wahhabi" and arrested by special forces officers in Andijan in 1998 reported that the SNB and then the MVD in Tashkent held him incommunicado for three months, the entire duration of his pre-trial detention. She told Human Rights Watch, "After his arrest...no one saw [him] at all. We were given no information and no visits with him. After three months, we heard from our neighbor that her son was also arrested and had told her that [my son] was in the basement of the SNB in Tashkent."[750] This did not resolve the problem, however: "At the SNB they refused to give us a visit with our son. After that, every month we went to Tashkent and

---

[748] Human Rights Watch interview with a person close to the case who spoke to neighbors who had seen police take Hasanov into custody on the day in question, name withheld, Tashkent, July 20, 2000. Hasanov's elderly father, Munavar Hasanov, born 1930, was convicted by a Tashkent court on fabricated charges of possession of Hizb ut-Tahrir leaflets, after being tortured and forced to sign a self-incriminating statement, and was sentenced to three years in prison. In 2000 Hasanov's younger brother Ismail was sentenced to twenty-four years in prison on terrorism charges. Human Rights Watch monitored his trial; no material evidence incriminating Ismail Hasanov was brought forth at trial or in the indictment. For details regarding the torture of Ismail and Munavar Hasanov, see below, "Torture and Mistreatment in Pre-trial Detention" in Chapter IV. See also, Human Rights Watch press release, "Uzbek Police 'Disappear' Torture Victim," July 20, 2000. It is believed Bahodir Hasanov was arrested as retribution for the independent religious activity of his family members.

[749] Human Rights Watch interview with "F.F" (not the person's true initials), Tashkent, July 2000. Human Rights Watch contacted several diplomatic missions to enlist their help in locating Bahodir Hasanov, but these efforts appear to have failed. In a telephone interview with a representative from the Alliance Francaise, a Human Rights Watch researcher was told that Hasanov's employer could confirm that he was missing in custody, considered that he had been disappeared, that his relatives were unaware of his whereabouts, and that appeals to the government for information had gone unanswered. Human Rights Watch telephone interview with Gerard Barbare, head of the Alliance Francaise, May 21, 2001. Human Rights Watch considers Bahodir Hasanov to be disappeared.

[750] Human Rights Watch interview, name withheld, Andijan, May 19, 2000.

were able to give him food and clothes, but we never got a meeting with him."[751]

- Komil Masudov was arrested on July 26, 1999. Police held him incommunicado for three months while family members frantically searched for him at the district police station, city police station, police headquarters, and National Security Service.[752] Finally, a relative learned from the procuracy that he was being held at the Ministry of Internal Affairs in Tashkent and hired a lawyer for him.[753] The lawyer was able to visit Komil and his sister, Shoknoza Musaeva, who was already in prison. The lawyer informed the Masudov family that those in pre-trial detention were being beaten regularly.[754]

- A female relative of one of seventeen accused "Wahhabis" arrested for taking private religion classes described the lengths to which police investigator Khojaev of the Ministry of Internal Affairs was prepared to go to deny family members their right to visit.[755] The Ministry of Internal Affairs held the young man in incommunicado custody for five months—the entire length of the preliminary investigation. During that time police compelled him to sign a self-incriminating statement. His wife was permitted to see him only after the investigation had finished. She told Human Rights Watch:

> Later, I learned that I had the right to see my husband every month [once the investigation was finished] and so I called the investigator and told him that I had learned that I could see my husband. He asked who had told me that and I said 'a neighbor' and he let me go see my husband… Then the other neighbors [i.e. relatives

---

[751] Ibid.

[752] Human Rights Watch interview, name withheld, Tashkent, November 3, 1999.

[753] Ibid.

[754] Ibid.

[755] Human Rights Watch unofficial transcript, Tashkent City Court, Judge Sharipov presiding, August 4, 2000. This case is described above, in "Imams, Their Followers, and 'Wahhabis'" in Chapter III.

> of his co-defendants] found out about this and called the investigator, but he told them they were too late. Only [my husband] was visited twice.[756]

Sometimes police have refused to let relatives even provide food for the detainees in pre-trial custody, who otherwise are fed so little that their health is compromised.

- Nakhmiddin Juvashev, convicted in 1999 for Hizb ut-Tahrir membership and then released on parole in August of that year, was re-arrested by police in August 2000. As of November 1, 2000, police had prevented all family members from visiting with Juvashev in custody and had allowed them to deliver food to the police station only three times. On October 31, Juvashev's wife took the last of the family's food to the Jizzakh province police station, where Juvashev was being held in the basement, but was told by guards that food could not be delivered to prisoners that day. Juvashev's wife described the incident: "I cried and explained that this was the last of our food, that my children were going hungry and I had brought the last of the food in the house to my husband, so the officer finally took it, but I don't know if he really gave it to my husband or not. The children have not eaten for two days now."[757]

The relative of another detainee told Human Rights Watch that courthouse guards demanded 5,000 som from family members to pass on food while defendants were on trial.[758]

Access to Legal Counsel and Preparation of a Defense

Although Uzbek law provides for access to legal counsel from the moment of arrest, throughout investigations police frequently pressure

[756] Human Rights Watch interview, name withheld, Tashkent, date withheld.

[757] Human Rights Watch interview with Juvashev's wife, Jizzakh, November 1, 2000.

[758] Human Rights Watch interview with the wife of an accused "Wahhabi," name withheld, Tashkent, August 14, 2000. At the time, 5,000 som was about the equivalent of the average monthly salary in Uzbekistan.

detainees not to seek counsel. When detainees or their families attempt to engage an independent defense lawyer, police and investigators often simply refuse requests from the lawyer for access to his or her client, until the police have secured a confession from the accused. Police frequently pressure detainees or their families to accept the services of state-appointed lawyers who do not defend their client's interests, and who are unlikely to lodge complaints against ill-treatment. Even when lawyers do gain access to clients, they do not have the right to freely arrange independent, objective forensic medical examinations that could provide evidence of torture.[759]

Police and procuracy officials are particularly wary of giving detainees time with their attorneys. Even when a detainee is permitted contact with relatives, police often deny access to his legal counsel of choice. In some cases, the investigator in charge denies a lawyer entry, or the family is told that the detainee has rejected legal counsel.[760] Most often, access is simply delayed, through false statements about a detainee's whereabouts in custody, health, or the stage of the investigation, until police have conducted all interrogation sessions and coerced a confession from the detainee. Police thereby prevent the attorney from being involved during the most crucial period in the investigation. These actions deprive the detainee of protection crucial to both his legal defense and his protection from torture. Police have threatened family members and used other methods to coerce detainees to accept state-appointed legal counsel that often amounts only to "shadow counsel," that is, a signature on documents but no actual participation. Like all detainees in Uzbekistan, religious detainees are routinely denied their right to meet with legal counsel in private.

- Following the arrest of Imam Iuldashev on July 23, 2000, his family engaged attorney Irina Mikulina, who went directly to the Ministry of Internal Affairs to meet with her client. Officers reportedly told her he

---

[759] Uzbekistan law grants the police or procuracy investigator handling a case the authority to approve or reject a detainee's or lawyer's request for a forensic medical examination; these requests are often simply denied. Those attorneys who do attempt to request a forensic examination face grave consequences, as do their clients, of retribution by police.

[760] See, for example, the case of Abdurashid Isakhojaev as described above, in "Imams, Their Followers, and 'Wahhabis'" in Chapter III.

had been transferred to Tashkent prison.[761] Upon investigation, she found this to be false and returned to the Ministry of Internal Affairs, where she obtained unofficial confirmation that he was indeed being held there. As of August 2000, however, authorities had failed to issue any official notification of Iuldashev's arrest or place of detention,[762] and although his lawyer made repeated requests to see him, investigators refused to give her access.[763] On or about August 9, investigators presented Mikulina with a document allegedly signed by Iuldashev, which stated that he rejected legal representation. Authorities forbade Mikulina to meet with her client to establish the authenticity of the document and confirm his choice not to be represented by legal counsel.[764] The imam's lawyer and relatives feared that Iuldashev had been physically coerced to reject a defense attorney.[765]

- On Feruza Kurbanova's fifth day of detention on charges of membership in Hizb ut-Tahrir, officers from the Tashkent Municipal Police Department instructed her to hire a defense lawyer. When she told the authorities that she did not have enough money to hire a lawyer and requested that a state lawyer be appointed to her, an officer responded, "In cases like yours, we don't provide lawyers."[766] A state lawyer eventually attended some interrogation sessions, but the only legal advice he gave Kurbanova was that she sign blank pieces of paper as the investigators demanded.[767]

Kurbanova's trial began on February 28, 2001, in the absence of any legal counsel. According to Kurbanova, she was questioned in court by

---

[761] Human Rights Watch interview, name withheld, Tashkent, August 1, 2000.

[762] Ibid.

[763] Human Rights Watch telephone interview with Irina Mikulina, August 9, 2000. The police investigator responsible for Iuldashev's case was Nishan Bekmanov, working under the supervision of investigator Karshiev, head of the criminal investigative group.

[764] Human Rights Watch telephone interview with Irina Mikulina, August 9, 2000.

[765] Human Rights Watch telephone interview with Irina Mikulina, August 9, 2000; and Human Rights Watch telephone interview, name withheld, August 2000.

[766] Human Rights Watch interview with Feruza Kurbanova, Tashkent, March 14, 2001.

[767] Ibid.

the judge, who also failed to provide her with legal representation.[768] At the second hearing, attended by Human Rights Watch as well as international media and diplomatic representatives, the judge began the trial again, as if the first hearing had never taken place. The judge read the charges against Kurbanova and repeatedly advised her of her right to an attorney, even announcing the delay of the proceeding until such time as a lawyer could be appointed and familiarized with the case.[769] The judge later attended Kurbanova's meeting with her state-appointed lawyer and instructed her to ask for forgiveness for her membership in Hizb ut-Tahrir.[770]

- At his trial, one defendant accused of being a Wahhabi, Shukhrat Balikov, told the court that arresting officers denied his requests for a lawyer: "They said, 'Why do you want a lawyer? You'll die in prison anyway.'"[771]

- At least five lawyers representing defendants in a group case spoke at trial about impediments to meeting with their clients. One attorney said:

> Article 250 [of the criminal procedure code] says a lawyer can meet his defendant anytime in detention, but I was not allowed to have a separate meeting with my client. Most of [the defendants] met their lawyers only once or twice [and] in the company of police. Defendants were threatened that they shouldn't be honest about conditions.[772]

---

[768] Ibid.

[769] Human Rights Watch unofficial transcript, Shaikantaur District Court, Tashkent, March 2, 2001.

[770] Human Rights Watch interview with Feruza Kurbanova, Tashkent, March 14, 2001.

[771] Human Rights Watch unofficial transcript, Tashkent City Court hearing held in the Akmal Ikramov District Court building, Tashkent, November 1, 2000.

[772] Human Rights Watch unofficial transcript, Tashkent City Court, Judge Sharipov presiding, August 4, 2000.

The attorney who represented Gafurjon Toirov and one other co-defendant in the same trial added:

> Today, my new defendant was beaten and forced to reject his lawyer…It's no use to go and see defendants. They are so scared they can't say the truth and the lawyers can't help. Lawyers meet in the presence of investigators, and a defendant can't open his mouth. Even if there are ten lawyers, with today's existing regime, nothing will change. [773]

The attorney's words were remarkable given the pattern of intimidation against defense lawyers and general climate of fear generated by Uzbekistan's criminal justice system.

The attorney for another defendant in that case, Otabek Makhmudbekov, stated in court, "He was detained on January 27, but I was allowed to start the case only on April 24. I wrote a letter to the ministry and got no reply. My complaints against the investigator remain without reply."[774] Meanwhile, the lawyer for yet another defendant, Gairat Sabirov, complained that his client was denied access to legal counsel for two full months during detention.[775] According to a person close to Sabirov, "They only let our lawyer in to see him after [he] had signed [the confession]."[776] Defendant Khamidullo Rakhmatullaev's attorney told the judge: "On January 27, I took this case. I went to the pre-trial detention [facility] and couldn't talk to him. I went there for ten days [in a row]...then I sent a complaint to the senior procurator. The complaint was sent to the procurator's office. I received an answer that the defendant didn't want a lawyer, and later I learned that he was forced to reject me."[777] Judge Sharipov did not respond to the attorneys' complaints.

---

[773] Ibid.

[774] Ibid.

[775] Ibid.

[776] Human Rights Watch interview, name withheld, Tashkent, August 14, 2000.

[777] Human Rights Watch unofficial transcript, Tashkent City Court, Judge Sharipov presiding, August 4, 2000.

- One woman whose son was arrested for membership in Hizb ut-Tahrir recounted her experience with police obfuscation: "The investigator did not let our lawyer meet with my son…. No one met with my son for the whole five months [of pre-trial detention]. I was only able to meet with him after the trial. My son never met with his lawyer. The investigator said my son refused a lawyer, but it turns out my son didn't even know about the lawyer."[778]

In some cases, the procuracy did not inform detainees of the charges against them, a crucial element in preparing an adequate defense. That the procuracy sends cases to trial based on a defendant's self-incriminating statements even when the defendant is not aware of the charges further illustrates that confessions have been fabricated or coerced.

- Accused Hizb ut-Tahrir member Abdilkhakim Shakasimov testified in court that police had never shown him the indictment against him.[779] Shakasimov also testified that officers held his arms and forced him to sign a self-incriminating statement. He said he was unsure of the contents of the statement and, in fact, could not even read or write in Uzbek, the language of the confession.[780]

- A person familiar with the case of Bahodir Ikramov—detained on December 21, 1998, at a Tashkent university where he was pursuing a master's degree—said that authorities denied the young man access to the lawyer of his choice until the very last day of the police investigation. Ikramov expressed shock when on the last day of the investigation, after he had already signed a "confession" to narcotics possession, he was presented with the full charges against him for the first time. Ikramov

[778] Human Rights Watch interview with the mother of a religious prisoner, name withheld at her request, Tashkent, February 14, 2000.

[779] Human Rights Watch interview with trial monitor Vasila Inoiatova, Tashkent, August 1, 2000.

[780] Ibid.

was charged with membership in Hizb ut-Tahrir, illegal possession of narcotics, and encroachment on the constitutional order.[781]

Torture and Mistreatment in Pre-trial Detention

Widespread torture of detainees is common in criminal investigations in Uzbekistan.[782] In the campaign against independent Islam, police have systematically employed torture to coerce confessions and statements incriminating others.

In the past two years, the international community has taken notice of the pervasive and serious nature of torture in Uzbekistan and its use in the campaign against independent Islam. The United Nations Special Rapporteur on Torture visited the country in November 2002 and published a report characterizing torture in Uzbekistan as "systematic."[783] The report also stated that "torture is being used in virtually all cases in which articles 156, 159, and 244 CC [of the Criminal Code] are invoked, in order to extract self-incriminating confessions and to punish those who are perceived by public authorities to be involved in either religious, or political, activities contrary to State interests (so-called security crimes)."[784]

In its own review of Uzbekistan in June 2002, the United Nations Committee against Torture expressed concern about "numerous,

---

781 Human Rights Watch interview, name withheld, Tashkent, July 10, 1999.

782 See Human Rights Watch, "And it Was Hell All Over Again."

783 Civil and Political Rights, Including The Questions of Torture and Detention: Torture and other cruel, inhuman or degrading treatment, Report of the Special Rapporteur on the question of torture, Theo van Boven, submitted in accordance with Commission resolution 2002/38. Addendum. Mission to Uzbekistan. United Nations document. E/CN.4/2003/68/add.2. February 3, 2003 (hereinafter, Report of the U.N. Special Rapporteur on Torture, Theo van Boven), p. 21.

784 Report of the U.N. Special Rapporteur on Torture, Theo van Boven, p.13. As noted elsewhere, criminal code article 156 refers to inciting religious enmity, article 159 relates to the attempted overthrow of the constitutional order, and article 244 refers to organizing public unrest. The Special Rapporteur's report may have intended to include in its reference to article 244, article 244-1, which refers to illegal dissemination of religious literature.

ongoing and consistent" allegations of torture. It made a recommendation that was extraordinary compared to those usually made to state parties. It recommended that the authorities: "Review cases of convictions based solely on confessions in the period since Uzbekistan became a party to the Convention, recognizing that many of these may have been based upon evidence obtained through torture or ill-treatment, and, as appropriate, provide prompt and impartial investigations and take appropriate remedial measures."[785]

The following section summarizes thirty-six cases of torture documented by Human Rights Watch, which represent only a fraction of the total number of cases Human Rights Watch has investigated. Several appeared in prior Human Rights Watch publications.[786] They describe a variety of methods of torture used against Muslim detainees, including beatings by fist and with truncheons or metal rods, rape and sexual violence, electric shock, use of lit cigarettes or newspapers to burn the detainee, and asphyxiation with plastic bags or gas masks.[787] They also reveal the role torture played in coercing testimony; judicial refusal to investigate victims' allegations; and the courts' routine practice of admitting as evidence testimony obtained under torture.[788] In twenty-seven of the thirty-six cases described below, detainees were tortured to compel them to give self-incriminating statements and were subsequently convicted. In four of the cases below, the torture of religious detainees led to their deaths. Human Rights Watch has

---

[785] Conclusions and Recommendations of the Committee against Torture: Uzbekistan. 06/06/2002. CAT/C/CR/28/7. (Concluding Observations/Comments.)

[786] See Human Rights Watch, "'And it Was Hell All Over Again."

[787] For a recent account of the use of rape against independent Muslim detainees, see *Uzbekistan: Chronicle of Life in Maximum Security Colony KIN-51 (April-May 2002)*. Available at: www.memo.ru/hr/politpr/asia/uzbekistan/uz020715.htm [retrieved March 26, 2003].

[788] The 1999 criminal procedure code does not explicitly forbid the use of information obtained through torture as evidence in criminal proceedings. The Uzbek Supreme Court, recognizing, perhaps, that police investigators and prosecutors rely most heavily on confessions to secure guilty verdicts, and that this creates an incentive to use torture, has erected a legal barrier against this. The Supreme Court issued a plenary court decision on May 2, 1997, which states that "…any evidence obtained unlawfully shall be devoid of evidential value and cannot form the basis of a judgment."

documented a total of ten cases in which religious pre-trial detainees died as a direct result of torture between May 1998 and May 2003.[789] Torture takes place in police precincts, provincial departments of the Ministry of Internal Affairs, and at the ministry building itself. It is also common in National Security Service facilities; in some cases, detainees are moved from facility to facility and tortured in each place.

Police and security agents torture independent Muslim suspects during the investigative phase to compel confessions or testimony against others. The interrogation of an independent Muslim generally centers on questions about the detainee's beliefs, affiliation with Islamic groups, or association with well-known independent imams. The end product the police are seeking is a statement—prepared by police, signed by the detainee—that describes the detainee's religious belief, practice, and affiliation rather than a criminal act. Because many of those detained on religion-related charges are held incommunicado, the interrogation may last up to six months.

Through torture and threats—on which we present details below—agents have coerced detainees to name members of religious organizations, people who have attended mosque with them, or even friends and neighbors who may not in fact have shared their religious beliefs or affiliation. They also have forced detainees to admit to associations with individuals unknown to them. Police then arrested those named, or brought them in as witnesses, often coercing them into testifying for the prosecution. This coercive strategy produces a perpetual flow of names for the police and security services to pursue. Police sometimes arrest a suspect and torture individuals unknown to him into testifying against him. The 1999 case of Bakhtior Musaev illustrates the latter strategy.

---

[789] Human Rights Watch documented the cases of another nine religious prisoners who died from torture in post-conviction facilities during the same period. Human Rights Watch documented six additional cases of suspicious death in prison custody. There was evidence of four cases of death from illness compounded by torture. Some of these cases are dealt with below in "Treatment in Prison" in Chapter IV. There were also numerous credible reports issued from other sources regarding deaths in prison and pre-trial detention during the period of Human Rights Watch's research.

The defense lawyer for Musaev, an accused Hizb ut-Tahrir member, wrote a letter of complaint to the Iunusabad District Court judge in charge of his client's case. In the letter the attorney drew particular attention to the fact that the witnesses against Musaev did not know him, had been instructed by police as to the content of their testimony, and had been tortured in order to compel that testimony. In his letter submitted to the judge prior to the June 1999 verdict against Musaev, attorney Shoknozar Jabrailov wrote:

> During questioning [in court] on June 17, 1999, witness Sherev, Bekzot testified that he did not know Musaev at all before March 1999. He first saw Musaev at the city police station [GUVD] in Tashkent, when police officers forced him to give testimony, prepared beforehand, against Musaev saying that they knew each other and that he [Sherev] had seen him [Musaev] once in 1996; that Musaev supposedly had said that it would be good if there were an Islamic government in Uzbekistan. Officers at the Tashkent city police station tortured him in order to force him to give testimony against Musaev, they beat him, put a gas mask on him and cut the oxygen supply.[790]

Musaev's lawyer alleged that the police used threats of arrest to compel incriminating testimony from two additional witnesses. Both of these witnesses, when questioned in court, recanted their written statements.[791] Sherev testified in court about the pressure against the other two witnesses with him at the Tashkent police station. He said that all three had been given identical statements to sign and joint

---

[790] Undated letter from Shoknozar Jabrailov to the presiding judge, Iunusabad District Court, on file with Human Rights Watch. Rights defender Vasila Inoiatova, who monitored the Musaev trial and was present during Beksot Sherev's testimony, verified the account of Sherev's court testimony provided in Jabrailov's letter. Sherev was convicted in a separate trial to seventeen years in prison on charges of religious extremism. Human Rights Watch interview with Vasila Inoiatova, Tashkent, June 19, 1999.

[791] Ibid.

instructions by police as to how to testify and what to say.[792] Bakhtior Musaev was sentenced to nine years in prison.[793]

Torture Resulting in Death

▪ Police from the Zangiota district of Tashkent detained Farhod Usmanov, son of well-known imam Nosir Usmanov, on June 14, 1999, for alleged possession of a Hizb ut-Tahrir leaflet.[794] Police reportedly placed Usmanov under formal arrest that same day and initially held him in the Zangiota district police station. After five days, authorities transferred him to a Tashkent police station, where he was held incommunicado for the rest of his detention—a matter of several days.[795] Investigator Kobil Khoitmetov was reportedly responsible for supervising Usmanov's case.[796] At 5:00 p.m. on June 25, authorities returned his body to his family with a death certificate attesting that the forty-two-year-old father of six had died in detention of heart failure the previous day.[797] Authorities who delivered Usmanov's body ordered the family to conceal his death and not to show his body to anyone.[798] However, that night a Human Rights Watch representative viewed the body, which was covered with large and small black bruises. The

---

[792] Human Rights Watch interview with rights defender Vasila Inoiatova, who monitored the Musaev trial, Tashkent, June 19, 1999.

[793] The Iunusabad District Court sentenced him to nine years in prison on June 21, 1999. Human Rights Watch unofficial transcript, Iunusabad District Court, Tashkent, June 21, 1999. Musaev was subseqently released under a presidential amnesty on August 29, 2001.

[794] Following his death, authorities alleged that Usmanov had recruited others to join Hizb ut-Tahrir and had taught them about the "Islamicization of society." Supreme Court verdict issued by Judge B. K. Rozikov, July 17, 2000, trial of ten alleged members of Hizb ut-Tahrir. Additional information regarding the state persecution of Usmanov's family members is presented above, in "Family Members: Arrests, House Arrest, Harrassment" in Chapter III.

[795] Human Rights Watch interview, name withheld, Tashkent, June 25, 1999.

[796] Ibid.

[797] Death certificate viewed by Human Rights Watch, specifying cause of death as heart failure and date of death as June 24, 1999.

[798] Human Rights Watch interview, name withheld, Tashkent, June 25, 1999.

Usmanov family alleged that he had been in good health prior to police detention and charged that authorities had tortured him to death.[799]

Usmanov's family reported that authorities failed to prosecute those responsible for his death.[800] A letter from the Ministry of Internal Affairs to his family, sent in September 1999, stated simply that the criminal case against Usmanov had been closed upon the occasion of his demise.[801]

- Police in Kashkadaria arrested Rustam Norbabaev,[802] born 1977, on March 13, 2000, for alleged membership in Hizb ut-Tahrir.[803] They detained Norbabaev along with his three brothers, Bahrom, Ergash, and Parda. All four men were allegedly tortured in the Yakkabaga district police department in Kashkadaria province. Rustam's three brothers were allegedly beaten to induce them to testify against him.[804] Rustam died after five days in custody—police claimed he hanged himself.[805] His three brothers were released immediately afterward.[806] The official investigation of his death did not consider possible police misconduct.

---

[799] Human Rights Watch interview with members of the Usmanov family, names withheld, Tashkent, June 25, 1999.

[800] Letter from Masuda Kosimova to the parliament of Uzbekistan, August 11, 1999.

[801] Letter from U.L Makhmudov, Ministry of Internal Affairs, Republic of Uzbekistan, to Masuda Kosimova, September 22, 1999. After Usmanov's death, authorities continued to accuse others of being his students and followers, accusations that turned into criminal charges.

[802] Some reports give the spelling as Norbaev. See, for example, Memorial Human Rights Center and the Information Center for Human Rights In Central Asia, *List of People Arrested and Tried in Uzbekistan for Political and Religious Reasons (December 1997 to August 2001)*, Moscow, October 2001.

[803] World Organization Against Torture request for urgent intervention, Case UZB 030400, April 3, 2000.

[804] Ibid.

[805] Human Rights Watch interview with rights defender Tolib Ikubov, Tashkent, May 1, 2000.

[806] Ibid.

▪ Hizb ut-Tahrir member Nu'mon Saidaminov died in police custody apparently from torture on September 8, 2000. When Saidaminov's body was washed in preparation for burial, an observer, "D.D." (not the person's true initials), reported that he was covered with dozens of open wounds and bruises, his fingernails were blackened, and there were puncture wounds on his fingers. He also had bruises around his eyes and a cut on the right side of his face. Bruises on his buttocks and anus suggested he may have been subjected to anal rape. The bottoms of his feet also showed markings consistent with a beating.[807] A doctor who reportedly observed the washing stated that the wounds were consistent with a fatal beating that had occurred at least two days earlier.[808]

▪ On October 17, 2001, Tashkent police arrested brothers Ravshan and Rasul Haitov on suspicion of membership in Hizb ut-Tahrir. Officers took the men—ages thirty-two and twenty-five respectively—to the Sobir Rakhimov district police station where they beat and otherwise physically abused the Haitov brothers. Within hours, Ravshan Haitov was dead. Authorities returned his body to his family the next day.[809] Those who viewed the body reported that Haitov's neck was broken, as was one leg, below the knee. The upper section of his back was injured, and his body was covered with bruises. The official cause of death was given as a heart attack.[810]

In an unusual departure from a pattern of police impunity for abuse, four officers allegedly involved in the torture of Ravshan and Rasul Haitov were brought to trial and convicted on January 30, 2002. They were charged with "inflicting bodily harm that caused death," a violation of criminal code article 104. They were each sentenced to twenty years in prison. Observers noted that persons sentenced under criminal code

---

[807] Human Rights Watch interview with "D.D." (not the person's true initials), Tashkent, October 2000.

[808] Human Rights Watch interview with D.D., who spoke to the doctor, Tashkent, October 2000; and written description of the body by D.D. provided to Human Rights Watch, October 2000.

[809] See "Uzbekistan: Torture Victim Dies in Custody: Crackdown on Independent Muslims Continues," Human Rights Watch press release, October 20, 2001.

[810] Ibid.

article 104 had qualified for release under past prisoner amnesties. They expressed concern that the state had failed to charge the officers with murder, in order to provide for their future pardon and release.[811]

Rasul Haitov also suffered severe injury as a result of police abuse. He was transferred to a Tashkent hospital, where he was kept under guard in an intensive care unit. He was subsequently released and testified at the trial of the police who had beaten him and his brother. Charges against Rasul Haitov for alleged membership in Hizb ut-Tahrir were subsequently dropped.[812]

Torture in Ministry of Internal Affairs Custody

Human Rights Watch gathered information about Muslim detainees tortured in Ministry of Internal Affairs custody, including in the Ministry's own holding facility, the Tashkent Municipal Police holding facility, and various district police departments. Some of the worst cases of torture reported occurred in the first two locations. Officers from the Tashkent police headquarters (MVD) reportedly beat Imam Abduvahid Iuldashev repeatedly upon his arrest in February 1999. The officers took Iuldashev to room 190 in the station, where a man identified only as Abdukhamid began to insult him. Then, according to Iuldashev, "Another four men began to taunt me, then they forced me to take off my jacket and sat me in the corner. Then they beat me, twisting my arms behind my back; they forced me to the ground and struck my arms and legs, inflicting a great many bodily injuries."[813] An OSCE trial observer present on the last day of the proceedings against Iuldashev reported

---

[811] See "Uzbek Court Convicts Police for Beating Death: Decision Welcomed as 'A First Step,'" Human Rights Watch press release, February 1, 2002.

[812] Authorities reportedly cited Rasul Haitov's poor health as the reason for closing the case. Human Rights Watch interview with persons close to the case, names withheld, Tashkent, October 10, 2003.

[813] Unofficial transcript, Iakasarai District Court, Tashkent, May 11, 1999, written by independent trial monitors, names withheld, June 1999.

that the imam testified that police had beaten him in the interrogation room and also in the elevator and corridor of the police station.[814]

According to Iuldashev, after the round of beatings in room 190, officers took him to room 194, where they continued to beat him. The officers then called in two witnesses to observe their search of his pockets—a search that produced a substance later identified as opium.[815] When Iuldashev denied that the drugs were his and refused to sign the police report, police beat him again.[816] Authorities charged him with illegal possession of narcotics.

According to a person close to the case, when Iuldashev's lawyer met with him the next day, February 22, 1999, she saw that his body was covered with marks of beatings, including bruises on his chest.[817] After that meeting, authorities prohibited Iuldashev from meeting with his lawyer or family again until the investigation was over. During the following month his relatives were not even informed of the location where he was being held.[818] Later, persons close to the imam's case learned from him that he had been held first in the basement and then in a regular cell in the Ministry of Internal Affairs for a week before being transferred to the Tashkent Municipal Police Department. There, when authorities asked him upon arrival if he had any physical complaints, he answered, "Yes, I have been beaten."[819] The Tashkent police officers took Iuldashev to a separate room where, instead of registering his complaint, a man began to beat him.[820] Throughout the attack, the officer demanded, "Did someone beat you? Do you have a

---

[814] Human Rights Watch interview with OSCE trial monitor, name withheld, Tashkent, July 2, 1999.

[815] Unofficial transcript, Iakasarai District Court, Tashkent, May 11, 1999, written by independent trial monitors, names withheld, June 1999; and Iakasarai District Court verdict, issued by Judge Kh. M. Kaiumov, July 1, 1999.

[816] Iakasarai District Court verdict, issued by Judge Kh. M. Kaiumov, July 1, 1999.

[817] Human Rights Watch interview, name withheld, Tashkent, August 1, 2000.

[818] Ibid.

[819] Ibid.

[820] Ibid.

complaint?" until Iuldashev agreed to sign a document saying that he had no complaint to make regarding physical mistreatment.[821]

In his verdict convicting Iuldashev, Judge Kaiumov wrote: "The court refutes Iuldashev's version [of events]...that police officers brought physical pressure to bear on him."[822] The court further accused Iuldashev of having invented this "alibi" with the aim of avoiding punishment.[823] After Iuldashev's release under a presidential amnesty, police arrested him again in July 2000 and tortured him for three months in pre-trial detention.[824] Testifying at his trial, Iuldashev recalled more than two weeks of grueling torture at the hands of police who forced him to say he had weapons and to name the place where they were supposedly hidden. He recalled being confined in room number 18 in Tashkent police headquarters, "a horrible place," he said. He testified: "For almost eighteen days I was tortured there. The skin on my legs was burned, and my genitals were burned twice...They kept asking me about guns."[825] Iuldashev eventually complied with his torturers' demands, but was then shocked when officers threatened that if the weapons were not where he had said, they would continue to torture him and would also arrest and torture his relatives.[826] He claimed he pleaded with them, explaining he had only said these things because of the torture in the first place.

Iuldashev was taken to Minister of Internal Affairs Zokirjon Almatov himself, indicating the importance Uzbek authorities attached to his case. Iuldashev recalled at trial, "[Almatov]...asked me to tell the truth, and I explained that they tortured me and forced me to say I had guns

---

[821] Ibid.

[822] Iakasarai District Court verdict, issued by Judge Kh. M. Kayumov, July 1, 1999.

[823] Ibid.

[824] Human Rights Watch unofficial transcript, Tashkent City Court hearing held in the Akmal Ikramov District Court building, February 7, 2001.

[825] Ibid.

[826] Ibid.

that were not really there...[and] he said...'Tell us where your guns are.' I said, 'I have no guns.' He said, 'Once, you said there were guns.'"[827]

Imam Iuldashev testified that after his meeting with the minister, he was again tortured and was forced this time to say that the guns were in Kazakhstan. He gave an address where they were supposedly hidden, but a Kazakh police officer who was informed said there was no such address.[828] Nonetheless, the Uzbek officials then chastised the Ministry of Internal Affairs of Kazakhstan for failing to keep guns out of their country.[829] Iuldashev reported, "Then the assistant minister of internal affairs of the Republic of Kazakhstan wanted to talk to me, and they [Uzbek police] told me what to say to him. My face was swollen on the left side. They didn't want me to talk to him with my swollen face. They prepared the [written statement] and made up the questions and answers themselves. [So] I said that Tokhir Ibrahimov, who lives in Kazakstan, told me about guns and wanted to show me where they were, but we never met. This was [all] fabricated by police. These minutes were registered and given to the assistant minister of internal affairs of Kazakhstan."[830] In the end, state authorities did not charge Iuldashev with possession of weapons.[831]

Iuldashev's account also provides a possible explanation for a phenomenon that is typical in religious prosecutions in Uzbekistan: the frequent appearance in indictments and verdicts of only the first names of supposed accomplices. He testified: "...I was asked, 'Who were your followers in Fergana and Kokand?' I said, 'I have no such followers.' After they tortured me, I said that I did have staff. When they asked me who, I just said common Uzbek names like Akhmat...The next day, I

[827] Ibid.

[828] Ibid.

[829] Ibid.

[830] Ibid.

[831] Indictment of Tashkent city procurator M. I. Naimov, signed by police investigator A. Karshiev, December 18, 2000.

couldn't remember the names and they kept changing. The torture was so bad. To avoid the torture, I just made up names."[832]

- The experience of one of Iuldashev's co-defendants also sheds light on how police made their case against the imam. When asked in court whether or not he had been tortured to incriminate Iuldashev, this defendant, Ulugbek Vakhidov, said, "Yes." He explained that in addition to beating him the police showed him documents and computer files that were supposedly Iuldashev's own confessions:

> They showed me a computer and on it, it said 'Testimony of Abduvahid Iuldashev.' It said that I was one of his students and that he taught us about jihad and that we collected money for the baitulmol fund. I was afraid I would be handicapped [from the torture], and I signed the document…I heard that if I didn't sign, I could be killed. I saw mattresses soaked with blood and, of course, I didn't want to die….[833]

The court sentenced Vakhidov to eight years in prison for membership in a criminal group and distribution of religious extremist literature.[834]

- The mother of one religious prisoner told Human Rights Watch, "In Tashkent prison, during the investigation, they beat him so that he would confess. So long as he refused to confess, two large men beat him and threatened to rape him. He heard that they raped others. He finally confessed after the beatings. He confessed to possession of bullets and marijuana."[835] Her son was sentenced to seventeen years in prison.

---

[832] Human Rights Watch unofficial transcript, Tashkent City Court hearing held in the Akmal Ikramov District Court building, Tashkent, February 7, 2001.

[833] Ibid.

[834] ibid.

[835] Human Rights Watch interview with the mother of an accused Hizb ut-Tahrir member, name withheld at her request, Tashkent, February 14, 2000. Tashkent prison serves as a pre-trial detention facility, in addition to being the central point from which prisoners are transferred to facilities for longer term incarceration, and a post-conviction facility for some prisoners, including those sentenced to death.

▪ Several defendants convicted in September 2000 on charges of religious extremism described being raped in Tashkent by officers and also with objects, including a bottle. Ma'rufkhoja Umarov stated that "they stripped me naked, and raped me several times. Then they sat me on the bottle, as a result of which I received several injuries."[836] Five of his co-defendants also stated in court that they were raped during interrogation. One of the defendants was Dilshod Isakhov, who testified that police beat him in the basement, that they forced him onto the floor and hit him on the head with their truncheons until he lost consciousness. Later, the officers applied electric shock to him and then raped him.[837]

▪ Ulughbek Mirzoev, tried along with Muzafar Avazov and other accused Hizb ut-Tahrir members in 2001, also testified in court that he had been tortured. Mirzoev accused law enforcement officers of pulling out his fingernails.[838]

▪ Describing injuries sustained as a result of police mistreatment in pre-trial detention, Khusan Maksudov, born 1952, testified in court, "I hear badly now, I have a scar in my left ear. I cannot lift my left arm or make sharp movements. I cannot lie on my right side, because my left kidney has been badly injured."[839]

▪ "Can't anybody monitor the behavior of the police?" pleaded Tokhir Obidov, on trial for "Wahhabism" along with sixteen co-

---

[836] Undated letter from Malrufkhoja Umarov to Human Rights Watch, smuggled out of pre-trial detention.

[837] Undated written report by rights defender Vasila Inoiatova, who monitored the trial and defendants' testimony, on file with Human Rights Watch.

[838] Human Rights Watch interview with a relative of Avazov who observed the trial, Tashkent, February 26, 2001. Judge Akhmadjonov sentenced the nine defendants, including Avazov and Mirzoev, to prison terms ranging from ten to twenty years. Some of the sentences were reduced on appeal. Ibid. Information on Muzafar Avazov's case is given below.

[839] Human Rights Watch unofficial transcript, Tashkent City Court hearing held in the Akmal Ikramov District Court building, Tashkent, February 7, 2001.

defendants in Tashkent City Court.[840] Obidov and many of his co-defendants and their lawyers gave the court details of the torture the men had suffered.[841] The attorney for co-defendant Gafurjon Toirov noted that a fellow defendant testified to seeing police beat Toirov and pull him by the hair.[842] According to the relative of one co-defendant, officers reserved their most brutal treatment for Toirov, beating him severely on the kidneys, in order to force him to sign a statement saying he had taught the others about Islam.[843] Toirov himself testified in court that he was tortured for more than two months in pre-trial detention. He said that officers beat him on the bottoms of his feet, and that the white clothes he had been wearing because he had just returned from a pilgrimage to Mecca were covered with blood.[844] While beating co-defendant Azgam Astankulov, police concentrated their blows on the young man's already injured kidneys, due to which, according to one source, Astankulov's "eyes popped and he immediately agreed to sign."[845]

Torture in National Security Service Custody

- Officers from the SNB in Tashkent arrested Muzafar Avazov on January 17, 2000, for alleged membership in Hizb ut-Tahrir. According to Avazov's relative, "C.C." (not the person's true initials), the officers allegedly stuck metal spikes all around Avazov's head and tortured him with electric shock for two days in the basement at SNB headquarters. Then, during interrogation, officers threw him on the floor and called in two large men who jumped on him.[846] According to C.C., the officers

---

840 This case is described above, in "Imams, Their Followers, and 'Wahhabis'" in Chapter III.

841 Human Rights Watch unofficial transcript, Tashkent City Court, Judge Sharipov presiding, August 4, 2000.

842 Ibid.

843 Human Rights Watch interview, name withheld, Tashkent, August 14, 2000.

844 Ibid. Police reportedly arrested Toirov directly from the airport upon his arrival from Saudi Arabia.

845 Human Rights Watch interview, name withheld, Tashkent, August 14, 2000.

846 Ibid.

ordered Avazov to sign a document that said that money found in his home was part of a Hizb ut-Tahrir fund for fighters in Chechnya, but he refused to sign. They told him that he should admit that the money was for IMU leader Tokhir Iuldash, but he again refused. Then, according to C.C., the officers tried to coerce him into saying that he had participated in a terrorist act in which a policeman was killed. He said, "Better that I die."[847] Then in July 2000, police arrested Avazov's younger brother and beat him in the elder's presence, again to coerce a self-incriminating statement.[848]

While the SNB otherwise held Avazov incommunicado during the six months of the criminal investigation, they summoned "C.C.," one of the young man's relatives, to meet with him after four months. According to C.C., "They finally let me see him so that I would advise him to give the testimony they wanted. I went, and he was swollen all over. His face was all swollen. He said the officers were from another region and were very cruel torturers. He said they hit him with truncheons. I opened his shirt, and on his chest there were bruises all over and marks that he had been beaten. There were bruises all over his legs as well."[849]

"C.C." was also present at Avazov's trial and said that Avazov recounted during the court hearing being tortured with electric shock but did not talk about the men who had attacked him.[850] C.C. further reported that Avazov was left in a traumatized state, "When [he] stood to give testimony, he couldn't remember how old his children were."[851] The judge reportedly taunted Avazov, saying, "You didn't forget Allah, but you forgot your children."[852]

---

[847] Human Rights Watch interview with C.C., Tashkent, February 26, 2001.

[848] Ibid.

[849] Ibid.

[850] Ibid.

[851] Ibid.

[852] ibid.

Muzafar Avazov was sent to Jaslyk prison, where authorities apparently tortured him to death. His body was returned to his family on August 8, 2002.[853]

▪ A person close to Gairat Sabirov, a defendant in a case against seventeen so-called Wahhabis, alleged that the young man was kept in a "sauna" or wet-room in the SNB for three days after his arrest in January 2000. The source said that officers there burned Sobirov's body with lit cigarettes before stripping and raping him. "For what?" the source asked, "He was only reading the Koran."[854] On January 8, 2000, he was transferred to police custody, where, according to a second person familiar with Sabirov's case, police investigators threatened to rape his wife if he refused to sign a self-incriminating statement.[855] A third person close to the case provided Human Rights Watch with the details of Sabirov's torture in both SNB and police custody. According to that source, when Sabirov was transferred from the SNB to MVD custody on January 8, 2000, his new custodians also tortured him, putting cigarettes out on his arms.[856] A state lawyer appointed to represent Sabirov visited his family on January 10, to instruct them to provide medicine and a pair of dark pants—the white ones he had been wearing were now covered with blood.[857]

Sabirov was kept incommunicado for sixty-eight days. During that time other detainees saw him lying unconscious and bloody in the basement of the Tashkent Municipal Police Department.[858] Transferred to pre-trial detention in Tashkent prison in April 2000, Sabirov was examined by

---

[853] See "Uzbekistan: Two Brutal Deaths in Custody Deaths Reveal 'Horror' of Uzbek Prisons," Human Rights Watch press release, August 10, 2002. Details regarding the evidence of prison authorities' torture of Avazov and a fellow prisoner, Husniddin Alimov, are given below in this chapter.

[854] Human Rights Watch interview, name withheld, Tashkent, August 4, 2000. Detailed information on the case of seventeen "Wahhabis" is provided in "Imams, Their Followers, and 'Wahhabis'" in Chapter III.

[855] Human Rights Watch interview, name withheld, Tashkent, August 21, 2000.

[856] Human Rights Watch interview, name withheld, Tashkent, August 14, 2000.

[857] Ibid.

[858] Ibid. Some of his co-defendants testified to this in court.

medical officers whose report stated that he had arrived covered with bruises.[859] A relative who met with him there reported, "We spoke on the phone through a window and guards walked to and fro. I asked if they tortured him and he just cried and said, 'The people who work here are not human.'"[860] In court, the defense gave extensive details about the torture in custody of the seventeen defendants, but the judge was unimpressed. "Testimony that the defendants were tortured wasn't proven. There was no written proof, and they didn't know the name of their torturer, and we value their testimony as having no grounds," the judge said.[861]

- SNB agents in Andijan tortured Tavakkaljon Akhmedov to compel him to admit to membership in Hizb ut-Tahrir and to name co-religionists. After succeeding in producing this testimony, agents continued to torture Akhmedov to compel him to admit to increasingly serious charges. Detained on May 15, 1999, he was held in the SNB basement where he was beaten, kicked, and hung by his wrists for seventeen days, until he confessed to Hizb ut-Tahrir membership.[862] Then, after he gave his confession, a whole new round of interrogation on additional charges began. SNB investigator Dilshod Akhmedov reportedly asked him "Will you confess or shall we continue with worse torture?" and threatened to cut off his tongue.[863] After that, Tavakkaljon admitted to the remainder of the charges the investigators had brought against him.[864] On or around July 27, he was transferred from the SNB basement to Andijan prison, where authorities continued to torture

[859] Ibid. The source learned of the existence of the report from Sabirov's state-appointed lawyer. The report was not available to Human Rights Watch at the time of this writing.

[860] Human Rights Watch interview, name withheld, Tashkent, August 14, 2000.

[861] Ibid. It is unclear why the medical report allegedly done in prison documenting Sabirov's bruises was not raised in court.

[862] Human Rights Watch interview with relatives of Tavakkaljon Akhmedov, names withheld, Asaka, Andijan, May 2000.

[863] Ibid.

[864] Ibid. According to family members, Akhmedov refused, however, to sign an additional statement incriminating him with the unsolved murder of a traffic officer who police alleged had been killed by members of Hizb ut-Tahrir.

him.[865] According to family members, Akhmedov lost consciousness in Andijan prison and fell into a coma for three days.[866]

- Another young man detained and interrogated by SNB officers in a province southwest of Tashkent told Human Rights Watch, "[the officer] took me to another room with no lights. He put me in a chair and ordered me to put my hands on the table and he beat me on my sides and all over. The major [presumably a senior SNB officer] was there, watching. Then [name of officer omitted] told me 'Write what I want or I'll put you in the basement and there I will teach you and by morning you will write what I want.'"[867]

- The Supreme Court released Nakhmiddin Juvashev, convicted in 1999, on parole in August of that year. But the National Security Service rearrested him in August 2000, along with his nephew, and beat them both.[868] The nephew was subsequently released but Juvashev was kept in custody and abused again during five days of incommunicado detention. His lawyer, Erkin Juraev, saw Juvashev on August 10 in his basement cell in the Jizzakh district police station, where National Security Service officials eventually brought him. He reported that, "Juvashev's face and right eye were bruised and swollen. On his shoulder, blue-black marks were visible, and on other parts of his body there were traces of wounds. When I asked him about these wounds, he told me that five to six National Security Service officers had beaten him in investigator Erkin Sattarov's office and that they kicked him in the stomach and other places. He also said that they beat him with a black electrical cable from a typewriter."[869] When Juraev informed investigator Sattarov and Jizzakh province procurator Ottabaev about these incidents and other abuse and demanded a medical exam for Juvashev, they did not respond to his

---

[865] Ibid.

[866] Ibid.

[867] Human Rights Watch interview, name withheld, place withheld, February 2001. Human Rights Watch has the name of the officer on file.

[868] Letter to Jizzakh regional procurator Ottobaev, from Juvashev's nephew, Yadgar Sodykov, August 14, 2000.

[869] Letter to General Procurator R.Kh. Kodirov, from Erkin Juraev, August 31, 2000; and letter to Jizzakh procurator M. Ottabaev, from Erkin Juraev, undated.

complaint in accordance with the law.[870] Juraev also pleaded for General Procurator Kodirov's help to put a stop to the torture.[871] No investigation was undertaken into the torture. The Jizzakh Province Court convicted Juvashev of anti-state activities and, on January 15, 2001, sentenced him to fourteen years in prison.

- Victims of torture testified to the effectiveness of police abuse. The wife of a man arrested for taking private lessons on Islam told Human Rights Watch, "My husband said that they threatened to remove his teeth. Then they told him to sign. They beat him on the legs, wrapped his legs in newspaper and lit it. In two days he told them what they wanted to hear...They took him to Tashkent prison, [where authorities] refused to take him because he was in such bad shape. But the police left him there, so they had to take him."[872]

- While President Karimov was promising pardons to independent Muslims who admitted having followed the "wrong" religious path, police actually tortured pious Muslim detainees to compel them to ask for pardons. The propaganda effort relied on the contrition of the accused to showcase the government's rectitude and generosity. Minister of Internal Affairs Zokirjon Almatov, claiming that dozens of people had applied to the police for the opportunity to repent, said, "No action has been taken against them, no punishment administered."[873] Just days after these declarations, another Ministry of Internal Affairs official, Maj. Fahriddin Islomov, announced that "...more than 700 young people who were led astray and joined various religious trends have come to the law-enforcement agencies to ask for forgiveness. None of them has been punished, they all have been forgiven and they have all returned to their families."[874] Several defendants, including Zafar Avasov and Ulmasbek

---

[870] Ibid.

[871] Letter to General Procurator R. Kh. Kodirov, from Erkin Juraev, August 31, 2000.

[872] Human Rights Watch interview, name withheld, Tashkent, November 3, 2000.

[873] Uzbek television first channel, April 4, 1999, English translation in BBC Monitoring, April 5, 1999.

[874] Uzbek television first channel, April 19, 1999, English translation in BBC Monitoring, April 19, 1999. Details regarding these people were not revealed by police, making it nearly impossible to confirm the state's claims that those who pleaded for the state's pardon were

Khakimov, who were part of a 1999 case against accused Hizb ut-Tahrir members, recounted in court the physical abuse inflicted on them by police to force them to apply for President Karimov's forgiveness.[875]

Threats of Torture

In addition to physical mistreatment, law enforcement officers also used a variety of threats to compel religious detainees to incriminate themselves and others. Twenty-five-year-old mother of four, Feruza Kurbanova, reported that arresting officers intimidated her with crude insults and threats of mistreatment. Kurbanova told Human Rights Watch that when officers arrested her on December 21, 2000, they took her to the Shaikhantaur district police station, where they "said the kinds of things a woman can't bear."[876] The officers asked her when she had last been with her husband and taunted that in Tashkent prison she would "have many husbands."[877] The officers threatened that if she did not confess to membership in Hizb ut-Tahrir, they would take her down to the basement of the police station and take turns raping her.[878] Kurbanova wrote the confession they demanded. The Shaikhantaur District Court found her guilty of membership in a banned religious organization and handed her a one-year suspended sentence.[879]

▪ Police also threatened to arrest or physically mistreat detainees' relatives to compel the detainees to confess. During the interrogation of Shukhrat Abdurakhimov, police threatened to arrest the young man's

---

indeed allowed to remain at liberty. There were, however, documented cases of the arrest and conviction of men who asked for forgiveness.

[875] Human Rights Watch unofficial transcript, Tashkent City Court trial held in the Chilanzar District Court building, Tashkent, July 20, 1999.

[876] Human Rights Watch interview with Feruza Kurbanova, Tashkent, March 14, 2001.

[877] Ibid.

[878] Ibid.

[879] The relatively lenient sentence for Kurbanova was believed to be due to intense interest in her case on the part of diplomatic representatives in Tashkent, international media, and local and international rights groups.

wife and mother if he did not sign a self-incriminating statement.[880] An accused "Wahhabi," Khusan Maksudov, recalled in court that during his detention at the Ministry of Internal Affairs, "They said they would bring in my wife and rape her, and my children and torture them" if he did not sign self-incriminating statements.[881] Twenty-five-year-old Kakhramon Saidkhojaev, arrested for taking part in private Islamic classes and charged with anti-state activity, asked in court, "Why would I [incriminate] my relatives as Wahhabis...? I have nothing against them; I was tortured into saying that. I was told that unless I condemned them, I'd be killed. I'm telling the truth. I was scared... They said that if I didn't admit [to the charges], they'd bring my wife in and rape her in front of me."[882]

- Detainees signed self-incriminating statements to stop the abuse of their relatives. On November 18, 1999, Tashkent police arrested Munavar Hasanov, whose son, Ismail Hasanov, had been arrested on charges of religious "extremism." They brought the elder Hasanov into the interrogation room to witness as his son was strung up by his ankles and repeatedly dropped on his head and beaten by officers.[883] Police told Munavar Hasanov that they could do anything they wanted with his son, even kill him, and no one would know.[884] Ismail Hasanov's father agreed to sign a confession to put an end to the torture.[885] Police later brought Ismail before his father, who had also been beaten. They threatened to continue to beat the elder Hasanov unless Ismail signed a

---

880 Written statement to then-U.S. Secretary of State, Madeleine Albright, from a relative of Shukhrat Abdurakhimov, name withheld, May 9, 2000; and Human Rights Watch interview with a relative of Shukhrat Abdurakhimov, name withheld, November 4, 1999. The author of the letter is the same relative as the interviewee. This case is described above in "Hizb ut-Tahrir" in Chapter II.

881 Human Rights Watch unofficial transcript, Tashkent City Court hearing held in the Akmal Ikramov District Court building, Tashkent, February 7, 2001.

882 Human Rights Watch unofficial transcript, Tashkent City Court hearing held in the Akmal Ikramov District Court building, Tashkent, November 1, 2000.

883 Human Rights Watch interview with a person close to the case, name withheld, Tashkent, June 15, 2000.

884 Ibid.

885 Ibid.

confession, which he did.[886] Neither man was released, instead both were convicted on trumped up charges and sent to prison.[887] Ismail Hasanov was sentenced to twenty-four years imprisonment on May 15, 2000.[888] Munavar was sentenced to three years of imprisonment on February 16, 2000.[889]

Judicial and Prosecutorial Indifference to Torture

The judiciary and the procuracy have legal obligations to protect detainees and defendants from torture. But in the overwhelming majority of cases, they failed to do so. Procurators fail to investigate diligently claims of torture filed by those detainees willing to risk speaking about the abuse. Indeed, it often takes the death of a detainee to prompt an investigation into torture. As noted in Chapter II, judges uniformly ignored defendants' court testimony about the torture they endured and admitted as evidence confessions and other testimony obtained through torture during the investigation.

The case of Nakhmiddin Juvashev, convicted on charges of Hizb ut-Tahrir membership, is an example of prosecutorial and judicial indifference to torture.[890] He was held first at the Jizzakh branch of the National Security Service and then in the basement of the Jizzakh city detention facility in February and March 1999. He was held incommunicado for almost two months, during which time he was

---

[886] Ibid.

[887] Human Rights Watch press release, "Uzbek Police 'Disappear' Torture Victim," July 20, 2000. For more information regarding the Hasanov family, see "Incommunicado Detention" in Chapter IV.

[888] Tashkent Province Court verdict issued by Judge Rustamov, May 15, 2000. The charges upon which Ismail Hasanov was convicted included attempt to commit terrorism (criminal code article 25-155).

[889] Tashkent Province Court verdict issued by Judge G. Khairullaev, February 16, 2002.

[890] Additional information about the persecution of Juvashev's relatives is found above in "Family Members: Arrests, House Arrest, Harrassment" in Chapter III.

repeatedly beaten.[891] In April 1999 his attorney wrote to the Jizzakh procuracy describing this treatment, but authorities failed to initiate an investigation. Instead, law enforcement agents tortured him in retaliation for making the complaint. After Juvashev's case was forwarded to the Jizzakh Province Court, his attorney filed a complaint to the presiding judge describing the torture. At trial the judge refused to mandate an investigation. Instead the judge ignored Juvashev's court testimony about the torture, admitted into evidence self-incriminating statements he had given while being tortured, and sentenced him to nine years in prison on the basis of these statements.

Juvashev's ordeal, detailed in these complaints, follows: on March 13, 1999, National Security Service investigator Shavkat Iakshiev took Juvashev to the Ministry of Internal Affairs in Tashkent. There, investigator Iakshiev, officers Bahodir Kurbanov and Rustam Mustafakulov, an officer named Abdulkhamid, and several other unidentified men took Juvashev down to the basement, fastened his wrists in handcuffs, and kicked him and beat him with their nightsticks for nine hours. They then insisted he write whatever they instructed.[892] "My legs and body became swollen. I lost consciousness several times," Juvashev recalled.[893] Juvashev was transferred to a detention facility in Uchtepa, where he was held from March 16 to April 6. There, a Ministry of Internal Affairs anti-corruption officer named Farkhod and another man beat and insulted him in an upper-floor room during three to four days.[894] In addition, Juvashev reported that every day he was visited by officer Bahodir Kurbanov from the anti-corruption department, who took him outside, tormented and insulted him, and beat him on the head

[891] Human Rights Watch interview, name withheld, Jizzakh, July 2, 1999; and letter to Jizzakh Procurator Ottabaev, from Juvashev's lawyer, M. Togaev, April 17, 1999, unofficial translation. M. Togaev was Juvashev's first lawyer, who was fired by Juvashev's family and replaced after he reportedly refused to pursue a case against the officers who allegedly tortured his client. Human Rights Watch interview, name withheld, Jizzakh, July 2, 1999.

[892] Written complaint to Judge Bakhriddin Norkhujaev of the Jizzakh Province Court, from Nakhmiddin Juvashev, June 25, 1999.

[893] Ibid.

[894] Ibid.

with a truncheon.[895] According to Juvashev, Kurbanov threatened, "I am going to subject you to such torture that you will do everything they demand, and then you will die."[896]

Authorities at the Uchtepa detention facility wrote a report registering Juvashev's condition and allegedly acknowledging that he had been beaten.[897] The day after his arrival at Uchtepa, presumably March 17, Juvashev was having trouble breathing; his condition was so dire that officers were forced to call an ambulance to give him emergency assistance.[898]

Juvashev reported that investigator Iakshiev instructed him to reject his lawyer, but that he managed to get a one-time visit—after almost two months in custody—by promising to fire his lawyer immediately afterwards.[899] Juvashev's first words to his attorney, M. Togaev, were about the torture he had endured, signs of which were visible, including swollen legs.[900]

Togaev's April 17, 1999 complaint to the Jizzakh procurator named the several officers who tortured his client and demanded a medical exam and an investigation.[901] Juvashev has stated that the procurator's first

---

[895] Ibid.

[896] Ibid.

[897] Letter to Jizzakh Procurator Ottabaev, from Juvashev's lawyer, M. Togaev, April 17, 1999, unofficial translation.

[898] Ibid; and written complaint to Judge Bakhriddin Norkhujaev of the Jizzakh Province Court, from Nakhmiddin Juvashev, June 25, 1999.

[899] Written complaint to Judge Bakhriddin Norkhujaev of the Jizzakh Province Court, from Nakhmiddin Juvashev, June 25, 1999.

[900] Human Rights Watch interview, name withheld, Tashkent, June 29, 1999; and Human Rights Watch interview with Juvashev's sister-in-law, name withheld at her request, Jizzakh, November 1, 2000.

[901] Letter to Jizzakh Procurator Ottabaev, from Juvashev's lawyer, M. Togaev, April 17, 1999, unofficial translation.

deputy, R. Tashkulov, visited him in detention, discussed his allegations with him, and obtained a full description of events.[902]

Juvashev's abusers responded by stripping Juvashev down to his underwear, handcuffing him, hanging him from an elevated, horizontal bar, and beating him for more than three hours with truncheons.[903] "With the aid of this kind of torture, humiliation and threat, Shavkat Iakshiev forced me to write a dictated letter stating that I supposedly broke my leg and received a massive number of bruises on my body from falling off the second tier bunk, and not from their having beaten me," Juvashev alleged.[904] But Juvashev persisted in attempts to hold his abusers accountable. On April 23, 1999, he wrote a complaint about the torture he had endured and the many blackouts and injuries he had suffered as a result.[905] According to a person close to the case, the deputy procurator of Jizzakh, Shamsilulov, allegedly responded to his complaint in a letter that said, "No one beat you and you should reject your lawyer."[906]

Juvashev was still in the hands of his torturers, and again they responded to his complaint with more violence, beating him on the bottoms of his feet in particular. By April 27 Juvashev had signed another statement prepared by police, to the effect that no one had beaten him and that he waived his right to an attorney.[907] For three days afterward, according to someone who talked with him later, he could not so much as lift his head.[908]

---

[902] Written complaint to Judge Bakhriddin Norkhujaev of the Jizzakh Province Court, from Nakhmiddin Juvashev, June 25, 1999.

[903] Ibid; and Human Rights Watch interview, name withheld, Jizzakh, July 2, 1999.

[904] Written complaint to Judge Bakhriddin Norkhujaev of the Jizzakh Province Court, from Nakhmiddin Juvashev, June 25, 1999.

[905] Human Rights Watch interview, name withheld, Jizzakh, July 2, 1999.

[906] Human Rights Watch interview, name withheld, Tashkent, June 29, 1999.

[907] Human Rights Watch interview, name withheld, Jizzakh, July 2, 1999.

[908] Ibid.

At his trial in the Jizzakh Province Court in July, Juvashev denounced the "severe and relentless" torture he had suffered,[909] but Judge Norkhujaev sentenced him to nine years in prison on the basis of his self-incriminating statements.

Juvashev was subsequently released on three years of parole. But on August 5, 2000, he was again arrested and physically mistreated by police. He was tried and sentenced on January 15, 2001, to fourteen years of imprisonment on charges of attempting to overthrow the government.

Another case, heard in the Tashkent City Court in 2000, also demonstrates judicial indifference to torture. Danior Sodykov testified in court that police had beaten and raped him to coerce him into signing a confession to membership in Hizb ut-Tahrir. Tashkent City Court Judge Rakhmonov responded by asking him if he had complained to anyone about the mistreatment, putting the onus of stopping his torture on Sodykov, the victim.[910] Sodykov replied, "I could not even tell the officers beating me to stop, how could I write a complaint? To whom could I complain?"[911] No investigation ensued.

Independent Muslim defendants in one 2002 group case alleged that Tashkent police had tortured them with electric shock, beatings, and suffocation with plastic bags and gas masks. When defendant Iskander Khudoiberganov was describing torture marks that he saw on one of his co-defendants, Judge Nizamiddin Rustamov responded by saying that the Ministry of Internal Affairs, where the torture allegedly occurred, "is not a holiday resort."[912]

---

[909] Human Rights Watch interview with Juvashev's sister-in-law, Jizzakh, November 1, 2000.

[910] Human Rights Watch interview with trial monitor, Vasila Inoiatova, Tashkent, August 1, 2000.

[911] Ibid.

[912] Human Rights Watch press release, "Uzbekistan: Alleged Torture Victim Sentenced to Death," December 4, 2002.

A judge in a June and July 2003 trial of fifteen alleged Hizb ut-Tahrir members did not respond at all to defendants' harrowing court testimony about the torture they had endured during the investigation. On June 10 one defendant, Ikrom Norkhojaev, stated in court:

> They put handcuffs on me. They made me lie down on the floor in the basement. They beat me on the soles of my feet. They also used a wooden stick to beat me. I couldn't walk—I had to crawl to the interrogation room.... Only God knows about the other things that happened. I am too ashamed to talk about it.[913]

Khikmat Buriev gave similar testimony on June 11: "They tortured me a lot. They put a gas mask on me and beat me on the soles of my feet. Ask the other guys as well—they even raped us.... The investigator forced me to sign a statement that was already written."[914] According to a person who attended the trial, the judge did not even question these defendants about their allegations.[915] During the two and a half hours it took the judge to read the verdict, his only reference to these testimonies was that Buriev had claimed that he had been pressured to sign statements.[916]

---

[913] Human Rights Watch interview with a local human rights defender who monitored and transcribed the trial hearings, name withheld, Tashkent, June 12, 2003.

[914] Ibid.

[915] Ibid.

[916] Human Rights Watch unofficial transcript, Akmal Ikramov District Court, Tashkent, July 4, 2003.

Tashkent courtroom.

Trials and Sentencing

Defendants generally have only a slim chance for a fair trial in Uzbekistan. Defendants charged with religion-related violations face additional problems and obstacles to obtaining due process during the trial phase. The country's judiciary is not independent of the executive.[917] The procurator—investigator and prosecutor of a case—holds the balance of power in a courtroom. Judges display marked deference toward and bias in favor of procurators. They approach

[917] "…in practice President Islam Karimov and the centralized executive branch that serves him dominate political life and exercise nearly complete control over the other branches …. Despite constitutional provisions for an independent judiciary, the executive branch heavily influenced the courts in both civil and criminal cases." U.S. Department of State, *2002 Country Reports on Human Rights Practices*, released by the Bureau for Democracy, Rights and Labor, March 31, 2003 [online], http://www.state.gov/g/drl/rls/hrrpt/2002/18400.htm (retrieved January 6, 2004).

defendants with hostility and suspicion rather than presumption of innocence. Corruption in the judiciary is rampant.[918]

In trials of independent Muslims, defendants are denied the right to examine witnesses against them.[919] An aggressive defense is the rare exception that proves the rule: defense counsel is sidelined, fearful, and passive. Defendants themselves must stick to the "script" of confession and contrition or else they are silenced. Judges routinely ignore or inadequately address court testimony regarding fabrication of evidence and coercive methods—including torture—used to procure defendants' testimony to police.

In Uzbekistan court cases are presided over by a professional judge and two assessors. Called "people's judges" during the Soviet system, lay assessors are private citizens who attend hearings and can question defendants and witnesses, but who are most often passive. Many lay assessors at trials observed by Human Rights Watch slept through significant portions of the hearings.

The procurator—who has supervised the investigation of the case and then prosecutes the case at trial—clearly has more power in the courtroom than the defense. In dozens of trials monitored by Human Rights Watch, judges consistently deferred to procurators on technical and material questions. Procurators have the right to appeal cases when they are not satisfied with the verdict or the length of the prison sentence.[920] Having one's decisions appealed and overturned or altered can damage a judge's career. A 1999 U.S. Department of Justice report on Uzbekistan's judiciary states, "In some cases the court may impose a

[918] Bribery and other means of extra-legal influence can rarely, if ever, make a difference in the verdict reached in a religion-related trial. Corrupt practices can, however, have an effect at the edges of the process; if sufficient, for instance, they can influence the length of a sentence or whether or not relatives of a suspect are allowed to attend the trial or visit the defendant.

[919] Article 14.3 (e) of the ICCPR states that in the determination of any criminal charges against them, everyone shall have the right "[t]o examine, or have examined, the witnesses against him and to obtain the attendance and examination of witnesses on his behalf under the same conditions as witnesses against him."

[920] Article 479 of the Uzbek criminal procedure code.

heavy sentence to avoid an appeal from the procurator. It is said that if a procurator appeals a judge three or more times, that judge's career is virtually over."[921]

In Uzbekistan (as in many countries of the former Soviet Union) trials almost always result in convictions. In trials of independent Muslims, a guilty verdict is virtually a foregone conclusion, as judges fall in line with the country's strict laws on religion.[922] With rare exception, conviction of the accused is inevitable. Human Rights Watch is aware of one independent Muslim having been acquitted. While judges can use discretion in determining sentences, they uniformly follow the lead of the procuracy's requests for prison terms. In earlier periods of the campaign, particularly after the 1999 bombings in Tashkent, sentences typically were from twelve to twenty years of imprisonment. In 2003 sentences were typically from eight to ten years of imprisonment.

Denial of the Right to Examine Witnesses

In trials of independent Muslims, courts routinely violate defendants' right to examine prosecution witnesses. A principal form of incriminating evidence was "confessions" obtained from defendants and prosecution witnesses—many themselves independent Muslim prisoners—often under torture or other forms of coercion. If such witnesses had appeared in court personally, the defense could have questioned them, including about the circumstances under which they made their testimony to law enforcement or security agents. But the prosecution routinely relied on what it claimed were written statements made by convicted persons incriminating the defendants on trial. In a few cases, the person whose written testimony was used in a case had been executed before the trial began. Other state witnesses were detainees simultaneously facing criminal charges in separate cases and were vulnerable to coercion. There is evidence that police and security

[921] Assessment of the Criminal Justice System of the Republic of Uzbekistan, United States Department of Justice, Criminal Division, June 18, 1999, p. 32.

[922] Mr. Craig Murray, the British Ambassador to Uzbekistan, referred to this high conviction rate in a speech at Freedom House: "In the Uzbek criminal justice system the conviction rate is almost 100%." Tashkent, October 17, 2002.

agents coerced false statements from detainees who were forced to stand witness in trials of people they did not know.[923]

Confessions and third person testimony form a critical element in cases against independent Muslims because in the majority of cases they are prosecuted in groups[924] consisting of unrelated defendants whom police compelled to testify against each other.[925] Prosecutors often argued their case against only one or two main defendants accused of leading anti-constitutional religious activity. They often failed even to identify criminal acts allegedly committed by other co-defendants. These remaining defendants were prosecuted mainly on the basis of allegations that they were connected to or affiliated with the principal defendants. This method of prosecution suggests an urgency to produce convictions

[923] For example, see the case of Bakhtior Musaev, "Torture and Mistreatment in Pre-trial Detention" in Chapter IV.

[924] They are not, however, charged with conspiring together as a group.

[925] For example, in one group case of fifteen men accused of Wahhabism, all of the defendants complained in court that police had pressured them to give false statements during the preliminary investigation. (See "Imams, Their Followers, and 'Wahhabis'" in Chapter III, Fifteen Accused Wahhabis, June–November 2000, for more details on this case and the use of defendant testimony to incriminate others.) Some testified that they had been forced to incriminate others, including people they did not know. Defendant Kakhramon Saidkhojaev gave court testimony that called into question the statements he had signed during interrogation, including testimony regarding other defendants' alleged participation in religious classes and in an alleged pro-jihad movement. In his statement to police, cited in the verdict, Saidkhojaev named several of his co-defendants, saying during religious classes they studied Koran and hadith, and were then called to jihad. However, when Saidkhojaev took the stand in court, he said that he was innocent, that the information in his testimony to police had been coerced and was untrue. Verdict issued by Judge K.A. Iusupov, Tashkent City Court trial held in the Akmal Ikramov District Court building, November 20, 2000.

Saidkhojaev's statements given under interrogation were also used as part of the basis for the conviction of Imam Iuldashev and his co-defendants, in a separate trial. (Unofficial U.S. Embassy transcript of the Tashkent City Court hearing, April 9, 2001. See "Imams, Their Followers, and 'Wahhabis'" in Chapter III for details on that case.) Co-defendant Shukhrat Balikov also testified that, under pressure, he had falsely incriminated a group of seventeen men who were tried separately. Like Saidkhojaev, he told investigators that the other men had studied Islam and were called to jihad. Human Rights Watch unofficial transcript, Tashkent City Court hearing held in the Akmal Ikramov District Court building, Tashkent, November 1, 2000. (See "Imams, Their Followers, and 'Wahhabis'" in Chapter III for further details regarding Balikov's testimony and the case of seventeen "Wahhabis").

and to move large numbers of detainees through the judicial system. It also permits prosecutors to focus on one main defendant, coerce other defendants into accusing him of serious crimes, and then, on the basis of coerced testimony, accuse those secondary defendants of association with him and with failing to inform the authorities of his illegal activities.[926]

Witness testimony is also crucial because the prosecution rarely has any other evidence to make the case that independent Muslims' actions could have amounted to an attempt to overthrow the government, the most common charge against them. Criticizing the prosecution, the attorney for accused "Wahhabi" Murod Kosymov—one of seventeen co-defendants—noted the vagueness of the charges, the lack of supporting details provided by the accusers. "You turn the pages of the indictment and you can see they've been accused of all these articles, but there is nothing saying when and where they committed these crimes, when and where they planned to overthrow the constitution."[927] Noting the absence of any witnesses for the prosecution or other evidence to prove his client guilty, the attorney for accused Hizb ut-Tahrir member Bakhtior Usmanov stated in court, "The procurator's words alone are not enough; there should be facts also."[928]

As described above, prosecutors relied heavily on evidence planted by police. Rarely was the defense able to question those who had vouched for that evidence, because in most cases the expert opinions of narcotics or ballistics and weapons experts were provided to the court in written form only, and in many cases were the only evidence presented at trial. In other cases, testimony from state witnesses whom police had brought along on the searches was the only certification offered to substantiate charges.

---

[926] See above, for example, the case of Imam Iuldashev and the men accused because of their connection to him, "Imams, Their Followers, and 'Wahhabis'" in Chapter III.

[927] Human Rights Watch unofficial transcript, Tashkent City Court, Judge Sharipov presiding, August 4, 2000. The case is that of seventeen "Wahhabis," described in "Imams, Their Followers, and 'Wahhabis'" in Chapter III.

[928] Human Rights Watch unofficial transcript, Tashkent City Court hearing held in the Chilanzar District Court building, Tashkent, July 9, 1999.

Defense often cannot examine witnesses from the state Committee on Religious Affairs, which, as noted in "Institutions of Control," provides "expert testimony" that routinely serves as a crucial basis for convictions. In his court testimony, Hafizulla Nosirov, the reputed leader of Hizb ut-Tahrir in Uzbekistan, argued that the right to confront his "expert" accuser was essential. He offered the judge the following critique of the state's experts: "In my first speech I told you about the contact I had with the Committee on Religious Affairs under the Cabinet of Ministers. From that communication, I conclude that the experts they have used to assess our leaflets don't know anything, and they avoid my questions. I request the invitation of religious experts into the courtroom to further discuss [the leaflets]. Let him [the expert] substantiate what he thinks we are doing wrong, here in the courtroom."[929] After consulting with the procurator, the judge declined Nosirov's request.

A Tashkent judge presiding over a trial against fifteen members of Hizb ut-Tahrir held in June and July 2003 also declined without explanation the defense's request to examine the Committee on Religious Affairs expert. [930]

Other Procedural Violations at Trial

Questions posed by judges suggested they had predetermined the trial outcomes, in violation of the principle of the presumption of innocence.[931] Presiding over a case of twelve accused Hizb ut-Tahrir

---

[929] Human Rights Watch unofficial transcript, Syrdaria Province Court, Gulistan, March 26, 2000.

[930] Human Rights Watch unofficial transcript, Akhmal Ikramov District Court, Tashkent, June 30, 2003.

[931] In some cases, the rush by police to take inventory of a defendant's possessions prior to trial also indicates violation of the principle of the presumption of innocence. For example, a member of the Sabirov family told Human Rights Watch that police surveyed the family's possessions for future confiscation before the trial against Gairat Sabirov had even begun. Sabirov's relative said that Hosan Manjurov, deputy to police investigator Khojaev, came to the family home with the explanation that the charges against Gairat included confiscation as part of the punishment and asked in whose name were the house and family car. Human Rights Watch interview, name withheld, Tashkent, August 14, 2000. According to

members in May 1999, Judge Mansrur Akhmadjonov of the Tashkent City Court turned to one defendant during the young man's testimony and asked, "How old is your daughter?" When the man replied that his daughter was still a young child, the judge reportedly told him, "By the time you get out of prison, she'll be grown up and married."[932] In another case, when Judge Akhmadjonov presided over a trial of nine alleged Hizb ut-Tahrir members, a person who had been in the courtroom recalled: "On the first day of trial, the judge threatened the defendants that he would send them to Jaslyk [prison, the harshest in Uzbekistan]."[933] The lawyer for the defense protested, and the defendants themselves reportedly refused to speak following the judge's outburst. Judge Akhmadjonov allegedly retaliated by moving the trial to Tashkent prison and blocking entry to the defendants' relatives.[934]

Also, as noted in "Torture and Mistreatment in Pre-trial Detention," judges often disregard evidence of torture or other illegal police conduct. The following example is illustrative. Judge Sharipov of the Tashkent City Court, who sentenced seventeen defendants for "Wahhabism" in August 2000, considered their recantation of earlier self-incriminating statements "an attempt to avoid punishment."[935] According to a relative of Gairat Sabirov (one of the defendants in that case), when Sabirov testified that police had held him in solitary confinement, burned him with cigarettes, and raped him, the judge continuously interrupted his testimony.[936] Rights defender Mikhail Ardzinov, who observed the trial, recalled that "the defense attorneys demonstrated the insufficiency of

---

Sabirov's relative, police paid a similar visit to the home of Sabirov's co-defendant, Azgam Astankhulov.

[932] Human Rights Watch interview with a person who attended the trial, name withheld, Tashkent, July 22, 1999.

[933] Human Rights Watch interview, name withheld, Tashkent, February 26, 2001. Tashkent City Court trial held in the Akmal Ikramov District Court building, Judge Mansrur Akhmadjonov presiding.

[934] Ibid.

[935] Tashkent City Court verdict issued by Judge Sharipov, August 21, 2000.

[936] Human Rights Watch interview, name withheld, Tashkent, August 4, 2000.

the evidence against the defendants and the weakness of the state's arguments...but the judge ignored them completely."[937]

Judges often make comments that are inappropriate, though not in violation of the right to a fair trial. At times, the judges' statements rise to the level of degrading treatment of defendants.[938] For example, a lay assessor in the Tashkent City Court trial against thirteen Hizb ut-Tahrir members asked a defendant "Are you faithful to your oath [to Hizb ut-Tahrir] or did you change your mind? Remember, you have two children."[939] When the defendant explained to the lay judge that his oath had been a vow to be faithful to religion, the presiding judge accused him of being against the constitution and queried, "With what in the Uzbek republic are you not satisfied? This country gave you an education, food, etc. Why are you not satisfied?" He later added, "Your parents are here, are you not ashamed? Don't you feel ashamed? Don't you feel ashamed?"[940] In response to a question from the presiding judge, Rakhmonov, also about asking for forgiveness, co-defendant Hikmat Rasulov sounded exasperated: "No one has said anything here about the six months of torture, and now you are demanding that we apologize...!"[941]

Judges' improper pronouncements extended to the correctness or error of certain religious beliefs or practices. In the trial of accused Hizb ut-Tahrir member Feruza Kurbanova, Judge Mirzahidov said to her, "You became a member and gave an oath. If you really believe in God, you shouldn't take oaths."[942] One woman described to Human Rights Watch how the judge presiding at her son's trial regarded her own religious

---

[937] Human Rights Watch interview with Mikhail Ardzinov, Tashkent, August 21, 2000.

[938] Article 7 of the ICCPR states that, "No one shall be subjected to torture or to cruel, inhuman or degrading treatment or punishment."

[939] Human Rights Watch unofficial transcript, Tashkent City Court trial held in the Chilanzar District Court building, Tashkent, June 30, 1999.

[940] Ibid.

[941] Ibid.

[942] Human Rights Watch unofficial transcript, Shaikhantaur District Court, Tashkent, March 7, 2001.

practice as evidence of her son's guilt: "When I went to the trial, the judge [pointing at my headscarf] said to my son, 'You are no good. If you were, then your mother wouldn't wear that.'"[943] Then the judge reportedly turned to the woman and said, "The state doesn't allow this. You should dress in European style..."[944]

Effect: Sidelining the Defense

The obstacles to establishing innocence are often so daunting that most defense attorneys give up long before they have begun. The defense is given little time to speak at trial. Defense attorneys are intimidated and threatened.[945] Fear of retribution has led lawyers to refuse to take on the cases of independent Muslims and affects the quality of their defense.[946] State-appointed attorneys, often the only counsel available to defendants in trials of independent Muslims, do not always act in the interests of their clients and regularly offer weak defense arguments. By and large, statements by defense counsel amount to little more than pleas for leniency in sentencing and rarely include a challenge to the charges against the defendants. Defense attorneys often fail to call witnesses for the defense and when they do, they have found themselves without the backing of the judge and police necessary to compel a witness to appear in court. Material evidence is often not presented in court, and the defense cannot summon independent experts to challenge opinions (almost always written) by government forensic, narcotics, or religion experts.

---

[943] Human Rights Watch interview, name withheld, Tashkent, February 27, 2001.

[944] Ibid.

[945] The Nazarov family's lawyer, for example, reported that authorities harassed her and tapped her telephone, that security agents followed her whenever she visited the Nazarov family, and that police regularly questioned neighbors about her. Interview with Irina Mikulina at a meeting with then-U.S. Ambassador-at-Large for Religious Freedom, Robert Seiple, and Human Rights Watch, Tashkent, May 23, 2000.

[946] For example, the family of Abdurakhim Abdurakhmonov told Human Rights Watch that at least three attorneys declined to represent the imam due to intimidation by security agents. See "Imams, Their Followers, and 'Wahhabis'" in Chapter III. Human Rights Watch interview with Mubarak Abdurakhmonova, Tashkent, May 26, 2000.

Defendants, for their part, are literally relegated to the sidelines during the process—they are kept in barred cages on one side of the courtroom and are given only limited time to speak. The part of the trial allotted to the defendant often includes an initial statement as to whether or not he or she acknowledges the charges against him/her and confirms the confessions he or she has made during the pre-trial investigation. Following the procurator's presentation of the charges, defendants are asked to give an oral statement outlining their crimes. When defendants digress from the "script" by pleading innocence, complaining of torture or coercion by police, or making other statements frowned upon by the court, they are often interrupted and silenced. After the procurator has made closing arguments and asked for specific sentences for those on trial, the accused are allowed to give what is called their "last word." This is the time, typically, for the defendants to express their contrition for their wrongdoing and ask for the forgiveness of the state and leniency of the court. While there were some indications that a failure to ask for forgiveness during this speech led to more severe sentences than were given to contrite defendants, in the vast majority of cases defendant statements appeared to fail to influence the judge's final decision.

Sentencing

Independent Muslims face lengthy and harsh sentences. Judges show little independence in determining sentences, condemning men to roughly the number of years in prison demanded by the procurator and very rarely finding against the state.

As noted earlier, the Russian rights group Memorial documented 2,297 cases of political and religious prisoners (1,967 of whom were not charged with acts of violence). Out of the 2,297 people arrested, Memorial succeeded in obtaining detailed information on the sentences of 1,649. The group's October 2001 report on the subject states that the majority, 1,002 people, were sentenced to strict-regime prisons. Another 515 people, convicted on charges related to their politics or religion, were sent to general-regime facilities, and thirty-four were sent to the country's "prison-regime" facility—the strictest form of incarceration.

Fifty-one people received sentences that did not involve prison time. One person was acquitted.[947]

Appeal

Unjust verdicts have seldom been redressed on appeal. Appeals courts have reduced sentences in some cases, but in general they have maintained the verdicts of the lower courts; so fifteen years may be reduced to twelve, but the underlying police methods and indicting arguments are not challenged. Indeed, fear that the appeals court would actually increase the lower court's penalty has often kept defendants and their families from launching an appeal. Moreover, conditions in pre-trial detention have been so harsh that some convicted religious prisoners have forgone their right to appeal in the interest of reaching what they believed would be the relative safety of a post-conviction facility.

Transparency: Corruption and Access to Trials

Although the majority of trials are officially open to the public, in practice, family members of the accused face a series of obstacles when trying to gain access to the court. Authorities often fail to notify family members that their relative's case has been sent to trial. Many therefore do not learn that the hearings have begun until well into the proceedings, and sometimes not until the trial is over. Because court clerks typically refuse to provide information about the time that a case will be heard, relatives end up waiting outside the courthouse for a trial to start for days or weeks on end. Authorities at courthouses sometimes lie to relatives about the timing of a case, in order to get them to leave and to allow proceedings to go on without observers. In what appears to

---

[947] The remainder includes thirty-six men condemned to death, presumably on charges of involvement in terrorism, and one human rights defender forcibly placed in an institution for the mentally ill. Nine people who were placed under official arrest, by sanction of the procurator, were released during the course of the investigation and had the cases against them closed. Memorial Human Rights Center and the Information Center for Human Rights in Central Asia, *List of People Arrested and Tried in Uzbekistan for Political and Religious Reasons (December 1997-August 2001)*, Moscow, October 2001.

be a trend at trials of independent Muslims, court authorities often limit access to the hearings to one relative of each defendant. Anxiety becomes acute as families are forced to decide in a matter of seconds whether a defendant's husband, wife, mother, father, brother, sister or other relative will be the one to attend the trial, and perhaps see him or her for the last time outside of prison. Guards physically prevent those without permission from attending court hearings, again, even for "open" proceedings.

The denial of access appeared at times to be yet another discriminatory element of the cases against independent Muslims. For instance, the judge presiding over Uigun and Oibek Ruzmetov's trial allegedly denied their mother, Darmon Sultanova, access and told her that "Wahhabists" are not authorized to attend trials.[948]

Other times, courthouse guards or other authorities of the court demand bribes in exchange for permission to attend the proceedings. One female relative of independent Muslim prisoner Tavakkaljon Akhmedov reported that courthouse guards demanded bribes from family members who wanted to attend his trial: "We paid to attend the trial. We put one packet of cigarettes and some money in our passports [when we handed them to the guards]."[949] Later, during this trial, co-defendant Nematullo Bobokhonov testified that today's society in Uzbekistan is marred by corruption and prostitution. "When the judge asked Bobokhonov for proof of corruption, no one spoke up, even though we had all paid a bribe to be there," said an observer. During the lunch break, police allegedly took Bobokhonov back to the prison transport truck and beat him "to the point where his pulse stopped." After the break, persons in the court noted Bobokhonov's poor condition: "We saw with our own eyes that Bobokhonov was bent over and in bad shape. The judge laughed at him and said, 'Oh, you must have eaten something bad,'" said one eyewitness.[950] One relative told Human Rights Watch: "On the day of the verdict, I [Akhmedov's wife]

---

[948] Report of the U.N. Special Rapporteur on Torture, Theo van Boven, p. 31.

[949] Human Rights Watch interview with relatives of Tavakkaljon Akhmedov, names withheld, Asaka, Andijan, May 2000.

[950] Ibid.

asked for a meeting for my children with my husband. I gave the police 700 som, all that I had, but they said they would only do it for more and refused."[951]

A relative of one of seventeen alleged Wahhabis reported that she and other family members were compelled to pay 5,000 som each to guards outside the courtroom for permission to give the defendants food. "To see a man for just two minutes," she said, "costs 3,000 som."[952]

Many of the relatives of thirteen men tried by the Tashkent City Court for Hizb ut-Tahrir membership in June and July 1999 told Human Rights Watch that they had been compelled to pay to attend the proceedings. One defendant's relative recalled, "I got a call from the clerk of the court, who said I needed to pay the lawyer in order to sit in the courtroom. This was Bahrom, the secretary. 'We paid already,' we said, but he said, 'You paid for the investigator; now you pay to go to the court.' If you don't pay, they don't allow you in."[953]

Priority access is given to plainclothes security agents who sit in the courtroom. Foreign observers, including diplomats, journalists, and representatives of international rights groups are given access on a secondary and uneven basis. Access for these groups has been repeatedly denied under a variety of pretexts, from lack of space in the courtroom, to a requirement for special permission from the Ministry of Foreign Affairs or Ministry of Justice to attend a specific trial. More often, particularly in the earlier years of the campaign, guards and court house officials lie to international observers who arrive to monitor a trial, telling them that the proceeding has been cancelled when in fact it has not or giving foreigners a false time as the start of the hearing—and later denying the person entry because he or she is "too late." Judges have also denied access to international observers—either through a message delivered by proxy or a direct in-person refusal, often accompanied by a story regarding scheduling delays or an instruction to

[951] Human Rights Watch interview with the wife of Tavakkaljon Akhmedov, name withheld at her request, Asaka, Andijan, May 2000.

[952] Human Rights Watch interview, name withheld, Tashkent, date withheld.

[953] Human Rights Watch interview, name withheld, Tashkent, July 12, 1999.

return with permission from the Ministry of Foreign Affairs to attend the trial.

Despite frequent difficulties gaining access to courts, Human Rights Watch representatives attended dozens of trials of religious Muslims in provinces throughout Uzbekistan.

Treatment in Prison

> *I heard the prisoners screaming, and the workers at the prison told me, 'They [the prisoners] are enemies of the state and that's why they're treated so harshly.'*
>
> —Female relative of a religious prisoner.[954]

Regardless of the reason for their incarceration, all inmates in Uzbekistan suffer from harsh, overcrowded, and unhygienic conditions in the Uzbek prison system.[955] Prison authorities commonly beat inmates and fail to address their basic medical and nutritional needs through corruption or neglect. Diseases, particularly tuberculosis, are rampant and often go untreated. These conditions jeopardize prisoners' health and life.[956]

Independent Muslims suffer acutely from these abuses. They are also singled out for special punishment, including physical and psychological

---

[954] Human Rights Watch interview with female relative of Tavakkaljon Akhmedov, name withheld, Asaka, Andijan, May 2000.

[955] See U.S. Department of State, *2002 Country Reports on Human Rights Practices*, released by the Bureau of Democracy, Human Rights, and Labor, U.S. Department of State, March 31, 2003.

[956] Several international treaties to which Uzbekistan is a state party recognize basic rights of prisoners. Article 10 of the ICCPR, for example, states: "All persons deprived of their liberty shall be treated with humanity and with respect for the inherent dignity of the human person." Several additional international documents enumerate the human rights of persons deprived of liberty, give guidance as to how governments may comply with their obligations under international law, and provide authoritative interpretations of the norms binding on governments. The most comprehensive such guidelines are the United Nations Standard Minimum Rules for the Treatment of Prisoners [hereinafter, Standard Minimum Rules], approved by the Economic and Social Council in 1957.

mistreatment, by prison authorities.[957] This section documents human rights violations against these prisoners. Some of the violations are common to the general prison population—the authorities' failure to inform families of their relatives' whereabouts in custody, the theft of food and medicine packages. Other violations, physical abuse in particular, are common but perpetrated against Muslim prisoners in retribution for their religious status, religious expression, adherence to religious practices, or their refusal to disavow their alleged "extremist" affiliations. In nine cases that Human Rights Watch documented, the torture of independent Muslim prisoners resulted in their deaths.[958] The following section of this chapter also focuses attention on the atrocious conditions in Jaslyk prison, which is believed to have been constructed in 1998 with the specific purpose of holding prisoners convicted on religion-related charges.

Background

Uzbekistan's prison system is under the jurisdiction of the Ministry of Internal Affairs and is administered by the ministry's Main Administration for the Execution of Punishments. According to the ministry, there are thirty-five facilities in the country, including five general-regime facilities, ten strict-regime, and another facility designated as a "special" regime prison.[959] The ministry runs a separate facility for

---

[957]Human Rights Watch interview with Nikolai Mitrokhin, Central Asia researcher for the Memorial Human Rights Center, New York, March 27, 2003. Memorial has undertaken a systematic study of prison conditions in Uzbekistan and found that independent Muslim prisoners are treated more harshly than average prisoners.

[958] Seven of the men died while still incarcerated. Six of these were prisoners at Jaslyk prison. Two additional prisoners died at home within days of their release from custody. One of these prisoners had been incarcerated at Jaslyk. Human Rights Watch received reports about another six suspicious deaths of independent Muslim prisoners. Four additional men died in prison from illness compounded by torture. See, Human Rights Watch, "Deaths in Custody in Uzbekistan," Human Rights Watch Briefing Paper, April 4, 2003.

[959] "On the Basis of Humanism: The Activities of the Penal System of the Republic of Uzbekistan," *Narodnoe Slovo*, September 2000. "General-regime" corresponds roughly to minimum security, "strict-regime," to medium security, and "special-regime," to maximum security. The type of regime to which one is sentenced depends on the convict's criminal

female inmates, as well as separate prisons for minors and persons diagnosed with tuberculosis.[960]

Despite the Ministry of Internal Affairs' assertions to the contrary, the country's prisons are reportedly grossly overcrowded, exacerbating the already abysmal conditions.[961] Human Rights Watch has consistently received reports throughout the past four years that prisoners were forced to sleep "in turns" due to a lack of beds and that some men were forced to sleep on the floor when prison officials filled cells beyond capacity.[962] One prisoner held in Kiziltepa told Human Rights Watch that he had to sleep on the floor along with many others during his incarceration there in 2000.[963] Another prisoner, held in the Zangiota facility, reported that he was held in a separate wing of the prison, along with more than one hundred other religious prisoners. He said that he regularly had to sleep on the floor because of overcrowding. He reported, however, that prison guards kept fewer men to a cell during the winter, because the floor was so cold.[964] The problems associated with overcrowding were widely believed to be the primary motivation for semi-regular presidential amnesty decrees providing for the release of certain categories of prisoners.[965]

---

record and the type of crime committed, and also determines the level of prisoner privileges.

[960] Ibid.

[961] Human Rights Watch interview with rights defender Tolib Iakubov, Tashkent, May 1, 2000; and U.S. Department of State, *2002 Country Reports on Human Rights Practices*, released by the Bureau of Democracy, Human Rights, and Labor, March 31, 2003, which stated, "Prison overcrowding was a problem, with some facilities holding 10 to 15 persons in cells designed for 4."

[962] Human Rights Society of Uzbekistan (HRSU) Information Bulletin number 2, September 12, 1999; and "Voices from the Detention Places," Information Bulletin on Human Rights Violations in Uzbekistan (during the period 2002-2003), Ezgulik [online], http://www.ezgulik.org/sboreng5/sboen5-1.html (retrieved February 24, 2004).

[963] Human Rights Watch interview with former inmate, name withheld, location withheld, November 6, 2001.

[964] Human Rights Watch interview with a relative of a prisoner in Zangiota, name withheld at her request, Tashkent, February 14, 2000.

[965] Amnesties generally do not lead to a sustained decrease in the total prison population. For more information on amnesties, see below, Chapter V, and "Religious Persecution of

Generally poor conditions appeared to contribute to desperation on the part of prisoners. During a single month in 2002, as many as eight prisoners incarcerated in prison number 64/51, in Kashkadaria province, reportedly attempted to commit suicide by slitting their wrists with razor blades.[966] Two other prisoners at the facility made unsuccessful attempts to hang themselves, while another man threw himself from a third-story height, allegedly out of desperation due to hunger.[967]

Deaths Attributed to Ill-Treatment and Disease

The combination of unhygienic conditions, malnutrition, and lack of medicine and medical attention, has led to serious problems of disease and illness in Uzbekistan's prisons, sometimes resulting in death. According to one U.S. State Department report on Uzbekistan, "Tuberculosis and hepatitis are epidemic in the prisons, making even short periods of incarceration potentially deadly."[968] The absence of official government statistics on the subject makes it difficult to determine how many deaths of prisoners each year are due to tuberculosis; however, from scattered reports it appeared a common cause of death.

Independent Muslims in Uzbekistan From September 2001 to July 2002," Human Rights Watch Briefing Paper, August 21, 2002 [online], http://hrw.org/backgrounder/eca/uzbek-aug/uzbek-brief0820.pdf (retrieved February 24, 2004).

[966] Anonymous letter regarding prison conditions based on information received from prisoners, delivered to Human Rights Watch June 2002, on file with Human Rights Watch.

[967] Ibid.

[968] Lack of medicine and supplies along with the apparent indifference of prison personnel has meant that most inmates' medical ailments go untreated. Tuberculosis among the prison population poses a serious health risk and disease rates are rising. U.S. Department of State, *2001Country Reports on Human Rights Practices*, released by the Bureau of Democracy, Human Rights, and Labor, March 4, 2002 [online], http://www.state.gov/g/drl/rls/hrrpt/2001/ (retrieved January 6, 2004). The same was reported by the U.S. Department of State, *2002 Country Reports on Human Rights Practices*, released by the Bureau of Democracy, Human Rights, and Labor, March 31, 2003.

Prison officials frequently beat prisoners and subject them to ill-treatment by such actions as stealing food and medicine hand-delivered by prisoners' relatives,[969] and placing them in cells with freezing temperatures without adequate clothing. Such treatment weakens prisoners' health and can lead to or compound illness, which sometimes ends with the prisoner's death. In such a case, the official cause of death is routinely given as "tuberculosis," "sclerosis of the liver," or "septic endocarditis."[970] Authorities, however, ignored aggravating factors of ill-treatment when determining the cause of death. Human Rights Watch documented thirteen cases involving the deaths of independent Muslims that occurred between November 2001 and March 2003, in which the ill prisoner's death was preceded by physical mistreatment, denial of medical treatment, and withholding of food parcels.[971]

Contact with the Outside World and Withholding Information regarding Prisoners' Whereabouts

Prisoners are often deprived regular contact with the outside world.[972] Sanctioned visits by relatives are generally rare—sometimes limited to one visit every six months or every three months, depending on the severity of the crime of which the person was convicted. Communications to the outside world, including letters from prisoners to their families, is highly restricted. The relative of one religious prisoner, for example, learned during a visit with her son at Zangiota prison that none of the letters she had sent had reached him and that he too had sent her letters that were never delivered.[973]

---

[969] Human Rights Watch interview with relatives of "B.B.," Margilan, March 5, 2003.

[970] Endocarditis is an infection of the heart valve. Death certificates on file with Human Rights Watch.

[971] Human Rights Watch, "Deaths in Custody in Uzbekistan," Human Rights Watch Briefing Paper, April 4, 2003

[972] Rule 37 of the Standard Minimum Rules states: "Prisoners shall be allowed under necessary supervision to communicate with their family and reputable friends at regular intervals, both by correspondence and by receiving visits."

[973] Human Rights Watch interview with the mother of an independent Muslim prisoner, name withheld at her request, Tashkent, February 14, 2000.

Many religious prisoners were deprived contact with family for months at a time because their relatives did not know where they were incarcerated. Ministry of Internal Affairs officials responsible for tracking prisoners frequently withheld this information for two to three months or longer. Shukhrat Parpiev, for example, was missing in custody for seven months and Abdurashid Isakhojaev's whereabouts were unknown for five months.[974] The denial of information on prisoner whereabouts hindered family efforts to provide food, medicine, and other assistance to prisoners. It also increased the prisoners' psychological isolation and made prisoners more vulnerable to torture and ill-treatment.

- The parents of Abdurashid Isakhojaev were permitted one meeting with him at Tavaksai prison in February 1999, after he was convicted of participating in a "Wahhabi trend." It was their first visit with him since his June 1998 arrest. When his brother returned to the prison in June 1999 to bring food, he was told Isakhojaev was no longer there. Family members describe a search that lasted five months, and took them from one prison and government office to another. First, a relative was told at Zangiota prison, in Tashkent province, that Isakhojaev was indeed there but could not receive food or visitors due to a quarantine. Returning to Zangiota ten days later, relatives were told that he was not there. At the office of Rakzhab Kodirov, the deputy minister of internal affairs and head of the Main Administration for the Execution of Punishments, they were told that Isakhojaev was certainly somewhere in the Tashkent province but that the office did not possess details. When Isakhojaev's father demanded proof that his son was alive, officials at the deputy minister's office assured him that they had spoken with him and that he was alive and healthy, but they refused to say where he was. The family wrote to that office every week. Finally, in November 1999, a year after his conviction, the family was informed that Isakhojaev was being held in Tavaksai prison. Guards at that facility confirmed that he was being held there and initially told relatives they could come back to leave food for the prisoner. After his father had waited half a day outside the prison with food, officials told him that his son was not there after all, but was

[974] Human Rights Watch interview with people close to Shukhrat Parpiev, names withheld, Andijan, May 18, 2000; and Human Rights Watch interview with Sharifa Isakhojaeva, Tashkent, June 1, 2000. Both men were subsequently revealed to be in Jaslyk prison.

in Zangiota. Officials at Zangiota denied having him. Back at Kodirov's office, the relatives were told to try again in a week. When Isakhojaev's father went back to the office, he found a gathering of relatives of men whose whereabouts in custody were unknown. Then officials read out a list of prisoners sent to Jaslyk, which included Isakhojaev's name, and the elder Isakhojaev returned home with a letter from his son, sent from that harsh desert prison.[975]

- Authorities transferred Shukhrat Abdurakhimov to an unknown location after his trial. Speaking to Human Rights Watch during this period, his mother said, "I cry day and night, I just want to know where he is."[976] Abdurakhimov's mother reported that when she appealed to the office of Ombudswoman Sayora Rashidova for help in locating her son, she was refused an audience and sent to the procuracy, where officials also refused to help her.[977] The family searched for three months before learning that Abdurakhimov was being held in Zangiota prison.

- The mother of a young man convicted on charges related to his alleged "Wahhabism" reported a similar ordeal. "[H]e had been in Tashkent prison, but when I went there for a visit, they said he'd been sent to the MVD...A month later, we returned to Tashkent prison, and then they said they had sent him to Zangiota, and we went there and they said that he was not there. Then I went to Tashkent prison, but no one would tell me where he was or how to find out. For a full year we looked for him, and in the end we learned he was in Jaslyk."[978]

- The 2003 report by the U.N. Special Rapporteur on Torture related the story of Alisher Khalikov, convicted in May 2003 on charges related to alleged membership in Hizb ut-Tahrir and sentenced to three and a

---

[975] Human Rights Watch interview with Sharifa Isakhojaeva, Tashkent, June 1, 2000.

[976] Human Rights Watch interview, with the mother of Shukhrat Abdurakhimov, name withheld at her request, Tashkent, November 1999.

[977] Human Rights Watch interview with the mother of Shukhrat Abdurakhimov, name withheld at her request, April 5, 2000. For a description of the office of the Ombudsperson, see Chapter V.

[978] Human Rights Watch interview, name withheld, Andijan, May 19, 2000.

half years in prison. According to the report, Khalikov's family searched for him for four months following his conviction, before locating him finally at Karshi prison, number 64/49.[979]

Targeted Abuse of Religious Prisoners

All prisoners in Uzbekistan are vulnerable to physical abuse by guards, but religious prisoners face the risk of harsher treatment and additional beatings to "break" them during the intake process and to ensure they will comply with prison rules, including prohibitions on religious practice.[980] Beatings and ill-treatment continue throughout incarceration, as targeted punishment for violating prohibitions on prayer or other religious observance, for failing to sing the national anthem when asked to,[981] or as a means to force independent Muslim prisoners to disavow their beliefs.[982]

---

979 Report of the U.N. Special Rapporteur on Torture, Theo van Boven.

980 While numerous sources have described the "breaking" of religious convicts, a source from Hizb ut-Tahrir told Human Rights Watch that one of the principal aims of this process is to ensure the observance of prohibitions regarding religious practice. Electronic communication to Human Rights Watch from a member of Hizb ut-Tahrir, name withheld, September 3, 2000.

981 Several sources separately described this practice. After his release from Kiziltepa prison in the Bukhara province, Ismail Adylov told Human Rights Watch that prisoners were regularly beaten in that facility for failing to sing the national anthem "loud enough." Human Rights Watch interview with rights defender and former political prisoner Ismail Adylov, New York, November 2001. Prisoners in Jaslyk were also reportedly beaten for not singing the national anthem. "A Letter from Jaslyk Prison," author is anonymous, provided to Human Rights Watch May 31, 2002, on file with Human Rights Watch; and Human Rights Watch interview with Abdumalik Nazarov's lawyer, Irina Mikulina, Tashkent, December 24, 1999. Similar accounts have been received from other prisons.

982 The U.S. Department of State acknowledged in its 2003 country report the particularly harsh treatment these inmates face in Uzbekistan's prisons, including as apparent summary punishment: "Prisoners suspected of extremist [sic] Islamic political sympathies reportedly were routinely beaten and treated more harshly than criminals, regardless of whether investigators were seeking a confession." U.S. Department of State, *2002 Country Reports on Human Rights Practices*, released by the Bureau of Democracy, Human Rights, and Labor, March 31, 2003.

According to Memorial, which has undertaken a systematic study of the Uzbek prison system, prison administrations have a special regime of control over political and religious prisoners involving both the prison officials and a network of informants chosen among inmates.[983] Religious and political prisoners are more likely than others to receive demerits for violation of prison rules.[984] Demerits lead to confinement in a punishment cell and undermine the prisoner's chances for release under amnesty.[985]

Prison administrations require religious and political prisoners to wear special markings indicating their criminal status. Ismail Adylov, a human rights defender convicted in 1999 under article 159 and amnestied in 2001, served in a number of facilities, and told Human Rights Watch that prisoners convicted for religious or political reasons were given badges to wear that had a red line going through their name, to indicate their status as having been convicted under article 159.[986]

---

[983] Human Rights Watch interview with Nikolai Mitrokhin, Central Asia researcher for the Memorial Human Rights Center, New York, March 27, 2003.

[984] Ibid.

[985] Ibid. Conditions in punishment cells are notoriously poor, and guards often abuse inmates serving in them. For example, the female relative of one Hizb ut-Tahrir prisoner told Human Rights Watch, "When he was in Karshi, they put them [the prisoners] in a punishment cell and poured cold water on the floor and they were naked. I went to Karshi for a visit and he told me that." Human Rights Watch interview, name withheld at her request, Tashkent, March 1, 2000.

[986] Human Rights Watch interview with Ismail Adylov, New York, November 2001. He also showed Human Rights Watch representatives a plaque (his own) as an example of the kind that he said was posted near the bed of each political or religious prisoner, also with a red line going through the person's name. In another example, in November 1999, when relatives visited convicted Hizb ut-Tahrir member Murodjon Sattarov at Karshi prison, he showed them his shirt, which bore a red mark that he said signified in the prison that he was a "bloodsucker," a Hizb ut-Tahrir prisoner. Human Rights Watch interview with the father, mother and sister of Murodjon Sattarov, names withheld, Andijan, May 17, 2000. The Uzbek human rights group *Mazlum* (The Oppressed) has also reported that religious prisoners are addressed with certain curses and referred to as "traitor" or "enemy of the people." "Islam Karimov: '7-8 people are not wanted in the republic,'" [online] http://mazlum.ferghana.ru/index.htm (retrieved February 24, 2004).

Beatings during Intake

An inmate convicted on religion-related charges and held at Zangiota prison told a relative that when he was transferred to the facility with 130 other comparable prisoners on December 19, 1999, guards took them from the transport vehicle, formed a circle around them, and beat them with truncheons.[987]

Memorial reported that another independent Muslim prisoner from Zangiota said of arrival at the prison, "The following command is given: 'Wahhabis and hizbuchiki—three steps forward!'" The Muslim prisoners are then sent through a "corridor" lined with officers who kick them and beat them with truncheons and wooden sticks. [988]

One man sentenced in April 2000 to six years in prison for membership in Hizb ut-Tahrir and subsequently released under a presidential amnesty decree told Human Rights Watch that when he arrived at Novoi prison number 64/29, authorities there took him and seven other observant Muslim prisoners to a separate area of the prison and beat them.989

Punishment for Religious Observance

Guards have punished and beaten independent Muslim prisoners for religious observance in custody, in violation of domestic law, the ICCPR, and international standards for the treatment of prisoners.[990]

---

[987] Human Rights Watch interview with a relative of a prisoner in Zangiota, name withheld at her request, Tashkent, February 14, 2000.

[988] Information Center for Human Rights in Central Asia and Memorial Human Rights Center, "Uzbekistan: treatment of political convicts in the strict order prison located near Tashkent," Moscow, March 2001. *Hizbuchik* is a slang expression for someone affiliated with Hizb ut-Tahrir.

[989] Human Rights Watch interview with a released prisoner, name withheld, Margilan, July 12, 2002.

[990] Uzbekistan's 1998 religion law, while placing limitations on most religious expression, explicitly provided for freedom of worship for prisoners and detainees. Article 14 states, "Worship and religious rites can be exercised in hospitals, nursing homes, detention centers, prisons and labor camps at the request of the people staying there." Article 14,

Prison officials forbid observance of Muslim rites and rituals. One member of Hizb ut-Tahrir told Human Rights Watch, "The prison 'rules' prohibit ablution, prayer, fasting, calling (da'wa) to Islam, reciting Quran and require singing the [national] anthem, [seeking] forgiveness of and glorifying the president, Karimov."[991] Prison officials, the author claimed, punish prisoners who fail to comply with the rules by beating them with truncheons and stripping them and putting them in cells with "homosexuals"—the intent of the officers was apparently to frighten the prisoners that they would be raped.[992] The rights group Memorial noted that prison restrictions on religious observance have tightened during the course of the government's campaign against independent Islam. Prior to 1999 some prison colonies maintained mosques, chapels, or areas where inmates could gather for group prayer. Prison administrations closed these in 1999, and subsequently strictly enforced a ban on group or individual prayer.[993]

The majority of cases Human Rights Watch documented regarding punishment of religious observance related to prayer:

Law on Freedom of Conscience and Religious Organizations, May 1, 1998. It remained unclear whether prison administrators were ignorant of the law, chose to violate this provision, or were ordered to do so by their superiors. As noted in the report on Uzbekistan issued by the U.N. Special Rapporteur on Torture in 2003, the internal rules of Uzbekistan's prisons are not available to the public. Report of the U.N. Special Rapporteur on Torture, Theo van Boven. Regarding international standards, the Standard Minimum Rules states in principle 6 that all prison regulations are to be carried out on an impartial basis and, further, that "...it is necessary to respect the religious beliefs and moral precepts of the group to which a prisoner belongs." The Standard Minimum Rules also recommends that space be provided for prisoners to practice their faith in conjunction with others, including through attendance at religious services in the facility. Rule 42 states, "...every prisoner shall be allowed to satisfy the needs of his religious life by attending the services provided in the institution and having in his possession the books of religious observance and instruction of his denomination."

[991] Electronic communication to Human Rights Watch from a member of Hizb ut-Tahrir, name withheld, September 3, 2000.

[992] Ibid. It is not clear that the other prisoners were in fact homosexuals. The reference to "homosexuals" appers to have been an attempt by the prison authorities to instill fear in the targets of their harassment, independent Muslim prisoners, that they would be raped by fellow inmates.

[993] Human Rights Watch interview with Nikolai Mitrokhin, New York, March 27, 2003.

▪ A thirty-one-year-old man who was not, apparently, imprisoned for his religious beliefs or affiliation, became religious after his conviction. In a letter addressed to the Procurator General and provided to Human Rights Watch in July 2002, "Bobomurod Bobomurodov" (not his real name) describes his experience in June 2002 at prison number 36 in Novoi province:

> Prison guards…gave my name to Captain of Internal Affairs ["A.A."] because they suspected me of praying. …they asked me for how many years and how many times a day I prayed. I answered that I prayed five times a day. They asked me whether I prayed here in the prison as well. I answered that I did. It is true that I prayed, but I did not disturb anyone. I sat by myself and read the sura to myself…. Captain of Internal Affairs ["B.B."] punched me on my ear. When he hit a second time…my head started spinning and I fell to the floor. Then he started kicking me in the side and my [ribs]. He also insulted me in any way he could think of, including insulting my mother. Then he ordered [A.A.] to bring me to the solitary confinement cell and deprive me of my male dignity by raping me. [A.A.] and another supervisor having brought me to the solitary confinement cell, beat me with rubber batons, and kicked me with their leather boots. My entire body was covered with marks and bruises. I wanted to go to the director of the prison, Lieutenant Colonel O. M. Safarov, but they wouldn't let me. They brought me to a room where I was held. After this my health deteriorated.[994]

▪ While in Tashkent prison, Usmon Inagamov continued his practice of praying five times daily. Prison officials reportedly beat Inagamov and

[994] Letter from an inmate in prison number 36, Navoi, name withheld, letter on file with Human Rights Watch. "A.A. and "B.B." are not the respective captains' true initials. Their names are on file with Human Rights Watch. The letter was provided to Human Rights Watch in July 2002.

deprived him of food as punishment for his practice.[995] Prison guards also repeatedly confined him to a punishment cell for praying.[996] Already ill with cancer at the time of his arrest, Inagamov reportedly contracted tuberculosis and suffered deteriorating health because prison authorities denied him proper care.[997] He died in prison on March 15, 2000. The immediate cause of death is unclear.

Prisoners in the Kashkadaria facility (prison number 64/51), Nasriddin Shamsiddinov, Ikrom Usvaliev, and Baktior Orzikulov, were also confined in punishment cells, reportedly for raising their hands by their heads while performing daily prayers.[998] Prayer was also forbidden at Zangiota prison and punished with beatings.[999] Similar reports came out of Karshi prison, where guards allegedly beat inmates with truncheons as punishment for breaking the prohibition against prayer.[1000]

- Shukhrat Abdurakhimov, confined in Zangiota prison, described to his family the beatings he had suffered during the first three months

[995] Written report by human rights defender Vasila Inoiatova, April 2000.

[996] Ibid.

[997] Ibid. Prison officials reportedly failed to deliver much-needed food and medicine to Inagamov provided by his family.

[998] Anonymous letter regarding prison conditions based on information received from prisoners, delivered to Human Rights Watch in June 2002, on file with Human Rights Watch. Fear of the punishment cell at the Kashkadaria prison was reportedly so great that one prisoner, Iuri Bushev, allegedly attempted suicide to avoid being sent there.

[999] Human Rights Watch interview with the mother of an independent Muslim prisoner, name withheld at her request, Tashkent, February 14, 2000.

[1000] Human Rights Watch interview with a Karshi prisoner's relative, name withheld at the interviewee's request, Tashkent, August 1, 1999. The report by the U.N. Special Rapporteur on Torture also described punishment for prayer at Prison Number 44/49 in Karshi. The report notes that prison guards allegedly beat and kicked Alisher Khalikov and forced him to do push-ups as punishment for praying. It further adds, "[Khalikov] is said not to be able to benefit from an amnesty as the prison authorities are said to note every day that he is violating internal prison rules (inter alia, by praying)." Report of the U.N. Special Rapporteur on Torture, Theo van Boven.

after his conviction. He also told relatives that guards routinely beat those prisoners who pray.[1001]

Prison authorities have banned such basic religious literature as copies of the Koran:

- The relative of one religious prisoner told Human Rights Watch that when she attempted to donate a copy of the Koran to the prison where her relative was being held, offering it even to the prison library in hopes he would have access to it there, the authorities refused to take it, saying that the Koran was a "political book."[1002]

- According to a press report, some 200 convicted members of Hizb ut-Tahrir incarcerated in Zarafshan prison, just 280 miles outside of Tashkent, wrote a letter to President Karimov on July 24, 2002 regarding restrictions on religion. They complained that prison officials had violated their right to worship and observe religious rites and they called for the government to allow them access to religious literature in prison.[1003]

Authorities also punish prisoners for proselytizing. On August 26, 1999, three days after Tavakkaljon Akhmedov's conviction for Hizb ut-Tahrir membership, his wife went to Andijan prison to meet with him. At the prison, however, authorities told her he would not be brought out to see her that day, as he was in a punishment cell in the prison basement for having violated prison rules—proselytizing, they said.[1004] He was kept in

---

[1001] Human Rights Watch interview, name withheld, Tashkent, May 9, 2000. On his first day in prison, guards beat Abdurakhimov in order to force him to reject prayer. Meeting with then-U.S. Ambassador-at-Large for Religious Freedom, Robert Seiple, and Human Rights Watch, name withheld, Tashkent, May 23, 2000. Abdurakhimov's family was unable to locate him following his conviction and he was missing in custody for the first three months of his incarceration.

[1002] Human Rights Watch interview with the relative of a Muslim prisoner, name withheld at her request, Tashkent, March 17, 2003.

[1003] "Uzbek prisoners held for religious extremism threaten to riot if conditions don't improve," Bagila Bukharbayeva, Associated Press, Tashkent, July 29, 2002.

[1004] Human Rights Watch interview with the wife of Tavakkaljon Akhmedov, name withheld at her request, Asaka, Andijan, May 2000.

the punishment cell for ten days. In December Akhmedov was sent to Tashkent prison, then transferred to Kashkadaria prison number 64/51 in southern Uzbekistan on January 11, 2000. A female relative who visited him told Human Rights Watch:

> In Kashkadaria, the conditions are bad and the guards torture Hizb ut-Tahrir prisoners. He [Akhmedov] looked terrible there...It was clear he had been tortured, but he wouldn't talk about it...I heard the prisoners screaming, and the workers at the prison told me, 'They [the prisoners] are enemies of the state and that's why they're treated so harshly.'[1005]

Punishments to Compel Statements of Contrition or Disavowals of Religious Beliefs

Prison officials reacted swiftly and severely when independent Muslims refused to sign statements of repentance. For instance, according to one authoritative report, Dshamurad Makhmudov, imprisoned on charges of possession of Hizb ut-Tahrir literature, was threatened and physically abused for his refusal to repent. Makhmudov was imprisoned in Zangiota when authorities threatened to send him to Jaslyk, a harsher facility, unless he asked for forgiveness. They allowed a visit from his relatives and then threatened he would never see them again unless he signed. According to the report, "When refusing to negate his beliefs, Dshamurad Makhmudov was reportedly taken to the medical unit early August 2002, as if to examine him, and was reportedly beaten there with bats. Four of his teeth were pulled out, and it is reported that he is bearing scars on the left side of his mouth."[1006]

- Twenty-six-year-old Muslim prisoner Jalaluddin Mamamirzaev, spent fifteen days (from January 25, 2002 to February 10, 2002) in a punishment cell, where officers beat him in the kidney area and kicked

---

[1005] Human Rights Watch interview with a female relative of Tavakkaljon Akhmedov, Asaka, Andijan, May 2000.

[1006] Report of the U.N. Special Rapporteur on Torture, Theo van Boven, p. 56.

him in the neck, for refusing to renounce his faith.[1007] He allegedly was beaten to the point where he could no longer walk.[1008] A fellow inmate in the Kashkadaria prison, Komil Khaitov, was also punished with sixty days in isolation to force him to renounce his faith and write a letter asking for the government's forgiveness for his "crimes."[1009]

- At least twenty religious prisoners were reportedly raped in Kashkadaria prison in 2002 to force them to renounce their religious beliefs or affiliation.[1010] A representative from the Kashkadaria province procuracy reportedly visited the facility on March 18, 2002. The representative took the names of sixteen rape victims and met with several Muslim prisoners who had complained of rape by prison authorities. Several men who had complained earlier were reportedly kept in isolation wards during the visit. The following day, prison officials gathered the sixteen alleged rape victims and threatened them with additional abuse, including additional sexual violence, unless they withdrew their complaints.[1011] When Colonel S. Islamov of the Ministry of Internal Affairs came to inspect the facility on March 22, 2002, he allegedly announced to the 2,600 prisoners assembled, "If someone was raped, it's in the past, it's not necessary to talk about it to everyone like sluts. We are not scared of any commissions, whether it's from the 'Red Cross' or the U.N.—we don't give a shit."[1012]

The Uzbek rights group *Ezgulik* (Good Deed) reported another case involving a convicted Hizb ut-Tahir member serving his sentence in Zarafshan prison. Prison officials beat Mashrab Mirzakhmedov with truncheons and put him in a punishment cell when he refused to write a

---

[1007] Anonymous letter regarding prison conditions based on information received from prisoners, delivered to Human Rights Watch June 2002, on file with Human Rights Watch.

[1008] Ibid.

[1009] Ibid.

[1010] Ibid. The names of the rape victims have been withheld by Human Rights Watch.

[1011] Ibid.

[1012] Ibid.

statement asking for President Karimov's pardon and recanting his beliefs.[1013]

Denying Opportunities for Amnesty

As noted above, observing such Muslim rituals as prayer and fasting is regarded as violation of the internal prison rules punishable by terms in punishment cells and a demerit on the inmate's prison record. Three demerits make a prisoner automatically ineligible for release under any amnesty passed during that period.

Prison authorities have accused religious prisoners, in particular, of violating prison rules, in order to make them ineligible for future amnesty provisions. They also fabricate other violations, such as drug possession or possession of money, or beat religious prisoners in order to force them to admit to false accusations of breaking prison rules.

- Guards at Kulyuk women's prison, located on the edge of Tashkent, used accusations of rule-breaking to extend the sentence of convicted Hizb ut-Tahrir member Shoknoza Musaeva.[1014] Specifically, they accused her of having violated the prison's prohibitions on certain religious practices, including wearing a headscarf "incorrectly" in the presence of guards and fasting during the Muslim holiday of Ramadan.[1015] In at least one instance, according to former fellow inmate Mahbuba Kosymova, guards planted a syringe on Musaeva, setting her up with a serious violation of the prison regime.[1016] As of February 2001, said Kosymova, Musaeva had been charged with twelve infractions of prison rules.[1017] Prison authorities, who labeled Musaeva

---

[1013] Ezgulik, "A Voice from Prison," [online], http://www.Ezgulik.org (retrieved January 6, 2004).

[1014] Human Rights Watch interview with rights defender Mahbuba Kosymova, Tashkent, March 15, 2001. Kosymova was in prison together with Musaeva.

[1015] Human Rights Watch interview with Mahbuba Kosymova, Tashkent, December 23, 2000.

[1016] Human Rights Watch interview with Mahbuba Kosymova, Tashkent, February 6, 2001.

[1017] Ibid.

"enemy number one" in the prison, placed the twenty-nine-year-old in solitary confinement in a punishment cell, first for eight days, then another ten days, and for an unknown length of time again in March 2001.[1018]

Jaslyk Prison

At minimum, hundreds of religious prisoners have been sent to Jaslyk prison.[1019] Local rights groups contend that the government has designated Jaslyk for religious and political prisoners.[1020] The majority of its inmates are reportedly independent Muslims; other inmates include persons convicted of terrorism or other violent crimes who had no connection to religious or political dissident groups.[1021]

Located in the desert of Karakalpakstan Autonomous Republic in the far northeast of the country, this prison is known for particularly high

[1018] Human Rights Watch interview with Mahbuba Kosymova, Tashkent, March 15, 2001.

[1019] Jaslyk prison's official number is 64/71.

[1020] "Uzbek activist tells Iranian radio about sorry plight of religious convicts," excerpt of *Iranian Radio Mashhad* interview with HRSU director Tolib Iakubov, English translation in BBC Monitoring, April 23, 2002; and Human Rights Watch interview with attorney Irina Mikulina, Tashkent, October 30, 1999. A similar view was expressed by Matthew Brzezinski, "In Uzbekistan, Whatever it Takes: Central Asian strongmen appear to have been inspired by Genghis Khan," *The New York Times*, December 16, 2001. The article referred to Jaslyk as a "desert gulag" that was "specifically constructed to house the growing influx of religious prisoners."

[1021] Those convicted on common criminal charges are reportedly held in a separate part of the facility, apart from those convicted on religious and political charges. Human Rights Watch interview with attorney Irina Mikulina, Tashkent, December 24, 1999. Lack of information makes it difficult to determine whether certain Jaslyk inmates, convicted on common criminal charges, were targeted because of their religious ties. For example, in 1998 the Supreme Court sentenced fifteen men to prison terms in Jaslyk for a series of armed robberies and violent attacks in the Fergana Valley. Fourteen of the men were, according to Vasilia Inoiatova, students of disappeared Imam Abduvali Mirzoev and prior to their arrest had actively sought to find him. Human Rights Watch interview with rights defender Vasila Inoiatova, Tashkent, January 27, 2000. Human Rights Watch did not have sufficient information at the time of this writing to determine whether the case against these men constituted a reprisal for their religious association and beliefs or was based on a legitimate law enforcement interest.

rates of torture and other mistreatment by guards and for inmate deaths from torture and disease. As noted elsewhere, Jaslyk is officially designated a general-regime prison.[1022] However, it is known for having the harshest penal conditions in the nation.

The isolation of the setting has been reinforced by authorities' policies on visitation. As of this writing, not a single attorney had been allowed to visit a client in Jaslyk. Family visits were not permitted until December 1999. Persons arriving by train (there is no paved road to the desert town of Jaslyk) were compelled by police to show a telegram proving that the prison had issued them an invitation before police guarding the train station would allow them to disembark at Jaslyk.[1023] When a Human Rights Watch representative visited the town of Jaslyk, close to the prison, in July 1999, the local police chief told her that entry to the area was prohibited and visitors must have the special permission of President Karimov even to enter the town.[1024] Even when families are permitted to visit, the cost of travel from virtually anywhere in Uzbekistan is prohibitive. Uzbek authorities allowed the U.N. Special Rapporteur on Torture to visit Jaslyk in December 2002, but the two hours allotted was insufficient for a meaningful visit.[1025]

At least during the early operation of the facility in 1999, authorities routinely failed to notify relatives that their imprisoned family members had been transferred from other prisons to Jaslyk. The prisoners were then, effectively, missing in custody for months and cut off from even

---

[1022] Human Rights Watch interview with Deputy Minister of Internal Affairs Sadulla Asadov, Tashkent, October 1999.

[1023] Human Rights Watch interview with rights defender Vasilia Inoiatova, who traveled by train to Jaslyk in December 1999, Tashkent, January 27, 2000; and Human Rights Watch interview with Irina Mikulina, attorney for a Jaslyk prisoner, Tashkent, October 30, 1999.

[1024] Human Rights Watch interview with Jaslyk police chief, Jaslyk, July 1999. The officer declined to give his name.

[1025] The Special Rapporteur stated that a proper visit to Jaslyk required six hours. Report of the U.N. Special Rapporteur on Torture, Theo van Boven. p. 15.

infrequent visits and transfer of food, clothing, and medicine from relatives.[1026]

Several people have described the general conditions in Jaslyk that violate international standards for the treatment of prisoners. Regarding religious prisoners, Irina Mikulina, attorney for one inmate, said prisoners were kept in their cells for as long as six months without being let outside for fresh air or exercise.[1027] Echoing accounts from others, Mikulina said that prisoners were kept in cells with up to sixteen other inmates and were forced to crouch on their heels with their hands behind their necks all day long.[1028] If a prisoner so much as stretches his leg, she said, he has to say, "Thank you President Karimov."[1029] Prisoners are not allowed to speak to one another.[1030]

Those who have visited their relatives in Jaslyk noted the severely weakened state of their family members, indicating the extremely poor conditions in the facility. The mother of an inmate at Jaslyk sentenced to fifteen years for "Wahhabism" managed to visit her son in December 1999—she was among the first relatives of Jaslyk inmates to obtain such permission. He was obviously weak from malnutrition. She said the prisoners ate barley once a day and were given one loaf of bread a day to be shared by three men.[1031] Another visitor at the prison told her that

---

[1026] Undated report by rights defender Vasila Inoiatova, based on interviews with several relatives of prisoners. On file with Human Rights Watch. For accounts of authorities' failure to notify families of their relatives' location in custody, see above in this chapter.

[1027] Human Rights Watch interview with Irina Mikulina, Tashkent, December 24, 1999. This treatment violates the United Nations Standard Minimum Rules for the Treatment of Prisoners, adopted 30 August 1995, Part 1, Section 21.

[1028] Human Rights Watch interview with Irina Mikulina, Tashkent, December 24, 1999; and undated report by rights defender Vasila Inoiatova, based on interviews with several relatives of prisoners. On file with Human Rights Watch.

[1029] Human Rights Watch interview with Irina Mikulina, Tashkent, December 24, 1999. A similar account was given by Vasila Inoiatova. Human Rights Watch interview with rights defender Vasila Inoiatova, Tashkent, January 27, 2000.

[1030] Human Rights Watch interview with Irina Mikulina, Tashkent, December 24, 1999.

[1031] Human Rights Watch interview with "F.F." [not the woman's true initials], Andijan, May 19, 2000.

the inmates were not allowed any fresh air and that guards forced them to crouch in their cells with their hands on their bowed heads, singing the national hymn, while guards beat each prisoner on the back.[1032]

Punishment for Religious Observance

As reported by inmates in other prisons, persons incarcerated at Jaslyk were allegedly beaten, threatened with sexual violence, and placed in solitary confinement for refusing to renounce their religious beliefs.[1033]

Observance of Muslim religious rites is prohibited in the prison.[1034] Those who observed daily prayers were reportedly punished with fifteen days in isolation cells and denial of food.[1035]

United Nations Special Rapporteur on Torture, Theo van Boven, reported on his conversation with the director, or warden, of Jaslyk prison: "The director stressed that muftis come to teach to prisoners 'real' Islam, because of the proselytism by religious terrorists detained in Jaslyk colony. The director proudly mentioned that 70-80 per cent of the detainees write letters of repentance, and that he personally exhorts them to do so."[1036]

Torture

Guards at Jaslyk beat prisoners to "break" them during the intake process, to punish them for religious observance, and to compel them to disavow their religious affiliations and faith.

[1032] Ibid.

[1033] "A Letter from Jaslyk Prison," author anonymous, provided to Human Rights Watch May 31, 2002. On file with Human Rights Watch.

[1034] Human Rights Society of Uzbekistan report on Uzbekistan, translated into English and distributed by the Kyrgyz Committee for Human Rights, January 3, 2000. On file with Human Rights Watch.

[1035] "A Letter from Jaslyk Prison," author anonymous, provided to Human Rights Watch May 31, 2002. On file with Human Rights Watch.

[1036] Report of the U.N. Special Rapporteur on Torture, Theo van Boven, p. 31.

The attorney for one Jaslyk prisoner, Abdumalik Nazarov, described, in detail, beatings during the intake process. The lawyer, Irina Mikulina, told Human Rights Watch that Nazarov arrived at Jaslyk prison by airplane along with 250 other prisoners—their hands and feet bound—on May 29, 1999.[1037] Upon arrival they were shoved to the ground "like sacks" and then forced to run a "living corridor" or gauntlet of prison guards approximately one hundred meters long (about one hundred yards) up to the prison entrance, while the officers beat them with metal rods and kicked them, causing some to fall.[1038]

Rights defender Vasila Inoiatova reported that beatings by a gauntlet of officers were in fact a regular occurrence at Jaslyk, not only upon arrival, but also as part of the daily routine.[1039] A Khorezm woman, whose son and husband were both imprisoned in Jaslyk, told Inoiatova that her husband was suffering from medical problems, including blood in his urine, as a result of a practice by guards that involved lining prisoners up in a row, tying their hands and feet together, and then kicking them repeatedly in the groin.[1040]

The mother of the young man serving a fifteen-year sentence for "Wahhabism" told Human Rights Watch, "They'd beaten him so badly that he couldn't even lift up a teapot. He had bruises all over him. We told him to take off his clothes, and we saw that he had bruises all over...

[1037] Human Rights Watch interview with Abdumalik Nazarov's lawyer, Irina Mikulina, Tashkent, December 24, 1999. Abdumalik Nazarov's mother, Muharramkhon Nazarova, reported what Abdumalik told his father during a fifteen-minute visit in 2000 about his horrific arrival at Jaslyk. She said he was transported by plane along with 250 other prisoners from Tashkent. The men were forced to sit crouched with their heads bowed. Human Rights Watch interview with Muharramkhon Nazarova, Tashkent, February 19, 2000. This account was corroborated also by a local rights defender. Human Rights Watch interview with Vasila Inoiatova, Tashkent, January 27, 2000.

[1038] Human Rights Watch interview with Abdumalik Nazarov's lawyer, Irina Mikulina, Tashkent, December 24, 1999; and Human Rights Watch interview with Muharramkhon Nazarova, Tashkent, February 19, 2000.

[1039] Undated report by rights defender Vasila Inoiatova, based on her interviews with relatives of prisoners. On file with Human Rights Watch.

[1040] Human Rights Watch interview with Vasila Inoiatova, Tashkent, January 27, 2000. Inoiatova reported that this information came from an interview with Mrs. Davletova.

'We are so tired,' he said, 'they torture us.'[1041] The woman noted how fearful he was. Guards interrupted the visit every ten minutes, she said, and each time an officer entered the room, her son would jump from his seat and rush over to greet the guard. Following the family visit, guards at Jaslyk beat the young man again, so badly that he was committed to the prison hospital in Tashkent. There, officials refused to allow any family visits or deliveries of food.[1042]

During the first months of Abdurashid Isakhojaev's incarceration, prison authorities refused to disclose his whereabouts to his parents, but on December 25, 1999, prison officials finally allowed relatives to meet with him in Jaslyk prison. The following is his mother's account of the visit:

> They showed us to a room. I heard someone screaming at my son and looked in the corridor and saw two men were carrying him—he could not stand on his own. Abdurashid was so afraid of the man who yelled at him. He said, "No, no, it's probably just because it's my first time in fresh air." They brought him to the room and he couldn't sit normally. When the men went out for a minute, his brother asked him how he was, but Abdurashid was afraid and said all was well. He refused his brother's request to show his body. But I insisted, and I saw the bruises all over, and they were clearly from a truncheon. I asked him what happened. He said, "No, all is well." He was glad to be alive because many couldn't take it. We put him on the bed because he couldn't sit up. [1043]

When relatives saw Isakhojaev again on April 14, 2000, he was in dire physical condition.[1044] Afterward, his parents were called into Warden

[1041] Human Rights Watch interview with "F.F.," Andijan, May 19, 2000.

[1042] Ibid.

[1043] Human Rights Watch interview with Sharifa Isakhojaeva, Tashkent, June 1, 2000.

[1044] Ibid.

Ozod Bobojonov's office, where he questioned them about letters they had written to government authorities complaining about Abdurashid's health and conditions in prison. The elderly parents were told to write a letter of thanks to the prison warden. According to the prisoner's mother, Sharifa Isakhojaeva, "We thought about our son in the next room, in their hands, and we wrote the letter."[1045]

Deaths Due to Torture

Human Rights Watch documented six deaths of independent Muslims in Jaslyk prison, from torture, between May 1998 and September 2003.[1046] One additional prisoner was tortured in Jaslyk and then died at home two days after his release.[1047] Below are several examples of deaths from torture in Jaslyk.

On August 8, 2002, the bodies of two independent Muslims, Muzafar Avazov and Husnidin Alimov, were returned to their families. Individuals who viewed Avazov's body told Human Rights Watch that it showed signs of torture, including burns on the legs, buttocks, and lower back.[1048] Doctors who saw the body reported that such burns could only have been caused by immersing Avazov in boiling water.[1049] Those who

---

[1045] Ibid.

[1046] Human Rights Watch documented a total of nine deaths of independent Muslims as a direct result of torture in prison. Seven of the men died while still incarcerated. Six of these were prisoners at Jaslyk prison. Two additional prisoners died at home within days of their release from custody. One of these prisoners had been incarcerated at Jaslyk. Human Rights Watch received reports about another six suspicious deaths of independent Muslim prisoners; four of the men were prisoners at the Jaslyk facility. Four additional men died in prison from illness compounded by torture; at least one of these prisoners had been held in Jaslyk. See, Human Rights Watch, "Deaths in Custody in Uzbekistan," Human Rights Watch Briefing Paper, April 4, 2003.

[1047] See below in this chapter, the case of Khusniddin Khikmatov.

[1048] Human Rights Watch interview, name withheld, Tashkent, August 9, 2002. The burns and bruising were later confirmed by photographic evidence. Photographs on file with Human Rights Watch.

[1049] Report of the U.N. Special Rapporteur on Torture, Theo van Boven, p. 16. The report noted that a forensics expert at the University of Glasgow in the United Kingdom had concluded from examination of photographs of Avazov's body that "[t]he pattern of scalding

saw Avazov's body also reported that there was a large, bloody wound on the back of his head, heavy bruising on his forehead and the side of his neck, and that his hands had no fingernails.[1050] The authorities restricted viewing of Alimov's corpse.

In May 2002 Human Rights Watch received reports that prison authorities had beaten Muzafar Avazov and put him in a punishment cell for stating that nothing could stop him from performing his prayers.

Prior to Alimov's death, relatives of people imprisoned in Jaslyk told Human Rights Watch that prison officials had also confined Alimov in a punishment cell. He was reportedly placed there before the end of June and spent many weeks there before his death.[1051]

In a May 2002 letter detailing mistreatment of prisoners in Jaslyk, Alimov was reported as being one of four men who were tortured—they were tied up with rope and raped with truncheons—at the prison from May 14 to May 15 for refusing to ask the government's pardon for their supposed crimes and for failure to sing the national anthem.[1052]

On May 26, 2002, Khusniddin Khikmatov died at home, after being released, critically ill, from Jaslyk prison.[1053] He had been serving a

---

shows a well-demarcated line on the lower chest/abdomen, which could well indicate the forceful application of hot water whilst the person is within some kind of bath or similar vessel. Such scalding does not have the splash pattern that is associated with random application as one would expect with accidental scalding." That report also noted that the director of Jaslyk prison contended that Avazov's burns were the result of boiling water from teapots being thrown at him during a fight between prisoners, and the prison director's theory that Avazov's skin burned particularly fast because of his dark complexion.

[1050] Human Rights Watch interview, name withheld, Tashkent, August 9, 2002.

[1051] Human Rights Watch telephone interview with a person close to the Alimov family, name withheld, August 9, 2002.

[1052] "Letter from Jaslyk Prison," author is anonymous, received by Human Rights Watch on May 31, 2002, on file with Human Rights Watch. The letter named the men responsible for the torture as being: senior lieutenant of the internal discipline department at the prison, Karim Atajonov, along with lieutenant Saitbai, officers Makhmud and Baktior, medical attendant Abad Utimurodov, and officers Otabek and Ziyod Jumaev.

[1053] Human Rights Watch interview, name withheld, Tashkent, July 22, 2002.

seventeen-year prison term on charges deriving from his membership in Hizb ut-Tahrir and possession of a book on Islam that the authorities deemed "extremist."[1054] His death certificate stated that he had died from a "severe intestinal illness."[1055] Days before his death, however, Khikmatov recounted to people close to him the punishment meted out to him in prison for praying and refusing to ask for forgiveness from President Karimov.[1056]

Khikmatov had said that beatings in Jaslyk prison began the day he arrived. When relatives visited him in February 2002, they witnessed bruising on his back and arms. He told them that prison guards beat him, including on the soles of his feet, for refusing to ask for forgiveness from President Karimov and refusing to sing the national anthem.[1057]

In April he began to pray openly, having previously only prayed in secret. For this he was placed in a punishment cell and two prison officers brutally beat him with batons for four days. By the fourth day he became ill with a high temperature and diarrhea. He was taken to the medical ward in Jaslyk prison. When his condition failed to improve, the authorities told him that he would be transferred to the prison hospital in Tashkent. First, however, they took him to Nukus, a town several hours from Jaslyk, and held him in custody for two weeks without medical treatment, he believed in order for his bruises to fade. At this stage he was unable to walk or eat—the authorities fed him via an intravenous drip. The authorities then transported him approximately 1,200 kilometers to Tashkent, twenty-six hours by train, declining the option of sending him on an available flight.[1058]

[1054] Verdict of the Tashkent City Court, issued by Judge M.A. Abduzhabbarov, September 25, 2001.

[1055] Human Rights Watch interview, name withheld, Tashkent, July 22, 2002.

[1056] Ibid.

[1057] Ibid.

[1058] Undated written statement from a person close to the case, name withheld, on file with Human Rights Watch; and Human Rights Watch interview, name withheld, Tashkent, May 26, 2002.

Khikmatov arrived in Tashkent on May 16, 2002. On May 24 he was released from prison custody and taken to Infectious Diseases Hospital Number 5 in Tashkent, where police continued to monitor him and his visitors. Khikmatov lost consciousness early on May 26; that day the family took him home without the permission of hospital staff. He died in the early afternoon.[1059]

Police questioned visitors to the family home during the ceremony preceding the burial, refusing entry to some. There was a large police presence during the funeral.[1060] The family told Human Rights Watch there had been no discussion with the authorities about an investigation, and made clear that they felt too intimidated to press the issue.[1061] No known investigation into Khikmatov's death has been initiated.

Shukhrat Parpiev, sentenced to five years in prison for concealing the alleged crimes of his boss, died in Jaslyk in May 2000, apparently from torture.[1062] The condition of his body when it was returned, in bloody sheets, indicated torture: part of his head was smashed, his collarbone was broken, he had broken ribs, and his body was covered with what appeared to be scratches and bruises.[1063]

Illness-related Deaths Compounded by Torture or Ill-treatment

In February 2002 Mirkamol Solikhojaev died at age thirty-seven in Jaslyk prison. The official cause of death was tuberculosis, but Human Rights Watch received reports from persons close to Solikhojaev that he had been systematically beaten by guards with truncheons and barbed wire,

---

[1059] Human Rights Watch interview, name withheld, Tashkent, July 22, 2002.

[1060] Ibid.

[1061] Human Rights Watch interview, name withheld, Tashkent, date withheld.

[1062] Human Rights Watch interview with persons close to Shukhrat Parpiev, names withheld, Andijan, May 18, 2000.

[1063] This description of the body was given by those who viewed the corpse. Human Rights Watch interview with persons close to Shukhrat Parpiev, names withheld, Andijan, May 18, 2000.

leaving puncture wounds, during his incarceration. Because the authorities did not investigate the abuse, the degree to which it contributed to Solikhojaev's death could not be determined.[1064]

Twenty-five-year-old Dilmurod Umarov, incarcerated in Jaslyk prison after a conviction on charges of religious infraction and anti-state activity, died there in July 2000. When his mother arrived on July 6 for what she was expecting to be a twenty-four hour visit, prison staff told her she would have only two hours. She reportedly overheard guards discussing her son: one said that Umarov was dying, and another reportedly ordered, "Then bring out a body, at least."[1065] Another prisoner's father, at the prison visiting his son, was with Umarov's mother when guards carried him out.[1066] According to him and another witness, Umarov could not stand on his own; his eyes were "strange" as if he were on strong medication; and he could not open his mouth to speak, he was so weak and incapacitated.[1067] When Umarov's mother expressed concern about her son, Warden Ozod Bobojonov reportedly told her all was in order.[1068] On July 19, less than two weeks later, Enakhon Umarova received a telegram saying her son had died from an illness and that she and her husband could travel to pick up his body. The official cause of death was reportedly given as tuberculosis, but sources who saw his body at the time of burial said he was covered with bruises.[1069]

Abdujalil Gafurov, whom police arrested out of the bazaar where he worked in 1999 on charges of membership in Hizb ut-Tahrir, was sent

[1064] Human Rights Watch, "Religious Persecution of Independent Muslims in Uzbekistan from September 2001 to July 2002," Human Rights Watch Briefing Paper, August 21, 2002.

[1065] Written statement by rights defender Vasilia Inoiatova, dated July 25, 2000; and Human Rights Watch interview with Vasila Inoiatova, Tashkent, March 8, 2000.

[1066] Rahim Juraev was visiting his son Beksot, whose case is described above in Chapter III.

[1067] Human Rights Watch interview with Rahim Juraev, Tashkent, July 16, 2000; and written statement by Vasila Inoiatova, dated July 25, 2000.

[1068] Written statement by Vasilia Inoiatova, dated July 25, 2000.

[1069] Ibid.

to Jaslyk.[1070] He was reportedly placed in an isolation cell where he was forced to stand in cold water. Gafurov contracted tuberculosis and died at age thirty on February 21, 2001.[1071]

[1070] Human Rights Watch interview, name withheld, Tashkent, February 27, 2001. Gafurov's brother, arrested along with him, was sent to Tavaksai prison.

[1071] Ibid.

V. IMPEDIMENTS TO REDRESS AND RELIEF

The government of Uzbekistan did not provide for redress for independent Muslims who were subjected to discriminatory arrest and conviction. High courts rarely remedied unjust verdicts against individuals on appeal. They did not conduct any systematic review of cases of independent Muslims to determine the legitimacy of the trend of convictions on religious grounds. Release by presidential amnesty decree proved an arbitrary, and even illusory, means of redress. Government agencies, including those tasked with championing citizen rights and helping victims of government abuse to obtain redress, displayed marked indifference or open hostility.

Citizens who pursued justice or relief outside of the framework of domestic law and government were hindered and often punished. When victims and their families appealed to relevant U.N. bodies competent to investigate cases after domestic remedies were exhausted, the government appeared to ignore the U.N. bodies' communications. In at least two cases, the authorities harassed those who appealed to U.N. agencies. Victims of the government's campaign who appealed to local or international rights groups were also harassed and threatened by law enforcement authorities.

Police thwarted efforts by relatives of convicted independent Muslims to organize and protest the government campaign. Demonstrations and other acts of peaceful public assembly were forcibly dispersed and participants were beaten, detained, arrested, and subjected to ongoing intrusive and intimidating surveillance. The complaints and requests of people at such gatherings were almost uniformly ignored by government officials to whom the public appeals were addressed.

Denial of Legal and Other Appeals

Because in practice the judiciary has no independence in Uzbekistan, the courts have provided little justice in the first instance or redress on appeal for independent Muslim defendants. Other possible avenues of redress, such as the office of the Ombudsperson, under parliamentary authority, and the influential entities of the official Muslim clergy, have also proven unresponsive, even outright hostile, to entreaties from victims' families. Recourse to intergovernmental organizations and nongovernmental rights groups also proved a dangerous business, as it brought retaliation from government authorities.

Appeals to Government Entities

Another avenue of possible redress is the potential intervention of government offices—the presidency, the procuracy, and the Ombudsperson's office.[1072] Families of detainees approached these agencies with a variety of issues, ranging from claims of illegal arrest to request for an ill detainee's transfer to a prison hospital. But efforts to engage these officials have been generally ineffective and even counterproductive, frequently resulting in a curt denial or dismissive reply that the complainant's appeal has been passed on to another agency. Victims and their families have been particularly distraught after their appeals to the Ombudsperson's office—the agency charged with liaising between victims and government and with facilitating redress for rights abuses—were not acted upon. In fact, complaints to the Ombudsperson were often merely forwarded to the police investigator or prosecutor responsible for the case, often the very subject of the prisoner or relative's complaint.

- The Ergashev family, for instance, appealed to Ombudsperson Sayora Rashidova (Rashidova herself is a member of parliament) with their allegations of procedural violations in the case of young Khojiakbar Ergashev. The Ombudsperson's office did not respond, but a procuracy offical charged with reviewing criminal cases did. He informed the family that Ergashev's guilt had been established during the investigation and court hearing. He pointed out that proof of Ergashev's guilt included "...material evidence discovered, such as religious books,

[1072] The office of the Ombudsperson is tasked with receiving individual citizen's complaints regarding violations of rights and assisting citizens to obtain remedy for injustices. Rather than conducting investigations itself, the office has a primarily advisory role. It sends communications regarding citizen complaints to the agency responsible for the alleged abuse—be it the procuracy, courts, or Ministry of Internal Affairs—makes recommendations to that agency, and awaits a response.

leaflets, magazines and narcotics," and stated that the procuracy upheld the court's decision.[1073]

- Relatives of Abdurashid Isakhojaev sent appeals on his behalf to Ombudsperson Rashidova; General Procurator U. Khudaikulov; SNB chief R. Inoiatov; Minister of Internal Affairs Z. Almatov; his deputy in charge of prisons, Rajab Kodirov; and President Karimov, requesting that Isakhojaev be sent to the main prison hospital located in Tashkent (called the Sangorod). Isakhojaev is disabled from a pre-existing injury and his motility and health has deteriorated in prison. According to Isakhojaev's mother, "They passed my letters [to] each other [like] a football."[1074] The Ombudsperson's office responded to the family's desperate appeal by copying the Isakhojaev family on a letter to the procuracy, asking that agency to look into the case.[1075] According to Isakhojaeva, one of the few direct responses she received was from Deputy Minister of Internal Affairs Kodirov, who sent her a letter dated February 5, 2000, stating that the prison hospital in Jaslyk was fully equipped to handle Isakhojaev's medical needs and there was no need to send him to Tashkent for treatment.[1076] A December 1999 letter from the MVD, signed by Kodirov's first deputy, Sarikov, stated that Isakhojaev could not be transferred to Tashkent because article 57 of the criminal procedure code of the Republic of Uzbekistan requires a convict to serve his entire sentence in one prison facility—an obviously specious claim given that independent Muslim inmates have frequently been transferred from one prison to another and Isakhojaev himself was

---

[1073] Letter to S. A. Ergasheva, from A.M. Salikhov, office of the Procurator General, Tashkent, document number 2/498-99, February 7, 2000.

[1074] Written statement to the Organization of the Islamic Conference, U.N. Commission on Human Rights and various human rights organizations, from Sharifa Isakhojaeva, January 30, 2000.

[1075] Letter from Ombudsperson Sayora Rashidova to General Procurator Khudaikulov, November 4, 1999, document number 07-05/1776k, on file with Human Rights Watch.

[1076] Written statement by Sharifa Isakhojaeva, February 20, 2000. In fact, the prison hospital at Jaslyk is known to be poorly equipped. Prisoners at Jaslyk are reportedly denied access to nearly any medical attention. Jaslyk prison authorities did not allow the U.N. Special Rapporteur on Torture access to the entire Jaslyk prison during his visit, and so the Special Rapporteur was unable to assess the state of medical facilities there. Report of the U.N. Special Rapporteur on Torture, Theo van Boven, p. 31.

initially incarcerated in Tavaksai prison, not Jaslyk.[1077] As of June 2000, Isakhojaev remained in Jaslyk.

Following a September 2000 presidential amnesty decree, Abdurashid Isakhojaev's father went to the procuracy to once again see what could be done for his son. The elder Isakhojaev recalled that the procurator told him: "'If he [Abdurashid] killed somebody, maybe I could help, but not for this crime.'"[1078]

- Accused Wahhabi Kudratullo Valiev testified in court that officials referred his complaints of torture in pre-trial detention back to his torturers. "I wrote letters to the general procuracy and to the president saying that I was wrongly accused and that the MVD [police] was forcing me to admit that I had conspired against the state. No one considered my appeals. The MVD tortured me, and it was the MVD itself that considered my appeal and said it was unfounded," Valiev said in court.[1079]

- The family of accused Hizb ut-Tahrir member Beksot Juraev complained to the procuracy about a police search of their home, during which officers ransacked the premises, allegedly planted drugs and weapons, and threatened to arrest the family to force them to agree to the search report. The Juraevs received the following response: "Your argument that the narcotic substance opium, [and] the RGD-5 grenade, found on Juraev, B. and in his home, were planted by police officers appears to be unsubstantiated, because during the investigation the aforementioned material evidence was seized in the presence of

[1077] Letter to Sharifa Isakhojaeva from R. Sarikov, Ministry of Internal Affairs, Main Administration for the Execution of Punishments [GUIN], document number 28/2/4-i-95, December 29, 1999.

[1078] Douglas Frantz, "Persecution Charged in Ex-Soviet Republic," *The New York Times*, October 29, 2000. For more on the limitations of the amnesty process, see below, in this chapter.

[1079] Human Rights Watch unofficial transcript, Tashkent City Court hearing held in the Akmal Ikramov District Court building, Tashkent, November 1, 2000.

participating witnesses and this was established in the report of the search."[1080]

Juraev's parents appealed to a host of other government agencies, including the Ombudsperson's office, the Supreme Court, and the office of President Karimov seeking review of their son's case. In particular, they complained that even if their son were a member of Hizb ut-Tahrir, evidence should not have been planted to incriminate him, and they asked again that these fabricated charges be removed.[1081] The Juraevs report that their appeals to Ombudsperson Sayora Rashidova and President Karimov complaining of an unfair Supreme Court trial and asking for assistance in compelling the Supreme Court to review the case were not examined in earnest, but simply forwarded to the Supreme Court, which responded that the case had been proven and that the family's request was denied.[1082]

Many relatives, desperate for sympathy and assistance, have continued to appeal to the Ombudsperson's office. For others, the prospect for useful intervention by the Ombudsperson's office to improve treatment of prisoners in Uzbekistan's post-conviction facilities was irremediably undermined by Ombudsperson Rashidova's own report of her visit to the most infamous facility, Jaslyk. After returning from an "inspection" of that prison in March 2000, she said in an interview in a state newspaper, "...conditions created for prisoners, and that the [corps] of guards are observing the law in their duties, made us happy."[1083] Regarding prisoners in Jaslyk, she added, "...I can say that the supply of

[1080] Letter from A.M. Solikhov, office of the Procurator General, Tashkent, to Rahim Juraev, January 29, 2000, document number 12/1048-99, on file with Human Rights Watch.

[1081] Letter from Rahim Juraev to President Karimov, December 18, 1999; and Human Rights Watch interview with persons close to the case, names withheld, Tashkent, February 10, 2000.

[1082] Letter from Rahim Juraev and Umida Juraeva to Sayora Rashidova, October 18, 1999; letter from Rahim Juraev to President Karimov, December 18, 1999; and letter from Judge S.O. Khojamuratov of the Supreme Court of the Republic of Uzbekistan, to Rakhim Juraev, October 21, 1999, document number 6-2681-99.

[1083] Ombudsperson Sayora Rashidova, as quoted in "Protecting Human Rights is our Sacred Duty," *Postda* [At One's Post] newspaper, March 30, 2000. *Postda* is published by the Ministry of Internal Affairs.

food and clothes for them is in good condition. What else can a person need who was found guilty by law, and who had admitted to [crimes with which he was charged]? Is the fact that such conditions have been created for prisoners not enough to state that human rights in Uzbekistan are being observed at every step?"[1084] Rashidova also reported that prisoners with whom she spoke at the prison had expressed their satisfaction with medical services, the quality of the food, and treatment by guards.[1085] By way of recommendation for improvements Rashidova had this to say: "Of course, we were also introduced closely to the conditions created for the guards. I can only say that we should thank them and create better conditions for their [corps]."[1086]

Appeals to Official Clergy

Appealing to the Islamic establishment, an integral player in the government campaign, endangered independent Muslims, making them vulnerable to increased surveillance and even arrest by police. In one extreme case, a young man who appealed to Mufti Abdurashid Kori Bakhromov, head of the Muslim Board of Uzbekistan and leader of the official Islamic establishment, in June 1999 was turned over to police by that same clergyman.[1087] The young man, Usmon Inagamov, allegedly one of Farhod Usmanov's religious students and a member of Hizb ut-Tahrir, had been upset by Usmanov's death in pre-trial detention. He reacted by appealing to the mufti to speak out, arguing that silence made the official clergy complicit in Usmanov's death and in the arrests of thousands of others. Beaten in detention, Inagamov was brought up on charges of anti-state activity and sentenced in a closed court to two and a half years in prison. Already ill with cancer, he died in prison nine

[1084] Ibid.

[1085] Ibid.

[1086] Ibid.

[1087] Written report by Vasila Inoiatova, April 2000; Human Rights Watch interview with Vasila Inoiatova, Tashkent, April 5, 2000; and Human Rights Watch interview with Vasila Inoiatova, Tashkent, December 12, 2000.

months later, presumably from untreated illness aggravated by denial of medical care and harsh prison conditions.[1088]

Appeals to Human Rights Organizations and the U.N.

Police and national security agents retaliated against victims of abuse and their relatives when they complained to local or international human rights defenders.

- Shukhrat Parpiev was arbitrarily arrested, convicted to five years in prison, and allegedly killed by guards in Jaslyk in May 2000. Persons close to him told Human Rights Watch that after they informed a local human rights activist about Parpiev's illegal arrest, officers from the SNB threatened to "make things worse" for the young man if further complaints were made.[1089]

With regard to international contacts:

- Following her release on parole, Feruza Kurbanova informed Human Rights Watch that the judge in her case had pressured her and her family to cut off contact with foreigners who had come to monitor her trial.[1090] According to Kurbanova, after representatives from Human Rights Watch, the British Embassy, and the BBC together with local rights activists attended a session of her trial, the judge instructed her to tell her mother "not to play with me and not to call those foreigners again."[1091] It is important to note, however, that international attention to the case did not cease and is believed to have had two important

[1088] The location of the court hearing is unclear. Sources alternately place the process at the Chirchik City Court in Tashkent Province or the Syrdaria Province Court. Memorial Human Rights Center and the Information Center for Human Rights In Central Asia, *List of People Arrested and Tried in Uzbekistan for Political and Religious Reasons (January 1999 to April 2000)*, Moscow, May 2000; and Hizb ut-Tahrir, March 24, 2000. Inagamov's case is described in Chapter IV.

[1089] Human Rights Watch interview with persons close to Shukhrat Parpiev, names withheld, Andijan, May 18, 2000.

[1090] Human Rights Watch interview with Feruza Kurbanova, Tashkent, March 14, 2001

[1091] Ibid.

effects: Kurbanova was eventually provided with an attorney, and the judge handed down a very unusual and lenient one-year suspended sentence.

- In 2000 a police officer paid an unannounced visit to the Akhmedov house in Andijan shortly after the family spoke with Human Rights Watch. The officer entered the house without a warrant and began to insult the family for having appealed to a human rights organization. He said he knew that the organization had given the family a "bulletin" and he demanded that the Akhmedovs hand it over to him, threatening that it would be "worse for them" if they did not.[1092] Speaking to Akhmedov's female relatives, the officer threatened to beat them if they did not give him the human rights documents.[1093] The Akhmedov family gave the officer the Human Rights Watch World Report 2000 chapter on Uzbekistan, translated into Uzbek, and contact information for the organization's representative in Uzbekistan. The officer confiscated these materials and warned the women that they must not appeal to any more human rights organizations or he would beat them.[1094] SNB officers also repeatedly returned to the house at night to interrogate family members.[1095]

- On June 9, 2000, the Andijan District Court sentenced Komoliddin Sattarov to nine years in prison on charges that partly stemmed from his having allegedly written a complaint on behalf of his imprisoned brother, Murodjon Sattarov, to the U.N. Human Rights Committee (UNHRC). Uzbekistan is a signatory to the International Covenant on Civil and Political Rights and its optional protocol, which provides for the submission of complaints to the UNHRC. Police arrested Komoliddin Sattarov on February 2, 2000, allegedly planting Hizb ut-Tahrir leaflets in his pockets. During a subsequent police search of his home, officers found a completed complaint form addressed to the

[1092] Human Rights Watch interview with rights defender Muzafarmirzo Iskhakov, Tashkent, July 7, 2000.

[1093] Ibid.

[1094] Ibid.

[1095] Human Rights Watch interview with relatives of Tavakkaljon Akhmedov, Asaka, Andijan, May 2000.

UNHRC on behalf of his brother, imprisoned on charges of Hizb ut-Tahrir membership, and another six blank complaint forms. Police confiscated the UNHRC forms as evidence against Komoliddin Sattarov. Although Sattarov was later charged with an array of crimes involving alleged religious extremism, his father reported that the investigator from the Andijan procurator's office informed him that the confiscated complaint forms amounted to the most serious and incriminating evidence against his son.[1096] In the verdict against Sattarov, the ruling judge referred to the UNHRC complaint forms as "appeals to a global human rights organization" and listed the discovery of these forms along with the Islamic leaflets as material evidence that Komoliddin Sattarov was involved in "anti-state activity."[1097] In an unusual step, presumably due to international diplomatic pressure, the Markhamat District Court in Andijan province reconsidered the case on October 18, 2000, with representatives from the U.N., U.S. Embassy, Human Rights Watch, and OSCE present, along with local rights defenders. Judge Kozim Karimov heard arguments and ruled the U.N. documents inadmissible as evidence. When he issued the final verdict, he also added another year to Sattarov's sentence.[1098]

Andijan police, led by officer Ortikali Rakhmatov, head of the Criminal Investigations Department, returned to the Sattarov home on March 20, 2001. This time, they confiscated the Human Rights Watch World Report 2000 chapter on Uzbekistan.[1099] When local rights activist Muzafarmirzo Iskhakov appealed in person to officer Rakhmatov to return the document, explaining that Human Rights Watch was a registered organization in Uzbekistan and that its report was neither

---

[1096] Human Rights Watch interview with father, mother, and sister of Komoliddin Sattarov and with rights defender Muzafarmirzo Iskhakov, Andijan, May 17, 2000.

[1097] Verdict of the Andijan City Court, issued by Judge M. Kholmatov, June 9, 2000

[1098] Human Rights Watch unofficial transcript, Markhamat District Court, Andijan Province, October 18, 2000; Memorial Human Rights Center and the Information Center for Human Rights In Central Asia, *List of People Arrested and Tried in Uzbekistan for Political and Religious Reasons (December 1997 to August 2001)*, Moscow, October 2001.

[1099] Human Rights Watch interview with rights defender Muzafarmirzo Iskhakov, Tashkent, April 4, 2001.

secret nor subversive, police refused to return the document and threw Iskhakov out of the office.[1100]

- Tashkent authorities interfered with efforts made by the family of Rakhima Akhmedalieva, wife of Imam Rukhiddin Fakhruddinov, to appeal to the United Nations on her behalf. On March 26, 2001, just nine days after police arrested Akhmedalieva, her daughter, Odina Maksudova, went to the Tashkent office of the U.N. Mission to deliver an appeal for assistance in securing her mother's release. Maksudova described what happened subsequently in a later letter addressed to U.N. Secretary-General Kofi Annan. When she first approached the U.N. building, police officers attempted to block her entrance and confiscate the letter she had written. When she succeeded in entering the building, she handed the appeal over to a U.N. receptionist, an employee of the United Nations Development Programme, who then gave the letter—which was addressed to the U.N.—to a nearby police officer.[1101] Maksudova reported that, fearing arrest by the officer, she and a friend who had accompanied her to the U.N. office exited the building. She claimed that, upon leaving, she overheard the receptionist ask the police officer, "Why couldn't you take them away in such a manner that we wouldn't have any trouble?"[1102] The officer proceeded to do just that, detaining Maksudova and her companion outside the building and holding them in the Mirabad district police station for four hours.[1103] Maksudova was brought before an investigator, who called her an "animal" and forced Maksudova and her companion to write statements disavowing the letter to the U.N.[1104] Maksudova was already acquainted

[1100] Ibid.

[1101] Letter to U.N. Secretary-General Kofi Annan from Odina Maksudova, March 29, 2001, provided in English.

[1102] Ibid.

[1103] Ibid.

[1104] As noted above, in "Family Members: Arrests, House Arrest, Harassment" in Chapter III, the officer Maksudova identified, Edik Tsoi, has been identified by others as involved in the torture of detainees at the Ministry of Internal Affairs and is the subject of numerous complaints by victims of torture. According to rights defender Vasila Inoiatova, the officer was fired along with a large number of other officers from the Ministry of Internal Affairs Department against Corruption, Racketeering and Terrorism in a "purge" of that division in 2002. Human Rights Watch telephone interview with Vasila Inoiatova, March 4, 2003.

with the officer—she had been detained once before, when she had appealed to police for help after her mother was arrested—and said that she agreed to write the false statement because she feared him.[1105]

Amnesty

Presidential amnesty decrees, orders for the release of certain categories of prisoners, are common in Uzbekistan and other countries of the former Soviet Union, primarily to relieve prison overcrowding.[1106] While release under amnesty does not provide redress to independent Muslims for the abuses they were subjected to, it does provide relief from the extraordinary hardship of prison. But only limited groups of independent Muslims have qualified for amnesty. In some cases, the amnesty process itself triggered a new round of abuse of religious prisoners. In other cases, those amnestied were rearrested or persistently harassed.[1107] Until 2001 presidential amnesties did not apply to those charged with sedition and other articles of the criminal code used to prosecute independent Muslims. The August 2001 amnesty applied to this category of prisoner, but only to those who had been sentenced to six years or less, thus exempting the majority of independent Muslim prisoners, who typically received longer terms.[1108] For example, of the

[1105] Letter to U.N. Secretary-General Kofi Annan from Odina Maksudova, March 29, 2001, provided in English. Human Rights Watch informed the United Nations High Commissioner for Human Rights about the incident on April 2, 2001.

[1106] In Uzbekistan, amnesties are usually issued on national holidays; while as many as two or even three amnesties may be decreed during a given year, a single amnesty, announced on or around independence day in September, is perhaps most common.

[1107] Decisions to amnesty a prisoner do not involve review of the grounds for his or her conviction. Because there is no case review that accompanies the amnesty process, law enforcement, procuracy, judicial, and prison officials who committed illegal acts and violated a prisoner's basic rights are not held accountable for their actions. The police records of convicts released under amnesty are not expunged and police harassment often haunts those released under such provisions.

[1108] The amnesty refers to such prisoners as "members of terrorist and extremist organizations, criminal associations…those who have committed crimes against the Constitutional order of the Republic of Uzbekistan or other acts against public security covered by articles 150-163, 242, 244, 244-1, 244-2 of the Criminal Code." Presidential amnesty decree issued on the tenth anniversary of Uzbekistan's independence, broadcast on Uzbek Television first channel, August 22, 2001, English translation in BBC Monitoring.

709 religious prisoners in Human Rights Watch's database who had been arrested or tried as of August 2001, only seventy-one had been sentenced to six years or less. The 2002 amnesty provided for the release of "Those convicted and sentenced for the first time to prison terms of up to ten years inclusive or who were given penalties other than imprisonment for involvement in the activities of extremist organizations and committing, as a member of these, a crime against the constitution[al] order of the Republic of Uzbekistan or other activities against public security."[1109]

The amnesty creates a revolving door for prisoners, some are released so others can be jailed—and the door swings full circle when those released are rearrested and imprisoned again. The U.S. State Department reported in 2003 that overcrowding was a problem in Uzbekistan's prisons, and noted that, "The overcrowding may have been one of the reasons for the large-scale amnesty in 2001, but the problem remained severe."[1110] Given the pace of ongoing arrests of independent Muslims at least, it is perhaps not surprising that amnesties are an inefficient means of addressing the problem of overcrowded prisons, as well as being a poor substitute for justice and redress.

Prison authorities, whose record of abuse is detailed above, have broad powers to determine who will be amnestied. Persons found to have "systematically" violated internal prison rules—i.e. those with three or more infractions on their record—were ineligible for release under amnesty decrees.[1111] Prison authorities arbitrarily charged religious inmates with prison infractions, making them ineligible for amnesty. They did so either by fabricating violations or taking punitive action

---

[1109] Decree of the President of the Republic of Uzbekistan on "Amnesty on the occasion of the tenth anniversary of the Constitution of the Republic of Uzbekistan," December 3, 2002, English translation provided to Human Rights Watch by the Embassy of the Republic of Uzbekistan to the United States.

[1110] U.S. Department of State, *2002 Country Reports on Human Rights Practices*, released by the Bureau of Democracy, Human Rights, and Labor, March 31, 2003.

[1111] For example, clause 8 of the 2001 amnesty states, "This decree is not applicable to those convicts who systematically violate the prison rules." Presidential amnesty decree issued on the tenth anniversary of Uzbekistan's independence, broadcast on Uzbek Television first channel, August 22, 2001, English translation in BBC Monitoring.

against legitimate activity such as prayer and counting that as a "demerit."

The 2001 and 2002 amnesty decrees include clauses that require, as a condition for release, that religious prisoners declare their "repentance" for crimes committed, and ask the state's forgiveness. Under both decrees, prison administrators are authorized to verify the "sincerity" of the declaration of contrition and give their opinion as to a given prisoner's active repentance.[1112] This is one way in which the amnesty process itself brings on further persecution. In addition, while not required by the decree, in practice independent Muslim prisoners also must disavow their religious beliefs or affiliations to qualify for release. Refusal resulted not only in foregoing the opportunity to be released, but also, as noted above, in beatings, solitary confinement, or other forms of retaliation.[1113] For example, one convicted Hizb ut-Tahrir member who had been serving a six-year term in Novoi prison, number 64/29, told Human Rights Watch that prison officials there forced him to sign a letter that went significantly beyond a plea for forgiveness. In order to qualify for the 2001 amnesty, he said, he was compelled to sign a statement of apology that also included a vow that he would not be involved in any religious movements in the future and would loyally serve President Karimov and the state.[1114]

Prison authorities often demanded a letter from the mahalla committee of a prisoner's previous neighborhood or district, promising to take

---

[1112] Clause 10, Presidential amnesty decree issued on the tenth anniversary of Uzbekistan's independence, broadcast on Uzbek Television first channel, August 22, 2001, English translation in BBC Monitoring; and clause 8, Decree of the President of the Republic of Uzbekistan on "Amnesty on the occasion of the tenth anniversary of the Constitution of the Republic of Uzbekistan," December 3, 2002, English translation provided to Human Rights Watch by the Embassy of the Republic of Uzbekistan to the United States.

[1113] See Chapter IV. Human Rights Watch research found that some of those who refused to ask for forgiveness and to recant their religious beliefs were punished by prison guards who placed them in pits, kept them naked in freezing conditions, and deprived them of sleep. "Memorandum on Cooperative Threat Reduction (CTR) Certification for Uzbekistan," Human Rights Watch, January 18, 2002.

[1114] Human Rights Watch interview with a released prisoner, name withheld, Margilan, July 12, 2002.

responsibility for the prisoner, vouching for his or her future good behavior. In one typical letter provided to Human Rights Watch, the mahalla committee agreed to "take responsibility for [the prisoner's] rehabilitation in the future."[1115] In other letters, the mahalla committees' obligation was more explicit, as they stated that the committee would act as a "guardian" to the prisoner upon release, or would keep "him under observation."[1116] While not required by the amnesty decrees, the mahalla letter, in some cases, proved a significant stumbling block to qualifying for amnesty. Relatives of a prisoner who potentially qualified for amnesty were instructed by prison officials, police, or local authorities to obtain such a letter, signed by the head of the mahalla committee and other committee members. Perhaps because of the responsibility that was understood to accompany a guarantee to keep released prisoners under close observation and control, and the fear that were a former prisoner to violate the law again the members of the mahalla committee would face censure from more senior government authorities, the mahalla committees were sometimes reluctant to provide the letters. During the first months of 2003—the implementation period for the 2002 amnesty, which was passed in December 2002—Human Rights Watch learned of several instances in which mahalla committees refused to sign letters of support, thereby effectively blocking the possibility of releasing prisoners.[1117] In these cases, even when the family provided their own letters of guarantee, prison authorities rejected the claim for amnesty and refused to release the prisoners.[1118]

[1115] Letter from a mahalla committee (location withheld) to "G.G." (recipient's name withheld, not the person's true initials), January 4, 2003. Human Rights Watch unofficial translation. The letter is on file with Human Rights Watch.

[1116] Letters from mahalla committees (locations withheld) to "H.H.," "I.I.," and "J.J.," (recipients' names withheld, not their true initials), dated January 21, 2003, January 26, 2003, January 27, 2003. Human Rights Watch unofficial translations. The letters are on file with Human Rights Watch.

[1117] Human Rights Watch interview with the mother of a religious prisoner, name withheld, Tashkent, January 30, 2003; and Human Rights Watch interview with "K.K." (name withheld, not the person's true initials), Tashkent, January 27, 2003.

[1118] Human Rights Watch interview with a friend of a religious prisoner, name withheld, place withheld, January 27, 2003; Human Rights Watch interviews with the father of another religious prisoner, name withheld, place withheld, January 27, 2003, and January 30, 2003; Human Rights Watch interview with the mother of yet another religious prisoner,

Another informal requirement for release under amnesty was payment of a sizeable bribe. According to local rights defenders, prison officials extorted sizeable bribes from prisoners and their families in exchange for freedom.[1119]

Sometimes because they had paid large bribes and sometimes because they feared retaliation from law enforcement, many amnestied prisoners were reluctant to talk to rights groups, including Human Rights Watch, about their experiences. They were particularly hesitant to discuss the conditions of their release. However, specific cases brought to the attention of rights defenders were believed to be representative of a wider trend of official treatment of amnestied persons. The vulnerability of amnestied prisoners to ongoing harassment by law enforcement officials is sharply illustrated by the case of Idobat Sultanova, a forty-year-old mother of six living in the Fergana Valley at the time of her arrest. Sultanova was detained in June 2000 for membership in Hizb ut-Tahrir and convicted in September to six years in prison on related charges. She appealed the Margilan District Court's decision and succeeded in getting her term reduced to a three-year suspended sentence. And so, after serving three months of her original term, was released.[1120] When the 2001 amnesty was declared, she was cleared of the suspended sentence as well. However, she remained a focus of attention for Margilan law enforcement agents. She reported that they detained her for several hours and insulted her soon after the amnesty went into effect, and that they constantly harassed her, questioning her frequently about where she was going and with whom she met.[1121] Sultanova told Human Rights Watch that police regularly compelled her to sign statements promising to stay at home and not participate in any

---

name withheld, place withheld, January 30, 2003; and Human Rights Watch interview with a human rights activist, name withheld, place withheld, February 5, 2003.

[1119] Human Rights Watch interview with a local rights defender, name withheld, Tashkent, July 1, 2003; Human Rights Watch interview with a second rights defender, name withheld, Tashkent, July 2, 2003; and Human Rights Watch interview with a third rights defender, name withheld, Tashkent, July 3, 2003.

[1120] Human Rights Watch interview with Idobat Sultanova, Margilan, July 12, 2002. Sultanova was presumably released around December 2000.

[1121] Ibid; and letter of April 17, 2002, on file with Human Rights Watch.

protests.[1122] She further reported to Human Rights Watch that, on March 5, 2002, officers, this time from the SNB, again detained her and held her for ten hours without charge.[1123] Finally, in July, the SNB pulled out its trump card. On July 12, 2002, officers from the Fergana province department of the SNB arrested Sultanova again and took her into custody, on charges of leadership of a Hizb ut-Tahrir women's group in Margilan.[1124] She was tried in the Margilan City Court and sentenced on September 13, 2002 to seven years in prison.[1125] As of this writing, Sultanova was back in the women's prison facility in Kulyuk, located on the outskirts of Tashkent.

Other independent Muslims shared a similar fate—they were amnestied, then rearrested on the same kinds of charges for which they were originally incarcerated, and then were sent back to jail. This was what happened to Merziot Usmanov, who was sentenced in 1999 to three years in prison on charges of subverting the constitution. He was released under amnesty in December 2001 and was rearrested just months later, in April 2002. At his new trial in July 2002, the Shaikhantaur District Court in Tashkent found him guilty of "extremism" and sentenced him to eight years in prison.[1126]

Suppression of Public Protests

Unable to obtain redress through recourse to domestic remedies or international organizations, some citizens in desperation turned to public protest as a means of voicing their dissatisfaction with government policies. They attempted to influence those in power to release those

[1122] Human Rights Watch interview with Idobat Sultanova, Margilan, July 12, 2002.

[1123] Ibid.

[1124] Human Rights Watch interview with Farkhod Kodirov, a local National Security Service investigator, Fergana city, July 30, 2002.

[1125] Human Rights Watch unofficial transcript, Margilan City Court, Margilan, September 12, 2002; and Human Rights Watch telephone interview with a human rights activist, name withheld, September 13, 2002.

[1126] Human Rights Watch interview with rights defender Ismail Adylov, Tashkent, August 5, 2003.

unjustly imprisoned. However, the Uzbek government does not allow public protests that express dissent and vigorously punished those who organized and participated in them. Police and security agents also sought to pre-empt such protests "both by refusing to allow potential demonstrators to leave their homes and by blocking access to planned demonstration sites."[1127] Police routinely broke up demonstrations—usually consisting of no more than about fifty people—against the arrest and torture of independent Muslims, and sometimes beat and detained protestors.[1128] In at least one case documented by Human Rights Watch, police physically abused and threatened the wife of a prisoner because they believed she was advocating for his release.

Some examples of the incidents known to Human Rights Watch include the funeral of a young man evidently tortured to death in custody, and several protests held during the period 1998 to 2003 by female relatives of religious prisoners.

- Farhod Usmanov was tortured to death in police detention just days after authorities arrested him, on June 14, 1999.[1129] Police treated the funeral as they would a public protest, and arrested dozens of mourners.

[1127] U.S. Department of State, *2002 Country Reports on Human Rights Practices*, released by the Bureau of Democracy, Human Rights, and Labor, March 31, 2003.

[1128] Freedom of assembly is guaranteed under Uzbekistan's constitution; however, citizens must obtain a permit in order to hold public demonstrations. According to the U.S. State Department, "in practice the Government restricted the right of peaceful assembly… and did not routinely grant permits to demonstrators." U.S. Department of State, *2002 Country Reports on Human Rights Practices*, released by the Bureau of Democracy, Human Rights, and Labor, March 31, 2003. Many people planning public gatherings in support of independent Muslims perceived their chances of obtaining government permission to be slim at best, and so did not apply. Some family members of independent Muslim prisoners had first-hand experience of the state's harsh reaction against association by independent Muslims and reason to expect a large public assembly would be greeted with similar hostility. Moreover, the secrecy that often surrounded the preparations for such protests suggests that the organizers perceived themselves as being at risk of government retaliation, and feared that, if they drew attention to themselves prior to the event, it would be blocked.

[1129] For details on his case, see Chapter IV.

Authorities who delivered Usmanov's body to his family for burial ordered relatives not to disclose his death or to show anyone the body, and plainclothes officers were posted outside the family home during the night of June 25.[1130] Police set up roadblocks during the night to block access to the neighborhood and surrounded the area with armed officers from the Ministry of Internal Affairs and National Security Service. Nonetheless, at least hundreds, and by some accounts thousands, of mourners gathered early the following day to attend the funeral.[1131] Police arrested dozens of them at the scene.[1132] One female relative who attempted to attend Usmanov's funeral recalled, "I went to Farhod's funeral and was arrested on the way, along with thirty or forty others. All of them were men, except for me and one other woman, who was ill, so they fined her 6,000 som and released her. An elderly man was arrested also and taken along with me to the local ROVD [district police station] and held one night and then released with a 6,000 som fine. My husband and I were held for ten days and not fined. We were held in the ROVD."[1133] She described the effect the arrest had on her, "Before that, I was never interested in Hizb ut-Tahrir. After the detention, I read the Hizb ut-Tahrir book, and it made sense to me. There was nothing in it about extremism, just about...living the right way."[1134] Police held other mourners under misdemeanor detention for ten to thirty days. Authorities reportedly made it a condition of their release that they not discuss their detention or make any claims of physical mistreatment in custody.[1135]

[1130] Human Rights Watch interview, name withheld, Tashkent, June 25, 1999.

[1131] Human Rights Watch interview, name withheld, Tashkent, July 12, 1999; Human Rights Watch interview, Vasila Inoiatova, Tashkent, July 21, 1999; and Human Rights Watch interview, name withheld, Tashkent, February 21, 2000.

[1132] Ibid.

[1133] Human Rights Watch interview, name withheld, Tashkent, February 21, 2000.

[1134] Ibid.

[1135] Human Rights Watch interview with Vasila Inoiatova, July 21, 1999; Human Rights Watch interview with a woman whose two nephews were detained for seventeen days for attending the funeral, name withheld, Tashkent, July 12, 1999.

- In January 1998 shortly after the government launched its full-fledged campaign to arrest independent Muslims, some one hundred women gathered outside a Tashkent police station to demand the immediate release of their male relatives. The protest was dispersed by police, who detained several of the women and levied fines against those they considered the protest's organizers.

- On November 18, 1999, Human Rights Watch was present when about forty women gathered outside the Tashkent mayor's office to protest the illegal arrest and incarceration of their male relatives. A number of women reported that their relatives' whereabouts were unknown and that they had been searching desperately for them. One of these women reported that her husband, detained two months earlier, was still missing in police custody. As with previous attempts to speak out against the government's arrest policy, this one was quickly shut down by security forces. A busload of police arrived on the scene as the women approached the entrance to the mayor's office building. At least six officials from the mayor's office, joined by approximately fifteen police officers and soldiers, surrounded the women. The city officials refused to grant the women's request for an audience with the mayor, advising them to return another day with a written appeal. After about forty minutes of discussion, officials disbanded the demonstration and escorted the women away from the government building.

Representatives of an international organization, who arrived on the scene as the women were being dispersed, reported that plainclothes officers presumed to be from the National Security Service followed several of the women as they descended into a nearby metro station. A Human Rights Watch representative noted that officials also approached participants, asking for and writing down their names. The police also succeeded in videotaping all of those gathered, widely perceived as an act of intimidation, since the National Security Service had videotaped past public demonstrations and subsequently arrested participants.

- Women in various parts of Uzbekistan staged a string of protests in March and April 2001. On March 21, an estimated 300 demonstrators, primarily women, took to the streets in Andijan—one of the areas hardest hit by the government's campaign against independent

Muslims—to demand the release of their male relatives imprisoned for their religious affiliations and beliefs.[1136] The participants reportedly carried signs reading, "2001: Year of the Widow and Orphan," a play on President Karimov's declaration of the year 2001 as the "Year of the Mother and Child."[1137] At 2:00 p.m., uniformed police and security agents in civilian clothes surrounded the women and then brought in minibuses to break up the gathering.[1138] The women called on the mayor, Kobiljon Obidov, to address them, but he refused, instructing them instead to meet with him in his office in groups of five. Meetings were held in this way with some fifty women.[1139] According to a local rights activist who interviewed the women afterward, the mayor, the head of the province court, Ikhtior Abdullaev, and the Andijan province procurator, Umatullo Shamsiev, instructed the women to write and sign statements detailing their complaints and promised each group of women that they would form a commission to review the men's cases by April 1, 2001.[1140] Around 5:00 or 6:00 p.m., police dispersed the crowd and detained at least two female participants, identified to Human Rights Watch as Zuhra and Umida. Zuhra's release was later confirmed.

[1136] Human Rights Watch interview with an eyewitness, a rights activist from Andijan, name withheld, Tashkent, April 20, 2001; Human Rights Watch telephone interview with Catherine Davis, BBC correspondent, Tashkent, March 23, 2001; and Bakhodir Musaev, "Uzbeks Losing Patience: Uzbeks take to the streets to air anti-government grievances," *The Institute for War and Peace reporting*, April 10, 2001 [online] http://www.iwpr.net/index.pl?archive/rca/rca_200104_47_02_eng.txt (retrieved June 5, 2003).

[1137] Human Rights Watch interview with an eyewitness, a rights activist from Andijan, name withheld, Tashkent, April 20, 2001; and Bakhodir Musaev, "Uzbeks Losing Patience: Uzbeks take to the streets to air anti-government grievances," *The Institute for War and Peace reporting*, April 10, 2001.

[1138] Human Rights Watch interview with an eyewitness, a rights activist from Andijan, name withheld, Tashkent, April 20, 2001.

[1139] Human Rights Watch interview with an eyewitness, a rights activist from Andijan, name withheld, Tashkent, April 20, 2001; and Bakhodir Musaev, "Uzbeks Losing Patience: Uzbeks take to the streets to air anti-government grievances," *The Institute for War and Peace reporting*, April 10, 2001.

[1140] Human Rights Watch interview with a rights activist from Andijan, name withheld, Tashkent, April 20, 2001. The head of the provincial court was allegedly removed from his post just days later, on March 26, 2001.

Umida presumably was also released.[1141] As of late April 2001 no review of the men's cases had been undertaken by the government.

- A follow-up protest was organized two days later in Andijan, where relatives again gathered outside the city mayor's office.[1142] This time, police quickly broke up the demonstration.[1143] Officers forced the women onto police buses and took them to the police station, where they showered them with threats and insults, and fined them each 2,200 som, approximately one month's salary. Officers pointedly threatened to extend the prison sentences of the women's jailed relatives if they did not write "explanatory letters" (a euphemism for confessions) and ask for forgiveness for their part in the demonstration.[1144] The women were released only after signing the statements and expressing their contrition.[1145] Several of the women expressed concern that police, who had recorded the faces of participants on videotape during the gathering, would come after them later.[1146] Police also reportedly reacted to the incident by throwing up roadblocks to cut off access between the Fergana Valley city and the nation's capital.[1147]

- On April 12, 2001, some forty women staged a protest outside the mayor's office in Tashkent.[1148] A local rights defender who observed the

---

[1141] Ibid. Human Rights Watch has no information confirming Umida's release. Because the vast majority of arrested demonstrators are subsequently released, we assume she was as well.

[1142] Human Rights Watch telephone interview with Catherine Davis, BBC correspondent, Tashkent, March 23, 2001.

[1143] Human Rights Watch interview with a rights activist from Andijan, name withheld, Tashkent, April 20, 2001.

[1144] Ibid; and Bakhodir Musaev, "Uzbeks Losing Patience: Uzbeks take to the streets to air anti-government grievances," *The Institute for War and Peace reporting*, April 10, 2001.

[1145] Ibid.

[1146] Human Rights Watch interview with a rights activist from Andijan, name withheld, Tashkent, April 20, 2001.

[1147] Bakhodir Musaev, "Uzbeks Losing Patience: Uzbeks take to the streets to air anti-government grievances," *The Institute for War and Peace reporting*, April 10, 2001.

[1148] Human Rights Watch interview with Mahbuba Kosymova, Tashkent, April 26, 2001.

demonstration, Mahbuba Kosymova, reported that police shouted insults at the demonstrators, called them terrorists, fired blanks over the heads of the protesters, and used force to disperse the crowd, shoving and pushing women into minibuses to take them into custody.[1149] According to a western diplomatic source, at least ten participants were injured by police.[1150]

Four women were detained beyond the day of the protest. Police reportedly held the sister-in-law of convicted Hizb ut-Tahrir member Shoknoza Musaeva and another young woman, Manzura Oripova, for three days at a local police station.[1151] Sources close to Oripova told rights defender Mahbuba Kosymova that Oripova was forced into a police car by officers who twisted her arms behind her back and taunted her, saying, "What a nice girl we've got," and that officers beat her at the local police station.[1152] Police held a young woman named Shaira in custody for one day for her part in the demonstration and held another protestor, whose name was not available at the time of this writing, for an unknown period of detention.[1153]

- At the end of July 2002, Tashkent police detained about thirty women for protesting the harsh prison conditions of their male relatives who were jailed for their connection to Hizb ut-Tahrir. Most of the protesters were released within several hours; however, some were kept in custody for several days.[1154]

[1149] Human Rights Watch interview with rights defender Mahbuba Kosymova, Tashkent, April 26, 2001; and Human Rights Watch interview with a diplomat, name withheld, Tashkent, April 2001.

[1150] Human Rights Watch interview with a diplomat, name withheld, Tashkent, April 2001.

[1151] Human Rights Watch interview with Mahbuba Kosymova, Tashkent, April 26, 2001.

[1152] Ibid.

[1153] Ibid.

[1154] Human Rights Watch interview with a female protester released from detention, name withheld, Tashkent, July 23, 2002; and Human Rights Watch interview with a local rights defender, Tashkent, July 25, 2002.

▪ When implementation of the 2002 presidential amnesty ended on March 4 or 5, 2003, thousands of independent Muslims were still in prison. Female relatives of religious prisoners held a peaceful gathering in Tashkent on March 7 to protest torture of detainees and the state's failure to release men who should have been released under the amnesty. An estimated sixty women took to the streets near the Chorsu bazaar, in the neighborhood referred to as the old city. According to one observer, police detained at least forty of the women who first arrived at the scene for the demonstration.[1155] A Human Rights Watch representative saw a busload of women wearing headscarves being taken away from the area by police.[1156]

In what appeared to be an act of intimidation organized by security agents, twenty men in plainclothes violently assaulted two journalists who had come to report on the protest.[1157] Uniformed officers nearby refused to come to the journalists' aid.[1158] The reporters' recording equipment, including interviews with the female protestors, was stolen during the attack.

▪ A protest in Margilan the same day, March 7, involved around twenty to twenty-five relatives of independent Muslim prisoners. The demonstrators gathered outside the mayor's office to protest the state's failure to release their family members under the 2002 amnesty. Police broke up the protest and detained six female protestors.[1159]

▪ Andijan police detained Nodira Solaeva on May 30, 2003, and took her to the Bulakbashinski district police station. The deputy police chief, Tajiddin Mansurov, accused Solaeva of participating in a protest in Tashkent along with other female relatives of religious prisoners earlier

---

[1155] Human Rights Watch interview with an observer at the scene, name withheld at his request, Tashkent, March 7, 2003.

[1156] As of this writing, there was no further information regarding the fate of the women.

[1157] Human Rights Watch interview, name withheld, Tashkent, March 7, 2003.

[1158] Ibid.

[1159] As of this writing, Human Rights Watch had no information regarding the terms of their detention.

that month.[1160] He shouted at her. He then said, "You need a man, that's why you went to Tashkent. You should have come to me."[1161] Alone in the room with Solaeva, Mansurov began to strangle her with his hands and then with plastic batons. She told Human Rights Watch, "He threatened to send two men to my house to rape me at night."[1162] Solaeva recounted that officer Mansurov exposed himself, saying again, "You need a man." When other officers entered the room, Mansurov again strangled and hit Solaeva. "He said that Almatov will kill my husband and that I can't do anything," Solaeva said.[1163] Mansurov ordered Solaeva to be placed in the courtyard in the sun. "[They] didn't give me water, drink, food for sixteen hours," Solaeva told Human Rights Watch. When Mansurov finally released Solaeva it was with a warning, she said, "He told me to sit at home, not to go to pickets or to Tashkent."[1164]

[1160] Solaeva told Human Rights Watch that she had traveled to Tashkent on May 27 to speak to officials at the Main Administration for the Execution of Punishments to ask for permission to visit her husband, a prisoner at Jaslyk. When she left that office, she said, officers from the Hamza district police station mistakenly detained her as one of a group of women who were protesting. She told them she was not part of the protest and was released. Officer Mansurov later told Solaeva he had received a telegram from Tashkent saying that she had participated in the protest. Human Rights Watch interview with Nodira Solaeva, Tashkent, July 18, 2003.

[1161] Ibid.

[1162] Ibid.

[1163] This was presumably a reference to Minister of Internal Affairs Zokirjon Almatov.

[1164] Ibid.

VI. APPENDIX

Survey, Distributed in 1998 by the Ministry of Internal Affairs of Uzbekistan among Chairmen of Mahalla Committees[1165]

1. Number and addresses of uninhabited privatized apartments.
2. List of residents often visited by people with no registration. Report on measures taken regarding such residents.
3. Information on individuals of 16 to 32 years of age not living in the city; list their occupation, and their sources of financial support.
4. List of names and addresses of individuals involved in retail import, who travel [for this purpose] to Saudi Arabia, Turkey, Pakistan and Iran.
5. List of names and addresses of individuals who bring commodities from abroad and sell them.
6. List of names and addresses of individuals who encourage or force women and minors to pray *namaz*.[1166]
7. List of individuals who pray namaz in unauthorized places in the city.
8. Identify residents and their family members who have connections to Wahhabis; list their occupation, workplace, educational institutions of their children, sources of income.
9. Provide information on unemployed individuals with secondary education. Record information about their families and sources of income.
10. Information on Wahhabis who have served a prison sentence and on their families, their occupation and source of income.
11. Take under special consideration those who have a beard or previously had a beard.

[1165] Provided to Human Rights Watch electronically by Memorial, June 2002. The name of the Fergana Valley city in which this document was obtained is withheld.

[1166] As noted elsewhere in this report, namaz is the observation of the five daily prayers in Islam.

12. List of married individuals who, in accordance with the *nikokh* custom, have an additional wife.
13. List of names and addresses of individuals who use their apartments as gambling places.
14. List names and addresses of individuals who use their apartments for prostitution.
15. Identify Wahhabi family members who are over eighteen years old but have not served in the army.
16. Information on girls who were married before the age of sixteen.
17. List of individuals in the mahalla, who are considered "authoritative," "leaders," or "unruly"